Mutual Boasting in Philippians

The Ethical Function of Shared Honor in Its Scriptural and Greco-Roman Context

Isaac D. Blois

t&tclark

LONDON • NEW YORK • OXFORD • NEW DELHI • SYDNEY

T&T CLARK

Bloomsbury Publishing Plc

50 Bedford Square, London, WC1B 3DP, UK
1385 Broadway, New York, NY 10018, USA
29 Earlsfort Terrace, Dublin 2, Ireland

BLOOMSBURY, T&T CLARK and the T&T Clark logo are trademarks of
Bloomsbury Publishing Plc

First published in Great Britain 2020
This paperback edition published in 2022

Copyright © Isaac D. Blois, 2020

Isaac D. Blois has asserted his right under the Copyright, Designs and Patents Act, 1988, to be identified as Author of this work.

For legal purposes the Acknowledgments on p. ix constitute an extension of this copyright page.

All rights reserved. No part of this publication may be reproduced or transmitted in any form or by any means, electronic or mechanical, including photocopying, recording, or any information storage or retrieval system, without prior permission in writing from the publishers.

Bloomsbury Publishing Plc does not have any control over, or responsibility for, any third-party websites referred to or in this book. All internet addresses given in this book were correct at the time of going to press. The author and publisher regret any inconvenience caused if addresses have changed or sites have ceased to exist, but can accept no responsibility for any such changes.

A catalogue record for this book is available from the British Library.

Library of Congress Cataloging-in-Publication Data
Names: Blois, Isaac D., author.
Title: Mutual boasting in Philippians : the ethical function of shared honor in its biblical and Greco-Roman context / Isaac D. Blois. Description: London ; New York : T&T Clark, 2020. | Series: The library of New Testament studies, 2513–8790 ; 627 | Includes bibliographical references and index. | Summary: "While past studies of Philippians recognize the theme of honour in Philippians and Paul's emphasis on his mutual relations with the culture, the integral relation between these two central themes and the role it plays in Paul's exhortations to the Philippians have not been developed. Taking the intersection of these two themes in the pivotal passages of Phil 1:26 and 2:16 as his focus, Isaac Blois argues that Paul's focus on the mutual boasting shared between Paul and his converts alludes back to the mutual boasting shared between Israel and her covenant God, as apparent in both Deuteronomy and Isaiah"– Provided by publisher. Identifiers: LCCN 2020014535 (print) | LCCN 2020014536 (ebook) | ISBN 9780567694041 (hb) | ISBN 9780567694058 (epdf) | ISBN 9780567694072 (epub) Subjects: LCSH: Bible. Philippians--Criticism, interpretation, etc. | Bible–Criticism, interpretation, etc. Classification: LCC BS2705.52 .B56 2020 (print) | LCC BS2705.52 (ebook) | DDC 227/.606–dc23
LC record available at https://lccn.loc.gov/2020014535
LC ebook record available at https://lccn.loc.gov/2020014536

ISBN: HB: 978-0-5676-9404-1
PB: 978-0-5676-9777-6
ePDF: 978-0-5676-9405-8
ePUB: 978-0-5676-9407-2

Series: Library of New Testament Studies, volume 627
ISSN 2513–8790

Typeset by Newgen KnowledgeWorks Pvt. Ltd., Chennai, India
Printed and bound in Great Britain

To find out more about our authors and books visit www.bloomsbury.com and sign up for our newsletters.

LIBRARY OF NEW TESTAMENT STUDIES

627

*formerly the Journal for the Study of the New Testament
Supplement series*

Editor
Chris Keith

Editorial Board
Dale C. Allison, John M. G. Barclay, Lynn H. Cohick,
R. Alan Culpepper, Craig A. Evans, Robert Fowler, Simon
J. Gathercole, Juan Hernández Jr., John S. Kloppenborg,
Michael Labahn, Matthew V. Novenson, Love L. Sechrest,
Robert Wall, Catrin H. Williams, Brittany Wilson

Contents

Acknowledgments	ix
List of Abbreviations	xi

1 Introduction — 1
    Argument and Arrangement of the Study — 2
    Status Quaestionis — 3
    Definition for Mutual Honor — 4
    The Centrality of Honor in Philippians — 6
    History of Research on Three Aspects of Pauline and Philippians Studies — 9
        Boasting in Paul — 9
            Programmatic Studies for the Recent Discussion of Pauline Boasting — 10
            The Hellenistic and Roman Context of Pauline Boasting — 13
            Paul's Boasting in the Context of Second Temple Judaism — 15
            Septuagintal Studies on Pauline Boasting — 16
            Summary of Scholarship on Pauline Boasting — 17
        The Presence and Function of Scripture in Philippians — 18
            Scriptural Allusions in Paul's Letters — 19
            Scriptural Allusions in Philippians — 21
            The Awareness of Scripture in Philippians 2:12–18 — 25
            Conclusion on Scripture in Philippians — 26
        Mutuality in Philippians — 26
            Κοινωνία as Legal *Societas* — 27
            Κοινωνία as Friendship — 27
            Κοινωνία as Patronage — 29
            Κοινωνία as Siblingship — 31
            A Three-Way Κοινωνία in Philippians — 33
            Conclusion on Mutuality in Philippians — 35

Part 1	Mutual Glory in the Jewish Scriptures	37
2	Καύχημα as a Sign of Mutual Honor in Deuteronomy	41
	Mutual Honor in the Song of Moses	42
	Deuteronomy 26:16–19 and the Mutual Honor of the Covenant Relationship	44
	The Honorific Triad as Covenant Blessing in Deuteronomy 26:18–19	46
	Mutual Honor between God and His People: Deuteronomy 26:19 and 10:21	54
	Conclusion	56
3	Mutual Glory in Isaiah	57
	The Exclusive Glory of God in Isaiah	60
	The Divinely Bestowed Glory of Israel in Isaiah	61
	Israel's Glorification in Isaiah 41:16 and 45:25	62
	Eschatological Glory for Israel in Isaiah 60–62	64
	Mutual Glory between YHWH and Israel in Isaiah 60:19 and 62:3	65
	The Servant's Glory and the Glory of Israel	68
	The Servant's Reward in Isaiah 49:4	68
	Futility Overturned in Isaiah 65:23	72
	Trifold Mutuality of Glory in Isaiah	73
	Conclusion	74
Part 2	Mutual Honor in Roman Antiquity	75
4	The Influence and Mutuality of Honor in the Hellenistic and Roman World	79
	Honor as Influence in the Hellenistic and Roman World	79
	Honor as Influence in Roman Letter Writing	80
	The Mutuality of Honor in the Hellenistic and Roman World	81
	Mutuality of Honor within the Family	83
	Mutual Honor in the Parent–Child Relationship	85
	Mutual Honor within Friendship	87
	Mutual Honor in the Teacher–Pupil Relationship	89
	Conclusion	90
5	Mutual Honor as Motivation in the Hellenistic and Roman World	93
	Mutual Honor as Rhetorical Strategy in Ancient Letter Writing	93

Mutual Consideration as Persuasive Strategy in Papyrus Letters	94
Mutual Honor as Motivational Strategy within Roman Epistolary Corpora	95
Mutual Honor as Motivation in Cicero's Letters	96
Cicero's Correspondence with Quintus	97
Cicero's Correspondence with Cassius	97
Cicero's Correspondence with Dolabella	98
Cicero's Correspondence with Plancus	100
Mutual Honor as Motivation in Seneca's Moral Epistles	103
Mutual Honor as Motivation in Fronto's Royal Correspondence	105
Conclusion	108
Part 3 Mutual Honor in Philippians	**109**
6 Mutual Honor in Philippians 1:25–26	113
Mutual Καύχημα in the Structure of Philippians 1–2	113
The Philippians' Καύχημα Resulting from Paul's *Syncrisis*	116
Grammatical Analysis of Philippians 1:25–26	117
Paul's Honorable Self-Sacrifice in Philippians 1:21–26	118
Paul's Honor Abounding to the Philippians	120
The Mutual Honor of Friends and Family in Philippians 1:26	124
The Mutual Honor of Friends in Philippians 1:26	124
The Mutual Honor of Siblings in Philippians 1:26	125
Conclusion	127
7 Mutual Honor in Philippians 2:14–16	129
Paul's Claim to Honor as the Goal of Philippians 2:14–16	129
Grammatical Analysis of Philippians 2:14–16	130
The Presence of Scripture in Philippians 2:12–18	131
Deuteronomy in Philippians 2:12–18: Israel's *Unheilsgeschichte* as Anti-Model	132
The Grumbling Motif in Philippians 2:14–16	132
The Philippians as Blameless Children of God in Philippians 2:15	134
The Final Appeals of Paul and Moses	139
Paul's Deuteronomic Καύχημα in Philippians 2:16	141
Isaiah in Philippians 2:10–16	144
Isaiah 45:24 in Philippians 2:10–11	144

	Paul and the Servant in Philippians 2:16	145
	Paul's Isaianic Servant-Reward	146
	Conclusion	149
8	Mutual Honor as the Motivational Spur in Philippians	151
	Triple Mutuality of Honor in Philippians	153
	Paul's Radical Reversal of Honor	155
	Mutual Fame as the Motivational Spur in Philippians	156
	Paul's Dangerous Mutual Boast	160
	Conclusion	161
9	Conclusion	163

Bibliography	165
Author Index	187
Ancient Sources Index	192
Scripture Index	195
Subject Index	204

Acknowledgments

The apostle Paul routinely begins his writing endeavors with a thanksgiving for those with whom he has joined in the task of gospel labor. I too have been supported in my writing efforts by many individuals, and it is fitting to begin by offering up my thanksgiving on their behalf. First, I would like to thank Chris Keith and the editorial staff at LNTS for their willingness to accept this study into their prestigious series. Their kind encouragement about my argument and their helpful feedback has greatly improved the nature of the work, which is a revised version of my PhD thesis submitted to the University of St Andrews in 2017. Thanks also are in order for my PhD examiners, Prof. Tom Wright and Dr. Andrew Clarke, who offered valuable criticism on the manuscript.

My passion for Paul's letter to the Philippians began when, as a teenager, I took up a pastor's challenge to memorize the entire epistle. This passion was then fueled when, as an undergraduate, I studied Koine Greek under the guidance of Joseph Hellerman. Joe's enthusiasm for the Greek text of Philippians, coupled with his keen attention to the social setting of the early church, has profoundly shaped my own reading of ancient texts. Joe, together with the entire biblical studies faculty at Biola University and Talbot, including John Lunde, Ken Berding, Darian Lockett, Moyer Hubbard, Tom Finley, Ed Curtis, and many others, set me on a trajectory of biblical study that has served me well in the field. I was also formed as a reader of biblical texts and other great books through my time as an undergraduate in the Torrey Honors Institute. There, being mentored by Fred Sanders and taught by Joe Henderson and others, I learned the skill of closely analyzing widely divergent texts. I am privileged now to be working alongside these same teachers in the department, as I continue to learn within and among the Torrey community from Torrey's faculty as their peer. I would also like here to express thanks to my research assistant, Benjamin Vincent, whose tireless efforts on the index for this book saved me countless hours of labor.

My greatest academic debt, however, is owed to my *Doktorvater*, Scott Hafemann, whose tireless efforts to instill in his students a deep grasp of the grammar and theological framework of the NT writers has profoundly shaped my own approach to Scriptural texts. Imitating Paul, Dr. Hafemann was happy not only to give to the six of us comprising his "Hafe Group" his formal teaching "but also his own life" (1 Thess 2:8), pouring countless hours into discussion over each of our individual projects, and hosting a weekly discussion group for us on works ranging from Paul's epistle to the Romans, to Ben Myers's book on Jesus, to Gese's German essay on the OT understanding of the atonement. He and his wife Debara were a major element in making those years of study in Scotland so enriching for myself and my wife. I am grateful also for the community of scholars I found at the University of St Andrews, who greatly impacted my own thinking about Scripture, including Jen Gilbertson,

Euichang Kim, Tim Fox, David Johnston, Tommi Karjalainen, Esau McCaulley, Kai Akagi, Jonathan Lett, Eric Covington, Matt Ketterling, Michael Paul Anderson, and countless others.

Finally, the biggest debt I accrued during the research making up this study is to my wife, without whose support and encouragement I would never have brought the work to completion. It is to my wife Laurie, "my fellow-laborer and fellow-soldier," "my joy and my crown," that I gratefully dedicate this book.

Isaac D. Blois
La Mirada, CA

Abbreviations

AASF	Annales Academiae Scientiarum Fennicae
AB	Anchor Bible
ABR	*Australian Biblical Review*
AJP	*The American Journal of Philology*
AJT	*The American Journal of Theology*
AnBib	Analecta Biblica
ANTC	Abingdon New Testament Commentary
AOTCS	Apollos Old Testament Commentary Series
APR	Ancient Philosophy & Religion
ATD	Das Alte Testament Deutsch
ATh	*Acta Theologica*
ATR	*Anglican Theological Review*
BA	La Bible d'Alexandrie
BBB	Bonner Biblische Beiträge
BCH	*Bulletin de correspondance hellénique*
BCT	*The Bible and Critical Theory (Monash University ePress)*
BDAG	Danker, Frederick W., Walter Bauer, William F. Arndt, and F. Wilbur Gingrich. *Greek-English Lexicon of the New Testament and Other Early Christian Literature*. 3rd ed. Chicago: University of Chicago Press, 2000
BDF	Blass, Friedrich, Albert Debrunner, and Robert W. Funk. *A Greek Grammar of the New Testament and Other Early Christian Literature*. Chicago: University of Chicago Press, 1961
BECNT	Baker Exegetical Commentary on the New Testament
BET	Biblical Exegesis and Theology
BETL	Bibliotheca Ephemeridum Theologicarum Lovaniensium
BHT	Beiträge zur historischen Theologie
BI	*Biblical Interpretation*
Bib	*Biblica*
BibSac	*Bibliotheca Sacra*
BijDragen	*International Journal in Philosophy and Theology (Peeters)*
BIS	Biblical Interpretation Series
BKAT	Biblische Kommentar Altes Testament
BN	*Biblische Notizen*
BNTC	Black's New Testament Commentaries
BSGUF	Beiträge zur Sprache und Geschichte der urchristlichen Frömmigkeit
BSR	Biblioteca di Scienze Religiose
BTB	*Biblical Theology Bulletin*
BTS	Biblical Tools and Studies

BWANT	Beiträge zur Wissenschaft vom Alten und Neuen Testament
BZ	*Biblische Zeitschrift*
BZAW	Beihefte zur Zeitschrift für die alttestamentliche Wissenschaft
BZNW	Beihefte zur Zeitschrift für die neutestamentliche Wissenschaft und die Kunde der älteren Kirche
Cat	*Catéchèse*
CB	Coniectanea Biblica New Testament Series
CBET	Contributions to Biblical Exegesis and Theology
CBNT	Commentaire Biblique: Nouveau Testament
CEA	*Cahiers des études anciennes*
CEP	*Contemporary Education Psychology*
CGLC	Cambridge Greek and Latin Classics
CNT	Commentaire du Nouveau Testament
COP	Colloquium Oecumenicum Paulinum
COQG	Christian Origins and the Question of God
CQ	*Classical Quarterly*
CP	*Classical Philology*
CSP	Collectània Sant Pacià
CTM	*Currents in Theology and Mission*
CTR	*Criswell Theological Review*
DCLS	Deuterocanonical and Cognate Literature Studies
DPL	*Dictionary of Paul and His Letters*
EB	Études Bibliques
EBC	The Expository Bible Commentary
ECL	Early Christianity and Its Literature
EDNT	*Exegetical Dictionary of the New Testament*
EEC	Evangelical Exegetical Commentary
EGLMBS	*Eastern Great Lakes and Midwest Biblical Societies*
EH	Europäische Hochschulschriften
EJL	Early Judaism and Its Literature (SBL)
EKK	Evangelisch-Katholischer Kommentar zum Neuen Testament
EQ	*Evangelical Quarterly*
ESEC	Emory Studies in Early Christianity
EstBib	*Estudios Bíblicos*
ETL	*Ephemerides Theologicae Lovanienses*
ExpT	*Expository Times*
FAT	Forschungen zum Alten Testament
FB	Forschung zur Bibel
FLSHUL	Faculté des Lettres et Sciences Humaines de l'Université de Lille
FRLANT	Forschungen zur Religion und Literatur des Alten und Neuen Testaments
GKC	F. W. Gesenius, E. Kautzsch, and A. E. Cowley, *Gesenius' Hebrew Grammar*. 2nd ed. Oxford: Clarendon Press, 2003
GTA	Göttinger Theologische Arbeiten
HBS	Herders Biblische Studien
HBT	*Horizons in Biblical Theology*

HTANT	Historisch-Theologische Auslegung Neues Testament
HTKNT	Herders theologischer Kommentar zum Neuen Testament
HTR	*Harvard Theological Review*
ICC	International Critical Commentary
ICSSup	Illinois Classical Studies Supplement
Int	*Interpretation*
JEOL	*Jaarbericht Ex Oriente Lux*
JBL	*Journal of Biblical Literature*
JGRChJ	*Journal of Greco-Roman Christianity and Judaism*
Joüon	Joüon, Paul. *A Grammar of Biblical Hebrew*. Translated and revised by T. Muraoka. 2 vols. Rome: Pontifical Biblical Institute, 1991
JSJSup	Journal for the Study of Judaism Supplement
JSNT	*Journal for the Study of the New Testament*
JSNTSup	Journal for the Study of the New Testament Supplement Series
JSPL	*Journal for the Study of Paul and His Letters*
JSR	*Journal of Scriptural Reasoning*
JSSM	Journal of Semitic Studies Monograph
JSOT	*Journal for the Study of the Old Testament*
JSOTSup	Journal for the Study of the Old Testament Supplement Series
KEK	Kritisch-exegetischer Kommentar über das Neue Testament
LBNT	I libri biblici: Nuovo Testamento
LCL	Loeb Classical Library
LD	Lectio Divina
LEC	The Library of Early Christianity
LNTS	The Library of New Testament Studies
LOTS	Library of Old Testament Studies
LS	*Louvain Studies*
MLN	*Modern Language Notes*
MNTC	Moffat New Testament Commentary
MNTS	McMaster New Testament Series
NACSBT	New American Commentary Studies in Bible and Theology
NCB	New Clarendon Bible
NCBC	New Century Bible Commentary
Neot	*Neotestamentica*
NET	Neutestamentliche Entwürfe zur Theologie
NETS	*A New English Translation of the Septuagint*. Edited by Albert Pietersma and Benjamin G. Wright III. New York: Oxford University Press, 2007
NICNT	New International Commentary on the New Testament
NICOT	New International Commentary on the Old Testament
NIGTC	New International Greek Testament Commentary
NIVAC	NIV Application Commentary
NKZ	*Neue Kirchliche Zeitschrift*
NSBT	New Studies in Biblical Theology
NTOA	Novum Testamentum et Orbis Antiquus
NeTT	*Nederlands theologisch tijdschrift*

NoTT	*Norsk Theologisk Tidsskrift*
NovT	*Novum Testamentum*
NovTSup	Novum Testamentum Supplement
NTS	New Testament Studies
OTL	Old Testament Library
PBM	Paternoster Biblical Monographs
PEGLBS	Proceedings of the Eastern Great Lakes Biblical Society
PEGLMBS	Proceedings of the Eastern Great Lakes and Midwest Biblical Societies
Ph	*Philologos*
PNTC	Pillar New Testament Commentary
PTL	*A Journal for Descriptive Poetics and Theory of Literature*
PRSt	*Perspectives in Religious Studies*
RB	*Revue biblique*
RBS	Resources for Biblical Study (SBL)
REG	*Revue des études grecques*
RevExp	*Review and Expositor*
RHPhR	*Revue d'histoire et de philosophie religieuses*
RivBib	*Rivista biblica*
RLC	*Recueil Lucien Cerfaux*
RPT	Religion in Philosophy and Theology
RQ	*Restoration Quarterly*
RSPT	*Revue des sciences philosophiques et théologiques*
RTP	*Revue de théologie et de philosophie*
SB	Stuttgarter Bibelstudien
SBLAB	Society of Biblical Literature Academia Biblica
SBLDS	SBL Dissertation Series
SBLSymS	SBL Symposium Series
SBLSP	*SBL Seminar Papers*
SBT	Studies in Biblical Theology
SCHNT	Studia ad Corpus Hellenisticum Novi Testamenti
SCS	Septuagint and Cognate Studies
SMB	Serie Monografica di "Benedictina": Sezione Biblico-Ecumenica
SNTSMS	Society for New Testament Studies Monograph Series
SO	*Symbole Oslon*
SP	Sacra Pagina
SPAW	*Sitzungsberichte der Preußischen Akademie der Wissenschaften* (Berlin)
ST	*Studia Theologica*
STAR	Studies in Theology and Religion
STDJ	Studies on the Texts of the Desert of Judah
StuEv	*Studia Evangelica*
TAPA	*Transactions and Proceedings of the American Philological Association*
TB	Theologische Bücherei
TDNT	*Theological Dictionary of the New Testament*. Edited by Gerhard Kittel and Gerhard Friedrich. Translated by Geoffrey W. Bromiley. 10 vols. Grand Rapids: Eerdmans, 1964–1976

Them	*Themelios*
Théo	*Théologie: Études publiées sous la direction de la faculté de théologie S. J. de Lyon-Fourvière*
THKNT	Theologischer Handkommentar zum Neuen Testament
THNTC	Two Horizons New Testament Commentary
TL	*Theologische Literaturzeitung*
TLNT	Theological Lexicon of the New Testament (Spicq)
TOTC	Tyndale Old Testament Commentaries
TQ	*Theologische Quartalschrift*
TrinJ	*Trinity Journal*
TynBul	*Tyndale Bulletin*
UNT	Untersuchungen zum Neuen Testament
VE	*Verbum et Ecclesia*
VT	*Vetus Testamentum*
VTSup	Vetus Testamentum Supplementum
WBC	Word Biblical Commentary
WF	Wege der Forschung
WGRWSup	Writings from the Greco-Roman World Supplements
WTJ	*Wesleyan Theological Journal*
WestTJ	*Westminster Theological Journal*
WUNT	Wissenschaftliche Untersuchungen zum Neuen Testament
ZAW	*Zeitschrift für die alttestamentliche Wissenschaft*
ZkTh	*Zeitschrift für katholische Theologie*
ZNT	*Zeitschrift für neues Testament*
ZNW	*Zeitschrift für neutestamentliche Wissenschaft*
ZTK	*Zeitschrift für Theologie und Kirche*

1

Introduction

This study focuses on the theme of mutual honor in Paul's letter to the Philippians. That is, it is about the honor shared between two or more individuals in relationship with one another, in this case between Paul, the Philippian Christ-believing community, and the God whom they worshipped. Insofar as we are dealing with the concept of honor, we have our feet firmly grounded in the Roman world of Paul and his addressees in Philippi. Paul's identity as an "apocalyptically minded pastor,"[1] however, brings him to reorient the common Greco-Roman notion of honor toward the future eschatological hope of glory on the day of Christ.[2] Thus, as James Harrison adduces, "The intersection of honorific perspectives from the eastern Mediterranean basin with the praise traditions of Second Temple Judaism allowed Paul to bring the culmination of glory in Christ into a rich cross-cultural dialogue in his letters."[3]

In some ways, however, the present study's use of Jewish Scripture, in combination with Roman and Hellenistic concepts, to interpret the theme of mutual boasting in Philippians is an attempt to swim against the tide of recent research on the letter. A glance at recent monographs on Philippians demonstrates an almost exclusive focus on the Roman background for interpreting the epistle, highlighting the stark *Romanitas* of Paul's audience in the letter.[4] In contrast, this study attempts to understand Paul's language of honor in the letter from the combined perspective of the Jewish theology

---

[1] Paul Foster, "Eschatology of the Thessalonian Correspondence," *JSPL* 1.1 (2011), 57–82, 81, uses this term to describe Paul in relation to his Thessalonian converts.
[2] See Peter Oakes, "Re-Mapping the Universe: Paul and the Emperor in 1 Thessalonians and Philippians," *JSNT* 27.3 (2005), 301–21, 320.
[3] James R. Harrison, "Paul and Ancient Civic Ethics," in *Paul's Graeco-Roman Context*, ed. Cilliers Breytenbach, BETL 277 (Leuven: Peeters, 2015), 75–118, 107.
[4] See Jörg Frey, Benjamin Schliesser, and Veronika Niederhofer, eds., *Der Philipperbrief des Paulus in der hellenistisch-römischen Welt*, WUNT 253 (Tübingen: Mohr Siebeck, 2015). Cf. the three articles on Philippians by Arnold, Verhoef, and Pevarello in *Paul's Graeco-Roman Context*. Among recent monographs on Philippians, Bradley Arnold, *Christ as the* Telos *of Life*, WUNT 2.371 (Tübingen: Mohr Siebeck, 2014), situates the letter within Greco-Roman philosophical thought; Heiko Wojtkowiak, *Christologie und Ethik im Philipperbrief: Studien zur Handlungsorientierung einer frühchristlichen Gemeinde in paganer Umwelt*, FRLANT 243 (Göttingen: Vandenhoeck & Ruprecht, 2012) and Sergio Rosell Nebreda, *Christ Identity: A Social-Scientific Reading of Philippians 2.5–11*, FRLANT 242 (Göttingen: Vandenhoeck & Ruprecht, 2011) both have minimal discussion of Jewish backgrounds. Two exceptions are David McAuley, *Paul's Covert Use of Scripture: Intertextuality and Rhetorical Situation in Philippians 2:10–16* (Eugene: Pickwick, 2015) and Jane Lancaster Patterson, *Keeping the Feast: Metaphors of Sacrifice in 1 Corinthians and Philippians*, ECL 16 (Atlanta, GA: SBL Press, 2015).

that shaped Paul's message and the Roman milieu in which that message is conveyed. Therefore, the structure of the present work reflects the three interrelated contexts in which the theme of mutual honor is developed in Philippians: its Scriptural context (Part 1), its Greco-Roman cultural context (Part 2), and its literary context (Part 3).

Argument and Arrangement of the Study

This study argues that the basis for Paul's mutual boasting with the Philippians rests in the Scriptures, and that, since this mutuality is culturally intelligible, Paul can use it to persuade the Philippians to heed his exhortation to maintain unity and perseverance. Specifically, the study analyzes Paul's use of the motif of mutual boasting (καύχημα) in two passages in Philippians (1:25–26 and 2:14–16), the second of which is steeped in Scriptural language. When viewed together against this Scriptural backdrop, these two appearances of καύχημα demonstrate the eschatological and ecclesial significance of the close mutuality between the apostle and his Philippian converts, with regard to their shared boasting in one another and in God, which Paul then capitalizes on culturally to motivate behavioral change in the community.

The study will thus begin by presenting a history of research on the three areas most pertinent to the investigation of mutual honor in Philippians: (1) boasting in Paul, (2) the presence of Scripture in Philippians, and (3) the Greco-Roman context for understanding the relationship of κοινωνία between Paul and the Philippians. Then, Part 1 of the study will engage the theological context of the theme of mutual honor, presenting close readings of two Scriptural texts, Deuteronomy and Isaiah, to which Paul overtly refers in his exhortation to the Philippians. Both Scriptural sources receive their own chapters, each of which begins with an analysis of the passage to which Paul directs his readers (Deut 32:5 and Isa 49:4), and then draws on resonances within their wider contexts of relevance for Paul's argument. The first chapter in this section, Chapter 2, argues that, within the closing chapters of Deuteronomy, Deut 26:19 LXX provides Paul with the key language of καύχημα in the context of a mutuality of honor between YHWH and his covenant people. Chapter 3 then argues that the latter portion of Isaiah affords Paul the mediatorial role of the Servant as the means for facilitating the mutual honor between God and his people envisioned in Deuteronomy (see Isa 42:7; 49:5–6), honor in which the Servant himself participates through the divine reward he earns from his ministry.

Part 2 of the study investigates the cultural context of the theme of mutual honor within the Roman and Hellenistic milieu, focusing especially on the use of this motif as a rhetorical strategy in friendship and family letters. The first chapter in this section, Chapter 4, discusses the way in which honor was shared in the Greco-Roman world among friends and family. Chapter 5 then shows how prominent letter writers, Cicero, Seneca, and Fronto,[5] employed this theme of mutual honor to persuade their correspondents paraenetically.

---

[5] Hans Dieter Betz, *Studies in Philippians*, WUNT 343 (Tübingen: Mohr Siebeck, 2015), 144, argues in favor of comparing Paul with such Roman authors as Cicero and Seneca, not because there

Finally, Part 3 brings these two strands of Jewish and Greco-Roman presentations of mutual honor to bear on the interpretation of Paul's letter to his Philippian converts, investigating the literary context in which this theme appears in the letter. The first chapter in this section, Chapter 6, offers a close reading of Phil 1:25-26, where Paul establishes his faithfulness in relationship with the Philippians, showing that his decision to remain alive for their sake will therefore garner a boast for their benefit. Chapter 7 then treats Paul's related admonition in Phil 2:14-16 regarding the Philippians' faithfulness, demonstrating how the Scriptural traditions of mutual honor elaborated in Deuteronomy and Isaiah describe the boasting that will accrue for Paul himself through the Philippians' honorable behavior. Finally, Chapter 8 shows how Paul utilizes the role of mutual honor within the Greco-Roman culture[6] to motivate the Philippians to maintain their side of the relationship, thereby preserving unity in order to bring about honor for their "brother," Paul. Whereas the Scriptures provide the content and significance of their mutual honor, the Philippians' own cultural context provides its rhetorical force and function.

Status Quaestionis

Previous scholars have called attention to the notion of "reciprocal boasting" shared between Paul (Phil 2:16) and the Philippians (1:26) in the letter.[7] For instance, Fee notes

---

would have been any literary influence between them, but because "they were close to him through the impact of their works on the wider public." Similarly, Jeffrey T. Reed, *A Discourse Analysis of Philippians: Method and Rhetoric in the Debate over Literary Integrity*, LNTS 136 (Sheffield: Sheffield Academic Press, 1997), 219, argues that Paul's letters differ from shorter papyrus letters because Paul "discloses information about himself and then uses this for paraenetic purposes," and in this they "resemble philosophical letters such as Seneca's." Reed here is following Peter Wick, *Die Philipperbrief: Der formale Aufbau des Briefs als Schlüssel zum Verständnis seines Inhalts*, BWANT 135 (Stuttgart: Kohlhammer, 1994), 158, who similarly compares Paul's letters with those of Seneca.

[6] My argument that Paul taps into traditions of honor that were culturally appropriate in Roman and Hellenistic first-century settings is built on the understanding that the colony of Philippi was highly influenced both by traditional Hellenistic practices and by Roman practices. On the historical backdrop of ancient Philippi, see Chaido Koukouli-Chrysantaki, "Colonia Iulia Augusta Philippensis," in *Philippi at the Time of Paul and After his Death*, ed. Bakirtzis and Koester (Eugene, OR: Wipf & Stock, 2009), 5-35. Cf. Cédric Brélaz, "First-Century Philippi: Contextualizing Paul's Visit," in *The First Urban Churches 4: Roman Philippi*, ed. James R. Harrison and L. L. Welborn, WGRWSup 13 (Atlanta, GA: SBL Press, 2018), 153-88, 163, who calls attention to the three main ethnic groups prominent within first-century Roman Philippi: the Roman citizens (only a fraction of the population), the native Thracians (the vast majority in the countryside around the colony), and those culturally Greek (Macedonians as well as Thracians and Athenians, among others), with this third group representing Paul's primary audience in the letter. See also Cédric Brélaz, "Philippi: A Roman Colony within its Regional Context," in *Les communautés du nord Égéen au temps de l'hégémonie romaine: Entre ruptures et continuités*, ed. Julien Fournier and Maria-Gabriella G. Parissaki, Meletemata 77 (Athens: National Hellenic Research Foundation, 2018), 163-82.

[7] Cf. John H. P. Reumann, *Philippians: A New Translation with Introduction and Commentary*, AB 33B (New Haven, CT: Yale University Press, 2008), 413: "Boasting, by Paul over his favorite congregation, is reciprocal to their boasting over Paul (1:26)." Frank W. Weidmann, *Philippians, 1 and 2 Thessalonians, and Philemon* (Louisville, KY: Westminster John Knox Press, 2013), 56: "The mutuality motif is reaffirmed and furthered [in 2:16] as in 1:26, where it is [the Philippians'] boasting. Here it is Paul's." Camille Focant, *Philippiens et Philémon*, CBNT (Paris: du Cerf, 2015), 130, affirms that in 2:16 "la communauté de Philippes contribuera à sa [viz., Paul's] gloire ..., mais en 1,26, c'était leur fierté qui abondait en Christ par lui." Antonio Pitta, *Lettera ai Filippesi*, LBNT

how the opening section of the letter dealing with Paul's situation (1:12–26) culminates in boasting for the Philippians, whereas the later paraenetic section dealing with the Philippians' situation (1:27–2:18) culminates in boasting for Paul, thereby displaying "reciprocal 'boasting.'"[8] Similarly, Fowl highlights the sharing between apostle and converts that emerges from their reciprocal boasting.[9] This demonstrable agreement about the presence of reciprocal or mutual boasting in Philippians, however, lacks scholarship addressing both (1) the source of this idea of mutual boasting for Paul in the letter and (2) the way in which mutual boasting is deployed rhetorically by the apostle in accord with cultural norms. It is the purpose of the present study to fill this lacuna of scholarship by identifying the Scriptural source of the theme of mutual honor in Philippians, and by demonstrating the cultural context in which mutual honor could garner rhetorical power for exhortation. In the end, I will argue that attention to these twin aspects of the theological source and the cultural context for the theme of mutual honor renders a more complete account of how Paul deploys mutual honor in Philippians to motivate his audience to maintain obedience in the face of persecution.

Definition for Mutual Honor

Since the notion of mutual honor is core to the argument of the present study, we first provide a definition for mutuality. The psychologist Judith Jordan offers the following description of how mutuality occurs within relationships:

> In a mutual exchange one is both affecting the other and being affected by the other; one extends oneself out to the other and is also receptive to the impact of the other. There is … a constantly changing pattern of responding to and affecting the other's state. There is both receptivity and active initiative toward the other.[10]

Although this entails a modern understanding of mutuality, it highlights social realities reflected in the ancient world. This constant give-and-take accompanying relationships is evident in the various texts analyzed below, whether Israel's Scriptures, the epistolary correspondences of the Hellenic and Roman world, or Paul's letter to the Philippians.

---

11 (Milan: Paoline, 2010), 181 n. 363, speaks of a "reciproco vanto," and Detlef Häußer, *Der Brief des Paulus an die Philipper*, HTANT (Witten: SCM R.Brockhaus, 2016), 111–12, writes that the Philippians' boast in Paul at 1:26 has its "entgegengesetzte Seite" in Paul's boast in them at 2:16.

[8] Gordon D. Fee, *Paul's Letter to the Philippians*, NICNT 46 (Grand Rapids, MI: Eerdmans, 1995), 249 n. 43. Cf. Fred B. Craddock, *Philippians* (Louisville, KY: Westminster John Knox Press, 1985), 31: "As the autobiographical section closed with Paul saying the Philippians would boast in him (1:26), here he closes with the hope that he can boast in them (2:16)." Cf. Luc Pialoux, *L'épître aux Philippiens: L'Évangile du don et de l'amitié*, ET 75 (Leuven: Peeters, 2017), 359, who notes that "chaque partie est invitée à devenir un sujet de fierté pour l'autre, dans le Christ Jésus (1:26; 2:16)."

[9] Stephen E. Fowl, *Philippians*, THNTC (Grand Rapids, MI: Eerdmans, 2005), 127–28, argues that "Paul and the Philippians engage in reciprocal boasting in God's work in each other's lives," which he then views as reasserting "the three-way partnership or friendship in the gospel into which God has called both Paul and the Philippians."

[10] Judith V. Jordan, *Women's Growth in Connection: Writings from the Stone Center* (New York: Guilford Press, 1991), 82.

Particularly important for our study will be how such mutuality intersected with the central value of honor in Paul's world. Indeed, honor was the main social value in the first-century world, though it was something that could be held "by an individual or by a group, the family in particular."[11] Following the social anthropologist Pitt-Rivers's standard definition of honor as "the value of a person in [one's] own eyes [and] in the eyes of [one's] society,"[12] we thus offer the following definition for "mutual honor": *mutual honor results from a relationship of two or more parties in which each party participates in the honor accruing from the actions of the other(s)*. The type of actions that accrue honor will vary among different cultures and groups, but when honor is bestowed, not merely the honorand but also those in relationship with the honorand rise in status.[13] The present study will employ terms from the language of honor—for example, glory, majesty, praise, boasting—not as technical terms[14] but as various designations referring to the broad semantic field of positive value judgment.[15]

---

[11] Philip F. Esler, "Keeping it in the Family," in *Families and Family Relations as Represented in Early Judaisms and Early Christianities: Texts and Fictions*, ed. Jan Willem van Henten and Athalya Brenner, STAR 2 (Leiden: Deo Publishing, 2000), 145–84, 152. Cf. Joseph Plevnik, "Honor/Shame," in *Handbook of Biblical Social Values*, ed. John J. Pilch and Bruce J. Malina (Peabody, MA: Hendrickson, 1998), 106–15, 107: "Honor is primarily a group value. Individual members of a group share in its honor." Halvor Moxnes, "Honor and Shame," in *The Social Sciences and New Testament Interpretation*, ed. Richard L. Rohrbaugh (Peabody, MA: Hendrickson, 1996), 19–40, 27, similarly calls attention to "collective honor, based on a system of patrilineal clans," which "is a common element in traditional communities all over the Mediterranean area" both in the ancient and modern societies.

[12] Julian A. Pitt-Rivers, "Honour and Social Status," in *Honour and Shame: The Values of Mediterranean Society*, ed. John G. Peristiany (Chicago, IL: University of Chicago Press, 1966), 19–78, 21. Cf. Annika B. Kuhn, "The Dynamics of Social Status and Prestige in Pliny, Juvevnal and Martial," in *Social Status and Prestige in the Graeco-Roman World*, ed. Annika B. Kuhn (Stuttgart: Franz Steiner Verlag, 2015), 9–28, 12, who writes about Pliny's Roman context of honor: "Honour is *accorded* by common recognition, by the judgment of others on someone's standing and qualities. It cannot be generated or maintained *ipso facto*, but constitutes a 'public commodity.'"

[13] The understanding of mutual honor reflected in this study bears similarities to the notion of "group esteem" presented in the study of Paul's opponents in Philippians by Nina Nikki, *Opponents and Identity in Philippians*, NovTSup 173 (Leiden: Brill, 2019), on group esteem see p. 52. This is also reflected in the study of Peter Reinl, "Plädoyer gegen die Schaffung neuer Ränder in der Gemeinde von Philippi: Phil 3,1b-11(21) und das kulturanthropologische Modell 'Ehre und Scham/Schande,'" in *Randfiguren in der Mitte: Hermann-Josef Venetz zu Ehren*, ed. Max Küchler and Peter Reinl (Luzern: Paulusverlag, 2003), 117–34, 122, who speaks of *Kollektivehre* in antiquity that was anchored in social groups such as family.

[14] For instance, some view glory (δόξα) as it appears in Septuagintal texts as entailing a more visibly recognizable attribute (cf. L. H. Brockington, "The Greek Translator of Isaiah and his Interest in ΔΟΞΑ," *VT* 1 [1951], 23–32, 29, who explains that LXX Isaiah's usage of δόξα contains "the idea of brightness, outward majesty and splendour"), whereas honor (τιμή) is generally held to be something socially ascribed (see following note). As noted by Moxnes, "Honor and Shame," 23, when analyzing terms for honor in the New Testament, "the semantic field is a broad one."

[15] See BDAG, 257, who define δόξα thus: "Honor as enhancement or recognition of status or performance, *fame, recognition, renown, honor, prestige*" (italics original). Gerhard Kittel, "δόξα," *TDNT* 2.234, extrapolates from the common meaning of δοκέω as "good standing" that δόξα "is mostly used favourably for 'reputation' or 'renown.'" Hans Hübner, "τιμή," *EDNT* 3.357, describes how τιμή "encompasses the range of meaning 'estimation, price, value, honor.'" H. Hegermann, "δόξα," *EDNT* 1.345, adduces one of the basic meanings of δόξα as "reputation, value, honor," which draws on the Scriptural tradition, where "[כָּבוֹד] refers to the weight of esteem and honor which a person ... has." Hegermann additionally notes that "Δόξα is used synonymously with τιμή with the meaning *esteem, honor*." Ceslas Spicq, "δόξα," *TLNT* 1.363, explains that in Koine Greek, especially

Such mutuality of honor is evident in numerous relational structures. Ancient friendship, ideally a relationship between equals,[16] reflected the reality that friends participated in the honor of the other. Among unequal relationships, clients participated in the *dignitas* of their more prestigious patron, while the patron too experienced an amplification of honor when a client displayed great virtue. Thus, the patron–client relationship, though necessarily unequal, reflected reciprocity of honor. Within the Jewish Scriptural framework, the covenant relationship between YHWH and Israel, which was essentially a nonparity relationship similar to that between patron and client, also reflects mutual honor in that Israel's tie with YHWH constituted her claim to honor, while, in conjunction, the holy people Israel represented YHWH's glory among the nations.

A combination of the Jewish covenantal pattern and the Greco-Roman patron–client and friendship pattern is found in the relation of kinship. Friends could share in each other's honor because they acted toward one another as siblings; clients acted toward their patrons as family members ideally acted toward their *paterfamilias*, and vice versa. YHWH entered into relationship with Israel on the basis that he was their "Father" and they his "children."[17] Thus, within the family, honor entails a communal possession, and so each member contributes to the honor of the others.

Paul's relationship with the Philippian Christ followers, while adopting wholesale neither the patron–client nor the friendship relational paradigm, similarly reflects the types of mutual honor reflected in these structures, especially insofar as he stresses the familial bond shared between himself, these believers, and God/Christ. Thus, on the one hand, the honorable actions of the Philippians render an honor that extends itself out to the other family members, namely, Paul as (superior) brother and God as Father. On the other hand, the honorable actions of Paul, while providing a model of behavior for his brothers and sisters in Christ, also contribute toward their honor, and that of Christ, alongside his own. Our study will focus on such mutuality of honor to elucidate Paul's language of boasting throughout Philippians.

Thus, mutuality of honor in Philippians rests on the fictive kinship relation evident in the letter between Paul, the Philippians, and God. As members of one family, they participate in one honor, with Paul's honor extending itself out to the Philippians and theirs to him so that together they contribute toward and participate in the honor of God their Father.

The Centrality of Honor in Philippians

A focus on the theme of honor in Philippians is warranted in light of the prominence of honor language in the letter and in view of the preoccupation with honor in

---

in the inscriptions and the papyri, δόξα means "esteem, honor (expressed by the Latin *gloria*)" and "is often linked with [τιμή], [ἀρετή], [ἔπαινος]." Spicq, "καυχάομαι," *TLNT* 2.295, defines καύχημα as a "claim to glory," noting that Paul "almost always uses this word in a positive sense" with respect to "virtues that entitle a person to honor" (p. 301). Liddell-Scott, "δόξα," meaning 3.2: "the opinion which others have of one, estimation," mostly "good repute, honour, glory."

[16] See Aristotle, *Nic eth.* 1155a.
[17] See F. M. Cross, "Kinship and Covenant in Ancient Israel," in *From Epic to Canon: History and Literature in Ancient Israel* (Baltimore, MD: Johns Hopkins Press, 1998), 3–21.

first-century Roman Philippi. Honor plays a significant role in the arguments of Phil 1:26 and 2:15–16, and these passages are pivotal in the structure of Philippians as a whole.[18] Although the "honor-shame" dynamic in Philippians has been much studied,[19] its connection with the prominent theme of mutuality in the letter has not been adequately observed, nor, as we will see, has scholarship recognized the pivotal role mutual honor plays in the rhetoric of the letter as the implied motivation for heeding Paul's paraenesis. In regard to this prominence, terms from the honorific word-field abound in Philippians,[20] though the apostle works from an understanding of the source and nature of honor that has been radically redefined by the Christ-event.[21]

Beginning in the first chapter of Philippians, Paul concludes his prayer for this beloved community by stating that their purity on the last day will contribute to the *glory* (δόξα) and *praise* (ἔπαινος) of God (1:11).[22] The apostle's central concern about his ensuing Roman trial revolves around his ability to avoid *being shamed* (οὐδενὶ

---

[18] Following the rising consensus among scholarship on the letter, this study will hold to the integrity of Philippians. This is reflected in the vocabulary links within the canonical letter, on which see, e.g., Robert Jewett, "The Epistolary Thanksgiving and the Integrity of Philippians," *NovT* 12 (1970), 40–53. For a defense of the unity of the letter on the basis of its structure, see, e.g., David E. Garland, "Composition and Unity of Philippians: Some Neglected Literary Factors," *NovT* 27 (1985), 141–73. See also the recent defense of the letter's unity by Mark A. Jennings, *The Price of Partnership in the Letter of Paul to the Philippians: "Make My Joy Complete"*, LNTS 578 (London: Bloomsbury T&T Clark, 2018), 4, who argues for the canonical letter's integrity on the basis of the single unifying theme of Paul's desire to "[persuade] the church to maintain its exclusive partnership with him and his gospel mission." The provenance for the letter, which is debated, does not impact the argument of this study; for a helpful survey, see Michael Flexsenhar III, "The Provenance of Philippians and Why It Matters: Old Questions, New Approaches," *JSNT* 42.1 (2019), 18–45.

[19] On first-century Philippi's preoccupation with honor, see the programmatic study by Joseph H. Hellerman, *Reconstructing Honor in Roman Philippi: Carmen Christi as Cursus Pudorum*, SNTSMS 132 (Cambridge: Cambridge University Press, 2005), 34–63. Cf. Rosell Nebreda, *Identity*, 88–106. Wojtkowiak, *Christologie*, 149–57, 253–83, finds the central concern of the letter to be Paul's response to a conflict of values (*Wertekonflikt*), in which the apostle calls the Philippian believers to a renunciation of status and honor (p. 282). See also James R. Harrison, "From Rome to the Colony of Philippi: Roman Boasting in Philippians 3:4–6 in Its Latin West and Philippian Epigraphic Context," in Harrison and Welborn, *Roman Philippi*, 307–70, 345, who notes that the "ethos of self-promotion," which originated in the military boasting culture of Rome and was duplicated in the Roman colony at Philippi, Paul shows in Philippians to be "totally antithetical to the exemplum of the cross and his own experience of God's justifying grace."

[20] Note the condensed list displaying Paul's emphasis on the values of honor and shame in Philippians by Nijay K. Gupta, "'I Will Not Be Put to Shame': Paul and the Honourable Wish for Death," *Neot* 42.2 (2008), 253–67, 258: "In Philippians, Paul emphasises: the necessity of living 'in a manner worthy (ἀξίως) of the gospel of Christ' (1:27); the 'worth' (δοκιμή) of Timothy and his work for Paul (2:22); the need to honour (ἐντίμους ἔχετε) people like Epaphroditus who risk their life for the Gospel (2:29); the 'shame (αἰσχύνη)' of Christ's enemies (3:19); the importance of keeping one's thoughts on 'honourable things (σεμνά)' (4:8)."

[21] See Mikael Tellbe, *Paul between Synagogue and State: Christians, Jews, and Civic Authorities in 1 Thessalonians, Romans, and Philippians*, CB 34 (Stockholm: Almqvist & Wiksell International, 2001), 274: "In shaping the Philippians' identity, Paul also assures them of their honor in the alternate 'court of reputation,' in particular by giving them new values and indications of their worth in the eyes of their group."

[22] Later scribes were apparently comfortable appropriating either ἔπαινος (𝔓[46]) or ἔπαινος and δόξα (F, G) to Paul himself, thereby reflecting the honor that accrued to the apostle for the Philippians' purity. See Brent Nongbri, "Two Neglected Textual Variants in Philippians 1," *JBL* 128 (2009), 803–8. Alternately, Wolfgang Schenk, *Die Philipperbriefe des Paulus: Kommentar* (Stuttgart: Kohlhammer, 1984), 126, arrives at a similar idea of honor *for humans* in Phil 1:11 by arguing for θεοῦ as a

αἰσχυνθήσομαι) and that Christ will be positively *honored* (μεγαλυνθήσεται) in Paul's life or death (1:20). Pondering the benefits of remaining alive in ministry, Paul views a return to the Philippians as necessary to engender for them an abundant *boast* (καύχημα) in Christ (1:26).[23] When launching into paraenesis, Paul is anxious that they conduct themselves *worthily* (ἀξίως) in their role as citizens of heaven (1:27).

In Chapter 2, Paul prohibits the attitude of *vain-glory* (κενοδοξία) for his communities (2:3), promoting instead the Christ-like virtue of *humility* (ταπεινοφροσύνη).[24] In the hymn, Christ both humbles himself (ἐταπείνωσεν, 2:8) and is then *exalted* (ὑπερύψωσεν) by God, being granted the honorific title (ὄνομα)[25] of *Lord* (κύριος, 2:9).[26] Just like Paul's opening prayer, the hymn climaxes with *glory* (δόξα) offered to God the Father (2:11). Paul hopes that the Philippians' faithfulness will engender an eschatological *boast* (καύχημα) for himself (2:16), an idea that he uses again later by referring to them as already constituting his *crown* (στέφανος, 4:1).[27] Paul states that Timothy's *proven character* (δοκιμή) is well-known to this community (2:22),[28] as is the *liturgist* (λειτουργός) Epaphroditus,[29] whom they are to hold in *honor* (ἐντίμος, 2:29).

In Chapter 3, while calling for *mimesis* (3:17) Paul points to both positive and negative *exempla* for the Philippians. The apostle himself represents the positive paradigm of pursuing Christ above all else with the hope of attaining the *prize* (σκοπός, 3:14).[30] As a negative model, Paul calls attention to enemies of the cross, whose *glory*

---

subjective genitive, reflecting "ein δοξάζειν der Menschen [i.e., of the Philippians] durch Gott" (p. 125).

[23] For the inclusion of καύχημα within the honorific word-field, see Mark T. Finney, *Honour and Conflict in the Ancient World: 1 Corinthians in Its Greco-Roman Social Setting*, LNTS 460 (London: T&T Clark, 2011), 13. Similarly, Gupta, "Honourable Wish for Death," 263, adduces that the word καύχημα "unquestionably involves honour."

[24] On the affirmation of humility in Philippians, see E.-M. Becker, *Der Begriff der Demut bei Paulus* (Tübingen: Mohr Siebeck, 2015), 74–129, 151–70.

[25] Jerome H. Neyrey, *Give God the Glory: Ancient Prayer and Worship in Cultural Perspective* (Grand Rapids, MI: Eerdmans, 2007), 70: "One's 'name' serves as a vehicle for one's reputation, worth, and respect."

[26] Samuel Vollenweider, "'Der Name, der über jedem anderen Namen ist': Jesus als Träger des Gottesnamens im Neuen Testament," in *Gott nennen: Gottes Namen und Gott als Name*, ed. I. U. Dalferth and P. Stoellger, RPT 35 (Tübingen: Mohr Siebeck, 2008), 173–86, 183, observes that Jesus' reception of the name reveals "die unvergleichliche Würde de Jesu." Cf. Samuel Bénétreau, "Appellation et transcendance: Le nom mystérieux de *Philippiens* 2,9," *RHPhR* 89.3 (2009), 313–31, 329, who argues that the "name" κύριος given to Jesus functions less as a "name" than as a "title," i.e., a "désignation honorifique exprimant une distinction de rang, une dignité."

[27] Frederick W. Danker, *Benefactor: Epigraphic Study* (St. Louis, MO: Clayton, 1982), 469, explains that the crown "is evidently the award that is ordinarily granted for achievement in which one takes pride as a head of state or as a generous citizen … [Paul's] real boast, however, has to do with the kind of life displayed by his addressees … [T]*hey make his reputation as a benefactor*" (emphasis added).

[28] Karl S. J. Prümm, *Diakonia Pneumatos* (Rome: Herder, 1962), vol. 2.2, 357, notes how δοκιμή and καύχημα belong within the same *Begriffsfelder*, i.e., referring to an individual's *Selbstwertbewusstseins*, arguing also that Paul employs these words especially when referring to "die eschatologische Billigung Gottes."

[29] Harrison, "Civic Ethics," 105: "The summons to hold 'in esteem' the self-sacrificing Epaphroditus belongs to traditional honorific parlance (Phil 2:29: ἐντίμους) and it is reinforced by the inscriptional language of 'liturgy' and 'zeal' (2:25: λειτουργόν; 2:28: σπουδαιοτέρως)."

[30] Philip F. Esler, "Paul and the *Agon*: Understanding a Pauline Motif in Its Cultural and Visual Context," in *Picturing the New Testament: Studies in Ancient Visual Images*, ed. Aannette Weissenrieder, Friederike Wendt and Petra von Gemünden, WUNT 2.193 (Tübingen: Mohr Siebeck, 2005),

(δόξα) is misdirected and therefore actually entails their *shame* (αἰσχύνη, 3:19). In contrast, believers are promised a divine vindication upon the parousia of Christ when their present experience of *humiliation* (ταπείνωσις) will give way to a *glorious* participation (σύμμορφος τῷ σώματι τῆς δόξης αὐτοῦ) in Christ's own resurrection experience (3:20–21).

And in Chapter 4, when seeking help in mediating the matter of Euodia and Syntyche, Paul commends both these women and other unnamed coworkers as having their *names written in the book of life* (4:3).[31] Paul calls for the Philippians to pursue virtue, listing common Hellenistic terms, among which are those describing behavior that is *well-spoken of* (εὔφημα) and *praiseworthy* (ἔπαινος, 4:8). Finally, Paul expects Christ's rich *glory* (δόξα) to reciprocate for the Philippians' benefaction to him (4:19), with the ultimate outcome being eternal *glory* (δόξα) for God the Father (4:20). While this overview of honorific language in the letter is by no means comprehensive, it demonstrates the prominent role honor has in shaping Paul's message for his community.

Against this backdrop, when we turn our attention to the specific argument of Phil 1:26 and 2:15–16, it will become clear that the theme of boasting as developed within the relationship of mutual honor between Paul, the Philippians, and God in Christ plays a central role in the rhetoric of Philippians. In short, Phil 1:26 highlights the apostle's contribution to the honor of the group, whereas Phil 2:15–16 depicts the community's contribution to this shared honor. In both cases, it is the boasting of the other that emerges, thereby entailing mutuality of honor.

History of Research on Three Aspects of Pauline and Philippians Studies

Our focus on mutual honor in Paul's boasting language in Philippians entails the convergence of three strands of scholarship: (1) works on the theme of boasting in Paul, (2) works on Paul's use of Scripture in Philippians, and (3) works on κοινωνία in Philippians. Each of these three strands has produced a large body of scholarship, and so in what follows we will treat each separately.

Boasting in Paul

Whereas our study will focus specifically on Paul's language of boasting in Philippians, most of the scholarship on this theme has either dealt with the Pauline corpus en masse, or else has focused specifically on the *Hauptbriefe*, especially the Corinthian

---

356–85, 368, points to "the central role of honour and shame" in Paul's language of prizes from the athletic realm in Phil 3:12–16.

[31] Stefan Schapdick, *Eschatisches Heil mit eschatischer Anerkennung: Exegetische Untersuchungen zu Funktion und Sachgehalt der paulinischen Verkündigung vom eigenen Endgeschick im Rahmen seiner Korrespondenz an die Thessalonicher, Korinther und Philipper*, BBB 164 (Göttingen: Vandenhoeck & Ruprecht, 2011), 247, situates this idea "in Analogie zur städtischen Liste römischer Bürger in Philippi."

correspondence[32] and Romans.[33] And whereas early works on this theme focused on the theological basis of Paul's boasting, more recently scholars have analyzed Paul's boasting in light of Greco-Roman rhetorical practices.[34] Others have treated the theological elements involved in Paul's language of boasting, particularly its correspondence with Jewish national pride and with claims to one's value before God.[35]

Programmatic Studies for the Recent Discussion of Pauline Boasting

Two works appeared early in the twentieth century on Paul's boasting that were programmatic for understanding this aspect in the Pauline corpus. In his 1925 article on Paul's boasting, Ragnar Asting asserts that the language of καύχημα "receives in the LXX a content that is, at times, quite different from the content of these words in profane Greek usage," that is, the pejorative sense of arrogance.[36] Asting contends that, whereas καύχημα "is naturally out of … [the] character" of the Greek papyri, which for him explains its rarity there,[37] its character does fit the context of the LXX[38] where it moves into the realm of declaring one's greatness *"in"* something else. This was the LXX's "new and original contribution" to previous usage of the term,[39] and it will be important for the present study because integral to the mutual honor shared between Paul, the Philippians, and God/Christ is their ability to boast *in each other*.

---

[32] See, e.g., Y. S. Choi, *"Denn wenn ich schwach bin": Die paulinischen Peristasenkataloge und ihre Apostolatstheologie*, NET 16 (Basel: Francke Verlag, 2010); Kate C. Donahoe, "From Self-Praise to Self-Boasting: Paul's Unmasking of the Conflicting Rhetorico-Linguistic Phenomena in 1 Corinthians" (PhD diss., University of St. Andrews, 2008); G. B. Davis, "True and False Boasting" (PhD diss., University of Cambridge, 1999); Jennifer A. Glancy, "Boasting of Beatings (2 Corinthians 11:23–25)," *JBL* 123 (2004), 99–135; Jan Lambrecht, "Paul's Boasting about the Corinthians: A Study of 2 Corinthians 8:24–9:5," *NovT* 40 (1998), 352–68; Ulrich Heckel, *Kraft in Schwachheit: Untersuchungen zu 2. Kor 10–13*, WUNT 2.56 (Tübingen: Mohr Siebeck, 1993); Eric Fuchs, "La faiblesse, gloire de l'apostolat selon Paul: Étude sur 2 Corinthians 10–13," *ETR* 55 (1980), 231–53; S. H. Travis, "Paul's Boasting in 2 Corinthians 10–12," *StuEv* 6 (1973), 527–32.

[33] See, e.g., Simon J. Gathercole, *Where Is Boasting?: Early Jewish Soteriology and Paul's Response in Romans 1–5* (Grand Rapids, MI: Eerdmans, 2002); Beverly Roberts Gaventa, "'Where Then Is Boasting?': Romans 3:27 and Its Context," *PEGLBS* 5 (1985), 57–66.

[34] See, e.g., Ryan S. Schellenberg, *Rethinking Paul's Rhetorical Education: Comparative Rhetoric and 2 Corinthians 10–13*, ECL 10 (Atlanta, GA: SBL Press, 2013); Duane F. Watson, "Boasting in Paul," in *Paul in the Greco-Roman World: A Handbook*, ed. J. Paul Sampley (Harrisburg: Trinity Press International, 2003), 77–100; J. Paul Sampley, "Paul, His Opponents in 2 Corinthians 10–13, and the Rhetorical Handbooks," in *The Social World of Formative Christianity and Judaism*, FS Howard Clark Kee, ed. Jacob Neusner et al. (Philadelphia, PA: Fortress Press, 1988), 162–77; Christopher Forbes, "Comparison, Self-Praise, and Irony: Paul's Boasting and Hellenistic Rhetoric," *NTS* 32 (1986), 1–30.

[35] See, e.g., Gathercole, *Where Is Boasting?*; Jan Lambrecht, "Why Is Boasting Excluded?: A Note on Romans 3:27 and 4:2," *ETL* 61 (1986), 365–9; Richard W. Thompson, "Paul's Double Critique of Jewish Boasting," *Bib* 67 (1986), 520–31.

[36] Ragnar Asting, "*Kauchesis*. Et bidrag til forståelsen av den religiøse selvfølelse hos Paulus," *NoTT* 26 (1925), 129–204, 143 (my translation throughout).

[37] Asting, "*Kauchesis*," 139.

[38] Asting, "*Kauchesis*," 143.

[39] Asting, "*Kauchesis*," 141. See also below, J. Sánchez Bosch, *"Gloriarse" segun san Pablo: Sentido y teología de καυχάομαι*, AnBib 40 (Rome: Biblical Institute Press, 1970), 120, who corroborates this notion that Jewish thinking was unique in proposing the possibility of a *shared boast*.

In enumerating the uses of καύχημα in the LXX, Asting points to two important Hebrew words underlying it: תהלה and תפארת, which "signify that which is the object of praise, of honor, and of fame."⁴⁰ He notes that these Hebrew terms "signify that which engenders acknowledgement from others."⁴¹ This description of what is essentially a claim to acknowledgment from others correlates with the definition for honor proposed by modern social-scientific scholars. For as Pitt-Rivers succinctly states,

> Honour ... is the estimation of [a person's] own worth, his *claim* to pride, but it is also the acknowledgement of that claim, his excellence recognized by society, his *right* to pride.⁴²

Thus, even in this early work on boasting Asting clearly situated the term καύχημα within the semantic word-field of honor.

Bultmann next provided a foundational study of Paul's boasting in his *TDNT* article, which falls in line with his overall project to find in the theology of the New Testament an invitation to existential self-awareness (*Selbstbewußtsein*). Bultmann thus finds in καυχᾶσθαι the "höchsten Ausdruck" of humanity's sinful desire to be self-sufficient, which is characteristic of the Jew (Rom 2:17, 23), of the Greek (1 Cor 1:19–31), as well as representing "ein natürlicher Trieb des Menschen" to compare oneself with others (cf. Gal 6:4).⁴³ In Bultmann's *TDNT* entry, he consequently contends that καυχάομαι in the LXX is used to express Jewish national pride and identity, brushing aside any Hellenistic influence upon Paul's use of the term because of its scarcity in Hellenistic texts.⁴⁴ However, in contrast to its primarily negative connotation when appearing in Hellenistic texts and when the "boast" is in Jewish national and ethnic identity, the LXX writers nevertheless envision a positive place for boasting when it involves "self-humbling before God,"⁴⁵ since "the one who glories thus looks away from himself, so that his glorying is a confession of God," and not a "boast" in one's own identity or accomplishments.⁴⁶ He notes the eschatological significance for boasting in the Scriptures, where it is "acutalised in the time of salvation" (Zech 10:12; Ps 149:5; 1 Chron 16:33). Bultmann finds in Second Temple Judaism a slight variation on this positive portrayal of boasting, noting especially Sirach's transferal of boasting "from the cultic and eschatological sphere to that of legal righteousness" (Sir 1:11; 9:16; 10:22;

---

⁴⁰ Asting, "*Kauchesis*," 141–2.
⁴¹ Asting, "*Kauchesis*," 141.
⁴² Pitt-Rivers, "Honour," 21. This aspect of boasting is rightly affirmed by Klaus Berger, *Exegese des Neuen Testaments* (Heidelberg: Quelle & Meyer, 1977), 151, who notes that *sich rühmen* represents "immer dem Fundament des sozialen Prestiges." See also Finney, *Honour and Conflict*, 13: "the καύχημα word-group ... contains the nuance of making public claims to honour."
⁴³ Rudolf Bultmann, *Theologie des Neuen Testaments* (Tübingen: Mohr Siebeck, 1948), 237–8. Cf. Bultmann, *Theologie*, 238: "Im καυχᾶσθαι zeigt sich die Verkennung der menschlichen Situation, das Vergessen der Tatsache" that everything we have is a gift (1 Cor 4:7).
⁴⁴ Donahoe, "Self-Boasting," xxvii, notes that Bultmann's bypassing of Greco-Roman texts sets a trajectory that has long since been followed.
⁴⁵ Bultmann, "καυχάομαι," *TDNT* 3.646.
⁴⁶ Bultmann, *TDNT* 3.647. Bultmann finds boasting terminology used in the LXX both negatively, depicting "the basic attitude of the ... ungodly" (Ps 51:3 LXX; 73:4 LXX; 93:3 LXX), and positively, being synonymous with the activity of hoping in God (Ps 5:11).

39:8).⁴⁷ Bultmann notes how Philo, though almost entirely avoiding the term, warns against self-glorying (*Spec.* 1.311), directing his fellow Jews rather to let their "boast" (using the related term αὔχημα) be in God alone (cf. Deut 10:21 LXX).

For Bultmann, the arrival of the new age in Jesus Christ means that Jesus now becomes the focus of Paul's identity and pride, with faith in him becoming central: "For Paul then, as for the OT and Philo, the element of trust contained in καυχᾶσθαι is primary," with self-confidence "radically excluded."⁴⁸ Bultmann thus points to Rom 15:17–18 to adduce that Paul grounds his boasting in what Christ does through him. Likewise, Bultmann denies that Paul's apostolic boasting in his churches is self-glorying, seeing it rather as expressing "his confidence in the congregation," a "mutual trust" that is "promoted in the fellowship of faith."⁴⁹ Finally, Bultmann associates those passages in which Paul speaks of his converts as his eschatological "boast" (e.g., 1 Thess 2:19–20, 2 Cor 1:14; Phil 2:16) with the Scriptural tradition of thanksgiving and exultation in which thankful joy accompanies the reception of God's grace, a thankfulness in which Paul's communities must participate as well (2 Cor 1:14; Phil 1:26; cf. 2 Cor 5:12).⁵⁰

These two early works were followed by a third important study: Sánchez Bosch's 1970 monograph on Pauline boasting. Similar to Bultmann, Sánchez Bosch finds that the LXX "completely abandons contact with the profane themes when organizing [καύχημα] in the sphere with the divine,"⁵¹ arguing that this Jewish understanding of the term is what shapes Paul's usage. Sánchez Bosch also calls attention to Paul's distinction from the Greco-Roman culture in depicting a mutuality of boasting, drawing on the LXX writers' usage of the καυχ- word group in which boasting occurred *in someone else*.⁵² Sánchez Bosch concludes with the affirmation that Paul offers the possibility of boasting before God, as long as it is on the basis of good works that "proceed from grace."⁵³ Sánchez Bosch concurs, however, with Bultmann that Paul's predication of

---

⁴⁷ Bultmann, *TDNT* 3.647, notes the connection between boasting and the law (Sir 39:8, ἐν νόμῳ διαθήκης κυρίου καυχήσεται). Cf. Philo, *Spec.* 4.164: "My sceptre is the book of the Sequel to the law, my pride (καύχημα) and my glory, which nothing can rival." For a recent study connecting Sirach's presentation of boasting with that of Paul in Phil 3, see Harrison, "Roman Boasting in Philippians 3:4–6," 312–19.

⁴⁸ Bultmann, *TDNT* 3.649.

⁴⁹ Bultmann, *TDNT* 3.650.

⁵⁰ Bultmann, *TDNT* 3.651. Bultmann's main line of thought is followed by Maurice Carrez, "La confiance en l'homme et la confiance en soi selon l'apôtre Paul," *RHPhR* 44 (1964), 191–9, 199, who asserts that the Christian's boasting represents "une nouvelle forme de confiance en soi." Bultmann's influence remains among recent scholars; see Élian Cuvillier, "L'homme entre mort et vie: L'existence humaine selon Philippiens 3," *Cat* 130 (1993), 43–55, 46, who argues that Paul often uses the καυχ- stem "pour exprimer l'attitude de l'homme qui cherche ce qui pourrait donner sens à sa vie, ce sur quoi il pourrait construire son existence."

⁵¹ Sánchez Bosch, *Gloriarse*, 55 (my translation throughout).

⁵² Sánchez Bosch, *Gloriarse*, 120, where he finds it certain that Hellenistic authors "know nothing of the idea that one person might be the καύχημα of another," while finding such a reality of mutual honor evident (eleven times) in the LXX (cf. pp. 88–9). See also Ceslas Spicq, "καυχάομαι," *TLNT* 2.300: "St. Paul innovates not only in giving the verb [καυχάομαι] the positive meaning 'be proud,' but also 'be proud of others'" (citing Gal 6:13; 2 Cor 5:12; 7:14; 9:2). I will attempt to show in Part 2 that Roman authors *could* envision mutuality of honor, though not necessarily employing the vocabulary of καύχημα to do so.

⁵³ Sánchez Bosch, *Gloriarse*, 312. Josef Zmijewski, "καύχημα," *EDNT* 2.279, speaks of Paul's boasting in his churches (or his churches boasting in him) as appropriate "inasmuch as it refers to either the

a καύχημα for himself through his churches reflects the Jewish idea of a thanksgiving before God within the community of faith.[54]

These early works on Pauline boasting by Asting, Bultmann, and Sánchez Bosch thus establish a framework for understanding Paul's use of the boasting theme across his letters. Important for our focus on mutual boasting in Philippians is Asting's presentation of the honorific nature of the term καύχημα, thereby warranting our presentation of mutual honor within the Greco-Roman honor-seeking cultural context (Part 2). Moreover, Bultmann's description of the "mutual trust" engendered by Paul's boasting in his churches provides a foundation for our investigation of the literary context of mutual honor in Phil 1:26 and 2:16 (Part 3). And finally, Sánchez Bosch's development of mutuality in Paul's boasting by building on the LXX usage of the καυχ-stem will be central to our presentation of the Scriptural context of mutual honor (Part 1). That is, we will argue that Paul drew on the Septuagintal language and idea of Israel as YHWH's καύχημα and YHWH as Israel's καύχημα found repeatedly in the Jewish Scriptures (Deut 10:21; 26:19; Jer 13:11; Zeph 3:19, 20) to which Sánchez Bosch calls attention. Our study will weave these three strands together, demonstrating how Paul relies on the mutual boasting created by his relationship with the Philippians, understood against both the theological context of the LXX Scriptures and the Hellenistic culture of honor, to issue exhortations to this beloved community.

The Hellenistic and Roman Context of Pauline Boasting

In addition to Asting's situating καύχημα within the Hellenistic culture of honor, many studies have analyzed Paul's boasting in light of Hellenistic rhetorical practices.[55] E. A. Judge has argued that even though "Paul was, in practice at least, familiar with the rhetorical fashions of the time,"[56] Paul's claims to glory "are always the opposite of what is normally boasted of" by his contemporaries, arguing that Paul even parodies the conventional norms.[57] Such conventional norms form the basis of numerous recent studies on Paul's boasting, using ancient rhetoricians' justification for boasting as a backdrop to defend Paul's boasting as legitimate.[58] This approach was taken by Smit

---

boasting in the Christian life that has been produced by grace or the boasting that anticipates the parousia."

[54] Sánchez Bosch, *Gloriarse*, 121–2.
[55] See Christine Gerber, "ΚΑΥΧΑΣΘΑΙ ΔΕΙ, ΟΥ ΣΥΜΦΕΡΟΝ ΜΕΝ ... (2 Kor 12,1): Selbstlob bei Paulus vor dem Hintergrund der antiken Gepflogenheiten," in Breytenbach, *Paul's Graeco-Roman Context*, 213–51. Cf. Benjamin Fiore S. J., "The Hortatory Function of Paul's Boasting," EGLMBS 5 (1985), 39–46; Ralph Brucker, *Christushymnen oder epideiktische Passagen?: Studien zum Stilwechsel im Neuen Testament und seiner Umwelt*, FRLANT 176 (Göttingen: Vandenhoeck & Ruprecht, 1997), 137–45.
[56] E. A. Judge, "Paul's Boasting in Relation to Contemporary Practice," ABR 18 (1968), 37–50, 41.
[57] Judge, "Boasting," 47. Similarly, Berger, *Exegese*, 151, speaks of Paul's boasting involving a fundamental *Umwertung* of the standards of men before God.
[58] Watson, "Boasting," 79–81, lists all the circumstances under which "boasting is acceptable" from the perspective of Hellenistic rhetoric. Sampley's *Handbook* has a new edition (London: Bloomsbury, 2016; 2 vols.), where Watson's article (1.90–112) is slightly altered. I will refer to the first edition unless otherwise noted. Forbes, "Comparison," 20, however, argues that, despite having "many plausible justifications" for his self-praise, for Paul self-praise was "never legitimate."

in regard to Phil 3,[59] where he relates Paul's boasting to Plutarch's view of morally acceptable and unacceptable self-praise. Smit argues that Paul's boasting "remains within the boundaries of acceptable and inoffensive self-praise" recommended by Plutarch because, among other reasons, "Paul's self-praise serves an ulterior motive: his care for the community, the salvation of which he considers to be endangered" (cf. Plutarch, *Mor.* 539E-F).[60]

Duane Watson's work presents an important argument in favor of the legitimacy of Paul's boasting. Following Bultmann, he affirms that in the LXX authors boasting is legitimate as long as it is "theocentric," based on "an intimate relationship with … God."[61] He argues further from this Jewish framework that "boasting in God's works is acceptable, particularly boasting about God's acts in sustaining the community of faith … [S]uch boasting is really worship and confession."[62] In regard to Paul's boasting, Watson focuses on 2 Cor 10–13, where he notes both that "an honor challenge and response (riposte) are central" to the apostle's boasting, and, with Judge, that "Paul's boasting challenges the value system of the Corinthians—and of the Greco-Roman world—through parody."[63] In line with this, while demonstrating that Paul's boasting generally conforms to the conventions of his contemporaries, "there is also a counter-cultural thread running throughout" it, since the apostle "rejects the dominant culture's criteria for honor," and instead engages in "boasting with non-conventional values."[64] Discussing Philippians, Watson simply affirms that Paul's boast in 2:16 that his labor has not been futile constitutes "proper boasting in the Lord's work through him."[65]

Finally, John Barclay's work on Paul's language of grace intersects with the issue of boasting in Gal 6, where Barclay situates this motif within the apostle's cultural context, which was "both ordered and threatened by the competition for honor."[66] Hence, for Barclay, Paul's terminology of καύχημα finds its home in the Roman world's prevalent quest for honor. Barclay argues that within this cultural context Paul works to overcome such "self-advertisement, rivalry, and public competition" within his own communities, since "the people reconstituted by the Christ-gift have discounted the value placed on forms of honor over which their contemporaries compete."[67] With these previous values and norms cast aside, God's radically incongruous grace has established for believers "an alternative system of worth, a new form of 'symbolic capital.'"[68] In this sense, boasting, along with all other forms of honor, is not denied, but is rather transformed. Thus, believers still have grounds for honor in their "work,"

---

[59] Peter-Ben Smit, "Paul, Plutarch and the Problematic Practice of Self-Praise (περιαυτολογία)," *NTS* 60 (2014), 341–59.
[60] Smit, "Self-Praise," 359, 353. See also Fiore, "Hortatory Function," 45. See below (Part 2) for further treatment of Plutarch's treatise on self-praise.
[61] Watson, "Boasting," 78.
[62] Watson, "Boasting," 78.
[63] Watson, "Boasting" (2nd ed.), 96, 102.
[64] Watson, "Boasting" (2nd ed.), 107–8.
[65] Watson, "Boasting," 97, where he also posits that Paul "anticipates sharing with the Philippians in boasting in their progress and joy in the faith ([Phil] 1:25–26)."
[66] John M. G. Barclay, *Paul and the Gift* (Grand Rapids, MI: Eerdmans, 2015), 433.
[67] Barclay, *Gift*, 435.
[68] Barclay, *Gift*, 435, drawing on Pierre Bordieu, *Outline of a Theory of Practice*, trans. R. Nice (Cambridge: Cambridge University Press, 1977), 171–82.

within the criteria of value established by the Christ-event: "on the right basis, and within the right limits, it is proper for honor to be offered and received."[69] Barclay's notion that Paul maintains a place for positive boasting within his Christ-communities is important for our study because, in Philippians, Paul deploys the theme of boasting as the positive reward available to believers, though it accrues not through their own activity but rather through the activity of others, thereby transforming it into a mutual boast.

To sum up, Paul's boasting demonstrates the apostle's interacting with his congregations in a culturally understandable manner, thereby avoiding the stigma that accompanied self-praise in antiquity.[70] Most importantly, Paul offers a reoriented appraisal of honor, finding in Christ that which is truly valuable, and seeking after this true honor both for himself and for his communities. The rhetorical dynamic of Paul's discussion of boasting, therefore, remains strong. Various scholars have interpreted Philippians against this background of ancient rhetorical practices.[71] Rather than interpreting Paul against rhetorical practices of the first century, however, our study will interpret Paul's boasting against the cultural phenomenon of mutual honor reflected in the relations between friends and family. While there is a rhetorical element to Paul's use of mutual honor in Philippians when he deploys that theme for the purpose of motivation in 2:14–16, our focus is less on the self-presentation involved in boasting and more on the pressure exerted through the kinship relation Paul establishes between himself and his auditors.

Paul's Boasting in the Context of Second Temple Judaism

Simon Gathercole's monograph shows that in Romans Paul employs the boasting motif in contrast to contemporary Judaism,[72] where the contrast is not regarding "the doctrine of judgment according to works *per se*," but is rather, "over the extent of God's grace."[73] Gathercole argues that Second Temple texts are cognizant of divine grace, but it is a different type of grace, lacking the "continual driving force" found in Paul's conception of Christ and the Spirit as "empowering … obedient service."[74] In light of this larger argument, Gathercole's work treats the issue of Jewish boasting in the Second Temple period, which he articulates as neither "negative by definition" nor "as a confidence based merely on divine election," but as entailing a twofold conviction: (1)

---

[69] Barclay, *Gift*, 437.
[70] On the offensiveness of self-praise in antiquity, see Plutarch, *Mor.* 539D; cf. Dionysius of Halicarnassus, *Letter to Pompeius*, 92.28-30, who describes self-praise as "most vulgar" (cited by Watson, "Boasting," 78).
[71] For an overview of various rhetorical approaches to the letter, see Duane E. Watson, "The Integration of Epistolary and Rhetorical Analysis of Philippians," in *Rhetorical Analysis of Scripture: Essays from the 1995 London Conference*, ed. Stanley E. Porter and Thomas H. Olbricht, LNTS 146 (Sheffield: Sheffield Academic Press, 1997), 398–426.
[72] Rather than following E. P. Sanders in speaking about "getting in" or "staying in," Gathercole, *Where Is Boasting?*, 24, proposes an eschatological perspective on Jewish soteriology focused on "getting there."
[73] Simon J. Gathercole, "After the New Perspective: Works, Justification and Boasting in Early Judaism and Romans 1–5," *TynBul* 52 (2001), 303–6, 306.
[74] Gathercole, "New Perspective," 306.

that God had graciously elected Israel and (2) that Israel would be vindicated at the eschaton on the basis of their fulfillment of the law. In doing so, Gathercole highlights that "boasting" is "usually oriented toward God's vindication."[75] This emphasis on eschatological boasting will be important for our own discussion of boasting in Philippians, which is overtly oriented toward "the day of Christ" (Phil 2:16).

In light of these works on boasting in Paul, we may summarize that boasting for Paul can be used in both a negative sense and a positive sense. Used negatively, boasting entails a human claim to honor over against God, which Paul prohibits (e.g., Rom 3:27). Used positively, boasting refers to the honor that accrues to believers for their labor on behalf of and through the power of Christ (e.g., Rom 15:17; 1 Cor 15:31). In Philippians, Paul's use of the boasting motif is always positive (1:26; 2:16; 3:3). Hence, the present study will show how Paul brings Scriptural texts on mutual honor into conversation with the Greco-Roman honor-seeking culture, presenting honor as something that is mutually attainable and that can thereby serve as proper motivation for virtuous behavior.

Septuagintal Studies on Pauline Boasting

Since one of the aims of this study is to draw out the Scriptural backdrop of mutual boasting for Philippians, it is necessary to call attention to two final studies of boasting in the Scriptures, which are helpful for the approach we will take in what follows. First, Josef Schreiner studies Paul's use of the Jeremaic admonition to boast only in the Lord (Jer 9:22–23 in 1 Cor 1:31 and 2 Cor 10:17), analyzing the appearance of the boasting theme in both the MT and the LXX.[76] Schreiner affirms both the positive use of the boasting theme ("Sache der Frommen") and its use as an expression of relationship with YHWH.[77] In accord with Sánchez Bosch's presentation of mutual boasting in the LXX, Schreiner uncovers a "zweifacher Hinsicht" by placing Deut 26:19 in conjunction with 10:21, since in 26:19 Israel is YHWH's καύχημα, whereas in 10:21 YHWH is Israel's καύχημα.[78] Schreiner believes that, from the perspective of these two verses, all the other texts about Israel's boasting become understandable.[79] Thus, Schreiner argues that by translating the Hebrew term for *praise* (תהלה) with καύχημα, "eine wichtige Entscheidung" was hit upon: "die Bedeutung 'Ruhm' war für [תהלה] neben 'Lobpreis' grundsätzlich anerkannt."[80] Finally, Schreiner also points to the prominent role that the language of boasting plays in Deutero- and Trito-Isaiah, albeit only reflected via the common terminology in the MT (since LXX-Isaiah avoids the καυχ- word group).[81] As we will see, Schreiner's understanding of the role of mutual boasting in Deut 10:21 and 26:19 will be formative for our own presentation of mutual boasting in Phil 1:26 and 2:16.

---

[75] This follows Berger, *Exegese*, 146.
[76] Josef Schreiner, "Jer 9,22.23 als Hintergrund des paulinischen 'Sich-Rühmens,'" in *Biblische Randbemerkungen*, FS R. Schnackenburg, ed. H. Merklein and J. Lange (Würzburg: Echter, 1974), 530–42.
[77] Schreiner, "Sich-Rühmens," 536.
[78] Schreiner, "Sich-Rühmens," 536–7.
[79] Schreiner, "Sich-Rühmens," 538.
[80] Schreiner, "Sich-Rühmens," 539.
[81] On LXX Isaiah's reticence to use the καυχ- word group, see Schreiner, "Sich-Rühmens," 539.

A second important study on καύχημα in the LXX is by Eric Fuchs.⁸² Fuchs too finds the translation at Deut 10:21 of תהלה with καύχημα to be "plus significatif."⁸³ Fuchs notes that when καύχημα renders terms other than תהלה it usually has "un sens positif," designating primarily "une qualité appartient à Dieu lui-même" (1 Chron 16:27; 29:11), but one that can be extended by God "reposer sur ses élus" (Jer 13:11), such that "καύχημα est donc un des attributs qui marque l'appartenance du peuple à Dieu."⁸⁴ Finally, Fuchs points to "une certain tension" in the usage of καύχημα "entre une signification eschatologique," in that it pertains only to God, who will not share it until the last days, and "une signification morale," in that it is available in the present as the reward for a life of faithfulness to the law.⁸⁵ Fuchs's emphasis on the positive quality of καύχημα in the LXX highlighting Israel's exalted status as God's elect is important for our own development of Paul's appropriation in Philippians of the Deuteronomic tradition that God makes Israel into a καύχημα (cf. Phil 2:16 with Deut 26:19 LXX).

Summary of Scholarship on Pauline Boasting

As this brief survey demonstrates, we can roughly distinguish between three approaches that discussions of Paul's boasting have taken: (1) dealing with boasting in connection with (Jewish) election and justification, (2) dealing with the apostle's boasting in relation to his own apostolic work and the life of his churches and vice versa, and (3) dealing with Paul's boasting in relation to Hellenistic rhetorical practice. This study will focus on the second of these concerns, since the boasting in Phil 1:26 and 2:16 is undoubtedly oriented relationally between apostle and community. Although the issue of Paul and the Philippians' eschatological fate does hang in the balance in these passages, where the reality of divine judgment looms on the horizon, the focus is on the mutuality of boasting between apostle and community. And though in Phil 3:3 Paul takes up the issue of "boasting" in regard to Israel's election and identity, yet our thesis deals less with the identity and confidence brought about by God's election of his people, which are subsidiary themes within the letter, and takes up instead the mutuality inherent in the honor emerging from a successful ministry for both the apostle and his community that stands at the rhetorical center of the letter. In this way, we hope to bring together the twin elements of Paul's Jewish heritage and the Philippians' Greco-Roman situation in order to understand the apostle's use of the mutual boasting theme. As Dieter Zeller has affirmed, while it is Scriptural tradition that provides the *Impuls* for Paul's language of boasting, this does not exclude the fact that the form of Paul's boasting was oriented according to Hellenistic *Regeln*.⁸⁶

---

[82] Eric Fuchs, "Gloire de Dieu, gloire de l'homme: essai sur les termes *kauchasthai, kauchèma, kauchèsis* dans la Septante," *RTP* 27 (1977), 321–32.
[83] Fuchs, "Gloire," 328.
[84] Fuchs, "Gloire," 329.
[85] Fuchs, "Gloire," 332.
[86] Dieter Zeller, "Selbstbezogenheit und Selbstdarstellung in den Paulusbriefen," in *Neues Testament und Hellenistische Umwelt*, BBB 150 (Göttingen: Philo, 2006), 201–13, 212.

Thus, in accordance with the argument of Phil 1:25–26 and 2:14–16, we approach the concept of boasting not from the standpoint of an activity in which Paul currently engages (as he does at Phil 3:4–6) but rather from the perspective of an honor that he prospectively hopes to embrace. In Phil 1:26 and 2:16 the term καύχημα constitutes an *Ehrentitel*,[87] an honor bestowed, rather than a legitimate/nonlegitimate rhetorical endeavor. Hence, our study will engage with those works that situate the concept of boasting within the realm of honor.[88] Especially helpful will be those works that discuss the honor emerging from the mutual interaction between the apostle and his converts.

The Presence and Function of Scripture in Philippians

Since we will argue that Paul's allusions to Scripture in Phil 2:14–16 provide an important source for his use of the mutual honor theme in the letter, a discussion of our method of engaging with Paul's use of Scripture is appropriate. In Philippians, rather than explicitly citing Scriptural texts, Paul "embeds" Scriptural material,[89] which has led some to dismiss the importance of Scripture in the letter.[90] A lack of citation formulae, however, does not rule out the presence of Scripture, as even Christopher Stanley observes.[91] Indeed, Stanley affirms the validity of attending to allusions, that is, unmarked citations, within Paul's letters as a means to uncover the apostle's "own deep roots in Judaism."[92] Finding that in Philippians Paul integrates Scriptural material within his own writing via allusions, we follow Hays's call to "recognize the embeddedness of [Paul's] discourse in scriptural language ... and explore the rhetorical

---

[87] Heckel, *Schwachheit*, 161, "καύχημα und καύχησις [können] vor allem in der jüdisch-christlichen Tradition einem Ehrentitel nahekommen."

[88] Cf. Donahoe, "Self-Boasting," 2: "References to ... 'boasting' frequently appear within the matrix of honor and shame that permeated the Greco-Roman world."

[89] See Reed, *Discourse Analysis of Philippian*, 291, where he posits the following Scriptural allusions in Philippians: Prov 3:9 and 11:30 LXX in Phil 1:11; Job 13:16 LXX in 1:19; Isa 53:3, 11 in 2:7; Isa 45:23 LXX in 2:10–11; Deut 32:5 and Dan 12:3 LXX in 2:15; Isa 49:4 and 65:23 LXX in 2:16; Hos 4:7 in 3:19; Ps 8:7 LXX in 3:21; Ps 69:28 in 4:3; Ps 145:18 in 4:5–6; and Gen 8:21, Exod 29:18, and Isa 56:7 in 4:18. Reed, 291 n. 499, however, questions our ability to "evaluate [the role of these allusions] in Paul's argument," and prefers to treat them "as part of [Paul's] idiolect rather than his rhetoric." Benjamin Fiore, "Invective in Romans and Philippians," *PEGLMBS* 10 (1990), 181–9, 187, claims that Paul's phrase in Phil 3:3 is "an allusion to Jeremiah's reminder (Jer 9:22–24) to boast not in human accomplishments but in the Lord's action, all in view of the coming account-taking of 'all those circumcised in the flesh.'"

[90] L. Michael White, "Morality between Two Worlds: A Paradigm of Friendship in Philippians," in *Greeks, Romans, and Christians*, FS Malherbe, ed. David L. Balch, Everett Ferguson and Wayne A. Meeks (Minneapolis, MN: Fortress, 1990), 201–15, 205, argues in passing that Philippians has "so little that is Jewish in its content, its tone, or its ethical exhortation. There is no midrashic play on the OT, as there is in ... 1 Corinthians 10, nor is there an overtly Jewish social idiom presupposed, as in ... the eschatological section of 1 Thessalonians." But as we will see, it is precisely in the "eschatological section" of Phil 2:12–16 that we find a "midrashic play" on Deut 32 just as in 1 Cor 10.

[91] Christopher D. Stanley, *Paul and the Language of Scripture: Citation Technique in the Pauline Epistles and Contemporary Literature*, SNTSMS 69 (Cambridge: Cambridge University Press, 1992), 254.

[92] Christopher D. Stanley, "What We Learned—and What We Didn't," in *Paul and Scripture: Extending the Conversation*, ed. Christopher D. Stanley, ECL 9 (Atlanta, GA: SBL Press, 2012), 321–30, 323.

and theological effects created by the intertextual relationships between his letters and their scriptural precursors."[93]

Scriptural Allusions in Paul's Letters

Scholars have debated the precise definition of "allusion" in Paul. G. K. Beale presents the following definition for a biblical allusion in the New Testament: "a brief expression consciously intended by an author to be dependent on an OT passage," and offers as "the telltale key to discerning an allusion" the recognition of "an incomparable or unique parallel in wording, syntax, concept or cluster of motifs in the same order or structure."[94] For our study, the "unique" term καύχημα, together with the parallel concept of obedience leading to mutual honor, constitutes the "telltale key" to discerning in Phil 2:16 an allusion to Deut 26:19 LXX, especially since this verse falls in the wider context of Deut 32:5, the verse to which Paul overtly alludes in Phil 2:15.

Since we will see that Scriptural material in Phil 2:14–16, one of two texts of particular relevance for this study, exists at the level of allusion or echo, the methodology developed by Hays to guide both recognition and analysis of echoes within Paul's writings is a helpful starting place for uncovering Scripture's presence in the letter.[95] Hays affirms that "Paul's citations of Scripture often function not as proofs but as tropes," generating "new meanings" by creating a link between Paul's words and Israel's Scriptures.[96] Hays offers seven "tests" for recognizing Paul's allusions to Scripture: (1) Availability, (2) Volume, (3) Recurrence, (4) Thematic Coherence, (5) Historical Plausibility, (6) History of Interpretation, and (7) Satisfaction.[97] For the present study Hays's fourth criteria, thematic coherence, is essential to our reading of Phil 2:14–16, since we argue that the theme of obedience engendering mutual boasting is precisely at issue in both texts to which Paul alludes in the passage (i.e., Deut 26:19 and Isa 49:4).

Hays is not the first to push for a more careful attention to the original context for Scriptural allusions. C. H. Dodd programmatically argued that New Testament authors selected for use sections of Scripture that "were understood as *wholes*, and particular verses or sentences were quoted from them ... as pointers to the whole context ... [I]t is the *total context* that is in view, and is the basis of the argument."[98] William A. Tooman

---

[93] Richard B. Hays, *The Conversion of the Imagination: Paul as Interpreter of Israel's Scriptures* (Grand Rapids, MI: Eerdmans, 2005), 29.
[94] G. K. Beale, *Handbook on the New Testament Use of the Old Testament* (Grand Rapids, MI: Baker, 2012), 31, where he further argues that "even an idea may be an allusion ... when both unique wording (verbal coherence) and theme are found." Christopher A. Beetham, *Echoes of Scripture in Colossians*, BIS 96 (Leiden: Brill, 2008), 29, concurs that "even single words can be allusions to a prior text if they are rare and prominent enough."
[95] Richard B. Hays, *Echoes of Scripture in the Letters of Paul* (New Haven, CT: Yale University Press, 1989).
[96] Hays, *Echoes*, 24. See also Beetham, *Echoes in Colossians*, 22, who argues that investigation into the context of the source text "frequently leads to a deeper understanding" of the new text making use of it.
[97] Hays, *Echoes*, 29–32.
[98] C. H. Dodd, *According to the Scriptures* (New York: Charles Scribner's, 1953), 126 (emphasis original). Cf. N. T. Wright, *Paul and the Faithfulness of God*, COQG 4 (London: SPCK, 2013), 176, who argues from the basis of Jewish exegetical practice in the Second Temple period that

has recently argued for a similar approach to understanding how allusions function within the Hebrew Bible, noting that "the category *allusion*, in particular, is sensitive to the ways that authors can use small discrete markers to evoke an entire context."[99] This aspect of how allusions function will be important to the present study because it is Paul's recognizable allusion to Deut 32:5 in Phil 2:15 that evokes the broader context of these closing chapters of Deuteronomy from which Paul draws the notion and language in Phil 2:16 of obedience producing καύχημα, as it does in Deut 26:18–19 LXX. Thus, following the lead of Wagner's study of Paul's use of Isaiah in Romans, I will "listen for the resonances" in Philippians "of the wider Isaianic [and Deuteronomic] settings of the texts that Paul appropriates through ... allusion."[100]

The closely related technique, originating among French literary critics, of *intertextualité* has also been used as a method to interpret Paul's Scriptural allusions.[101] Discussing intertextuality, Ben-Porat provides specific constraints for understanding how literary allusions function. She explains,

> The literary allusion is a device for the simultaneous activation of two texts. The activation is achieved through the manipulation of a special signal: a sign (simple or complex) in a given text characterized by an additional larger "referent." This referent is always an independent text. The simultaneous activation of the two texts thus connected results in the formation of intertextual patterns whose nature cannot be predetermined.[102]

"the context of a scriptural allusion or echo is again and again very important," and that writers "could evoke a whole world of textual reference with a word or phrase." Similarly, J. Ross Wagner, "Isaiah in Romans and Galatians," in *Isaiah in the New Testament*, ed. Steve Moyise and Maarten J. J. Menken (London: T&T Clark, 2005), 117–32, 132, argues that "Paul's allusive appropriations of Isaiah 49 derive ... from a sustained, careful reading of the prophetic oracles in the conviction that he has been crucified with Christ, that Christ now lives in him, and that Christ's mission has become his own." Florian Wilk, "Isaiah in 1 and 2 Corinthians," in Moyise and Menken, *Isaiah in the New Testament*, 133–58, 157, argues about Isaianic allusions that "Paul did not isolate the oracle ... from its original context but has interpreted it in accordance with that context."

[99] William A. Tooman, *Gog of Magog: Reuse of Scripture and Compositional Technique in Ezekiel 38-39*, FAT 2.52 (Tübingen: Mohr Siebeck, 2011), 9. Cf. Michael Fishbane, *Biblical Interpretation in Ancient Israel* (Oxford: Clarendon Press, 1985), 270, who argues that the phenomenon of biblical allusions among Jewish exegetes presupposes "the predisposition to study the textual *traditum*, to be sensitive to its ambiguities, conflicts, and contradictions, and to know how to resolve them."

[100] J. Ross Wagner, *Heralds of the Good News: Isaiah and Paul in Concert in the Letter to the Romans*, NovTSup 101 (Leiden: Brill, 2003), 18.

[101] Jonathan Culler, "Presupposition and Intertextuality," *MLN* 91.6 (1976), 1380–96, 1385, argues that intertextuality requires attention to "the general discursive space which makes a text possible." See, however, the caution advised by Thomas R. Hatina, "Intertextuality and Historical Criticism in New Testament Studies," *BI* 7.1 (1999), 28–43, that by describing Paul's appropriation of Scripture with the notion of "intertextuality" necessarily evokes the post-structuralist framework associated with that notion. Cf. the helpful distinction between "hard" and "soft" intertextuality in John Barton, "Déjà Lu: Intertextuality, Method or Theory?" in *Reading Job Intertextually*, ed. Katharine J. Dell and William L. Kynes (London: T&T Clark, 2013), 1–16. The following study is much more in line with the version of "soft" intertextuality described by Barton.

[102] Ziva Ben-Porat, "The Poetics of Literary Allusion," *PTL* 1 (1976), 105–28, 107–8. Similarly, Carmela Perri, "On Allusion," *Poetics* 7 (1978), 289–307, 293, argues that allusion's "great power of signification ... resides in the additional inter- and intra-textual patterns of associated attributes it can evoke once the primary sense is comprehended."

Ben-Porat uses the terminology "actualize" to describe this intentional invocation of specific elements from the source text.[103]

Applying Ben-Porat's model to Paul, the apostle offers "signs" through using specific language and/or concepts from Scriptural texts; the specific terms he deploys as signs are then framed by the larger text to which they allude. The result is an intertextual pattern, involving elements from both the Scriptural source-text and Paul's own text, creating meaning that is beyond what either text could have achieved individually.[104] The phenomenon of intertextuality and its occurrence in Paul's Scriptural allusions therefore necessitates attention to those elements evoked from the Scriptural source text in order to uncover how Paul's own letter is transformed by the intertextual pattern.

Numerous scholars have followed Dodd and Hays in interpreting Paul's allusions as footnotes to the wider Scriptural context which elucidates Paul's arguments. Lincicum has done this for Paul's engagement with Deuteronomy, arguing that this text was formative for the apostle's thinking.[105] Similarly, Gignilliat has done this by using Isaiah to illumine Paul's self-defense as minister of the gospel in 2 Corinthians.[106] The present study will follow the methodology of these previous scholars by finding Paul's Scriptural allusions to be integral for understanding Philippians, particularly for the mutual boast that Paul shares with the Philippians.

Scriptural Allusions in Philippians

Scholars fall into two distinct groups when determining the function of Scripture in Philippians. Bormann represents the *minimalist* approach, arguing that, despite the presence of allusions in the letter, Paul's argumentation "does not depend on the allusions to Scripture."[107] Schoon-Janssen concurs, since while he admits that Paul's

---

[103] Ben-Porat, "Allusion," 107. Stanley E. Porter, "Allusions and Echoes," in *As It Is Written: Studying Paul's Use of Scripture*, ed. Stanley E. Porter and Christopher D. Stanley, SBLSymS 50 (Atlanta, GA: SBL Press, 2008), 29–40, 33, speaks of allusions "involving the indirect invoking of a person, place, or literary work" and "bringing the external person, place, or literary work into the contemporary material."

[104] Dodd, *According to the Scriptures*, 130: "The transposition into a fresh situation involves a certain shift, nearly always an expansion, of the original scope of the passage." Cf. Stefan Alkier, "New Testament Studies on the Basis of Categorical Semiotics," in *Reading the Bible Intertextually*, ed. Richard B. Hays, Stefan Alkier and Leroy A. Huizenga (Waco: Baylor University Press, 2015), 223–48, 144: "The meaning potential of both texts will be changed through the intertextual point of reference."

[105] Cf. David Lincicum, *Paul and the Early Jewish Encounter with Deuteronomy* (Grand Rapids, MI: Baker, 2013), 52, where he demonstrates the pervasive influence that Deuteronomy had on Second Temple Jews via liturgical usage, arguing that Paul most likely had the entire book memorized.

[106] Cf. Mark Gignilliat, *Paul and Isaiah's Servants: Paul's Theological Reading of Isaiah 40–66 in 2 Corinthians 5.14–6.10*, LNTS 330 (London: T&T Clark, 2007), 37, who argues on the basis of Paul's numerous allusions to Isaianic material in 2 Corinthians that "deep reflection on the message of Isaiah 40–66 in its own canonical form and shape is demonstrated in Paul's thought."

[107] Lukas Bormann, "Triple Intertextuality in Philippians," in *The Intertextuality of the Epistles*, ed. Dennis MacDonald, Stanley E. Porter and Thomas L. Brodie (Sheffield: Sheffield Phoenix Press, 2006), 90–7, 93. Bormann later clarifies his position, arguing that the reader does "not need to know the pretext nor the context of the allusion for understanding the argument of Paul in Philippians" (p. 94) In a later article, however, Bormann, "Die Bedeutung des Philipperbriefs für

numerous Scriptural allusions in Philippians reflect "den jüdischen Hintergrund des paulinischen Denkens," he does not find Paul *arguing* from the Old Testament in Philippians, as the apostle does in, for example, Romans and Galatians.[108] Fee is right to respond, however, that while Paul does not use Scriptural allusions for the purpose of polemics in Philippians, he does appeal to Scripture for the purpose of community formation and practical living.[109]

Alternatively, the *maximalist* approach has been recently championed by McAuley in his monograph on Paul's Scriptural allusions in Phil 2:10-16.[110] McAuley argues that Paul's deployment of Scriptural allusions in Philippians reflects "an OT framework" lying behind Paul's thought that plays "a *generative* role in his argument."[111] To find how such Scriptural allusions generate new meaning for Paul's letter, McAuley posits a comparison of rhetorical exigencies between the source text and the alluding text.[112]

In addition to McAuley's recent monograph, three additional works on the presence of Scripture in Philippians demand attention because they establish a scholarly consensus in regard to Scriptural material in the letter.[113] First, Peter Oakes analyzes

---

die Paulustradition," in *Beiträge zur urchristlichen Theologiegeschichte*, ed. W. Kraus, BZNW 163 (Berlin: de Gruyter, 2009), 321–41, 327, does recognize four allusions in Philippians as "Prägnante Textsignale" (in Phil 1:19 to Job 13:16, in 2:10–11 to Isa 45:23, and in 2:15 both to Deut 32:5 and to Dan 12:3 LXX).

[108] Johannes Schoon-Janssen, *Umstrittene "Apologien" in den Paulusbriefen: Studien zur rhetorischen Situation des 1. Thessalonicherbriefes, des Galaterbriefes und des Philipperbriefes*, GTA 45 (Göttingen: Vandenhoeck & Ruprecht, 1991), 145.

[109] Fee, *Philippians*, 18, where he describes that when Paul in Phil 2:14–16 "presupposes the Philippians' place in the story of Israel," this "is not the stuff of polemics but of mutuality, thus of friendship," since Paul's concern is with the "practical implications" of the common understanding of the gospel that he shares with the Philippians.

[110] McAuley, *Scripture*. Cf. Wick, *Philipperbrief*, 174, "Paulus steht … mit dem Philipperbrief, obwohl er kein direktes Schriftzitat aufführt, auf dem Boden der hebräischen Bibel, der Septuaginta und des zeitgenössischen Judentums," pointing back to Lohmeyer, whom Wick credits as demonstrating "die tiefe Verankerung des Philipperbriefes im jüdischen und alttestamentlichen Denken." So too Guy P. Waters, *The End of Deuteronomy in the Letters of Paul*, WUNT 221 (Tübingen: Mohr Siebeck, 2006), 158, who argues that Paul is not arguing polemically at Phil 2:15, yet maintains that the Scriptures are generative for helping construct the identity of his readers.

[111] McAuley, *Scripture*, 7 (emphasis original).

[112] McAuley, *Scripture*, 52, where he draws on Lloyd F. Bitzer's notion of "rhetorical situation" (cf. "The Rhetorical Situation," *Philosophy & Rhetoric* 1.1 [1968], 1–14).

[113] Aside from the works discussed in the following paragraphs, cf. Florian Wilk, *Die Bedeutung des Jesajabuches für Paulus*, FRLANT 179 (Göttingen: Vandenhoeck & Ruprecht, 1988), 322–5, who treats Isa 45:24 in Phil 2:10, and Isa 49:4 in Phil 2:16 (p. 302); Mehrdad Fatehi, *The Spirit's Relation to the Risen Lord: An Examination of its Christological Implications*, WUNT 2.128 (Tübingen: Mohr Siebeck, 2000), 222–4, who argues for an allusion to Psalm 35 in Phil 1:20; and Hays, *Echoes*, 21, who treats the allusion to Job 13:16 in Phil 1:19. Markus Öhler, "Rezeption des Alten Testaments im 1. Thessalonicherbrief und im Philipperbrief?" in *Paulinische Schriftrezeption: Grundlagen - Ausprägungen - Wirkungen - Wertungen*, ed. Florian Wilk and Markus Öhler, FRLANT 268 (Göttingen: Vandenhoeck and Ruprecht, 2017), 113–35, speaks not only of the possible but also of the probable familiarity of the Philippian church with the LXX (p. 129), citing Phil 1:19, 2:14–15, and 4:19 as examples, though Öhler remains noncommittal about how much these Scriptural allusions had an actual "argumentative Funktion" (p. 134). See also Mark J. Keown, "The Use of the Old Testament in Philippians," in *All That the Prophets Have Declared: The Appropriation of Scripture in the Emergence of Christianity*, ed. Matthew R. Malcolm (Milton Keynes: Paternoster, 2015), 139–65, who, along with the allusions treated by Öhler, posits also Phil 4:5 as echoing Pss 33 and 144.

Paul's allusions in the letter in order to aid modern translation strategies.[114] Oakes devotes the bulk of his article to a discussion of Phil 2:15-16, for which, incidentally, he finds the Greco-Roman background to be more illuminating than the Scriptural background. Before coming to that passage, however, Oakes surveys several other possible Scriptural allusions in the letter.[115] In his previous monograph on the epistle, Oakes argued that Paul drew on the broader context of Isa 45 when alluding to Isa 45:24 in Phil 2:10-11.[116] Discussing Phil 2:15, Oakes asserts that "les échos de la *LXX* en Phil 2,15 sont très nets. Il est possible que les chrétiens de Philippes soient comparés à Abraham et presque certain qu'on les compare aux Israélites et aux 'sages' du livre de Daniel."[117] Oakes argues for a possible allusion to Gen 17:1 in Paul's description of the Philippians as ἄμεμπτοι in Phil 2:15[118] and for the "enormous" probability of allusion to Deut 32:5 when Paul refers to the Philippians as living amid a crooked and depraved generation (Phil 2:15).[119] Oakes does not develop, however, the way in which these numerous allusions to Pentateuch material might shape Paul's argument, focusing instead on the idiom λόγον ζωῆς ἐπέχοντες in this verse and arguing for its background in Hellenistic cosmological texts.

Second, Stephen Fowl offers perhaps the most comprehensive treatment, apart from that of McAuley, of Paul's engagement with Scripture in Philippians, where he treats at length the allusion to Isa 45:23 in Phil 2:10-11, to Job 13:16 in Phil 1:19, and the cluster of allusions in Phil 2:12-18. On the Isaianic allusion in the Christ hymn, Fowl recognizes an activation of the broader context of Isa 40-55, in which "God's vindication and exaltation of the obedient, suffering Christ is in line with the vindication of the suffering obedient servant of God."[120] With regard to the Deuteronomic allusion in Phil 2:15, Fowl argues that "both the specificity of the vocabulary and the relatively secure fit between the aims of Deut 32:5 and Paul's larger argument in Philippians support the judgment that Paul intended to allude to Deut 32:5."[121] Fowl argues for a distinction between the allusions in Phil 2:12-18 and the previous two Scriptural allusions (in 1:19 and 2:10-11) because Paul's "overarching aim" that the Philippians would develop "the ability to read and interpret God's economy of salvation" requires that they recognize his intentional allusion in Phil 2:14-15.[122] That is, Fowl posits that "one of the habits that

---

[114] Peter Oakes, "Quelle devrait être l'influence des échos intertextuels sur la traduction?" in *Intertextualités: La Bible en échos*, ed. Daniel Marguerat and Adrian Curtis (Geneva: Labor et Fides, 2000), 251-87. I am indebted to Prof. Oakes for providing me with an English version of this essay.

[115] That is, Job 13:16 in Phil 1:19; Isa 45:24 in 2:10-11; Exod 15:16, parr. in 2:12; Num 14:2 parr. in 2:14; Num 15:5 in 2:17; 1 Kgs 18:28 in 3:2; Isa 45:24, Hos 4:7, etc. ("un thème important de l'AT," p. 261) in 3:19; and Ps 145 (144 LXX):18 in 4:5. He remains skeptical about the certainty of the allusions at 2:12 ("Il ne faudrait même pas, dans le cas présent, parler d'un écho général de la *LXX*," p. 255) and 4:5.

[116] Peter Oakes, *Philippians: From People to Letter*, SNTSMS 110 (Cambridge: Cambridge University Press, 2001), 169.

[117] Oakes, "L'influence," 262.

[118] Cf. Fee, *Philippians*, 242.

[119] Oakes, "L'influence," 262.

[120] Stephen E. Fowl, "Use of Scripture in Philippians," in Stanley, *Paul and Scripture*, 163-84, 166.

[121] Fowl, "Scripture," 177.

[122] Fowl, "Scripture," 178. For a similar view that Paul sought to train his communities to think Scripturally, cf. Kathy Ehrensperger, "Scriptural Reasoning: The Dynamic That Informed Paul's Theologizing," *JSR* 5.3 (2005), 1-16.

Paul wants to help form in the Philippians is a ... Christ-focused practical reasoning," which includes the ability "to see connections both positive and negative between Israel's and the Philippians' situations."[123] In this way, Fowl concludes that recognition of the Scriptural allusions in Phil 2:12-18 is essential for uncovering the apostle's rhetorical aims in the letter, since the Israel-faithless/Philippians-faithful contrast is central to the paraenesis of this section of the epistle. This point will be important to our present study because the honor accruing to Paul from the Philippians' behavior in Phil 2:14-16 is grounded in their success at precisely that point where Israel failed. Hence, Paul's role as the successful servant to God's new covenant people is primarily justified, thereby engendering a boast for him on the day of Christ (Phil 2:16).

The third study that treats the Jewish background of Philippians is James Ware's monograph, in which he affirms that "Philippians, ... although widely considered the least Jewish of Paul's letters, is steeped in Jewish traditions, and it is Jewish sources which will prove most fruitful in illuminating the letter."[124] In reference to Phil 2:12-18, in particular, Ware argues that the passage reflects "the Jewish character of Paul's thought" and displays "the role of interpretation of scripture in Paul's understanding."[125] Ware supports this on the basis of the recurrence of Isaianic language in this portion of the letter: "The echo of Isaiah 49:4 in Philippians 2:16b, in combination with allusions to Isaiah 52:13-53:12 in Philippians 2:6-9 and Isaiah 45:22-23 in Philippians 2:10-11, reveals a connected reading of Isaiah 40-55, with special focus upon the Servant Songs."[126] Ware particularly draws the connection between Paul's description of the Philippians as "shining as lights in the world" (2:15b) and the mission given to Israel to be a light to the Gentiles in Isa 42:6 and 49:6.[127]

This brief survey shows that recent studies of the Scriptural backdrop to Philippians have recognized Paul's allusions as being not only multiple but also multilayered. This confirms what Ciampa, among others, has observed, namely, Paul's tendency to "[clump] together" Scriptural references "in sections where a variety of scriptural texts are drawn together and interpreted in light of each other."[128] We will show in Part 3 of this study that the "clump" of Scriptural allusions in Phil 2:10-16[129] (two allusions to Isaiah that frame a central allusion to Deuteronomy) serves to "interpret each other," but we may recognize at the outset that the dense web of Scripture embedded in this passage connects Isaiah and Deuteronomy with the situation of Paul's community at Philippi.[130] That is, by alluding to Isaiah in 2:10, to Deuteronomy in 2:15, and again

---

[123] Fowl, "Scripture," 178. He later clarifies that in Phil 2:14-15 "Paul is both interpreting the Philippians' situation in the light of Israel's past relations with God and inviting the Philippians to do likewise as part of their growth in Christ-focused practical wisdom" (p. 181).

[124] James P. Ware, *Paul and the Mission of the Church: Philippians in Ancient Jewish Context* (Grand Rapids, MI: Baker, 2011), 18.

[125] Ware, *Mission*, 237.

[126] Ware, *Mission*, 275.

[127] Ware, *Mission*, 256 n. 56.

[128] Roy E. Ciampa, "Deuteronomy in Galatians and Romans," in *Deuteronomy in the New Testament*, ed. Steve Moyise and Maarten J. J. Menken, LNTS 358 (London: A&C Black, 2007), 99-117, 99.

[129] McAuley, *Scripture*, 1, speaks of "the density and interplay of the tacit references, in seven contiguous verses, to five texts in four books of the OT" occurring in Phil 2:10-16.

[130] Scholars regularly note the apostle's penchant for drawing on both Isaiah and Deuteronomy. Hays, *Echoes*, 163, places Deuteronomy as a conspicuous "member of Paul's functional canon within

to Isaiah in 2:16, Paul draws on these Scriptural sources to narrate reality for his readers: Christ's exaltation (Phil 2:10, using Isa 45:23) enables holy living among God's people (Phil 2:15, inverting Deut 32:5), which leads to honor for God's Servant who facilitates this transformation into holiness (Phil 2:16, inverting Isa 49:4a). The recent focus on this Scriptural backdrop for Paul's argument in the letter is an important step forward in interpreting these key texts in Philippians, but the present study will show that a central motif binding these allusions together is their common concern for the mutual honor of God, his people, and his Servant(s), a motif that has yet to be sufficiently explored in regard to the study of Scripture in Philippians, a study that is still in its infancy.

The Awareness of Scripture in Philippians 2:12-18

One final word on the issue of audience comprehension of Scriptural allusions in Paul is needed since many scholars reject granting conceptual significance to such allusions in Philippians on the grounds that the primarily Gentile believers at Philippi would recognize neither the allusions themselves nor the context from which the allusions emerge.[131] This objection has been championed by Stanley, who maintains, on the basis of this presupposition, that Paul's use of Scriptural language functions merely to convey pious language, rather than to control meaning in the apostle's writing.[132] McAuley answers this critique by pointing to the authorial intention that controls meaning in any given text, thereby allowing Paul the author to activate elements from the wider context of the Scriptural allusions whether the auditors perceived them or not.[133] Alternately, Fowl deals with this objection by pointing to the nonstatic nature of Paul's epistles, allowing for ongoing engagement with the contents of the letters within the community and thereby facilitating, over time, increased understanding of the meaning borne by the Scriptural allusions.[134] The following study is in accord with McAuley in viewing the Scriptural allusions as existing primarily at the level of Paul's intentions as an author.

---

the canon." J. Ross Wagner, "Moses and Isaiah in Concert," in *"As Those Who Are Taught": The Interpretation of Isaiah from the LXX to the SBL*, ed. Claire Matthews McGinnis and Patricia K. Tull, SBLSymS 27 (Atlanta, GA: SBL Press, 2006), 87–103, 102, argues about Rom 10 that "it is the interplay between [Isaiah and Deut 29–32] that proves decisive for Paul's argument."

[131] For example, Markus Bockmuehl, *Philippians*, BNTC 11 (Peabody, MA: Hendrickson, 1998), 157, argues that there is no "indication or indeed likelihood of intimate familiarity with [the Old Testament] on the part of Paul's readers."

[132] Christopher D. Stanley, *Arguing with Scripture: The Rhetoric of Quotations in the Letters of Paul* (London: T&T Clark, 2004), 46–52.

[133] McAuley, *Scripture*, 76. So too Porter, "Allusions and Echoes," 36: "it is authorial intent that defines the presence of an allusion"; "an allusion or an echo can still be present if the recipients fail to know or recognize its presence" (p. 40).

[134] Fowl, "Scripture," 164, appears skeptical about the ability of exegetes to "speak authoritatively about the ways in which the actual first recipients of Paul's letters engaged with those epistles or the Old Testament over time." Cf. Keown, "Use of the Old Testament," 150, who writes that Paul's letters "were not read in a vacuum and there are good reasons to argue that, while at first hearing these [Scriptural echoes] may not be discerned, with the assistance of the bearers of the letter and as the letter sat in the community they would be noted."

Conclusion on Scripture in Philippians

This survey of scholarship on Paul's use of Scripture in Philippians sets the framework for one of the two main goals in our study, namely that of placing the mutual boasting theme in its theological context. Following Fowl's proposal that the Scriptural allusions in Phil 2:14–16 are integral to understanding the *telos* toward which Paul guides the Philippians in the letter, we will demonstrate the importance of Paul's allusions to Deut 32:5 in Phil 2:15 and to Isa 49:4 in Phil 2:16 for understanding the theme of mutual honor in the letter. In line with the methodologies of Beale, Hays and Beetham, we will argue that Paul's allusion to the Song of Moses guides Paul's auditors to the broader context of the end of Deuteronomy, where significantly the key term καύχημα occurs in Deut 26:19 LXX in the context of mutual honor established by obedience, just as καύχημα is used in Phil 2:12–16. Second, and again in line with the methodologies established by these scholars, we will argue that Paul's allusion to the Servant's lament in Isa 49:4 directs his readers to reflect upon the Isaianic Servant's reward in the broader context of Isaiah, a reward that entails mutual participation in the honor shared between YHWH and his people Israel.

Mutuality in Philippians

The Scriptural backdrop to Philippians provides the theological framework in which mutual honor emerges in the letter, but the cultural relevance of mutual honor requires attention to the Hellenistic context of Paul's audience. This is especially the case since Philippians is widely recognized to be thoroughly Greco-Roman in its conceptuality.[135] One of the key ways in which mutuality emerges in the letter is through the idea of κοινωνία. Without a doubt the theme of κοινωνία is central to Paul's letter to the Philippians (cf. 1:5, 7; 2:1; 3:10; 4:14, 15).[136] The precise nature of Paul's κοινωνία-relationship with his addressees, however, has been widely debated. Schliesser provides a recent overview of the various "zeitgenössischer sozialer Konventionen und Beziehungsformen" proposed by scholars for interpreting Paul's relationship with the Philippians,[137] the three most important of which include (1) *societas*, (2) friendship,

---

[135] See Laura S. Nasrallah, "Spatial Perspectives: Space and Archeology in Roman Philippi," in *Studying Paul's Letters: Contemporary Perspectives and Methods*, ed. Joseph A. Marchal (Minneapolis, MN: Fortress Press, 2012), 53–74, 64: "the effects of the Roman Empire are concretely in view in [Philippians]." Cf. Samuel Vollenweider, "Politische Theologie im Philipperbrief?" in *Paulus und Johannes: Exegetische Studien zur paulinischen und johanneischen Theologie und Literatur*, ed. Dieter Sänger and Ulrich Mell, WUNT 198 (Tübingen: Mohr Siebeck, 2006), 457–69, 462, who speaks of "die Dominanz politischer Rhetorik" throughout Philippians.

[136] Luke T. Johnson, *Writings of the New Testament*, 3rd ed. (Minneapolis, MN: Fortress Press, 2010), 329, describes κοινωνία as "the organizing principle of the letter." Julian M. Ogereau, *Paul's Koinonia with the Philippians: A Socio-Historical Investigation of a Pauline Economic Partnership*, WUNT 2.377 (Tübingen: Mohr Siebeck, 2014), 311, argues that "κοινωνία, i.e., partnership, constitutes *the* interpretive key that unlocks a proper understanding of Paul's relationship with the Philippians" (italics original).

[137] Benjamin Schliesser, "Paulus und 'seine' Philipper," in Jörg, Schliesser, and Niederhofer, *Philipperbrief in der hellenistisch-römischen Welt*, 33–119.

and (3) patronage.¹³⁸ To Schliesser's list should be added kinship in light of Paul's common reference to these believers as ἀδελφοί (Phil 1:12; 2:25; 3:1, 13, 17; 4:1, 8).¹³⁹ Moreover, Hainz has rightfully emphasized that any definition of the κοινωνία between Paul and the Philippians must transcend a mere "relation between individuals" and take into account the specific goal of their relationship: it was a κοινωνία εἰς τὸ εὐαγγέλιον (1:5) and therefore entails a "Gemeinschaft mit jemandem durch gemeinsame Teilhabe an etwas."¹⁴⁰

Κοινωνία as Legal Societas

Sampley laid the groundwork for viewing Paul's κοινωνία with the Philippian believers as a consensual *societas*, "a prevalent partnership contract of Roman law, where each of the partners contributed something to the association with a view towards a common goal."¹⁴¹ In this model, the primary relation between apostle and community is that of partners, each side subsisting in relative equality, though Paul maintains the role of model. Still, Sampley argues that when the *societas* was operating as intended, it allowed for the ideal situation in which "the different partners' commitment to a shared goal and their sense of brotherly equality [could] meld together into a strong sense of community."¹⁴²

Ogereau follows Sampley's model, though adding some nuances of his own. Ogereau critiques Sampley's position that the *societas* model *promoted* a sense of community, arguing that such community was instead presupposed.¹⁴³ Instead, Ogereau posits as the major benefit offered by the *societas* relationship the engendering of "a greater level of participation and a greater sense of *ownership* amongst all involved, since each had a vested interest in the outcome of the partnership."¹⁴⁴

Κοινωνία as Friendship

Another widespread way of interpreting κοινωνία in Philippians is under the rubric of friendship. Important here is L. M. White's article, where he characterizes Philippians

---

[138] One further lens through which scholars have interpreted Paul's κοινωνία with the Philippians that has been left out from this survey is that of joint members in an association or *collegium*. Cf. Richard S. Ascough, *Paul's Macedonian Associations: The Social Context of Philippians and 1 Thessalonians*, WUNT 2.161 (Tübingen: Mohr Siebeck, 2003), 161, who classifies the Philippian Christ-believing community as "analogous to religious voluntary associations." Cf., however, the cautionary analysis of Brélaz, "First-Century Philippi," 179: "The Christian groups were not intended to be associations like any other cultic club. On the contrary, they were meant to become a community on their own ... which would be able to challenge the ordinary secular institutions."

[139] Schliesser, "seine Philipper," 35 n. 6, recognizes the possibility of "andere Rollen und Funktionen" to illumine Paul's relationship with the Philippian community, such as kinship.

[140] Josef Hainz, *Koinonia: "Kirche" als Gemeinschaft bei Paulus* (Regensburg: Pustet, 1982), 89.

[141] J. Paul Sampley, *Pauline Partnership in Christ* (Philadelphia, PA: Fortress Press, 1980), 11. Followed by Betz, *Philippians*, 128–9: "The legal terms of the contract (κοινωνία) were as follows: The Philippian church accepted the status as 'partners in the gospel mission' (κοινωνοί τοῦ εὐαγγελίου), with the concrete establishment of a fund (εἰς λόγον) based on the principle of 'giving and receiving' (δόσις καὶ λῆμψις)."

[142] Sampley, *Partnership*, 107, where he also notes how *societas Christi* "minimizes social stratification."

[143] Ogereau, *Koinonia*, 347.

[144] Ogereau, *Koinonia*, 346.

as a "letter of friendship," that is, a hortatory letter between friends. White shows that ancient friendship was based on the pursuit of virtue so that by adopting it Paul created "a moral paradigm" for the Philippian believers to follow (cf. 4:8-9).[145] Similarly, Stowers asserts that "Philippians confronts the reader with a massive ... number of connections with ... friendship motifs."[146] He argues from this that the platform for moral instruction offered by the friendly letter is then adopted by Paul as he writes to his friends at Philippi, exhorting them to become the ideal community of friends.[147] Pushing back, Fitzgerald notes that Philippians is "'mixed' in terms of style and content,"[148] so it would be "misleading" to refer to Philippians as a *Freundschaftsbrief*. Still, he maintains that this designation is "quite useful in calling attention to the presence in the letter of a remarkable number of terms that were associated in antiquity with the topic of friendship."[149] Fitzgerald adduces the following friendship motifs in the letter: μιᾷ ψυχῇ (1:27; 2:20), τὸ αὐτὸ φρονεῖν (2:2; 4:2), κοινωνία (1:5, 7; 2:2; 3:10; 4:14-15) as reflecting the friendship maxim κοινὰ τὰ φίλων, and the presence/absence motif (1:27; 2:12).[150] In addition to these earlier appearances of friendship motifs, he finds Phil 4 "replete with terms and ideas connected with friendship."[151]

Scholars, however, have critiqued the friendship paradigm for understanding how Paul relates to his churches. Sevenster remarks about Paul's avoidance of the term φιλία: "Even if Paul has not intentionally avoided [the term], it is remarkable that he does not use [φιλία] automatically when he is dealing with such intimate relationships."[152] E. A. Judge argues that Paul "found no use for the regular social terminology of friendship ... because of the status implications that it had."[153] Reumann presents a mediated position: "[Paul] at times employed some [language from the *philia topos*]. But he did not create a special ecclesiology out of it with the Philippians."[154] Rosell Nebreda similarly adduces that, rather than it being a letter of friendship in form, it is more fruitful to speak in terms of Paul's "rhetoric of friendship" in Philippians as

---

[145] White, "Morality," 215.

[146] Stanley K. Stowers, "Friends and Enemies in the Politics of Heaven: Reading Theology in Philippians," in *Pauline Theology, Volume 1*, ed. Jouette Bassler (Minneapolis, MN: Fortress, 1991), 105-21, 106-7.

[147] Stowers, "Friends and Enemies," 108, 110-11.

[148] John T. Fitzgerald, "Philippians in the Light of Some Ancient Discussions of Friendship," in *Friendship, Flattery, and Frankness of Speech*, ed. John T. Fitzgerald, NovTSup 82 (Leiden: Brill, 1996), 141-60, 142.

[149] Fitzgerald, "Discussions of Friendship," 143. Fitzgerald elsewhere, "Paul and Friendship," in Sampley, *Paul in the Greco-Roman World* (2nd ed.), 1.331-362, 352, notes that "although the word φιλία ... does not occur in Paul's correspondence, many of the terms or concepts in its linkage group do."

[150] See Fitzgerald, "Discussions of Friendship," 144-7.

[151] Fitzgerald, "Discussions of Friendship," 153.

[152] J. N. Sevenster, *Paul and Seneca*, NovTSup 4 (Leiden: Brill, 1961), 178. Alan Mitchell, "'Greet the Friends by Name': New Testament Evidence for the Greco-Roman Topos on Friendship," in *Greco-Roman Perspectives on Friendship*, ed. John T. Fitzgerald, RBS 34 (Atlanta, GA: Scholars Press, 1999), 225-62, 260, notes the "level of social obligation" imposed by the ancient friendship model, as well as "the problems it created for Pauline churches, composed of differing social statuses."

[153] E. A. Judge, "Paul as a Radical Critic of Society," in *Social Distinctives of the Christians in the First Century*, ed. David Scholer (Peabody, MA: Hendrickson, 2008), 99-115, 106.

[154] John H. P. Reumann, "Philippians as a Letter of Friendship: Observations on a Checkered History of Scholarship," in Fitzgerald, *Friendship, Flattery*, 83-106, 95.

an "effective means to persuade the Philippian community."¹⁵⁵ The present study is in accord with Rosell Nebreda that, rather than providing the *Gattung* for the letter, friendship (along with family, see below) furnishes the rhetorical power through which Paul exhorts the Philippians to virtuous action, relying upon their goodwill toward him and their desire to uphold his honor.

Κοινωνία *as Patronage*

The foregoing critique of the friendship model for comprehending Paul's relation with the Philippians has led some to posit a more structured, class-oriented model for the relationship, especially given Paul's status as an apostle: that between patron and client. Walton explains that "'friendship' language was commonly used in patron/client relationships and need not imply that the two 'friends' were social equals."¹⁵⁶ Bormann argues that friendship, classically defined, was reserved for a relationship between two individuals who are of equal status.¹⁵⁷ Moreover, for Bormann, since Paul relates to his churches as a group, rather than as to a single individual, the character of these relationships is so fundamentally different from a friendship relation that one can no longer speak of them as such.¹⁵⁸ Rather, Bormann points to the patron-client bond as the best matrix in which to interpret Paul's relationship with the Philippian believers since the relation of client to patron was the foundational form of organization between unequal individuals in the Roman world.¹⁵⁹ A patron's clients, argues Bormann, could view themselves in solidarity with one another, and the patron would have been concerned with the inner organization of his clientele.¹⁶⁰

Marchal also posits a domineering hierarchical strain in Paul's κοινωνία with the Philippians, finding in Paul's deployment of "friendly rhetorics" in the letter certain "problematic dynamics of Paul's argumentation."¹⁶¹ Namely, Marchal finds in Paul's implicit hierarchical authority in the letter a "subject-master dynamic," through which "Paul is seeking an elevated, authoritative status in these relationships."¹⁶² Paul's rhetoric thus, in Marchal's analysis, seeks "to consolidate his own authority."¹⁶³

---

155 Rosell Nebreda, *Christ Identity*, 252.
156 Steve Walton, "Paul, Patronage and Pay: What Do We Know about the Apostle's Financial Support?" in *Paul the Missionary: Identity, Activity, Theology and Practice*, ed. Trevor Burke and Brian Rosner, LNTS 420 (London: T&T Clark, 2013), 220–33, 228.
157 Lukas Bormann, *Philippi: Stadt und Christengemeinde*, NovTSup 78 (Leiden: Brill, 1995), 170.
158 Bormann, *Philippi*, 170.
159 Bormann, *Philippi*, 187–205, 207. Bormann, 197, argues for the readily understandable nature of the clientele system to occupants of first-century Philippi in light of its character as a Roman colony under the patronage of the Julio-Claudian house.
160 Bormann, *Philippi*, 207.
161 Joseph A. Marchal, "With Friends Like These …: A Feminist Rhetorical Reconsideration of Scholarship and the Letter to the Philippians," *JSNT* 29 (2006), 77–106, 96. Marchal argues that "the majority of Paul's audience likely experienced friendship rhetorics as part of an exploitative system" (p. 99).
162 Marchal, "Friends," 97–8. Elsewhere, in Joseph Marchal, *Politics of Heaven: Women, Gender and Empire in the Study of Paul* (Minneapolis, MN: Fortress, Press, 2008), 52, Marchal describes Paul's paradigmatic actions in the letter as involving "an effort to ascend in a hierarchical arrangement."
163 Marchal, *Politics*, 57. Marchal, *Politics*, 52, rightly adduces that part of Paul's authority is drawn from patterning his life on the model of Christ in the hymn so that Paul "is a model because he

Park stands against these views, however. Park argues that, while Paul does hold a privileged position in the relationship, since "he is the speaker with privileged knowledge," yet such a position "does not necessarily signify *coercive* power."[164] Rather, "Paul's authority is neither absolute nor autonomous, but provisional and subjugated to the authority of Christ."[165] Furthermore, Park affirms that "mutuality does not preclude hierarchy," so the mutuality between Paul and the Philippians does not eliminate "the hierarchy between Paul and the Philippians."[166] Ultimately, Park finds Paul presenting a mutuality based in volitional submission and in radical self-sacrifice for the sake of others.[167] Our study follows Park's analysis of the mutuality between Paul and the Philippians in the letter as opposed to that of Marchal.

Briones critiques both the friendship model and the patron-client model for framing Paul's relationship with the Philippians since they "[downplay] one significant detail—God's presence in the relationship. Paul's friendship with the Philippians ... is a three-way bond with God."[168] Briones contends that both of these foregoing relational frameworks "can only account for two parties in exchange," not providing the means to comprehend "the relational modifications that the divine third party generates in the two-way relationship between Paul and the community."[169] In contrast, for Briones, "God's presence ... resolves the equality/inequality tension of their relationship."[170] This threefold perspective on Paul's relation to the Philippians, which intentionally includes God's/Christ's role in the relationship, is important for the approach taken in the following study and will be addressed more fully below.

To summarize from these brief surveys of scholarship on friendship and patronage in Philippians, the present study will give attention to Paul's intentional use of themes and vocabulary from the friendship model in Philippians to illumine his presentation of the mutual honor shared between himself, the Philippians, and God/Christ. Recognizing that friendship does not entail equality, this study yet affirms that Paul's rhetoric in the letter emphasizes mutuality rather than domination when depicting

---

is willing to suffer or give up status to gain something greater," listing Phil 1:23–26. Marchal does not elaborate, however, on *who* gains from Paul's renunciation in this passage; in fact, it is *the Philippians* and explicitly *not* Paul who gain from Paul's choice to go on living.

[164] M. Sydney Park, *Submission within the Godhead and the Church in the Epistle to the Philippians: An Exegetical and Theological Examination of the Concept of Submission in Philippians 2 and 3*, LNTS 361 (London: T&T Clark, 2007), 106. In fact, Park asserts that "it is the Philippians who possibly hold power *over Paul*. And arguably, the call to imitation [in 3:17] can be assessed as Paul's exertion of his religious authority over and against the social authority the Philippians have over Paul" (p. 108, emphasis added).

[165] Park, *Submission*, 107. Similarly, cf. the work of Park's *Doktorvater*, Andrew D. Clarke, "Source and Scope of Paul's Apostolic Authority," *CTR* 12.2 (2015), 3–22, 18, who speaks of Paul's authority vis-à-vis his churches as "socially negotiated."

[166] Park, *Submission*, 159.

[167] Park, *Submission*, 163.

[168] David E. Briones, *Paul's Financial Policy: A Socio-Theological Approach*, LNTS 494 (London: T&T Clark, 2013), 77. Cf. John H. P. Reumann, "The Theologies of 1 Thessalonians and Philippians: Contents, Comparison, and Composite," *SBLSP* 26 (1987), 521–36, 529: "The 'in Christ' motif connects God, Paul, and the Philippians."

[169] Briones, *Financial Policy*, 77.

[170] Briones, *Financial Policy*, 77.

Paul's relation to his audience.[171] As we will demonstrate in Part 2 of the study, there was a recognizable tendency among Greco-Roman letter-writers to make use of the mutual relationship of honor shared between writer and recipient to motivate the proper response to ethical paraenesis. It is this mutual element of Paul's friendship rhetorics, that is, Paul's mutual participation in honor *alongside* the Philippians, rather than the hierarchical element of Paul's authority *over* the Philippians, that will be the focus of the present study.

Κοινωνία as Siblingship

A fourth way to view Paul's relation with his Philippian converts is through the lens of fictive kinship groups.[172] Loveday Alexander originally proposed that Philippians ought to be read in the context of the Greco-Roman family letter.[173] Alexander argues that a "semi-formal" pattern reflected in family letters provides help for understanding how Paul fluidly adapts the body section of his letter to the Philippians.[174] Noting the lack of any business portion within the family letter, Alexander argues that "the whole point of [family] letters—their real business—*is* this exchange of news between the sender and his family."[175] She then maps the flow of Philippians onto this pattern, arguing that Phil 1:12–26 reflects the *reassurance about the sender*, and Phil 1:27-2:18 reflects the *request for reassurance about the recipients*. Thus, Alexander argues that all of Paul's hortatory

---

[171] For a similar analysis of Paul's use of friendship language as promoting mutuality rather than instituting hierarchy, see Jennings, *Partnership*, 37, who speaks of Paul's partnership language in Phil 1:6-8 as displays of "sincere mutuality." Cf. Pialoux, *Philippiens*, 29, who argues that Paul's purpose in writing a letter of friendship to the Philippian believers was "de fortifier sa relation d'intimité avec les Philippiens." Pialoux later describes the relationship between Paul and the Philippian Christ-followers as not operating on the basis of "un principe de réciprocité *do-ut-des* utilitaire," but rather as "une communion purifiée selon la logique nouvelle de l'amour chrétien" (p. 86).

[172] So, e.g., Hans-Joseph Klauck, "Kirche als Freundesgemeinschaft: Auf Spurensuche im Neuen Testament," *MTZ* 42 (1991), 1–14, 11, who speaks of the need to work out the affinities and the convergences of *Bruderethik* and *Freundesethik*. Mitchell, "Greet the Friends," 260, affirms that "the ethics of brother/sister relationships and the ethics of friendship relationships converge in the New Testament, while the language of fictive kinship is preferred." Reider Aasgaard, "Paul as Child: Children and Childhood in the Letters of the Apostle," *JBL* 126 (2007), 129–59, 156, notes how Paul's use of the fatherhood metaphor utilizes "the whole spectrum of nuances for this role" available in antiquity, focusing especially "on an understanding and supportive type of father" rather than on an "authoritative one."

[173] Loveday Alexander, "Hellenistic Letter Forms and the Structure of Philippians," *JSNT* 37 (1989), 87–101. She draws on John L. White's presentation and brief analysis of family letters in *Light from Ancient Letters* (Minneapolis, MN: Fortress, 1986), 196–7, as well as on Heikki Koskenniemi's characterization of ancient family letters as *Verbindungsbriefen*, in *Studien zur Idee und Phraseologie des griechischen Briefes bis 400 n. Chr* (Helsinki: Kirjakauppa, 1956), 104–14. On the close connection between the language of friendship and the language of kinship, see Peter Arzt-Grabner, "'Brothers' and 'Sisters' in Documentary Papyri and in Early Christianity," *RivBib* 50 (2002), 185–204, 193, who points to papyri letters in which friends whose "relationship is obviously very close and cordial" address each other as ἀδελφοί, thereby acting "as if the two families were one."

[174] Alexander, "Letter Forms," 90. Wick, *Philipperbrief*, 156: "vor allem scheint das Muster des Familienbriefes eine angemessene Form für einen Brief zu sein, dessen Hauptthema die innige Gemeinschaft des Absenders mit den Empfängern ist."

[175] Alexander, "Letter Forms," 93.

goals in the letter can be subsumed under "the primary purpose of strengthening the 'family' links between the apostle and the Christian congregation in Philippi."[176] She softens this point, however, by recognizing that "the formal pattern of the familiar letters ... cannot serve as more than a launching-pad" for Paul's exhortation within the letter, in which "a predictable 'family' letter develops into a 'sermon-at-a-distance.'"[177] Nevertheless, she affirms the suitability of allowing the formal patterns from the family letters to inform our reading of Philippians, especially in view of Paul's "liberal usage of fictive kinship terms" to describe the Christ-believing community.

Others have followed Alexander in developing Paul's use of fictive kinship terms in Philippians to decipher Paul's relationship with the Philippians. Gerber recognizes the father–child relationship in Philippians in Paul's relation to Timothy and in God's relation to the Philippians, pointing out that all other fictive kinship terminology reflects the language of siblingship.[178] Schäfer finds in Phil 2:1–4 ethical implications for the church as a *Bruderschaft*.[179] In support, Schäfer points to the abundance of ἀδελφός terminology in the letter, which he sees demonstrating "die Grundlage der Bruderschaft zwischen Apostel und Gemeinde."[180] Significantly for our study of mutual honor in Philippians, Aasgaard has demonstrated the expectation linked to the sibling relationship in antiquity, in which "one important task of siblings was to maintain their own honour and that of the family."[181]

One must be careful, however, not to misrepresent the family model as implying total equality among members within the relationship.[182] Witherington rightly notes, after having argued in favor of the family model, that "Paul does not see his relationship with the Philippians as one of absolute parity," since his clear (though, unstated) depiction as father figure for the Philippians entails that "there is some sort of hierarchical relationship still existing between Paul and these converts that cannot be described simply as friendship between equals."[183] Yet, Paul's use of sibling language, as opposed to father–child language, to characterize his relationship with the

---

[176] Alexander, "Letter Forms," 95.
[177] Alexander, "Letter Forms," 99.
[178] Christine Gerber, *Paulus und seine "Kinder": Studien zur Beziehungsmetaphorik der paulinischen Briefe*, BZNW 136 (Berlin: de Gruyter, 2005), 242.
[179] Klaus Schäfer, *Gemeinde als "Bruderschaft": Ein Beitrag zum Kirchenverständnis des Paulus*, EH 333 (Bern: Peter Lang, 1989), 114.
[180] Schäfer, *Bruderschaft*, 343.
[181] Reider Aasgaard, "Role Ethics in Paul: The Significance of the Sibling Role for Paul's Ethical Thinking," NTS 48 (2002), 513–30, 519.
[182] David G. Horrell, "From ἀδελφοί to οἶκος θεοῦ: Social Transformation in Pauline Christianity," JBL 120 (2001), 293–311, 303, argues that, although Paul primarily employs the language of ἀδελφοί to designate egalitarian communities, "Paul certainly does not restrict himself to a role as an ἀδελφός among equal siblings." Andrew D. Clarke, "Equality or Mutuality? Paul's Use of 'Brother' Language," in *The New Testament in its First Century Setting*, ed. P. J. Williams et al. (Grand Rapids, MI: Eerdmans, 2004), 151–64, 164, adduces from ancient sources that "brotherly love is concerned with mutuality, rather than equality."
[183] Ben Witherington III, *Friendship and Finances in Philippi: The Letter of Paul to the Philippians* (Valley Forge, PA: Trinity Press, 1994), 119–20. See also Bengt Holmberg, *Paul and Power: The Structure of Authority in the Primitive Church as Reflected in the Pauline Epistles* (Lund: Gleerup, 1978), 78–9, who notes that even when Paul does not explicitly state his role as father over his communities, it remains central to his relationship vis-à-vis them.

Philippians emphasizes solidarity more than it does hierarchy. As Trebilco notes, "It is significant that Paul uses ἀδελφοί, a term of intimacy, when addressing his readers, rather than using a term which would create distance and formality. Such speech is a sign of solidarity and through it a sense of camaraderie is engendered."[184] The type of solidarity evident within the sibling relationship in antiquity noted by Trebilco and others is important for our study because it provides the basis for Paul's notion of mutual honor shared between himself and the Philippians. As we will see, it is precisely as "siblings" that they can contribute through their own noble actions to the honor of each other.

A Three-Way Κοινωνία in Philippians

A common thread running through these various models is their predominantly bilateral nature (Paul in relationship to the community). As will become clear in our own study of the theme of mutual honor, as expressed in the overlap between the culturally understood relationships of family and friends, the relational matrix portrayed in the letter is in fact threefold in that it brings together three entities into one unified relationship.[185] There are numerous ways in which this triple mutuality finds expression in the letter. One is through the theme of joy, since Paul's joy in Christ and Paul's joy in the Philippians impacts the Philippians' joy in Paul and their joy in Christ.[186] Another is via the threefold relationship between Paul, Epaphroditus and the Philippians, in which as the Philippians' emissary, Epaphroditus, acts as a go-between in the relationship between Paul and the Philippians, enacting their service to the apostle and bringing his grace back to them.[187] As yet another example, John Marshall describes Paul's use of "double identifications" in the letter: "these are phrases which identify him both with God and with the Philippians."[188]

---

[184] Paul Trebilco, *Self-Designations and Group Identity in the New Testament* (Cambridge: Cambridge University Press, 2011), 11. In addition to camaraderie, Trebilco notes how Paul uses the language of siblingship among his communities to motivate them to honor each other: "That they are ἀδελφοί should enhance and elevate the status of each group [i.e., Jewish believers and Greek believers] in the eyes of the other" (discussing Rom 14) (p. 32). So, too, Arzt-Grabner, "Brothers and Sisters," 202: "'brother' expresses *closeness, solidarity* and some kind of bond or *engagement*."

[185] After pointing to the mutuality between Paul and the Philippians engendered by their mutual boasting (evinced in 1:26 and 2:16), Craddock, *Philippians*, 45, describes how "Christ, Paul, and the Philippians were in a real sense fulfilled in each other." Gerber, *Kinder*, 242, affirms that "das gegenseitige Verhältnis" between Paul and the Philippians is no "Zweierbeziehung," but entails "eine Verbindung" of Christ Jesus, God, and the Gospel.

[186] Timothy C. Geoffrion, *The Rhetorical Purpose and the Political and Military Character of Philippians: A Call to Stand Firm* (Lampeter: Mellen Biblical Press, 1993), 120, argues that the "'triangle-type' relationship between God and/or Christ, Paul and the Philippians is especially evident in the particular area of 'joy.'"

[187] See Rainer Metzner, "In aller Freundschaft: Ein frühchristlicher Fall freundschaftlicher Gemeinschaft (Phil 2.25–30)," *NTS* 48 (2002), 111–31, 119, who explains how "das Dreiecksverhältnis zwischen Paulus, Epaphroditus und der Gemeinde in Philippi" is best characterized through the "freundschaftliche Grundton" of the letter.

[188] John W. Marshall, "Paul's Ethical Appeal in Philippians," in *Rhetoric and the New Testament: Essays from the 1992 Heidelberg Conference*, ed. Stanley E. Porter and Thomas H. Olbricht (Sheffield: Sheffield Academic Press, 1993), 357–74, 366, cf. Phil 1:3, 8, 19, 23, 26; 2:17–18.

This same threefold mutuality has been highlighted in relationship to the κοινωνία-theme in Philippians, especially as this theme functions within its Greco-Roman context.[189] For example, Hansen builds on Sampley's model of understanding Paul's κοινωνία with the Philippians as "a Roman *societas*," arguing, however, for a further transformation of this concept.[190] Hansen asserts that "the partnership is not merely between two parties (Paul and the Philippians) but triangular—it involves God, Paul, and the Philippians."[191] By combining Phil 2:2, which depicts the believers' κοινωνία in the Spirit, with Paul's statement in Phil 3:10 that he hopes to experience the κοινωνία of Christ's sufferings, Hansen shows how κοινωνία is "used to denote both the solidarity of all believers and the communion of human and divine."[192]

Others then develop Hansen's presentation of Paul's κοινωνία with the Philippians as "triangular." Fee argues that in Philippians Paul radically transforms friendship "from a two-way to a three-way bond—between him, the Philippians, and Christ," which bond Fee describes as "the glue that holds the letter together from beginning to end."[193] Thus, while Paul and the Philippians are caught up in "most of the conventions of Greco-Roman friendship," this occurs overtly "in light of Christ and the gospel."[194] Ebner

---

[189] Treating the Greco-Roman culture of gift exchange reflected in Phil 4, Pialoux, *Philippiens*, 151, calls attention to "une relation non pas binaire (je/vous) mais ternaire, avec l'immixtion de Dieu qui devient le réel récipiendaire du don (4:18b), puis celui qui opérera le retour, en gloire pour les Philippiens (4:19), et aussi à sa propre gloire, comme le souligne une véritable doxologie finale (4:20)."

[190] G. Walter Hansen, "Transformation of Relationships: Partnership, Citizenship, and Friendship in Philippi," in Donaldson and Sailors, *New Testament Greek and Exegesis*, 181–204, 187–8.

[191] Hansen, "Relationships," 188, where he notes how Paul connects God's "good work" in 1:6 to the Philippians' κοινωνία εἰς τὸ εὐαγγέλιον of 1:5. He summarizes: "The joint venture of the Philippians is really God's venture."

[192] Hansen, "Relationships," 191.

[193] Fee, *Philippians*, 13. Note Fee's triangular graphic below which I will use as a model for similar triangular graphics in Parts 2 and 3 to depict mutual honor in Isaiah and in Philippians:

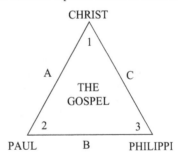

Fee explains (p. 14) that line C (involving the Philippians' relationship with Christ) is the focus of Paul's exhortations in the letter, whereas line B (Paul's relationship with the Philippians) renders the friendly context in which he can make such exhortations. He argues that "everything in the letter can be explained in light of one of these items," that is, by the relationships depicted in lines A, B, and C.

[194] Fee, *Philippians*, 13–14. Cf. François Vouga, "L'épître aux Philippiens," in *Introduction au Nouveau Testament: Son histoire, son écriture, sa théologie*, ed. Daniel Marguerat (Genève: Labor et Fides, 2008), 251–64, 262, who similarly notes that a triangular relationship between Paul, the Philippians, and God permeates much of the letter: "L'objet tant de la première (1.3–2.18) que de la troisième partie de la letter (4.10–23) est d'inclure l'apôtre et sa communauté dans l'histoire d'une relation triangulaire dont Dieu est à la fois l'auteur et l'origine, et dont Jésus Christ est le but."

similarly argues that Paul resituates his friendship with the Philippians by asserting his ultimate dependence on God (Phil 4:13), and not on them, thereby transforming their two-way *Freundschaftskoinonia* into a three-way "Koinonia mit Gott," which *Beziehungsdreieck* counteracts the moral obligations that would have arisen from Paul's friendship with the Philippians (i.e., the need to reciprocate their financial gift).[195]

Briones concurs with Ebner on the triangular nature of Paul's κοινωνία with the Philippians, but disagrees that, by bringing in his relationship with God, Paul is thereby cutting the horizontal ties he has with the Philippians. Rather, Briones argues that Paul is in fact retying them "into a three-way knot, with God as the third party to whom Paul and the church share a mutual obligation."[196] Briones thus treats "God's role as the third party and its relational implications for Paul and the Philippians," arguing that it "reconfigures Paul's full, trusting κοινωνία with the Philippians."[197] He explores this dynamic via an analysis of the letter's presentation of the threefold flow of χάρις between the three parties in the relationship. Pertinent to our own study of Paul's presentation of κοινωνία in Philippians, Briones views Phil 1:26 working in conjunction with Phil 2:16 to manifest an "intricately interdependent relationship" between apostle and community in which "the eschatological σωτηρία/καύχημα of one party lies in the mutual concern of the other, with both parties directing their gaze to God in Christ as the main supplier of χάρις through the other."[198] The reconfiguration of reciprocity is brought about by Paul's presentation of God as the provider of both "the immaterial and the material benefits that Paul and the Philippians reciprocate," which means that "no party can claim ownership of their gifts" and that both parties "equally share a vertical tie of obligation to God."[199]

Conclusion on Mutuality in Philippians

In summary, while numerous models have been proposed for understanding Paul's relationship with the Philippian community, the two that provide the best framework for understanding the mutuality depicted in the letter are that of friendship and family.

---

[195] Martin Ebner, *Leidenslisten und Apostelbrief: Untersuchungen zu Form, Motivik und Funktion der Peristasenkataloge bei Paulus*, FB 66 (Würzburg: Echter Verlag, 1991), 363–4.
[196] Briones, *Financial Policy*, 78.
[197] Briones, *Financial Policy*, 79.
[198] Briones, *Financial Policy*, 92.
[199] Briones, *Financial Policy*, 120. Briones, 129, depicts this divinely sourced "circle of χάρις" in the following illustration:

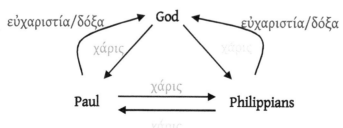

This is evident, first, in that by variously alluding to friendship motifs Paul draws on a concept integral to this relationship, that is, friends shared all things. Most important for our focus on mutual honor, friends also shared in each other's honor. In Parts 2 and 3, we will demonstrate the reality that friends shared honor in antiquity and that Paul's depiction of mutual honor in Philippians draws on this common cultural script from his audience's primarily Hellenistic world. Second, by explicitly placing himself in a sibling relationship with his audience, Paul evokes the common cultural script that brothers honored brothers, thereby engendering a family honor that was mutually shared between the "siblings," Paul and the Philippians, and their "Father," God.

Oakes argues that the three-way interplay between Paul, the Philippians, and Christ serves as "the main thematic structure of the letter" by which Paul attempts to affect the attitudes and behavior of the Philippian believers.[200] One of the key ways that Paul accomplishes this, we argue, is by means of the threefold mutuality of honor described throughout the letter between himself, the Philippians, and God/Christ. Before discussing how mutual honor functioned within the structures of friendship and family in the Hellenistic context, we first begin our investigation by delving into the theological underpinnings of mutual honor in Paul's Scriptural heritage, to which the apostle directs the Philippians in his exhortation at Phil 2:12–16.

---

[200] Oakes, *Philippians*, xiii.

Part 1

Mutual Glory in the Jewish Scriptures

Sons are indeed a heritage from the Lord,
the fruit of the womb a reward ...
Happy is the man who has his quiver full of them.
He shall not be put to shame
when he speaks with his enemies in the gate.

Ps 127:3, 5

For parents have little thought for their own personal interests
and find the consummation of happiness in the high excellence of their children.

Philo, *Spec.* 2.236

Honor plays a conspicuous role throughout the Hebrew Bible. Indeed, "ancient Jewish culture participated in the order of honor."[1] For at the most fundamental level, YHWH, Israel's God, is "great in glory" (Ps 138:5) and his people "glorify his name" (Ps 66:2). Von Rad points to the fact, therefore, that God's glory is not only something that his people are to ascribe to him (Ps 29:1; Jer 13:16) but also "an established part of [his people's] eschatological expectation"[2] so that his prophets work to prepare the way for YHWH's כבוד to be revealed to all nations (cf. Isa 40:5). Glatt-Gilad thus speaks of the wide-ranging nature of the theme of "God's reputation in the eyes of Israel's adversaries."[3] This focus on the reality and manifestation of God's glory accords with a basic biblical fact: "Gott selbst hat Ehre und orientiert sein Verhalten daran (Ex 33,12; Jes 48:11)."[4]

---

[1] Gudrun Guttenberger Ortwein, *Status und Statusverzicht im Neuen Testament und seiner Umwelt*, NTOA 39 (Göttingen: Vandenhoeck & Ruprecht, 1999), 89 (my translation).
[2] Gerhard von Rad, excursus on "כָּבוֹד in the OT" in Kittel's entry on δόξα in *TDNT* 2.238–242, 242.
[3] David A. Glatt-Gilad, "Yahweh's Honor at Stake: A Divine Conundrum," *JSOT* 98 (2002), 63–74, 63.
[4] Ortwein, *Status*, 89.

The usage of כבוד יהוה as a *terminus technicus* to refer to the visible revelation of God's majesty (e.g., Ex 24:16) does not detract, however, from other ways in which glory appears in the Scriptures. As Chibici-Revneanu notes, in the historical books and the wisdom literature the meaning of "reputation" and "honor" came to dominate the *Begriffsverwendung* for כבוד.[5] For example, "honor" is regularly applied to humans as well as to God in the Hebrew Bible. Thus, when describing an attribute of a human individual, כבוד "dient zur Bezeichnung des hohen Ansehens ('Ehre'), die ein Mensch haben kann."[6] In this regard, Jan Dietrich calls attention to the two most common forms of human honor in the Scriptures as *Leibesehre*, which refers to the physical manifestation of one's greatness, and *Statusehre*, which signifies the honor ascribed to an individual by society.[7] Moreover, Dietrich points to the self-proclaimed acquisition of an honorable name for the sake of one's "glory" as an "anthropological need" motivating individuals in many of the Scriptural narratives.[8]

In fact, these two spheres of divine glory and human glory coincide in the Hebrew Bible in the context of covenant.[9] As Olyan observes, "Covenant honor ... is reciprocal," noting that "Yhwh himself ... participates in reciprocal honor" with his covenant people.[10] He cites 1 Sam 2:30 ("those who honor me, I will honor; those who despise me, I will curse"), finding here the paragon of reciprocal honor: "to repay honor is the appropriate response to one who bestows honor; likewise, to return humiliation is the goal of one who is diminished or despised by a treaty partner."[11] The covenantal link between God's honor and Israel's honor is consequently equally true as regards their shame: "If God acquires a shameful reputation in the opinion of others this will reflect on Israel also. Her own pride as well as God's is at stake."[12]

Against this background, Olyan thus finds it curious regarding the mutuality of honor among Jewish kinsman in the Hebrew Bible that, whereas "the conferral of honor is reciprocal in a number of passages (e.g., 1 Sam 2:30), ... no text states explicitly that brothers are bound to honor one another," though treaties often make use of fraternal rhetoric while presupposing such mutuality of honor.[13] Instead, Olyan

---

[5] Nicole Chibici-Revneanu, *Die Herrlichkeit des Verherrlichten: das Verständnis der δόξα im Johannesevangelium*, WUNT 2.231 (Tübingen: Mohr Siebeck, 2007), 358.

[6] Thomas Wagner, *Gottes Herrlichkeit: Bedeutung und Verwendung des Begriffs kābôd im Alten Testament*, VTSup 151 (Leiden: Brill, 2012), 6.

[7] Jan Dietrich, "Über Ehre und Ehregefühl im Alten Testament," in *Der Mensch im Alten Israel: Neue Forschungen zur altestamentlichen Anthropologie*, ed. Bernd Janowski, Kathrin Liess with Niko Zaft, HBS 59 (Freiburg: Herder, 2009), 419–452, 446.

[8] Dietrich, "Ehregefühl," 437.

[9] Saul Olyan, "Honor, Shame, and Covenant Relations: Honor Relations in Ancient Israel and its Environment," *JBL* 115 (1996), 201–18, 217: "honor and shame were clearly components of a larger complex of ideas related to covenant, a complex characterized by notions of reciprocity." Again, Olyan, 218: "It would seem that honor was frequently an implicit requirement in covenant relations."

[10] Olyan, "Covenant Relations," 205. Such despising of the covenant by a treaty partner is precisely what YHWH calls Israel to account for in the Song of Moses, where Israel is condemned for breaking fealty to their covenant God YHWH, who, incidentally, is also depicted as their father.

[11] Olyan, "Covenant Relations," 205–6.

[12] Lyn Huber (Bechtel), "Biblical Experience of Shame/Shaming" (PhD diss., Drew University, 1983), 170.

[13] Saul Olyan, *Friendship in the Hebrew Bible* (New Haven, CT: Yale University Press, 2017), 19.

affirms, one finds numerous texts "consistently emphasizing the honor owed to parents by children," thereby accenting generational hierarchy and sharing of honor between parents and children.[14]

The following section will attempt to build on the importance of the honor theme throughout the Hebrew Bible, focusing on its presence in the two texts to which Paul directs his auditors in Phil 2:14–16, that is, Deuteronomy and Isaiah. While a full analysis of the language of honor in these corpora is beyond our purpose, this section will direct attention to the reciprocal honor reflected in Deut 26 and 32 and to the mutual honor envisioned eschatologically for YHWH and Israel in Isa 40–66. Chapter 2 will argue that both the Song of Moses (Deut 32) and the covenant ceremony (Deut 26:16–19) portray the blessing of honor offered to Israel for obedience to the covenant, that is, her καύχημα (Deut 26:19 LXX), an honor that would then redound back to YHWH himself. Chapter 3 will then argue that Isaiah envisioned Israel finally coming to fulfill her call to covenant obedience through the mediation of the Servant figure, who is subsequently offered a share in the mutual glory enjoyed by God and his people resulting from their obedience (see פעלה ‖ πόνος, in Isa 49:4). As we will see, these two ideas from Deut 26:19 (mutual boasting arising from covenant obedience) and Isa 49:4 (the Servant as mediator of the mutual glory shared between God and his people), along with their wider contexts, form the theological underpinnings for Paul's use of the mutual boasting motif in Philippians.

This study is aware that Paul was not the only Jewish author from the Second Temple period to cull resources from the closing chapters of Deuteronomy to shape an understanding of the identity of God's people. When it comes to the focus of our present subject, however, which treats the *mutual honor* arising from covenant obedience as described in Deut 26:19, Paul seems to stand apart from his contemporaries. We see many Jewish writers before and after Paul looking to Deut 27–32 to understand both Israel's apparent failure and how their restoration might come about.[15] One searches in vain, however, to find other Jewish writers of Paul's time speaking about themselves sharing in the mutual honor emerging from the divinely empowered obedience of an eschatologically restored covenant people. This is precisely what Paul has the audacity to declare in Philippians, as we will demonstrate in Part 3.

---

[14] Olyan, *Friendship*, 19.
[15] See, e.g., Josephus, *Ant.* 4.303; Philo, *Vit. Mos.* 2.288; for discussion see N. T. Wright, *Paul and the Faithfulness of God*, COQG 4 (London: SPCK, 2013), 129–31.

2

Καύχημα as a Sign of Mutual Honor in Deuteronomy

As we have seen above, mutual honor is essential for understanding the covenant relationship established between God and his people as portrayed in Deuteronomy. By entering into a covenant relationship with Israel, YHWH has bound up his own reputation with them, thereby tying his own honor to their success as a nation. Should they maintain their honor through covenant faithfulness, they will be for YHWH a claim to honor; but should they dishonor themselves by forsaking their loyalty, then God's honor will be diminished before the eyes of the nations.

These two options of either honor or shame, mutually experienced by both YHWH and Israel, surface in the various scenes that conclude the book of Deuteronomy. This is especially evident in two passages, Deut 26:16-19 and Deut 32. The Song of Moses in Deut 32 depicts YHWH's covenant relationship with Israel as that between father and son, highlighting the filial failures of Israel and the resultant scandal brought upon God their "Father."[1] The Song of Moses has important links, moreover, with Deut 26:16-19,[2] which presents a covenant ceremony wherein the mutual honor available to both the covenant God and his people as a result of their mutual covenant faithfulness is a central aspect. It is at Deut 26:19 LXX[3] that this mutual covenant honor shared

---

[1] On the centrality of kinship terminology to conceive of the covenant relationship between YHWH and Israel, see F. M. Cross, "Kinship and Covenant in Ancient Israel," in *From Epic to Canon: History and Literature in Ancient Israel* (Baltimore, MD: Johns Hopkins Press, 1998), 3-21. Cf. *Jub* 1:24-25, 28, where the covenant relationship between God and Israel is presented primarily in terms of a father-son relationship.

[2] Scholars commonly denote portions of Deut 27-34 as "endings" or "appendices" to the book. For Richard H. Bell, *Provoked to Jealousy: The Origin of the Jealousy Motif in Romans 9-11*, WUNT 2.63 (Tübingen: Mohr Siebeck, 1994), 210, Deut 31-34 is an "appendix"; for Casper J. Labuschagne, "The Setting of the Song of Moses in Deuteronomy," in *Deuteronomy and the Deuteronomic Literature*, BETL 133, ed. Marc Vervenne and Johan Lust (Leuven: Leuven University Press, 1997), 111-29, 113, they are a "postscript." E. Talstra, "Deuteronomy 31: Confusion or Conclusion? The Story of Moses' Threefold Succession," in *Deuteronomy and Deuteronomic Literature*, 87-103, 88-9, notes that for some the "appendices" start in chapter 27, for others at chapter 29. For S. R. Driver, *Deuteronomy* (Edinburgh: T&T Clark, 1902), 320, Deut 29-30 are "of the nature of a supplement."

[3] For the purpose of this study, I follow the continuing custom of referring to the Old Greek (OG) translations of the various biblical books as the LXX. While LXX has commonly been a shorthand way to refer to the entire collection of the Hebrew Scriptures translated into Greek despite their varying translators and textual traditions, this study will take into account the differing translational strategies and textual histories reflected throughout the corpus, rather than seeing the LXX as a

between God and his people occurs via the language of καύχημα, which will serve as an important tie to Paul's own usage of the term in Philippians. But the Song of Moses in Deut 32 presents the issue in summary fashion and hence we treat that passage first before moving on to a more extensive treatment of the covenant ceremony in Deut 26:16-19.

Mutual Honor in the Song of Moses

The Song of Moses, in summarizing Deuteronomy as a whole, presents Israel's precarious history as the covenant people of God, highlighting in particular their failure despite God's covenant faithfulness. This contrast between Israel's failure and God's faithfulness is apparent in the Song's introduction at Deut 32:4-5, where God is described as possessing "works [that] are genuine" and "ways [that] are justice (κρίσις)"; he is "a faithful (πιστός) God, and there is no injustice (ἀδικία),[4] a righteous (δίκαιος) and holy (ὅσιος) Lord" (32:4 LXX).[5] The people of Israel, in contrast, appear as "blemished children, not his" (οὐκ αὐτῷ τέκνα μωμητά), who "have sinned"; they are "a generation crooked and perverse" (γενεὰ σκολιὰ καὶ διεστραμμένη, 32:5 LXX).[6] The contrast between the two parties is stark, with God's positive traits piled up (πιστός, δίκαιος, ὅσιος), while Israel's negative traits are equally multiplied (μωμητά, σκολιὰ καὶ διεστραμμένη).[7]

This characterization of Israel as God's rebellious children, with God as their spurned father,[8] continues throughout much of the Song. Hence, God is explicitly given the epithet of being Israel's "father" (32:6), the one who "bore" Israel (v. 18), with Israel characterized as "his young" (v. 11), his "beloved ones" (v. 15), and "his sons and daughters" (v. 19). In the Song, God performs many of the roles a father was expected to fulfill for his children, for example, protection, education, sustenance. Israel, however, neglects their filial obligations, "abandoning" and "forgetting" God (vv. 15, 18), and ultimately "provoking" him. They are described a second time as

---

single work with a unified textual history. All references to the Greek translation of Deuteronomy are from John W. Wevers, *Deuteronomium*, Septuaginta 3.2 (Göttingen: Vandenhoeck & Ruprecht, 1977), which represents a consensus regarding the OG of Deuteronomy.

[4] John W. Wevers, *Notes on the Greek Text of Deuteronomy*, SCS 39 (Atlanta, GA: Scholars Press, 1995), 511, argues that this phrase "must mean" that "there is not injustice with God."

[5] All English translations of the LXX are from NETS unless otherwise noted.

[6] The MT for Deut 32:5 is uncertain, which leads to variations in the versions; see Alison Salvesen, *Symmachus in the Pentateuch*, JSSM 15 (Manchester: University of Manchester, 1991), 162-3. Wevers, *Notes*, 511, offers the gloss: "disgraceful children who are not his have sinned."

[7] While specific vocabulary of shame does not appear in the text of the Song, the incongruity between YHWH's faithfulness and Israel's faithlessness makes implicit the shame of the one and the honor of the other. Lyn Huber (Bechtel), "Biblical Experience of Shame/Shaming" (PhD diss., Drew University, 1983), 170-4, notes a similar type of "subtle shaming" introduced through the notable incongruity between previous faithfulness and current abandonment.

[8] Ronald Bergey, "Song of Moses and Isaianic Prophecies," *JSOT* 28 (2003), 33-54, 39, notes that "both Deuteronomy 32 and Isaiah 1 share … father-son imagery" and notes that only in these two chapters do we find "sons dealing corruptly" and "God's sons either being spurned or spurning God" (p. 33). The theme of Israel's filial unfaithfulness shared between Isaiah and Deuteronomy recurs in Paul's reappropriation of these two Scriptural precursors in Phil 2.

"a perverse generation, sons who have no faithfulness in them" (v. 20; cf. v. 5).[9] Thus, the father–son relationship enumerated in the Song functions to highlight the unfaithfulness of Israel in performing their covenantal/filial duty to God their father.[10]

Israel's faithless behavior as God's children prompts God to step into the role of the reprimanding father, who restores the family's honor by forcefully punishing his sons who have stepped out of line. Cross's analysis of the kinship idea as the basis for conceptualizing YHWH's covenant relationship with Israel demonstrates that such punishment stems from the father–son relationship adduced in the Song. That is to say: "the Divine Kinsman … receives the privileges of kinship," that is, his family "obeys his patriarchal commands [and] maintains familial loyalty (ḥesed)."[11] The failure of Israel to maintain this filial loyalty thus unbalances the mutual relationship within the family.[12] Hence, God's "anger" will burn against Israel (v. 22), bringing waste upon them and dispersing them (vv. 24–26), thereby causing "their memory to cease from among humans" (v. 26). Dille argues from the father–child relationship between YHWH and Israel that such paternal wrath would have been "expected" as the rightful response of a father to his children's rebellion.[13] Ultimately, however, God will "avenge the blood of his sons" (v. 43), repaying their enemies. De Vaux's classic study of ancient family institutions thus distinguishes between the "blood-vengeance" enacted toward those outside the group and the disciplinarian punishment inflicted upon those within one's group.[14] Only after this fatherly reprisal has restored the internal status of family honor (i.e., punishing his "disgraceful" children, cf. v. 5) can God then move outward to assert the family's honor against the enemies, which is reflected in Deut 32:43.[15]

In this way, the law code that constituted the majority of the book of Deuteronomy becomes the fatherly education offered by YHWH for his son Israel. The Song is adamant that Israel's rejection of God's law will be a reality, but it also envisions a time

---

[9] Annette Böckler, *Gott als Vater im Alten Testament: Traditionsgeschichtliche Untersuchungen zu Entstehung und Entwicklung eines Gottesbildes* (Kaiser: Gütersloher Verlagshaus, 2000), 291: "Durch dieses Bild wird der Aufweis der Schuld Israels verstärkt." Böckler, *Gott als Vater*, 298: "Israel hat diese Eigenständigkeit dazu missbraucht, sich von seinem Vater zu entfernen."
[10] Böckler, *Gott als Vater*, 298: "Das Vater-Sohn-Bild steht in Dtn 32 im Zusammenhang eines Schuldaufweises … Ihr Ungehorsam ist so, als rebellierten Kinder gegen ihren eigenen Vater."
[11] Cross, "Kinship and Covenant," 7. Later in the essay, Cross asserts that "kinship obligations are necessarily mutual" (p. 14).
[12] Cf. Sarah J. Dille, "Honor Restored: Honor, Shame and God as Redeeming Kinsman in Second Isaiah," in *Relating to the Text: Interdisciplinary and Form-Critical Insights on the Bible*, ed. Timothy J. Sandoval and Carleen Mandolfo, LOTS 384 (London: T&T Clark, 2003), 232–50, 241: "YHWH's honor is tied to Israel—they are his offspring and their honor or lack of honor reflects on the father."
[13] Sarah J. Dille, *Mixing Metaphors: God as Mother and Father in Deutero-Isaiah*, LOTS 398 (London: T&T Clark International, 2004), 101; earlier, on p. 77, she writes that God's wrath in Deut 32:30 is an "intentional action on the part of the father" that restores the family honor.
[14] Roland de Vaux, *Ancient Israel: Its Life and Institutions*, trans. John McHugh (London: Darton, Longman & Todd, 1973), 11: "Blood-vengeance does not operate within the group, but the guilty man is punished by his group or expelled from it."
[15] David A. Glatt-Gilad, "Yahweh's Honor at Stake: A Divine Conundrum," *JSOT* 98 (2002), 63–74, 70, explains that the transition to God's punishment upon Israel's enemies at Deut 32:43 relies upon vv. 26–28. Cf. Dille, "Honor Restored," 238, who shows how God restores honor *within* the group before restoring honor *in the eyes of others*.

when restoration will come (following, of course, the punishment of exile), when God will restore not only his people's honor but also his own when he "avenges the blood of his sons" (v. 43).[16] Thus, even though it anticipates a day of future restoration, the Song mainly highlights the negative possibility of Israel's mutuality of honor with God: their unfaithfulness compromises his honor and justly solicits his wrath. The apostle Paul overtly takes up this image of Israel as God's perverted and rebellious offspring when he warns the Philippians to stop grumbling in Phil 2:14. For Paul, however, as we will see, the image of the twisted generation stands in opposition to his hope for these Christ-believing converts, for whom he envisions honor and glory resulting from their firm adherence to God's commands. The prophetic depiction of the shame from God's paternal discipline upon Israel displayed in Deut 32 stands in stark contrast to the offer of honor held forth previously when they enter into covenant with YHWH in Deut 26:16–19.

Deuteronomy 26:16–19 and the Mutual Honor of the Covenant Relationship

Lohfink designates Deut 26:16–19 to be "an interpretation of the whole law as a contract concluded between Yahweh and Israel."[17] It is marked off from the law code proper through its repetition in 26:16 of language from the beginning of the law code at 4:45 (החקים and המשפטים ‖ τὰ δικαιώματα and τὰ κρίματα).[18] Deuteronomy 26:16 thus provides a key structural transition into a summary section at the point where the specific laws conclude, and so the paragraph in 26:16–19 offers an initial "ending" for the book, cementing the covenant relationship between the Torah-giving God and the Torah-receiving people.[19]

The ceremony in 26:16–19 exhibits the common Deuteronomic theme of YHWH's setting Israel apart as his own people (4:20; 7:6; 9:29; 14:2, 21), a theme that is emphasized in the various closing portions of the book (26:18–19; 27:9; 29:13; 32:8–9). In both 26:17–19 and 29:12, this theme of Israel as God's particular people (λαὸς περιούσιος) is joined with an equivalent depiction of YHWH as Israel's God, commonly designated by scholars as the constitutive elements of the covenant

---

[16] Jos Luyten, "Primeval and Eschatological Overtones in the Song of Moses (Dt 32:1-43)," in *Das Deuteronomium*, ed. Norbert Lohfink, BETL 68 (Leuven: Leuven University Press, 1985), 341–7, 345, points to this verse as relating "the idea of the day of the execution of a twofold vindication—punishment for the enemies and salvation for Yahweh's people" and as representative of YHWH's vindication of his people in the "eschatological finale" to the Song.

[17] Norbert Lohfink, *Great Themes from the Old Testament*, trans. Robert Walls (Edinburgh: T&T Clark, 1982), 25.

[18] The unique designation of Moses's instruction to Israel on the plains of Moab as "statutes and rules" (as opposed to a number of other designations) appears first at 4:1 and again at 4:45 to mark the close of Moses's first speech (chapters 1–4); again at 5:1 and 11:32 to mark off his second speech; and finally at 12:1 and 26:16 to delineate his third speech.

[19] Some scholars are hesitant to recognize in this passage the idea of "covenant," since the actual term ברית is lacking in the passage, but see Andrew D. H. Mays, "Deuteronomy 4," *JBL* 100 (1981), 23–51, 42, who describes Deut 26:16–19 as "the formal declaration of the establishment of a (covenant) relationship between Yahweh and Israel."

relationship between YHWH and Israel.[20] Rendtorff describes how these elements combine to form the covenant formula ("I will be your God and you will be my people"). He highlights the "mutuality" expressed in the relationship conveyed by the formula, clarifying that for Israel to be a people *for YHWH* is not a matter of "belonging-to" but of "belonging together."[21]

The significance of this passage for our study lies in the relationality of the covenant emphasized therein, rather than in the admittedly unequal relationship between the divine and human partners.[22] Of all the covenant-formula passages, here the motif of mutuality between God and his people is most prominent, since both sides of the mutual arrangement are clearly laid out. The text of 26:17–19 is as follows:

LXX: [17] τὸν θεὸν εἵλου σήμερον εἶναί σου θεὸν καὶ πορεύεσθαι ἐν ταῖς ὁδοῖς αὐτοῦ καὶ φυλάσσεσθαι τὰ δικαιώματα καὶ τὰ κρίματα αὐτοῦ καὶ ὑπακούειν τῆς φωνῆς αὐτοῦ, [18] καὶ κύριος εἵλατό σε σήμερον γενέσθαι σε αὐτῷ λαὸν περιούσιον, καθάπερ εἶπέν σοι, φυλάσσειν πάσας τὰς ἐντολὰς αὐτοῦ [19] καὶ εἶναί σε ὑπεράνω πάντων τῶν ἐθνῶν, ὡς ἐποίησέν σε ὀνομαστὸν καὶ καύχημα καὶ δόξαστόν, εἶναί σε λαὸν ἅγιον κυρίῳ τῷ θεῷ σου, καθὼς ἐλάλησεν.

NETS: [17] Today you have chosen God to be your god and to walk in his ways and to keep his statutes and his judgments and to obey his voice.[18] Today also the Lord has chosen you to be his exceptional people, as he said, to keep all his commandments,[19] and that you be high above all nations, as he has made you renowned and a boast and glorified, that you be a people holy to the Lord your God, as he spoke.

What is noteworthy about the passage is the unusual structure for the covenant stipulations. In conjunction with Israel's covenantal agreement to have YHWH as their God is a list of three stipulations: to walk in his ways, to keep his statutes, and to heed his voice (v. 17). Then, in parallel fashion, linked with YHWH's covenantal agreement to choose Israel as his people (v. 18), there again follows a threefold list of stipulations: to keep his commands, to be high above the nations, and to be a holy people. The balanced structure would cause us to expect three activities that YHWH now undertakes on behalf of Israel, but instead Israel's obedience recurs yet again, with YHWH performing only the second two activities, that is, exalting Israel and sanctifying them.[23] This

---

[20] See Cross, "Kinship and Covenant," 13: "Israel is the kindred of Yahweh; Yahweh is the God of Israel. This is an old formula. But this formula must be understood as legal language, the language of kinship-in-law, or in other words, the language of covenant."

[21] Rolf Rendtorff, *The Covenant Formula*, trans. Margaret Kohl (Edinburgh: T&T Clark, 1998), 11 n. 4. Similarly, Rudolf Smend, *Die Bundesformel* (Zürich: EVZ-Verlag, 1963), 27, describes "der vollen Reziprozität" represented in the bilateral covenant formula.

[22] Saul Olyan, "Honor, Shame and Covenant Relations," *JBL* 115 (1996), 201–18, 205: "Covenant honor, like covenant love, is reciprocal; it applies to partners in parity treaties and to those in covenants of unequals (vassal-suzerain treaties), even if the reciprocal nature of honor is not always made explicit."

[23] Cf. Norbert Lohfink, "Dt. 26, 17–19 und die 'Bundesformel,'" *ZkTh* 91 (1969), 517–53, 537–8, "[YHWH] leistet einen Eid darauf, daß er bei seiner Zusage bleiben will, Israels Gott zu sein und Israel zu seinem Volk zu machen, wobei der zweite Aspekt noch ausführlicher umschrieben wird mit Vorstellungen wie Sondereigentum, Erhobensein über die anderen Völker, Heiligkeit." Lohfink,

misbalance thus places a strong emphasis on Israel's obedience. Indeed, Rendtorff recognizes here a focus on Israel's obligation that is "almost to a one-sided degree."[24] The essential foundation of the covenant, however, as Lohfink asserts, remains the fact that YHWH's actions are "gnädig gewährend."[25]

Alongside this concentration on the need for obedience in vv. 17–18, v. 19 then provides positive motivation by elaborating upon the benefits of status available to Israel as YHWH's covenant people. The brief section in 26:17–19 can thus be connected to the larger unit of blessings and curses that follows in chapter 28.[26] As the complement to chapter 28, Deut 26:18–19 focuses specifically on the positive benefits[27] that arise for Israel as a result of their covenant obedience to YHWH, as opposed to the emphatic presentation of the curses for Israel's unfaithfulness in Deut 28.

The Honorific Triad as Covenant Blessing in Deuteronomy 26:18–19

As noted above, the blessings of Deut 28:1–14 are to be read in close connection with the covenant ceremony of 26:17–19. Both passages speak of Israel's obedient relationship to YHWH resulting in his distinguishing Israel by setting her "*high above* (עליון ‖ ὑπεράνω) the nations." Whereas in chapter 28 this declaration is followed by a comprehensive list of material blessings promised by YHWH to Israel,[28] in 26:19 the blessings are protracted into a concise, triadic honorary description of Israel as a people "renowned and a boast and glorified" (ὀνομαστὸν καὶ καύχημα καὶ δόξαστον; cf. MT: לתהלה ולשם ולתפארת). The use of the rare word καύχημα is an interesting choice by the LXX translator here, though among the LXX authors it does regularly render two of the three terms in the MT's honorific triad here (תהלה and תפארת). Numerous scholars point out that, in contexts like this one, the LXX translator fundamentally

---

"Dt. 26, 17–19," 544, perceptively connects the holiness of Israel in Deut 26:19 to the blessings YHWH promises for his covenant people in Deut 28:1–14.

[24] Rendtorff, *Covenant Formula*, 52–3, where he goes on to describe, "Both Yhwh's being God and Israel's being a people find their decisive expression in Israel's keeping of the commandments God has given."

[25] Lohfink, "Bundesformel," 537. So too Rendtorff, *Covenant Formula*, 25: "Israel expresses this obligation in response to Yhwh's preceding declaration that he will be Israel's God."

[26] Both 26:19 and 28:1 declare that the Lord will "render you high above all the nations of the earth" (δώσει σε … ὑπεράνω πάντων τῶν ἐθνῶν τῆς γῆς). Lohfink, *Themes*, 25, suggests Deut 26 and 28 were originally conjoined, with Deut 27 representing a later insertion. Cf. J. G. McConville, *Deuteronomy* (Grand Rapids, MI: InterVarsity Press, 2002), 387: "28:1 flows neatly from 26:19, both in terms of literary smoothness and in that it introduces the expected blessings and curses of the Moab covenant."

[27] This leads Andreas Michel, "Deuteronomium 26,16-19: ein 'ewiger Bund,'" in *Für Immer Verbündet: Studien zur Bundestheologie der Bibel*, ed. Christoph Dohmen and Christian Frevel, SB 211 (Stuttgart: Katholisches Bibelwerk, 2007), 141–9, 148–9, to conclude that the description of Israel's promised exaltation in Deut 26:18–19 should be linked together only with the blessings in 28:1–14 (as well as with the promised repentance in Deut 30) rather than with both the blessings and curses that constitute all of chapter 28.

[28] For similar, though less extensive, lists of blessings offered to God's people, see Deut 7:13, 20; 11:13, 26; 15:6; 30:9, 16.

alters the connotation of καύχημα from negative to positive.[29] Kate Donahoe thus emphasizes the relational, and therefore mutual, nature of the term καύχημα when it bears a positive connotation, asserting that, whereas the majority of Greek usage of the term καύχημα is negative,[30] "the positive connotations emerge when the καυχ- stem *is used of someone else.*"[31] Hence, the promise that YHWH will exalt another, namely, Israel, into this position as a boast among the nations guards against any negative connotations that might accrue had he been exalting himself, thereby freeing Israel up to enjoy fully the benefits of receiving glorification.

The LXX translation that introduces the triad is irregular,[32] since the MT reads that Israel will be "set high above the nations *whom [YHWH] has made*," whereas the LXX offers "high above the nations, *as [YHWH] has made you renowned.*"[33] The variation is slight, but the addition of the second-person pronoun (σε) in the LXX emphasizes that it is *Israel* that has become renowned and a boast and glorified. This is more specific than the MT's bare assertion that Israel's exaltation vis-à-vis the nations occurs *for a glory, for a name, and for a boast* (לתהלה ולשם ולתפארת).

As indicated above, the Hebrew underlying this phrase enumerates the exaltation as a threefold honorific title: "for praise, and for fame, and for glory."[34] On par with the title given to Israel in 26:18 ("a treasured possession [סגלה | | περιούσιος] for YHWH"),[35] this tripartite title in 26:19 appears at first to designate Israel as the honorable possession of YHWH.[36] They add to his beauty, or in the words of Raurell, "The elect people can be compared to the precious garment by which God is present to

---

[29] Josef Schreiner, "Jer 9,22.23 als Hintergrund des paulinischen 'Sich-Rühmens,'" in *Biblische Randbemerkungen*, ed. H. Merklein and J. Lange (Würzburg: Echter, 1974), 530–42, 539, views καύχημα as rendering the Hebrew term תהלה (rather than שם, as the word order would suggest) and sees the choice by the Deuteronomy LXX translator to deploy καύχημα here as "sehr bedeutsam" because it ultimately directs the connotation of this term away from its primarily negative prior usage. So too Cécil Dogniez et al., *Les douze prophètes*, BA (Paris: Les Éditions du Cerf, 1999), 374, who note that καύχημα in the LXX "est employé avec une valeur positive qu'il n'a pas dans l'usage grec."

[30] Ulrich Heckel, *Kraft in Schwachheit: Untersuchungen zu 2. Kor 10–13*, WUNT 2.56 (Tübingen: Mohr Siebeck, 1993), 159, points to "einen weitgehenden Grundkonsens zwischen Griechen, Juden und Christen" for the negative, deprecating usage of the καυχ- word group.

[31] Kate C. Donahoe, "From Self-Praise to Self-Boasting" (PhD diss., University of St Andrews, 2008), 43 (emphasis added).

[32] Another oddity in the LXX translation is that it does not render the threefold prefixed *lameds* on each of the nouns in the MT's triad. One would expect at least the central substantive in the LXX triad to be introduced by the preposition εἰς: "*for* a boast." See Cécile Dogniez and Marguerite Harl, *Le deutéronome*, BA (Paris: Les Éditions du Cerf, 1992), 279: "une traduction littérale aurait employé [εἰς] suivi de trois noms."

[33] On the variation, see Wevers, *Notes*, 414. There is a telling variant, noted in Wevers, *Deuteronomium*, 285, in which the manuscript A* reads the pronoun in the dative ἐποίησέν σοι (*he did on your behalf*).

[34] The grammar is truncated here, but most likely the verb נתן governs the triad; see BDB, "נתן," 681 (3.b): נתן plus complementary accusative with ל-prefix (Deut 28:13; Isa 42:24). The LXX translator has taken some liberty in rendering the first and last of the substantives in the Hebrew triad as adjectives. On this see Wevers, *Notes*, 414.

[35] For Israel as YHWH's סגלה cf. 7:6; 14:2; Ex 19:5; Mal 3:17; Ps 135:4.

[36] Georg Braulik, *Deuteronomium II* (Würzburg: Echter, 1992), 198, notes that 26:18–19 "enthalten ein kleines Summarium 'ekklesiologischer' Titel, das die höchsten Würdenamen Israels im Blick auf Jahweh und auf die Völker zusammenfaßt."

the eyes of all the world."[37] But Israel too seems to share in the honor accruing from their obedience described in this verse.[38] If we look elsewhere in the Scriptures, this triad represents a "stehende Formel,"[39] recurring verbatim in Jer 13:11,[40] and in modified form in Jer 33(40):9,[41] Zeph 3:19-20,[42] and 1 Chron 22:5.[43] In the Jeremaic passages the reference is explicitly to *God's* honor (cf. לִי ‖ μοι),[44] yet the Zephaniah passage seems to focus on the benefit for *Israel* at the time of restoration,[45] while 1 Chron 22:5 remains ambiguous. Since the triad of Deut 26:19 is to be seen in connection with the other benefits offered to Israel in vv. 18–19 in reward for maintaining their side of the covenant stipulations,[46] we should not rule out that the triad, alongside designating honor for YHWH via Israel's obedience, also designates exaltation for obedient Israel. That is, since in Deut 26:19 YHWH makes Israel "name-worthy" and "glorious," both of which adjectival descriptions imply honorable attributes belonging to Israel herself, so too YHWH's making Israel a "boast" (καύχημα) conveys their reception of honor.[47]

However, application of these honors *to Israel* does not detract from Israel's exaltation simultaneously redounding to the glory of God.[48] Rather, the glorification of YHWH's people amplifies that of YHWH himself. Indeed, this is so with the promise that Israel will be λαὸς περιούσιος, upon which the honorific triad in Deut 26:19 elaborates. The fact that Israel is YHWH's "rich possession" means that they are "the people which constitutes the crown jewel of God … Israel is the precious stone, the pearl in His possession."[49] Raurell similarly notes that the notion of Israel being made "into a

---

[37] Frederic Raurell, *'Doxa' en la teologia I: Antropologia dels LXX*, CSP 59 (Catalonia: Herder, 1996), 113: "El poble escollit és com el vestit preciós amb què Déu es presenta als ulls de tot el món."

[38] In his analysis of the καυχ- word group in the LXX, J. Sánchez Bosch, *"Gloriarse" segun san Pablo: Sentido y teología de καυχάομαι*, AnBib 40 (Rome: Biblical Institute Press, 1970), 59, describes the importance of these three Hebrew terms for understanding Israel's special place among the nations: "In [the triad of Deut 26:19] we see *the key to the entire biblical doctrine of the glory of man*" (my translation).

[39] Gerhard von Rad, *Deuteronomium*, ATD 8 (Göttingen: Vandenhoeck & Ruprecht, 1964), 116.

[40] Jer 13:11: להיות לי לעם ולשם ולתהלה ולתפארת; τοῦ γενέσθαι μοι εἰς λαὸν **ὀνομαστὸν** καὶ **εἰς καύχημα** καὶ **εἰς δόξαν** (LXX). The key words that reflect the Deuteronomic phraseology in the Hebrew text are underlined and in the Greek text are set in bold in this and subsequent verses.

[41] Jer 33:9: והיתה לי לשם ששון לתהלה ולתפארת; the LXX translator chooses not to use καύχημα when rendering the triad: ἔσται **εἰς εὐφροσύνην** καὶ **εἰς αἴνεσιν** καὶ **εἰς μεγαλειότητα** (40:9 LXX).

[42] Zeph 3:19: ושמתים לתהלה ולשם בכל־הארץ; θήσομαι αὐτοὺς **εἰς καύχημα** καὶ **ὀνομαστοὺς** ἐν πάσῃ τῇ γῇ (LXX). Zeph 3:20: כי־אתן אתכם לשם ולתהלה בכל עמי הארץ; δώσω ὑμᾶς **ὀνομαστοὺς** καὶ **εἰς καύχημα** ἐν πᾶσιν τοῖς λαοῖς τῆς γῆς (LXX).

[43] 1 Chron 22:5: והבית לבנות ליהוה להגדיל למעלה לשם ולתפארת לכל־הארצות; ὁ οἶκος τοῦ οἰκοδομῆσαι τῷ κυρίῳ εἰς μεγαλωσύνην ἄνω, **εἰς ὄνομα** καὶ **εἰς δόξαν** εἰς πᾶσαν τὴν γῆν (LXX).

[44] Sánchez Bosch, *Gloriarse*, 61, interprets the assertion that Israel's glory is *for God* as the most salient component in such passages about Israel's glory: "in all these texts it is clear that they indicate glory *for God*."

[45] Note the emphasis on the third-person plural and the second-person plural pronouns in Zeph 3:19 and 3:20, respectively. Cf. Braulik, *Deuteronomium II*, 198–9.

[46] Israel as סגלה of YHWH; Israel "set high above" the nations (explicated by the triad); and Israel as a "holy people" to the Lord (seen as a state divinely bestowed upon her).

[47] Peter C. Craigie, *The Book of Deuteronomy*, NICOT (Grand Rapids, MI: Eerdmans, 1976), 325: "The covenant community would reflect the glory of the covenant God … This glory was the potential of the community of God's people."

[48] Schreiner, "Sich-Rühmens," 536, comments succinctly that "Nach Dtn 26:19 ist Israel Jahwehs Ruhm." Bultmann, "καυχάομαι," *TDNT* 3:646, cites Deut 26:19 as indicating how God "deals with Israel to His own glory."

[49] H. Preisker, "περιούσιος," *TDNT* 6:57.

name (שם), a praise (תהלה), and a glory (תפארת)" "signifies their bearing testimony to YHWH's efficacious presence among his people," thereby becoming "a signal to the nations" of God's greatness.[50] Thus, both parties in the covenant relationship receive the glory arising from YHWH's setting Israel as a "praise, a name, and a boast." As Dogniez and Harl observe, the LXX authors employ καύχημα both when speaking of the boast that comes to Israel *through God* and when speaking of the boast that God possesses *through Israel*.[51] We thus see in the honorific triad of Deut 26:19 a picture of mutual honor, that is, honor for YHWH and honor for Israel, able to arise from Israel's covenant obedience.

As noted above, though the three terms תהלה, שם, and תפארת are common in the Hebrew Bible,[52] when appearing in succession they represent a recognizable formula.[53] The recurrences of the triad are listed in the following table.

This table shows the Deuteronomic triad recurring as a cluster designating honor.[54] The various terms (always paired with at least one other term) appear within a somewhat consistent pattern,[55] where an individual or entity is established *as an honor*. One could speak here of an act of *institution* in which an individual or entity is established into a specific role or position of honor (designated in nominal form as a predicate).[56] Oftentimes this process of institution occurs with a beneficiary specifically designated, for example, Israel is instituted into a position of honor *for YHWH* (Jer 13:11).[57] In fact, in most cases where the beneficiary is marked (via the *lamed* as *dativus*

---

[50] Raurell, *Doxa*, 112–13.
[51] Dogniez et al., *Les douze*, 374.
[52] תהלה appears 57 times; שם is extremely common, appearing 881 times; תפארת appears 51 times.
[53] Moshe Weinfeld, *Deuteronomy and the Deuteronomic School* (Oxford: Clarendon Press, 1972), 328, in his appendix for "Deuteronomic Phraseology," points to the triad's representative nature pertaining to Israel's election, citing its appearance in Jer 13:11 and 33:9.
[54] Along with the original triad, תפארת, שם, תהלה, at least two other clearly parallel terms can be added: כבוד and גאון, aside from the various other terms employed by Isaiah. Out of these five Hebrew terms, כבוד is the overarching term for describing an individual's exalted status. See Sánchez Bosch, *Gloriarse*, 58, who observes that the three Hebrew words from the triad in Deut 26:19 are "organized under the heading of כבוד."
[55] The pattern from the passages appears to have שם as the leading word for the triad. Of the six recurrences of the triad, only two diverge from this pattern: Deut 26:19 and Zeph 3:19. The ordering in Zeph 3:19 is immediately inverted in Zeph 3:20, reflecting perhaps rhetorical variation. Note the comment by Michel, "Ewiger Bund," 143 n. 12: "Der 'Name' (שם) ist … das entscheidende mittlere Stichwort in der nachgestellten Zweckangabe von Dtn 26:19."
[56] This language comes from BDB, "היה," 226 (II.2f): "followed by ל predicate" היה can mean *be instituted*. On the use of metonymy reflected in this act of institution, see Isaac D. Blois, "Formulas for (Dis)Honorable Installation in Deuteronomy 26:19 and 28:37: The Honorific Implications of Israel's Covenant (Un)Faithfulness," *CBQ* 82.3 (forthcoming in 2020).
[57] BDB, ל, 513, meaning 5a (d): "denoting *relation* (to be *to* or *towards* one in a particular regard or capacity)," after which they cite Ex 19:5a (והייתם לי סגלה, *and you shall be to me a special possession*, of Israel), which they note as distinct from meaning 5b ("denoting *possession*"), in which they place Ex 19:5b (כי לי כל הארץ, *for to me is all the earth*, of the other nations). Joüon, 459, notes that "the ל of the *dativus commodi* is used in a very particular way with a pronominal suffix referring to the *same person* as the subject of the verb," which is how we find it used in 1 Sam 12:22 (cf. Ex 19:5–6; Deut 7:6; 14:2; 26:19; 28:9). The remarks by C. H. J. van der Merwe, J. A. Naudé, and J. H. Kroeze, *A Biblical Hebrew Reference Grammar* (Sheffield: Sheffield Academic Press, 2000), 285, are helpful: "ל is used especially *to characterize relationships* that are marked by the dative form in Latin and Greek." Thus, the common use of the "for myself" phrase in these covenantal passages could easily denote what Greek grammarians refer to as the dative of advantage (*dativus commodi*). This is borne out by the fact that most of these verses appear in the LXX in the dative case, hence, e.g., Ex 19:5 LXX: "you

Table 1 MT Passages Reflecting the Honorific Triad of Deuteronomy 26:19

Passage	First Term	Second Term	Third Term	ל-Prefix	Preceding Verb	ל+Suffix Marking *dativus comodi*
Deut 26:19	תהלה	שם	תפארת	Yes	נתן?	No
Jer 13:11	שם	תהלה	תפארת	Yes	היה	Yes ("for me")
Jer 33(40):9	שם ששון	תהלה	תפארת	Yes	היה	Yes ("for me")
Zeph 3:19	תהלה	שם	-	Yes	שים	No
Zeph 3:20	שם	תהלה	-	Yes	נתן	No
1 Chron 22:5	שם	-	תפארת	Yes	Implied היה	Yes ("for YHWH")
Similar Passages						
Ex 28:2	כבד	-	תפארת	Yes	Implied היה	Yes ("for Aaron")
Ex 28:40	כבד	-	תפארת	Yes	Implied היה	Yes ("for Aaron")
Isa 4:2	צבי + כבד	נאה	תפארת	Yes	היה	Yes ("for the survivors of Israel")
Isa 28:5	עטרת צבי	-	צפירת תפארה	Yes	היה	Yes ("for the remnant of his people")
Isa 60:19	אור עולם	-	תפארת	Yes	היה	Yes ("for you")

commodi), we see Israel honored for the benefit of YHWH, thereby demonstrating the mutuality inherent within the covenant relationship between God and people. That is, the covenant people are exalted, and this in turn exalts the covenant God. Thus, a pattern emerges in which the honorific triad found in Deut 26:19 marks the blessing God gives to obedient Israel—an exaltation that then redounds back to himself.

The first two terms from the triad in Deut 26:19 (תהלה and שם) do not always convey honorific connotations. The term תהלה usually means "praise," and, though it often appears in contexts of worship (nearly always to God),[58] it seldom represents a title of honor. The distinction is subtle, but it essentially involves the difference between declaring, "We give praise to God," versus declaring, "O God, you *are* my praise." This ascription of honorable status to God combined with the possessive marker ("*my* praise") highlights the relational connection between the two parties. Whereas the nations can be seen giving glory to God, only the covenant people can declare that YHWH *is* their glory, just as YHWH declares that Israel *is* his glory. Such usage of the noun תהלה as a title appears only eight times in the Hebrew Bible: four times in the honorific triad (Deut 26:19; Jer 13:11; Zeph 3:19, 20), twice in hymn-like passages as a title for God (Deut 10:21 and Jer 17:14), and twice as a title of a city (eschatologically of a restored Jerusalem in Isa 62:7 and ironically of a despoiled Babylon in Jer 51[28 LXX]:41).[59] The term שם is common, most often meaning simply "name," though it can also mean "reputation,"[60] while its use as an honorific title (to be instituted *as a name*) is far rarer.[61]

The third term in the triad, תפארת, has a range of meanings from "beauty" to "glory, splendor," and semantically is thus the most likely of the three terms to appear in contexts bearing an honorific sense. For instance, it is used in combination with the term כבוד to describe the official priestly garments assigned to Aaron by YHWH in Ex 28:2, 40.[62] It is also often used by Ezekiel to describe the beautiful jewelry and ornaments given

---

shall be *for me* (μοι) a special people (λαὸς περιούσιος)." This implies not just possession (i.e., "my") but possession *for the benefit* of the possessor, indicating "the person … interested in the verbal action" (Daniel B. Wallace, *Greek Grammar: Beyond the Basics* [Grand Rapids, MI: Zondervan, 1996], 142). Wallace's caution, 143, however, should be borne in mind, that "every pure dative use is a dative of interest in a general sense," and thus the category of *dativus commodi* should be reserved for times "when the idea of advantage … is prominent," of which prominence the "connotation of the verb used is frequently a major clue." Another, and perhaps more exegetically sound clue for deciphering between a dative of possession and that of interest is the overall context. As seen in the numerous texts in which God's relationship to Israel is indicated by means of the prefixed ל (in Hebrew) or the dative pronoun (in Greek), *for myself* (e.g., Ex 19:5–6; Deut 7:6; 14:2; 26:19; 28:9), it is the *covenantal* context that makes the mutuality of interest most prominent.

[58] Though, with תהלה used for praise to humans, see Ps 22(21 LXX):26 and 148:14.
[59] Thus, out of fifty-seven canonical occurrences, only eight times does תהלה indicate a title of honor (instituted *as a praise*).
[60] BDB, "שם," 1028 (#2b). Of humans generally: Gen 6:4; 11:4; 2 Sam 23:22; 2 Chron 26:15; of those whom God exalts: Gen 12:2; 2 Sam 7:9; 1 Chron 14:17; Ezek 16:14; 34:29; of God himself: 2 Sam 7:23, 26; 1 Chron 17:21, 24; Isa 60:9; 63:12, 14; Jer 32:20. See also Johannes Pedersen, *Israel: Its Life and Culture Volume I* (Atlanta, GA: Scholars Press, 1991), 249: "To have a name means the same as to have greatness. Israel received a name and greatness from his god (2 Sam 7:23)."
[61] Only in the deuteronomic triad and in Ezek 39:13.
[62] "You shall make holy garments for Aaron … for glory (לכבוד ‖ εἰς τιμήν) and for splendor (ולתפארת ‖ δόξαν)."

by God to Israel (Ezek 16:12, 17, 39; 23:26, 42). Significantly, the term appears often in the latter chapters of Isaiah to describe God's own glory (Isa 46:13; 63:14), which he then bestows on his people Israel (Isa 60:19; 62:3; of the garments of Israel: 52:1; of the Temple: 60:7; 63:15; 64:10). Like the other two terms in the triad, however, the term תפארת appears rarely as a title of honor (i.e., instituted into the position of *glory*). Apart from its occurrence in the deuteronomic triad (Deut 26:19; Jer 13:11; Zeph 3:19, 20), such usage appears in only two descriptions of priestly garb (Ex 28:2, 40), along with four occurrences in Isaiah (4:2[63]; 28:5[64]; 60:19[65]; 62:3[66]) and one in Ps 89:18.[67]

The honorific triad found in Deut 26:19 LXX is consequently no less conspicuous in its recurrence as a tripartite expression of God's blessing upon his faithful people. We noted previously the variation in using two adjectives (ὀνομαστός and δόξαστος) to flank one central substantive (καύχημα),[68] which thereby places the emphasis on καύχημα.[69] While the ordering somewhat varies, the same passages that took up the triad from Deuteronomy in the MT (with the exception of Jer 33[40]:9) also take up the triad in the LXX (ὄνομα term + καύχ- term + δόξα term). These LXX passages also manifest a similar usage, at least when one or more of the nouns are retained, of the type of institution that we saw in the MT. The Greek reproduces the Hebrew grammatical structure, though employing one of the verbs *to be/give/place*, combined with a "substitute for predicate nominative (εἰς + accusative)," as can be seen in the following table.[70]

When comparing the honorific terminology of the triad in these LXX passages, it is clear that numerous possibilities were available.[71] Thus, καύχημα stands apart in emphasis over against the other two Greek terms, since it alone consistently remains a substantive in the recurrences of the triad.

---

[63] Isa 4:2: The branch of YHWH will be (היה) "for beauty and for glory," and the fruit of the land will be "for pride and for *glory*" for the remnant of Israel.

[64] Isa 28:5: YHWH "will be *as* a crown of glory, and *as* a diadem of *beauty*" for the remnant of his people.

[65] Isa 60:19: "Your God will be *for your glory*."

[66] Isa 62:3 (in converse to Isa 28:5): "you shall be *as* a crown of *beauty* in the hand of the Lord."

[67] Ps 89:18: The Lord is "the *glory* of their strength." Additionally, Prov 17:6 could possibly be included in this list: "the *glory* of sons is their fathers."

[68] The LXX translators most often use καύχημα to render תהלה (7x), but it also renders תפארת (5x), גאוה (1x), חדוה (1x), and תוחלת (1x). Barton Alexander Dowdy, "The Meaning of Kauchasthai in the New Testament" (PhD diss., Vanderbilt University, 1955), 40, explains that these other uses of the honorific triad "retain the word order of the Hebrew" reflected in Deut 26:19, rather than the alternate ordering of Deut 26:19 LXX.

[69] Dogniez and Harl, *Le deutéronome*, 279.

[70] Wallace, *Grammar*, 47–8. Wallace argues that this phenomenon is "usually due to a Semitic influence (Hebrew *lamed*)." Cf. BDAG, 290, where εἰς is described as used "with the … end indicated *for*, *as*," and then lists its use with the verbs τίθημι and εἰμί meaning "to *serve as something*." This use is also noted under the entry on εἰμί, 285.

[71] Johannes Schneider, *Doxa: Eine bedeutungsgeschichtliche Studie*, BSGUF 3 (Gütersloh: C. Bertelsmann, 1932), 37–9, lists the numerous Greek terms that LXX translators used to render various Hebrew terms found within the honorific semantic field. Cf. Dowdy, "Kauchasthai," 33: "The Greek parallels to καυχᾶσθαι and its cognates form a circle of words that translate the same Hebrew words that καυχᾶσθαι translates." Again, when looking at 1 Chron 16:27, 35, Dowdy, 54, concludes: "honor [הוד], majesty [הדר], strength [עז, ἰσχύς], joy [הודיה], glory [δόξα], praise [ἔπαινος], and boasting [καύχημα] are all compatible ideas; meaning … that καύχημα is not out of place in the noblest of company."

Table 2 LXX Passages Reflecting the Honorific Triad from Deuteronomy 26:19

Passage	First Term	Second Term	Third Term	εἰς Marker for Accusative?	Preceding Verb	Joined with Dative of Advantage?
Deut 26:19	ὀνομαστόν	καύχημα	δόξαστον	No	ποιέω	No
Jer 13:11	ὀνομαστόν	εἰς καύχημα	εἰς δόξαν	Yes (with nouns)	γίνομαι	Yes (μοι)
Jer 33(40):9	εἰς εὐφροσύνην	εἰς αἴνεσιν	εἰς μεγαλειότητα[72]	Yes (with all three nouns)	εἰμί	No
Zeph 3:19	εἰς καύχημα	ὀνομαστούς	–	Yes (with noun)	τίθημι	No
Zeph 3:20	ὀνομαστούς	εἰς καύχημα	–	Yes (with noun)	δίδωμι	No
1 Chron 22:5	εἰς ὄνομα	–	εἰς δόξαν	Yes (with nouns)	Implied εἰμί	Yes (τῷ κυρίῳ)
Similar Passages						
Ex 28:27[73]	εἰς τιμήν	δόξαν	–	Yes (with 1 noun)	Implied εἰμί	Yes (τῷ ἀδελφῷ)
Ex 28:40	εἰς τιμήν	δόξαν	–	Yes (with 1 noun)	Implied εἰμί	Yes (αὐτοῖς)
Isa 4:2[74]	τοῦ ὑψῶσαι	δοξάσαι	–	(no nouns)	–	No
Isa 28:5	ὁ στέφανος τῆς ἐλπίδος	ὁ πλακεὶς τῆς δόξης	–	No	εἰμί	Yes (τῷ καταλειφθέντι μου λαῷ)
Isa 60:19	φῶς αἰώνιον	σου δόξα	–	No	εἰμί	Yes (σοι)

[72] Aquila reads ἔσται **μοι** εἰς **ὄνομα** εὐφροσύνης καὶ εἰς αἴνεσιν καὶ εἰς **καύχησιν**. Joseph Ziegler, *Jeremias*, Septuaginta 15 (Göttingen: Vandenhoeck & Ruprecht, 1957), 377–8, when discussing the switch in both α´ and σ´ from μεγαλειότητα to καύχησιν in v. 9, refers for comparison to Isa 63:14, in which the LXX translation, ποιῆσαι σεαυτῷ ὄνομα **δόξης**, of the Hebrew phrase, לעשות לך שם תפארת, is changed by Aquila into: ποιῆσαι σεαυτῷ ὄνομα **καυχήσεως**. Schreiner, "Sich-Rühmens," 540, points out the way in which Aquila's rendering conveys more clearly the emphasis that Israel will be the *ground upon which* YHWH will boast. Eric Fuchs, "Gloire de Dieu, Gloire de l'homme," *RTP* 27 (1977), 321–32, 326 n. 13, notes how Isaiah LXX conspicuously avoids the term καυχήμα.

[73] See Sir 45:7–8 for a similar collocation of three honorific terms (ארתו || δόξης; תפארת || καύχημα; עז || ἰσχύς) applied to priestly garments, in which the Hebrew term from Ex 28 (תפארת) reappears, though rendered by the Sirach LXX translator with καύχημα, as opposed to the δόξα of Exodus LXX. Cf. Sir 45:12, on which Dowdy, "Kauchasthai," 76, comments: "the glory, power, and beauty of the [high priestly] golden crown are all caught in the word καύχημα."

[74] On the LXX "deviation from [established] equivalences" in this verse, see Ronald L. Troxel, *LXX-Isaiah as Translation and Interpretation*, JSJSup 124 (Leiden: Brill, 2008), 106.

Thus, the language used to describe Israel's exaltation in Deut 26:19 is paradigmatic for depicting Israel's status as God's people. As Fuchs has argued, the triad, and the term καύχημα in particular, "marque l'appartenance du peuple à Dieu."[75] This status, however, is dependent upon Israel's obedience to God and would be forfeited in the case of disobedience. The triad is thus used by the prophets both to point back to Israel's failure to uphold the covenant (Jer 13:11) and to point forward, in the face of exilic disgrace, to a future, eschatological restoration, at which time the Lord would reestablish his repentant people into their promised position of glory (Jer 33[40 LXX]:9; Zeph 3:19–20).[76] This eschatological extension by the prophets of the covenant blessing of honor (καύχημα) for God's people is essential for understanding later Jewish hope, particularly that of the apostle Paul, whose vision of eschatological fulfillment undoubtedly included this notion of eschatological honor (καύχημα) for a new covenant people restored to obedience (Phil 1:26; 2:16, cf. 3:21), which honor would then redound to God himself (cf. Phil 1:11).

Furthermore, there pertains an intricate connection, reflected in Deut 26:17–19, between covenant obedience and the glory of God's people. The honorific terms תהלה, שם, and תפארת, especially when used in combination, are specifically linked with obedience to God; they are the reward that his people can both hope and expect to receive when acting faithfully. Conversely, disobedience is linked with the consequence of becoming "a *horror*, a *proverb*, and a *byword* among all the peoples" (Deut 28:37).[77] Just as the honorific triad is paradigmatic for obedient Israel's glorification, so is the dishonorific triad in Deut 28:37 paradigmatic for disobedient Israel's exilic degradation. The social realities of honor and shame are thereby subsumed under the ultimate category of covenant relationship: God exalts those loyal to a position of honor, and he demotes those disloyal to a position of shame.[78]

Mutual Honor between God and His People: Deuteronomy 26:19 and 10:21

The foregoing linguistic data demonstrate the relationship of mutuality between the glory of God and the glory of his people and its significance for Israel's identity and history. This can be seen even more clearly when comparing the covenant ceremony in Deut 26:18–19 with an earlier description of Israel's praise for their covenant

---

[75] Fuchs, "Gloire," 330.
[76] Note Norbert Mendecki's comment "Deuteronomistische Redaktion von Zef 3,18-20," *BN* 60 (1991), 27–32, 29: "Die Schande der Zerstreuung wird in לתהלה ולשם (Preis und Ruhm) verwandelt. Damit greift v. 19 mit dieser Formulierung auf die Vorstellung Israels zurück, nach der Israel (Dtn 26:19) לתהלה ולשם ולתפארת (Preis und Ruhm und Ehre) unter allen Völkern werden wird ... Das Buch Jeremia verwendet auch diese Formel (vgl. Jer 13:11; 33:9)."
[77] See 1 Kings 9:7 (=2 Chron 7:20); Jer 24:9; Lev 26:31–33; 2 Kgs 22:19; Jer 18:16; 25:9; 25(32):18; 42(49):18; Ezek 5:14-5; Mic 6:16; Zeph 2:15; 2 Chron 29:8; Joel 2:17; Isa 43:28. Cf. Blois, "Formulas."
[78] See Olyan, "Covenant Relations," 204: "There are several points of contact between the sphere of covenant relations in particular and the notions of honor and shame," since "Yhwh himself ... participates in reciprocal honor" (p. 205). He ultimately argues that "honor is ... tied to covenant loyalty" (p. 215).

God in Deut 10:21. As we have seen, in the covenant ceremony of 26:18–19 Israel is portrayed as representing *God's* καύχημα,[79] as is especially evident in the use of the datives in v. 18 (where Israel is chosen to be a people *for God* [αὐτῷ]) and again in v. 19 (where Israel is to be a holy people *for the Lord their God* [κυρίῳ τῷ θεῷ]), each of which flank the key description of Israel becoming a καύχημα.[80] This portrayal is matched by the earlier passage in Deut 10:21, where God is praised as being *Israel's* καύχημα.

Deuteronomy 10:12–22 succinctly summarizes the obedience to which Moses exhorts this new generation of Israelites on the plains of Moab. It is preceded by a retelling of the wilderness generation's previous failure (9:7–24)[81] and then Moses's own intercession on their behalf (9:25–29),[82] along with a description of the remaking of the stone tablets (10:1–11).[83] The passage is followed by God's promise of blessing for obedience and God's threat of cursing for disobedience (11:1–32), largely congruent with Deut 26:16–19.[84]

In Deut 10:12–22, Moses reminds the community that God chose Israel out of all the nations to be his own people (10:14–15). The corollary to such divine grace, Moses asserts, is for the people to "not harden (οὐ σκληρυνεῖτε) [their] neck any longer," like their fathers,[85] but rather to "fear the Lord your God, and him you shall serve (λατρεύσεις), to him you shall hold fast, and by his name you shall swear" (10:20; cf. 10:12). Moses closes this exhortation with a twofold hymnic statement (10:21a), before recalling once more God's gracious activity on their behalf (vv. 21b–22).[86] The use of the laudatory exclamation in 10:21, "He is your praise (οὗτος καύχημά σου); he is your God," follows naturally after the call to "swear" in God's name; most likely they are to swear that YHWH is their covenant God.[87] In any case, Moses overtly presents God as

---

[79] This does not, however, exclude Israel's participation as well in the honor conveyed by her status as God's καύχημα.
[80] Dowdy, "Kauchasthai," 40, finds Deut 26:19 depicting Israel "as [an occasion] of boasting ... *for God*" (emphasis added).
[81] Focusing on the golden-calf incident, Moses characterizes Israel as "stiff-necked" (9:13, 27) and describes their failure as disobedience and disbelief (9:23).
[82] In his intercession, Moses reminds God that Israel is God's own possession (נחלה ‖ μερίδα, κλῆρος) (9:26, 29).
[83] This passage is interrupted in vv. 6–9 by an aside describing Levi as having neither portion (חלק ‖ μερίς) nor inheritance (נחלה ‖ κλῆρος) because "God himself is his inheritance." This sense of God as the "inheritance" of Levi (cf. Deut 18:2), and by extension of Israel (see Jer 10:16; 51:19; Ezek 44:28), similarly reflects the mutuality between God and his people in light of the numerous descriptions in Deuteronomy of Israel as the "inheritance" of God (4:20; 9:26, 29; 32:9; cf. 1 Kgs 8:51, 53; Ps 33:12; 1 Sam 10:1; Isa 63:17; Joel 2:17).
[84] See the reference to blessings and curses on Mt. Gerizim and Mt. Ebal in both 11:29 and 27:12–13, as well as the parallel listing of material blessings for obedience (11:13–15, 23–25 as compared to 28:1–14) and, in converse, material curses for disobedience (11:16–17 as compared with 28:15–69). See Jeffrey H. Tigay, *Deuteronomy* (Philadelphia, PA: JPS, 2003), 247, who speaks of an outer frame (11:29 and 27:1–8, 11–26) encompassing an inner one (12:1 and 26:16–19).
[85] On Israel as stiff-necked, see Deut 9:13, 27; cf. Ex 32:9; 33:3, 5; 34:9.
[86] Sánchez Bosch, *Gloriarse*, 69, sees 10:17b (YHWH's glorious deeds on behalf of Israel) as providing the reason why Israel can refer to YHWH as their "boast" in 10:17a.
[87] Cf. the similar command to "swear" by YHWH followed by the content of the verbal oath/declaration in Isa 45:23–24, on which Paul explicitly draws in the conclusion to the Christ hymn, envisioning all people swearing allegiance to the exalted Christ (Phil 2:10). See Dowdy, "Kauchasthai," 51, commenting on Deut 10:21 LXX: "God as [καύχημα] conveys the same idea as the expression of swearing by God (v. 20)."

Israel's καύχημα[88] in a context describing the unique (covenantal) relationship between God and his people (cf. 10:15).

Placing Deut 10:21 in conjunction with 26:17–19, we see that both texts uniformly present YHWH as the covenant God of Israel (10:21: "he is your God"; 26:17: "You have chosen YHWH to be your God"). The two texts present a balanced alternation, however, between God as Israel's καύχημα (10:21) and Israel as YHWH's καύχημα (26:19). Josef Schreiner thus observes that the mutuality of boasting in Deut 10:21 and 26:19 "geschieht in zweifacher Hinsicht," since on the one hand "Israel soll für Jahwe zu Lob, Ruhm und Ehre ... werden" (26:19), and on the other hand "Jahwe [ist] Israels Ruhm" (10:21).[89] Thus, the covenant relationship that Israel enjoys with YHWH entails that both become the other's boast, just as the twofold covenant formula emphasizes that YHWH and Israel belong to one another as "Israel's God/Lord" and "God's people."[90] As Sánchez Bosch aptly describes in his major treatment of the term καύχημα in the Scriptural texts, "God and [Israel] appear in a perfect interchangeability with respect to the terminology of glory."[91] This is only true, however, when Israel remains loyal to the covenant.

Conclusion

Thus, to conclude this section on the promise of Israel becoming a καύχημα as a manifestation of divine blessing for covenant obedience, we note that such glorification is always to be considered in conjunction with the glorification of YHWH himself. Just as obedient Israel will be made into a praise and a glory for YHWH, so YHWH himself remains Israel's glory and praise due to his faithfulness to Israel. The covenant therefore establishes a relationship of mutual honor between YHWH and his people. Paul will later draw on this theme of mutual honor within the covenant when he writes to the Philippian Christ-community about the καύχημα that will result from faithful adherence to the gospel way of life. Much as the honor arising from Israel's obedience was reciprocal in that it both exalted God and also solicited divine exaltation for the community, so too will Paul present his converts' obedience as facilitating honor and praise for God (Phil 1:11) as well as honor for their own beleaguered community (Phil 1:26; 3:21).

---

[88] MT: תהלה (*praise*).
[89] Schreiner, "Sich-Rühmens," 537–8.
[90] Ceslas Spicq, "καυχάομαι," *TLNT* 2.297 n. 12, draws out the mutuality reflected in the various LXX uses of καύχημα: "The just put their pride in God (Sir 1:11; 9:16; Ps 89:18), the object of their praise (Jer 17:14; cf. 1 Chr 29:11). In return, God gives honor, renown, and glory to his people (Jer 13:11; Zeph 3:19–20; cf. Zech 12:7)."
[91] Sánchez Bosch, *Gloriarse*, 70: "'Dios' y 'el pueblo' se encuentran en una perfecta intercambiabilidad respecto del término 'gloria.'"

3

Mutual Glory in Isaiah

As we have noted, in Phil 2:15-16 Paul casts his discussion of the mutual honor that exists between himself, the Philippians, and God in Christ in the context of the mutual honor between God and his covenant people in Deuteronomy and Isaiah. It is striking that Paul's linking of these two Scriptural contexts reflects the commonality that exists between Deuteronomy and Isaiah themselves, namely, through the language and concepts of mutual honor.

In line with the depiction of shared family (dis)honor in the Song of Moses, the prophecies of Isaiah highlight the filial disloyalty of Israel to their "Father," YHWH (cf. Isa 1:2; 63:8).[1] Moreover, the language of honor ascribed to Israel in the honorific triad of Deut 26:19 (MT = תהלה, שם and תפארת; LXX = ὀνομαστός, καύχημα and δόξαστος)[2] also occurs repeatedly throughout Isa 40–66,[3] though not in the same triadic format. McConville comments on this connection as it appears in the latter portions of Isaiah,

> The lines from [Deut 26:19] to Is. 56–66 are most noticeable, because of the vocabulary chain "praise, name and glory," adopted there in a more scattered way ... Especially in Isaiah chs. 56–66, the triad of terms in [Deut 26:19] appears with some frequency, to denote both *the new glory Yahweh will bring to his people* when he redeems them after exile, and *the glory they will bring him* among the peoples of the earth.[4]

---

[1] R. Norman Whybray, *Isaiah 40–66* (Edinburgh: Oliphants, 1975), 257, comments on Isa 1:2 and 63:8 that "the rebellion of sons against their fathers was an unthinkable impiety, yet Israel was guilty of it."
[2] I refer to the Old Greek translation of Isaiah as the LXX, though I am aware that this term is only shorthand to refer to the various Greek textual traditions for each book (see footnote 3 in Chapter 2). Unless otherwise noted, I follow the textual decisions reflected in Joseph Ziegler, *Isaias*, Septuaginta 14 (Göttingen: Vandenhoeck & Ruprecht, 1983).
[3] Despite the modern tendency to divide canonical Isaiah into three independent productions, this study follows the practice of ancient readers, who engaged with the book as a unity (as would have the apostle Paul), even though we will focus primarily on the latter portion of the book due to the high concentration of glory language there.
[4] J. G. McConville, *Deuteronomy*, AOTCS 5 (Downers Grove, IL: InterVarsity Press, 2002), quoting from 383 and 385 (emphasis added). Cf. Josef Schreiner, "Jer. 9,22 als Hintergrund des paulinischen 'Sich-Rühmens,'" in *Exegetische Randbemerkungen*, ed. H. Merklein and J. Lange (Würzburg: Echter, 1974), 530–42, 537–8, who declares that, besides Deut 26:19, the other corpus where YHWH's boast plays "eine besondere Rolle" is "vor allem bei Deutero- und Tritojesaja."

Not only does McConville's observation underscore the connection between (trito-)Isaiah and the triad of Deut 26:19 in their deployment of honorific terminology, it also highlights the mutuality apparent in Isaiah's use of this terminology. The glory that YHWH brings to Israel finds its counterpart in the glory that Israel brings to YHWH.[5] This mutuality of honor will represent an important aspect of our analysis of texts from Isaiah in the treatment that follows, since it is primarily this aspect of reciprocal honor that the apostle Paul draws on for his exhortation to the Philippian community (cf. Phil 2:14–16). A second element from Isaiah that will be crucial for illuminating Paul's argument in Philippians is the mediatorial role of Isaiah's Servant figure. We will demonstrate how the Servant facilitates Israel's glorious restoration and thus propels Israel into an obedience that will garner glory both for YHWH and for the Servant himself. As we will see in Part 3 of our study, Paul casts himself into the role of the Isaianic Servant in Phil 2:16 and thereby allows for his participation in the mutual honor enjoyed by the Servant together with God and the people of Israel.

It must be noted at the outset, however, that while the linguistic linkage between the triad of Deut 26:19 and the glory language of Isa 40–66 holds true for the MT, this is not so for LXX-Isaiah. The LXX-Isaiah translator chose to avoid entirely the central term from the triad of Deut 26:19 LXX, καύχημα, while yet abundantly employing the word-groups from the other two terms in the triad, ὀνομαστός and δόξαστος. This choice by the LXX-Isaiah translator stands against the common rendering by other LXX translators of terms from the הלל root[6] and the פאר root[7] with terms from the καυχ- word-group.[8] As Fuchs has observed, "les traductuers d'Esaïe dans la LXX semblent systematiquement ignorer l'ensemble καυχ-."[9] The LXX-Isaiah translator thus evinces a noticeable aversion to this term,[10] one that is not shared

---

[5] Walter Brueggemann, *Isaiah 40–66* (Louisville, KY: Westminster John Knox Press, 1998), 206, points to (at least one side of) the mutuality of honor shared between YHWH and Israel: "The well-being and preeminence of Yahweh ... is intimately linked to the well-being and preeminence of the realm of Jerusalem."

[6] The καυχ- stem renders the substantive תהלה in Deut 10:21; Jer 13:11; 17:14; 51(28 LXX):41; Zeph 3:19–20 (*bis*). The καυχ- stem renders the verb הלל in 1 Kgs 21:11; Ps 49(48 LXX):7; 52(51 LXX):3 (= ἐγκαυχάομαι); 97(96 LXX):7 (= ἐγκαυχάομαι); Prov 25:14; 27:1; Jer 9:22 (*ter*), 23 (*bis*); 50(27 LXX):38 (= κατακαυχάομαι); Sir 11:4; 38:25.

[7] The καυχ- stem renders the substantive תפארת in 1 Chron 29:11, 13; Ps 89(88 LXX):18; Prov 16:31; 17:6; 19:11; Ezek 16:12, 17, 39; 23:26, 42; 24:25; Zech 12:7; Sir 9:16; 10:22; 31:10 (where the preferred reading of תפארה has multiple variants with either לתפארה, תפארת, or the infinitival verbal form להתפאר); 44:7; 50:11. The καυχ- stem renders the verb פאר in Judg 7:2; Sir 38:25; 48:4; 50:20.

[8] Cf. Barton Alexander Dowdy, "The Meaning of Kauchasthai in the New Testament" (PhD diss., Vanderbilt University, 1955), 34.

[9] Eric Fuchs, "Gloire de Dieu, Gloire de l'homme," *RTP* 27 (1977), 321–32, 326 n. 13, where he further notes that "ce qui n'est pas le cas pour Aquila (41,16: [הלל]; 60,19: [תפארת]; 63,14) Théodotion (41,16: [הלל]; 60,18; 62,7: [תהלה]), ou Symmaque (55:5; 60:7: [פאר])." Schreiner, "Sich-Rühmens," 539, points likewise to Theodotion's more generous use of the καυχ- word group in contrast to that by other LXX translators when rendering תהלה: "die LXX in der Annahme der Bedeutung 'Ruhm' zurückhaltender war. Theodotion scheint hier großzügiger zu sein."

[10] This is in keeping with LXX-Isaiah's idiosyncratic tendencies, as noted by Francis B. Watson, "Mistranslation and the Death of Christ," in *Translating the New Testament: Text, Translation, Theology*, ed. Stanley E. Porter and Mark J. Boda (Grand Rapids, MI: Eerdmans, 2009), 215–50, 231: "The translation technique [of LXX-Isaiah] is, to say the least, eccentric—and was perceived as such by later translators such as Symmachus, whose rendering is normally much closer to the plain sense of

by the various Hexaplaric translators, who use it on fifteen different occasions in Isaiah.[11]

One text can be adduced as a case in point. In Isa 63:14 the prophet looks back to YHWH's actions on behalf of Israel in the past, focusing especially on God's miraculous power displayed in the Exodus event. Isaiah asserts that God's saving activity on behalf of Israel was "to make for [himself] an everlasting name" (63:12) and "to make for [himself] a glorious name (שם תפארת)" (63:14). The phrase from v. 14 contains two of the honorific terms from Deuteronomy's triad: שם and תפארת (lacking only the תהלה term for "praise"), which the LXX renders into ὄνομα δόξης, thereby also retaining two of the three honorific terms from Deut 26:19 LXX. In the Hexaplaric versions, however, Aquila offers the rendering ὄνομα καυχήσεως, which still retains two of the three honorific terms from Deut 26:19 LXX, but follows the majority of other LXX translators in deploying the καυχ- stem to render תפארת, as opposed to the use of the δόξα word-group by LXX-Isaiah (a term that occurs regularly throughout LXX-Isaiah).[12]

We can thus see from this test-case in Isa 63:14 two things: (1) the honorific language from Deut 26:19 is indeed "scattered" throughout Isaiah in both the MT and the LXX, and (2) in every case where one of the triadic terms from the MT could have been rendered with the καυχ- stem (in keeping with the tradition of the LXX translation of the Pentateuch), LXX-Isaiah chose instead to use some other honorific term (most often δόξα, but others appear as well). Thus, the following study will necessarily proceed on the basis of conceptual connections between the mutual honor evinced in Deut 26:19 and in Isa 40–66, rather than relying primarily on the *Wortfeld* of καύχημα, which is rightfully situated within the *Bildfeld* of honor.[13]

---

the Hebrew." See also Ronald L. Troxel, *LXX-Isaiah as Translation and Interpretation: Strategies of the Translator of the Septuagint of Isaiah*, JSJSup 124 (Leiden: Brill, 2008), 106.

[11] The καυχ- word group appears in the Hexaplaric translations of Isaiah at 3:18 (α′, using the cognate αὔχημα); 10:12 (σ′, καύχημα); 13:19 (σ′, αὔχημα); 20:5 (<α′>, καύχημα); 41:16b–17a (α′ and θ′, καυχήσῃ); 52:1 (α′, αὐχήσεως); 60:7 (σ′, καύχημα), 18 (θ′, καύχημα), 19 (α′, καύχημα); 61:3 (θ′, καυχήματος); 62:3 (α′ and σ′, καυχήσεως), 7 (σ′ and θ′ [86], as well as θ′ [Q], καύχημα, which reading Frederick Field, *Origenis Hexaplorum* [Oxford: Clarendon Press, 1875], 2.556 n. 18, notes is also reflected in the "Curter. Syro-hex" manuscript); 63:14 (α′, καυχήσεως). On the validity of appealing to the Hexaplaric versions for interpreting Paul, who admittedly had no access to these later translations, Otto Michel, "Zur Exegese von Phil 2,5-11," in *Theologie als Glaubenswagnis*, eds. K. Elliger, A. Weiser, E. Würthwein, and O. Bauernfeind (Hamburg: Furche-Verlag, 1954), 79–95, 92, suggests, on the basis of the agreement between Phil 2:7 and Aquila's rendering of Isa 52:14 against the LXX, that both the hymn's author and Aquila "vielleicht weisen … auf ein ältere griechische Übersetzung von Jes 52,14 hin." Cf. Lucien Cerfaux, *Christ in the Theology of St. Paul*, trans. Geoffrey Webb and Adrian Walker (New York: Herder and Herder, 1959), 386: "this is not the only case where Paul's quotations agree with Aquila, suggesting the existence of an older Greek version."

[12] On the prominence of the δόξα word group in LXX-Isaiah, see A. Haire Forster, "Meaning of Δόξα in the Greek Bible," *ATR* 12 (1929), 311–16, 312–13; and L. H. Brockington, "The Greek Translator of Isaiah and His Interest in ΔΟΞΑ," *VT* 1 (1951), 23–32, 26, who concludes that "δόξα is [a] word which [the Isaianic translator] made very much his own, and which, contrary to the variety of synonym [sic] used for [תהלה], is the almost constant equivalent of [כבוד] and in addition is used to translate a number of other Hebrew words … The translator's individuality appears most strongly in his very frequent use of δόξα and of cognate words."

[13] For the distinction between *Wortfeld* and *Bildfeld*, see Lukas Bormann, "Das 'letzte Gericht' – ein abständiges Mythologumenon?" *ZNT* 9 (2002), 47–53, who describes how numerous terms within a semantic range (i.e., the *Wortfeld*) can be deployed to create a "frame," via metonymy or *pars pro toto*, setting up the *Sachzusammenhang* involved in the conceptual *Bildfeld*.

The Exclusive Glory of God in Isaiah

Within its emphasis on the mutual honor that exists between YHWH and his people, Isaiah consistently depicts YHWH as jealous, above all, for his own glory. In this regard we find in Isaiah, especially in chapters 40–46, numerous passages in which YHWH engages in polemics, denouncing idolatry and asserting his sole prerogative to receive worship from Israel as well as from the nations.[14] This polemical stance accounts for much of the language of exclusivity with regard to YHWH recurring in these chapters (e.g., 42:8; 43:10, 11, 13; 44:6, 8; 45:5, 6, 14, 18, 21, 22; 46:9).[15]

While Isaiah offers numerous reasons why YHWH alone should receive glory as the sole object of worship,[16] a key reason emphasized throughout is his redemptive work on behalf of his people. For instance, Isa 43 presents YHWH's words of comfort to Israel, narrating the many dangers from which he promises to protect them, during which YHWH twice points to his own glory as the driving motive for his gracious activity: 43:7: "[the people] whom I created *for my glory* (לכבודי || ἐν ... τῇ δόξῃ μου[17])"; and v. 21: "The people whom I formed *for myself* (לי),[18] so that they might declare my *praise* (תהלתי || τὰς ἀρετάς μου)." Similarly, in 60:21, amid an eschatological vision of Zion's glorious restoration, the prophet declares that YHWH's people "shall all be righteous," to which YHWH responds: "They are the shoot that I planted, the work of my hands, *so that I might be glorified*."[19] And finally, in chapter 48, amid an accusation against Israel for her obstinacy in dealing treacherously and rebelling (48:4, 8, cf. Deut 32:5, 20), YHWH nevertheless promises to relent regarding his judgment, making sure to clarify, though, that he does so "for the sake of my name and my praise (למען שמי ... ותהלתי || ἕνεκεν τοῦ ἐμοῦ ὀνόματος ... καὶ τὰ ἔνδοξά μου)" (48:9).[20]

Thus, we find in Isaiah a marked emphasis upon YHWH's exclusive right to glory. He maintains this right in the face of idols, demonstrating and revealing it through his saving work for Israel. In his unique relationship with Israel, he acquires glory through his creation of them as a people (Isa 43), through their renewed vocation and ministry (Isa 49), and through their eventual righteous character as a result of their redemptive restoration (Isa 60), despite their current unfaithfulness in service (Isa 48). What

---

[14] See Isa 41:21–24; 42:17; 44:9–20; 45:16, 20; 46:6–7.

[15] Notice the concentration in Isa 45 of the "exclusivity clause" (*there is no other*), where six out of its three uses occur. W. A. M. Beuken, "Confession of God's Exclusivity," *BijDragen* 35 (1974), 335–56, 337, points to the "statement of exclusivity" in 45:18 and concludes, "The divine self-praise in Is. 45.18-25 is not an accidental feature of style but a dominating trend" (p. 345).

[16] For example, for his incomparability (40:18, 25; 44:7; 46:5), his eternality (40:28; 41:4; 48:12), his role as Creator (40:28; 42:5; 45:7, 12, 18; 51:3), as Judge (41:1, 21; 43:9; 45:21), and as Provider (41:17, 20; 42:16).

[17] The LXX translator reads ἐν rather than the εἰς that one might expect as the equivalent to the MT's prefixed *lamed* preposition: "I prepared him *in* my glory" (LXX).

[18] The LXX offers instead λαόν μου, ὃν περιεποιησάμην ("my people, whom I prepared").

[19] The MT provides a bare להתפאר ("for glorification"), and the LXX gives a similarly ambiguous εἰς δόξαν ("for glory"). It is by means of context that most English versions fill out the phrase to include the first-person singular ("for *my* glory"). Context suggests that the glory is YHWH's (since the reference immediately prior is to the work of "[YHWH's] hands"); however, Israel too can participate in his glory (i.e., they will be glorified as YHWH's people who will possess the land forever).

[20] Notice that two of the three terms from the Deuteronomic triad are represented at Isa 48:9 in both the MT (שם and תהלה) and the LXX (ὀνόματος and ἔνδοξά).

remains to be addressed, however, is how Israel can be ushered within the gamut of a glory that belongs exclusively to God. Oswalt hints how the prophet carefully threads the needle between the exclusivity of YHWH's glory and Israel's participation therein:

> The wonder of [Isa 60] is that the glory of the Lord is to be reflected from Israel. … God promised that he would somehow share his glory with [Israel] (ch. 4). … He will not share his glory with an idol …, *but he does intend to share it with his people* (11:10; 35:2; 43:7), and that intention comes to its apex [in ch 60] and in ch. 66.[21]

Alongside YHWH's jealous safeguarding of his own glory one finds in Isaiah an equally adamant presentation of glory espoused for Israel, a reality that, far from detracting from YHWH's glory, rather enhances it. It is this Jewish prophetic understanding of reciprocal glory shared between God and his people that undergirds Paul's own presentation of the eschatological honor available to believers. As we will see in Phil 1:9–11, the glorious purity to which the Philippian saints will attain through Christ on the final day will ultimately redound to God's own praise.

The Divinely Bestowed Glory of Israel in Isaiah

In his seminal treatment of כבוד in Kittel's wordbook, von Rad aptly describes the link between God's exclusive claim to glory in Isaiah and the glory envisioned there for Israel.

> Yahweh Himself can sometimes say that He is not prepared to concede His כָּבוֹד to other gods (Is. 42:8; 48:11). To an extraordinary degree, however, the כָּבוֹד of God is also a theme of religious hope and an established part of eschatological expectation. … The saving act to which these eschatological statements [viz., Isa 40:5 and 66:18–19] refer is finally so embracing that *the colours merge into one another and it makes little difference whether it is said that Yahweh will become כָּבוֹד for Israel or that Israel is created for Yahweh's כָּבוֹד* (Zech. 2:9; Is. 43:7).[22]

Von Rad points here to a recurring aspect of Isaiah's prophecies in which glorification becomes a dominant theme toward the end of the book. Sometimes it is YHWH who receives the glory,[23] other times the glory is ascribed to Israel,[24] while elsewhere the glory lacks a specific recipient thus leaving room for both parties to participate

---

[21] John Oswalt, *Isaiah: Chapters 40–66* (Grand Rapids, MI: Zondervan, 1998), 537 (emphasis added). Michael P. Maier, *Völkerwallfahrt im Jesajabuch*, BZAW 474 (Berlin: de Gruyter, 2015), 488, describes a similar willingness on God's part to share his glory with Israel in Isa 60:2, where "[YHWHs] Glanz zu [Israels] Glanz geworden ist."

[22] Gerhard von Rad, "כָּבוֹד in the OT," excursus in Gerhard Kittel, "δόξα," *TDNT* 2, 238–42, here 241–2 (emphasis added). The German for the italicized section reads "und so nicht viel ausmacht, ob gesagt ist, Jahwe werde für Israel zum [כבוד] werden, oder Israel sei zu Jahwes [כבוד] geschaffen."

[23] See Isa 42:8, 12, 21; 43:7, 21; 44:23; 48:9, 11; 49:3; 55:13; 60:6, 21; 61:3; 63:7, 12, 14; (66:5, a taunt by Israel's enemies).

[24] See Isa 41:16; 45:25; 46:13 LXX; 49:5; 55:5; 56:5; 60:9, 18, 19; 62:2, 7.

therein.²⁵ But throughout them all there is a mutual sharing by both Israel and YHWH in the glorious effects of YHWH's redemptive work for his people.

Israel's Glorification in Isaiah 41:16 and 45:25

Two texts in which Israel's glory enters the purview are Isa 41:16 and 45:25. These verses both employ the verbal root הלל ("to exult"), upon which the substantive תהלה ("praise") from the Deuteronomic triad is based. In both cases Israel is the subject of the verb הלל, they perform the activity of exulting or glorying, and it will be shown that in doing so they participate in the glory of the very God in whom they boast.

The הלל root appears at Isa 41:16 in the context of YHWH's encouragement to Israel, whom YHWH exalts to a privileged status in light of their election (vv.8–9: בחר || ἐκλέγω) and his calling of them (v. 9: קרא || καλέω). Israel is exhorted not to fear (41:10 [*bis*], 14), since YHWH promises both to strengthen Israel (v. 10: אמץ || ἐνισχύω) and to help Israel (41:10, 14). Furthermore, YHWH promises to make of Israel a "threshing sledge" (v. 15) so that they might "winnow" the mountains, with the final result that "then you shall rejoice (תגיל) in YHWH; *in* (ב) the Holy One of Israel *you shall glory* (תתהלל)."²⁶ The *hitpael* of the verb הלל brings together both Israel and YHWH: Israel is the one performing the activity of exulting, while YHWH becomes the sphere *in which* Israel exults.²⁷ The exultation, or boasting, of Israel claims honor not only for the God in whom they boast but also for themselves, for as Goldingay and Payne observe about the *hitpael* verb in 41:16, it is "performed with regard to or for oneself, in one's own special interest."²⁸ Hence, the activity of *boasting in someone* entails a mutual claim to honor, with honor claimed both for the boaster and for the one in whom the boast occurs.²⁹

The *hitpael* of הלל appears again in Isa 45:25 in a context similar to that of 41:16, but now Israel's exaltation is more explicit. In this passage, the oath of universal homage to YHWH in 45:23–24a is flanked by references to Israel's exaltation over the nations. Isaiah 45:4 depicts the nations bowing down in homage *to Israel*, and vv. 16–17 contrast Israel's assured success with her enemies' certain demise (cf. v. 24b). Then, in v. 25, Israel's exaltation is explicitly described: "In YHWH all the offspring of

---

²⁵ See Isa 62:3.
²⁶ The LXX has significant variations: "σὺ δὲ εὐφρανθήσῃ ἐν τοῖς ἁγίοις Ισραηλ. καὶ ἀγαλλιάσονται." While still in contrast to the enemies' receiving shame, the addressees are promised they will "rejoice," though not in YHWH but rather "in the *holy ones* of Israel." The final exulting verb is rendered with the following sentence; hence it is the "poor and needy" from 41:17, rather than a restored Israel (as in the MT), who exult (ἀγαλλιάσονται).
²⁷ J. Sánchez Bosch, *"Gloriarse" segun san Pablo: Sentido y teología de καυχάομαι*, AnBib 40 (Rome: Biblical Institute Press, 1970), 77, notes that the middle voice of the *hitpael* in both Isa 41:16 and 45:25 makes possible the notion that Israel, along with glorifying God, is able at the same time *to glorify themselves*.
²⁸ John Goldingay and David Payne, *Isaiah 40–55* (London: T&T Clark International, 2006), 1.176, citing GKC §54.
²⁹ This grammatical formulation reappears in Phil 1:26, where the Philippians possess a *boast* that "abounds *in Christ Jesus in Paul*," which similarly entails mutual honor from which all three parties benefit.

Israel *shall triumph/be justified* (יִצְדְּקוּ ‖ δικαιωθήσονται) and glory/be glorified (יִתְהַלְלוּ ‖ ἐνδοξασθήσονται)." Olley writes on the Septuagintal variation in this verse: "Instead of MT בַּיהוָה followed by two verbs referring to Israel, LXX has one group who '*from* the Lord δικαιωθήσονται,' and 'the seed of Israel' who 'will be glorified *in* God,' i.e., probably, 'share in God's glory' or 'be glorified because of their relationship with God.' "[30] The parallel verb in 45:25, צדק ("to vindicate, triumph"), elucidates the *hitpael* of הלל as Israel's act of "exulting" in some kind of victory or triumph, either in a military[31] or judicial sense.[32] Thus, the occurrence of this honorific verb in 45:25 with Israel as its interested subject (MT: reflexive as middle, "exulting") or object (LXX: passive, "being glorified") conveys the notion that Israel participates in the honor conveyed by the activity of exultation.[33] That is to say, alongside YHWH's receiving glory from his people's exultation, Israel too participates in that same glory.[34] The LXX rendering of יתהללו ... ביהוה with ἐν τῷ θεῷ ἐνδοξασθήσονται ("they shall be glorified by means of God") makes explicit Israel's participation in the glory (as passive object of divine agency) envisioned resulting from Israel's restoration by God.[35]

The connection between Isa 41:11–16 and 45:18–25 is evident not only through their similar usage of the הלל root to envisage Israel's participation in glorification but also in the terminology used to describe Israel's enemies. The phrase in 41:11 describing Israel's enemies as "all those who are incensed against/oppose you [viz., YHWH] (כל הנחרים בך ‖ οἱ ἀντικείμενοί σοι)" recurs in Isa 45.[36] The LXX phrase οἱ

---

[30] John W. Olley, *"Righteousness" in the Septuagint of Isaiah*, SCS 8 (Atlanta, GA: Scholars Press, 1979), 57, citing for reference LXX Isa 60:19 and 62:2ff.

[31] C. R. North, *The Second Isaiah* (Oxford: Clarendon Press, 1964), 162, notes that " 'paeans of victory' might serve" as an interpretative rendering.

[32] Olley, *Righteousness*, 55: "The disputation setting, together with the opponents' being ashamed (v. 24b; בוש often appears in forensic settings with the connotation of 'be shown to be in the wrong'), suggests that linked with 'find salvation' is the forensic idea, 'be vindicated,' 'be shown to have been in the right (to have trusted in Yahweh).' "

[33] North, *Second Isaiah*, 100: "The suggestion of arrogance, though usual, does not necessarily attach to [הלל] in the *hitpael*], especially when the glorying is 'in Yahweh'; cf. Ps. 34:2(3); Jer. 4:2." Maier's discussion, *Völkerwallfahrt*, 279, is helpful here: "Wie die reflexive Form des Verbs [הלל] ausdrückt, besteht dieser Jubel nicht in einer sachlich-objektiven Feststellung, sondern in einem Lobpreis, *der das Subjekt miteinbezieht*. Ob er zum Selbstlob, zur arroganten Überheblichkeit wird, hängt an dem durch ב bezeichneten Grund. Die falschen Gründe werden in *Jer 9,22* angeführt. ... Hier aber ist wie schon in *Jes 41,16* ... Gott selbst der Grund des Rühmens (ביהוה)" (emphasis added).

[34] It should be noted that whenever the phrase הלל ביהוה (exult in YHWH/God) appears in the various LXX books, this positive activity is *never* rendered with the verb καυχάομαι (e.g., Ps 34[33LXX]:3, where ביהוה תתהלל is rendered ἐν τῷ κυρίῳ ἐπαινεσθήσεται, see also Ps 44[43LXX]:9; 56[55LXX]:5; 63[62LXX]:12; 105[104LXX]:3; alternately, see Jer 4:2, where a similar phrase, בו יתהללו, is rendered ἐν τῷ αὐτῷ αἰνέσουσιν. Rather, the verb καυχάομαι, when rendering הלל, appears explicitly linked in the LXX to the *negative* activity of arrogant boasting; see 1 Kgs 20:11; Jer 9:22, 23; Ps 49:7; 52:3; 97:7 [ἐγκαυχώμενοι ἐν]; Prov 25:14; 27:1. The verb καυχάομαι can, however, depict the positive activity of praise for YHWH when rendering other Hebrew roots (e.g., 1 Chron 16:35; Ps 5:11[12]; 32[31LXX]:11; 149:5). See Schreiner, "Sich-Rühmens," 538: "Für die Wiedergabe des unsachgemäßen sich Rühmens, des Prahlens bot sich das griechische Wort καυχάομαι an, das meist im abwertenden Sinn gebraucht wurde." Thus, Paul's allusion to Isa 45:24 in Phil 2:10–11 opens up the context of Israel's "boasting" via the הלל root in Isa 45:25, which context Paul likely takes up in his use of καύχημα later in 2:16 (cf. also Phil 1:26, where Paul envisions the Philippians' καύχημα abounding *in Christ Jesus*).

[35] The LXX, along with employing a verb with a prefixed preposition (ἐνδοξασθήσονται), adds ἐν τῷ θεῷ to reiterate that it is *in God* that the seed of Israel is (*en*)glorified.

[36] See Olley, *Righteousness*, 56.

ἀντικείμενοι [αὐτῷ] recurs at 45:16, where the enemies "will be put to shame." The MT phrase כל הנחרים בו ("all those incensed against him") recurs at 45:24, where they again shall be put to shame. The collocation of these three texts, all of which speak of Israel's enemies being put to shame, presents the other side of the coin from YHWH's act of vindication on behalf of Israel: for Israel, God's salvation means that they can "glory"; for Israel's enemies, conversely, God's salvation of Israel means that the enemies will be put to shame.[37]

Eschatological Glory for Israel in Isaiah 60–62

Isaiah's prophecies crescendo into a climax of glory for Israel in Isa 60–62, depicting their restoration by YHWH that burgeons with honorific terminology. One key honorific term in this section is the פאר root, which appears four times in verbal form. Westermann comments on the centrality of this term for these chapters:

> Das Verb "verherrlichen" (*qal* und *hitpaēl*) ist für Tritojesaja besonders charakteristisch[38] ... Um das Sich-Verherrlichen Gottes *in der und durch die Verherrlichung des Zion geht es* in seiner ganzen Heilsverkündigung.[39]

Not only is פאר characteristic for this portion of Isaiah, it also applies especially to the glorification *of Israel*. Stromberg describes this distinct usage of the root in Isa 60: "Everywhere else in [Isa] 40–55 [פאר] occurs in the Hithpael to describe the Lord's self-glorification through the restoration of Zion (44,23; 49,3). However, ... [Isa 60:7, 9, 13] all speak of ... the glorification *of Zion* which was to result from the influx of the nations with their wealth."[40] In this sense, God glorifies Israel via the nations, even as the nations were earlier called upon to glorify YHWH.

---

[37] This Isaianic idea resonates with Paul's assurances to the Philippians that their enemies (ἀντικείμενοί; rare in the NT [eight total; cf. Lk 13:17, where Jesus shames his "opponents"]) will be shamed and face destruction (Phil 1:28; 3:19).

[38] Claus Westermann, *Das Buch Jesaja 3*, ATD 19 (Göttingen: Vandenhoeck & Ruprecht, 1986), 286, points to the uses of the verb פאר in 60:7 (δοξασθήσεται), 9 (ἔνδοξον), 13 (δοξάσαι, for אכבד), 21 (εἰς δόξαν); 61:3 (εἰς δόξαν); of the noun פאר in 61:3 (δόξαν), 10 (μίτραν); and of תפארת in 60:7, 19 (δόξα); 62:3 (κάλλους); 63:12 (δόξης), 14 (δόξης), 15 (δόξης); 64:10. As is evident by the preceding Greek renderings, the פאר root is often translated by LXX-Isaiah with the favored term δόξα.

[39] Westermann, *Jesaja 3*, 286 (emphasis added). Thomas Wagner, *Gottes Herrlichkeit: Bedeutung und Verwendung des Begriffs kābôd im Alten Testament*, VTSup 151 (Leiden: Brill, 2012), 127, similarly points to the central importance of glory for these latter chapters of Isaiah, though arriving at this conclusion via the Hebrew term for glory, כבוד: "[in Isa 60–62] kommt dem Begriff [כבוד] ebenfalls eine zentrale Stellung zu," noting especially 60:1–3 and 62:1–3.

[40] Jacob Stromberg, "The Second Temple and the Isaianic Afterlife of the הסדי דוד (Isa 55:3–5)," *ZAW* 121 (2009), 242–55, 246 (emphasis added). James P. Ware, *Paul and the Mission of the Church: Philippians in Ancient Jewish Context* (Grand Rapids, MI: Baker, 2011), treats extensively the importance of the prophetic theme of the pilgrimage of the nations for understanding Paul's eschatological hope as it appears in Philippians.

Mutual Glory between YHWH and Israel in Isaiah 60:19 and 62:3

The mutuality of honor shared between YHWH and Israel can be demonstrated when two texts from these climactic chapters (Isa 60:19 and 62:3) are compared with two earlier texts (Isa 28:5 and 46:13). These four passages alternate descriptions of either God as Israel's glory or Israel as God's glory, thereby forming a reciprocal connection much like that adduced above between Deut 26:19 and Deut 10:21. In Isa 28:5, after denouncing the arrogant boasting of Ephraim, the prophet speaks of a coming day when "YHWH of hosts will be a crown of glory and a *diadem of beauty* (תפארת || πλεκεὶς τῆς δόξης) to the remnant of his people." Here the idea is that the glory of the remnant, as opposed to the fading glory of others (cf. vv. 1–4), will be lasting because the Lord himself constitutes their glory.[41] In Isa 60:19, God similarly comprises glory for Israel: "the Lord will be to you an everlasting light, and *God will be your glory* (ὁ θεὸς δόξα σου, 60:19 LXX)." Aquila offers a more literal rendering of this final phrase from 60:19 (MT: לתפארתך), declaring that "God will be your *boast* (καύχημα)."[42] The eschatological exaltation of God's people entails God as representing in himself their glory and their boast.[43]

A corollary to this idea can be found in Isa 62:3,[44] where the vindication and restoration of Zion are described in similar terms, only this time the roles are reversed; it is now Israel who is the glorious ornament while God is the one adorned: "You [viz., restored Zion] shall be a *crown of beauty* (תפארת || στέφανος κάλλους) in the hand of the Lord, and a *royal diadem* in the hand of your God."[45] This verse clearly portrays Israel in a state of honor, in which she gloriously adorns God himself.[46] It is noteworthy that both Symmachus and Aquila uphold the more common rendering of תפארת with the καυχ- word group so that Zion becomes a "στέφανος καυχήσεως in the hand of the Lord,"[47] which harmonizes with the idea in Deut 26:19 LXX that Israel becomes a

---

[41] The beneficiary of the honorable regalia is marked in the MT with the prefixed *lamed* (לִשְׁאָר) and in the LXX by the dative (of advantage) (τῷ καταλειφθέντι).

[42] See Field, *Hexaplorum*, 2.553; Joseph Reider and Nigel Turner, *Index to Aquila*, VTSup 12 (Leiden: Brill, 1966), 133; Ziegler, *Isaias*, 347; Fuchs, "Gloire," 326 n. 13.

[43] James A. Motyer, *The Prophecy of Isaiah* (Grand Rapids, MI: InterVarsity Press, 1993), 499, renders v. 19b, "for the display of my splendour," interpreting this as "the Lord 'embodied' and displayed in his people [which] has ever been the divine intention (44:23) and hitherto realized only in the Servant (49:3)." Motyer, in p. 499 n. 1, notes that Isaiah alone among the prophets employs the פאר root (as in 10:15; 44:23; 49:3; 55:5; 60:7, 9, 13, 21; 61:3).

[44] E. J. Young, *The Book of Isaiah* (Grand Rapids, MI: Eerdmans, 1965), 1.174–175, sees a connection in Isa 28:5 both forward to Isa 60 and back to Isa 4:2 ("on that day the branch of YHWH shall be for a beauty and for a glory [לכבוד || μετὰ δόξης], and the fruit of the land shall be for pride and for glory [לתפארת || δοξάσαι] for the survivors of Israel"). Young, *Book of Isaiah*, 1.176 n. 45, posits a connection between the honorific term in Isa 4:2, תפארת (found also in Isa 28:5 and 60:3), and the honorific triad of Deut 26:19.

[45] Whybray, *Isaiah 40–66*, 247, finds in Isa 62:3 the "strange" promise that "Zion is not to *receive*, but to *be* a crown," indicating that "the city is to be regarded as a crown worn by Yahweh, its city walls having the appearance of a tiara."

[46] Oswalt, *Isaiah 40–66*, 580, "The people of God ... are [in God's hand] as a priceless possession, a thing of delight, honor, and beauty."

[47] See Reider and Turner, *Index to Aquila*, 133; Ziegler, *Isaias*, 351.

καύχημα on behalf of YHWH.[48] Another text that could possibly corroborate Israel's position as entailing YHWH's glory is Isa 46:13, where the MT reads: "I will give in Zion salvation, for Israel *my glory* (תפארתי)."[49] The Hebrew grammar is truncated here and therefore ambiguous, but could very well indicate via apposition that Israel constitutes YHWH's תפארת, rather than merely that YHWH will give *to Israel* his own תפארת.[50] Both verses, Isa 62:3 and 46:13, show Israel as constitutive of YHWH's glory, thereby highlighting the relationship of mutual honor enjoyed between them. As Westermann rightly asserts, the promise in Isa 62:3

> describes the very close relationship in which the glorified Jerusalem stands to Yahweh, how precious she is to him ... Jerusalem is described as a magnificent ornament in which God takes pleasure, indeed *which serves to adorn him*. (emphasis added)[51]

Therefore, when collocating these four texts we find Isaiah depicting a mutuality of honor between God and his people. At times YHWH is the one who constitutes glory for Israel, while at other times they are the ones who comprise glory for YHWH, throughout all of which the honorific terms laid out in Deuteronomy's triad abound.

Alongside these texts that move in alternating directions, with YHWH as Israel's glory and vice versa, are texts that speak of shared glory in a more opaque way. Isaiah 55:5 depicts the nations as flocking to God's restored people "because [God] has glorified you" (כי פארך ‖ ὅτι ἐδόξασέ σε). In both the MT and the LXX, the idea is clear: God enhances Israel's honor,[52] where yet again another Hexaplaric variant adopts the καυχ- word group, following the general pattern reflected in the rest of the LXX of using καυχ- to translate the פאר word group. Hence, in Symmachus, the nations come to Israel "because [God] made you a *boast* (καύχημα)."[53] This rendering is striking in that

---

[48] P.-E. Bonnard, *Le Second Isaïe: Son Disciple et Leurs Éditeurs, Isaïe 40–66*, EB (Paris: J. Gabalda, 1972), 427 n. 6, describes this Hebrew phrase (*crown of beauty*) as "une expression classique," citing as evidence Prov 4:9 and 16:31; Jer 13:18; Ezek 16:12; 23:42, in three of which passages (Prov 16:31 and the Ezekiel texts) this "classic expression" is rendered by LXX translators using the καυχ- word group. This traditional expression presumably stands behind Paul's deployment of the καυχ- word group in 1 Thess 2:19 and may also contribute toward his description of the Philippians as his "crown" in Phil 4:1.

[49] LXX drops the MT's first-person possessive pronoun modifying the noun: "I have provided salvation in Zion to Israel *for glorying* (εἰς δόξασμα)." Symmachus is closer to the MT, but still lacks the first-person pronoun: "I will give salvation in Zion and *glory* (δόξαν) to Israel." Olley, *Righteousness*, 82, notes that the phrase εἰς δόξα in Isa 61:3 LXX is "ambiguous as to whose 'glory' is meant."

[50] In support of the appositional interpretation, see H.-J. Hermisson, *Deuterojesaja*, BKAT XI.8 (Neukirchen-Vluyn: Neukirchener Verlag, 2007), 138.

[51] Claus Westermann, *Isaiah 40–66*, trans. David Stalker (London: SCM Press, 1969), 375.

[52] On the application of the פאר root toward *Israel's* glorification in 55:5, see Peter Höffken, "Eine Bemerkung zu Jes 55,1-5," *ZAW* 118.2 (2006), 239–49, 241, who notes "dass die Rede davon, dass Jahwe Zion verherrliche (Piel פאר) in [Jes] 40–66 nur hier in 55,5 und dreimal in Jes 60 vorkommt. An anderen Stellen ist davon die Rede, dass Jahwe sich durch Zions/Israels Restitution selber verherrliche (Hitpael): 44,23; 49,3; 60,21; 61,3." Thus, for Höffken the *Stichwort* פאר creates a "sprachliche Verbindung" between Isa 60 and 55:5b.

[53] See Ziegler, *Isaias*, 328; Field, *Hexaplorum*, V. 2, 538; Fuchs, "Gloire," 326 n. 13. Similar is Symmacus's rendering of 60:7, in which YHWH "glorifies his glorious house" by *making [it] a boast* (καύχημα ποιήσω); see Ziegler, *Isaias*, 345; Field, *Hexaplorum*, V. 2, 551–2.

by using the substantive καύχημα it ambiguates *who* receives the honor from the boast, thereby allowing for the honor to be mutually experienced, just as it is in Deut 26:19 LXX. A similar ambiguity arises in a later Hexaplaric deployment of the καυχ- stem at Isa 62:7, where the prophet exhorts his audience never to cease praying until YHWH "sets Jerusalem as a *praise* (תהלה || LXX: ἀγαυρίαμα) in the earth." Both Symmachus and Theodotion bring in the καυχ- stem here so that Jerusalem is envisioned as becoming "a *boast* (καύχημα) upon the earth."[54] Once again, the beneficiary of Israel's institution into this exalted role of becoming a καύχημα upon the earth remains unstated, leaving room for honor to accrue both to God and to his glorious people in this act of public restoration. Pauritsch thus aptly notes that Zion's glorification in the latter chapters of Isaiah ultimately serves God's own glorification: "Das Ziel [of the glorification of Zion] ist die Verherrlichung, der Ruhm Jahwes."[55]

Such a mutuality of glory is understandable within the framework of Isaiah, since, as we have seen, it is clear throughout that any glory acquired by Israel redounds back to the glory of YHWH and vice versa. YHWH's glory reflects upon Israel, since YHWH is Israel's God.[56] We must not, however, overlook the emphasis throughout Isaiah placed upon YHWH's exaltation of Israel, along with the honorific effects of such exaltation. For instance, one finds in Isa 43 a strong emphasis upon the glory that accrues to YHWH by means of his work on Israel's behalf (*for myself/for my glory* in 43:7, 21). However, amid this emphasis stands a poignant affirmation of glory *for Israel*: "You are precious (יקרת || ἔντιμος) in my sight, and honored (נכבדת || ἐδοξάσθης)" (43:4). Sarah Dille picks up on the mutuality of honor reflected in this passage, arguing that 43:7 highlights "that YHWH's honor is tied to Israel—they are his offspring and their honor or lack of honor reflects on the father."[57]

Similarly, Saul Olyan points to this same verse to demonstrate his proposal that "covenant honor, like covenantal love, is reciprocal," that is, "it applies to partners in parity treaties and to those in covenants of unequals."[58] Hence, the relationship between God and Israel, though they remain unequal, allows for a reciprocity of honor, in which each party promotes the glory of the other. This mutuality of glory between YHWH and Israel is apparent throughout Isaiah. As Westermann summarizes about God's glorious restoration of Zion in Isa 60,

> In one and the same event glory accrues both to God and his people. *Each is involved in the other.*[59]

---

[54] Following σ' and θ' [86] as well as θ' [Q].
[55] Karl Pauritsch, *Die neue Gemeinde: Gott sammelt Ausgestossene und Arme (Jesaia 55–66)*, AnBib 47 (Rome: Biblical Institute Press, 1971), 123.
[56] Cf. Brueggemann's apt statement, *Isaiah 40–66*, 212: "There is no doubt that the promised future will be an enhancement of Zion [noting 60:7, 9, 13, 15] ... All of that, however, in the end is penultimate. In the end, it is all 'so that I may be glorified' (v. 21). *Zion is able, at its best, to refer all of its enhancement beyond itself to the ultimate enhancement of Yahweh*" (emphasis added).
[57] Sarah J. Dille, "Honor Restored: Honor, Shame and God as Redeeming Kinsman in Second Isaiah," in *Relating to the Text: Interdisciplinary and Form-Critical Insights on the Bible*, ed. Timothy J. Sandoval and Carleen Mandolfo, LOTS 384 (London: T&T Clark International, 2003), 232–50, 241.
[58] Saul Olyan, "Honor, Shame and Covenant Relations," *JBL* 115 (1996), 201–18, 205.
[59] Westermann, *Isaiah 40–66*, 359 (emphasis added), where he also provides the following linguistic data: "The whole thing thus serves the renown ([שם], 'name' in the sense of God's praise or honour is

The Servant's Glory and the Glory of Israel

The mutuality of honor between God and Israel presented above carries on the mutuality of covenant honor in Deuteronomy that we adduced in our previous chapter. A new element, however, emerges in Isaiah in the form of a mediator within the exchange of honor between YHWH and Israel. This mediator appears as the enigmatic Servant figure. While the Servant's identity remains elusive, his mission is clear: to assist in YHWH's work of restoring his sinful people (49:5: "to gather Jacob to [YHWH]"). We have already seen how such restoration envisioned glory accruing to Israel, but what remains to be observed is how the Servant becomes a third entity participating in the honor accruing from YHWH's redemptive work on Israel's behalf.

The Servant's Reward in Isaiah 49:4

Honor for the Servant stands out prominently in the second Servant song (Isa 49:1–6), where multiple honorific terms refer both to God's glory and to that of the Servant. The wider context will be helpful in determining the mutuality of glory represented in this verse.

> ¹ YHWH called me from the womb … he called my name …³ and he said to me, 'You are my servant,⁶⁰ Israel, *in whom I will be glorified* (אשר־בך אתפאר || ἐν σοὶ δοξασθήσομαι).' ⁴ But I said, 'I have labored (יגעתי || ἐκοπίασα) in vain (לריק || κενῶς), I have spent my strength *for nothing and vanity* (לתהו והבל || εἰς μάταιον καὶ εἰς οὐδέν); yet surely my recompense is with YHWH, and my reward with my God. ⁵ And now YHWH says, who formed me in the womb to be his servant, to bring Jacob back to him … for *I am honored* (אכבד || δοξασθήσομαι) in the sight of YHWH, and my God has become my strength. (Isa 49:1–5)

In v. 3 YHWH is the one who will "be glorified" (אתפאר || δοξασθήσομαι), and his glorification will occur *by means of* (ב || ἐν) the Servant,⁶¹ thereby demonstrating

---

also found in Trito-Isaiah in 56:6; 59:19; 60:9, but it never occurs in Deutero-Isaiah) or the glorifying of God. The verb 'to glorify' … is particularly characteristic of Trito-Isaiah … God's glorifying of himself in and through the glorification of Zion is a topic which runs through [Trito-Isaiah's] entire proclamation of salvation."

⁶⁰ Notice that LXX-Isaiah fluctuates (even in the space of two sequential verses, see 49:5–6) between using the term δοῦλος and the similar term παῖς to render עבד (servant). Παῖς appears in 41:8, 9; 42:1; 43:10; 44:1, 2, 21 (*bis*), 26; 45:4; 49:6; 50:10; 52:13. Δοῦλος appears in 42:19 (plural); 48:20; 49:3, 5; 53:11 (if one takes δουλεύοντα as rendering MT's עבד). After Isa 53 there is greater fluidity in LXX-Isaiah, and "servant" often appears in the plural: in 54:17, the MT "servants of YHWH" is rendered with the participial plural form of θεραπεύω; in 56:6, the MT plural "servants" becomes δούλους καὶ δούλας; in 63:17, "servants" is rendered δούλους; in the string of five occurrences of עבד in Isa 65, in v. 8 "for my servants" is rendered with the participial τοῦ δουλεύοντός μοι; in v. 9, "my servants" is rendered οἱ δοῦλοί μου; and in vv. 13, 14, and 15, the participial form of δουλεύω is used; and finally, 66:14 renders "with his servants" as τοῖς σεβομένοις αὐτόν ("with those who *fear* him"). Thus, Paul's preference for using the term δοῦλος in describing himself (e.g., Phil 1:1; Rom 1:1; Gal 1:10) and believers as the servant(s) of God (2 Cor 4:5; cf. Phil 2:22) should not exclude the possibility of his alluding to various Isaianic Servant texts that instead are translated with παῖς (or other variations) in the Old Greek versions.

⁶¹ It is unclear whether this is to be understood instrumentally, i.e., occurring *through* his ministry, or merely in a locative sense: "in the physical person of" the Servant. Francis Landy, "Construction

the idea that what happens to the Servant reflects back upon YHWH. Beyond this, however, the Servant's glory enters the purview as well. In v. 1 the prophet declares that YHWH "mentioned my name," which, although primarily signifying a vocational call, yet introduces the Servant's privileged status before God (cf. 43:1; 45:4).[62] Of greater significance is the reference to the Servant's "reward" in v. 4 and to his being "glorified" in v. 5. Verse 5 restates the Servant's vocation (he is to "bring Jacob back to [YHWH]") with the result that the Servant "will be honored" (אכבד ‖ δοξασθήσομαι[63]) and will experience divine enablement (עז ‖ ἰσχύς) for his task.[64] Whereas the Hebrew terms used to describe YHWH's glorification (פאר in v. 3) and the Servant's glorification (כבד in v. 5) are conceptually parallel in the MT, the LXX makes this correlation even clearer, rendering both terms with δοξασθήσομαι. Thus, while YHWH is glorified through the Servant, so the Servant too is glorified through YHWH.

The Servant's lament in Isa 49:4a that he has "labored in vain" stands apart from the surrounding context in the song. The two references to the exaltation of the Servant in v. 3 and v. 5 in the future form an *inclusio* around the Servant's declaration in v. 4, which presents a far more pessimistic outlook regarding his ministry in the present.[65] Moreover, the transition from God's speech in v. 3 to that of the Servant in v. 4 is emphasized by the inclusion of the first-person pronoun, setting up a clear contrast between the glorious outcome envisioned *by God* and the shameful result lamented *by the Servant*: "*but as for me, I* said, 'I have labored vainly; for futility and for nothing I have given my strength'" (v. 4a LXX).[66]

The metaphor of laboring describes the activity undertaken by YHWH's Servant, both by means of the verb "to labor" (יגע ‖ κοπιάω)[67] and the noun that it parallels: "strength"

---

of the Subject and the Symbolic Order," in *Among the Prophets*, ed. P. R. Davies and David G. A. Clines (Sheffield: JSOT Press, 1993), 60–71, 64, presents the intriguing notion that here the Servant "becomes the container of God" such that God "enters the prophet and radiates from him."

[62] See Dille, "Honor Restored," 240: "Having a 'good name' means having honor." Sarah J. Dille, *Mixing Metaphors*, LOTS 398 (London: T&T Clark International, 2004), 86, "'to call PN [viz., personal name] by his name' ... indicates familiarity (and recognition). ... It is also connected to YHWH's status as creator."

[63] Although there is ambiguity in the MT whether the first verb represents past or future activity (there is a textual variant for אכבד, but היה is clearly past tense), the LXX has explicitly placed both verbs in the future tense.

[64] An important link can be drawn here between the divine enablement experienced by the Servant in Isa 49:5 (cf. 41:10; 42:6) and the divine enablement similarly experienced by Paul in Phil 4:13, where the apostle employs the same ἰσχύς word group in verbal form (ἰσχύω).

[65] H.-J. Hermisson, "Israel und der Gottesknecht bei Deuterojesaja," in *Studien zu Prophetie und Weisheit*, ed. Jörg Barthel, Hannelore Jauss, and Klaus Koenen, FAT 23 (Tübingen: Mohr Siebeck, 1998), 197–219, 215, describes v. 4a as presenting not a temporal advance upon vv. 1–3 but rather "ein sachlicher Rückschritt: als die (subjektive) Lagebeurteilung des Propheten," which only the new word from YHWH in vv. 5–6 (cf. vv. 1–3) is able to overturn.

[66] Joachim Begrich, *Studien zu Deuterojesaja* (Munich: Chr. Kaiser Verlag, 1969), 55, points to the common element of *Klageliedes* within songs of thanksgiving, which is how he classifies Isa 49:1–6 (cf. Ps 31:23; 66:18). Hermisson, "Der Lohn des Knechts," in *Studien zu Prophetie*, 177–96, 180, describes how the contrast between failure and success is emphasized by the *Subjektswechsel* between YHWH and the "I" of the Servant.

[67] Hauck, "κόπος," *TDNT* 3.828: "In the LXX κοπιᾶν is used ... in the sense of 'exertion' (יגע), e.g., in connection with work on the land." Adolf von Harnack, "Κόπος im frühchristlichen Sprachgebrauch," *ZNW* 27 (1928), 1–10, 1, notes that "das tragische εἰκῆ, εἰς κενὸν bzw. μάτην κοπιᾶν des Paulus

(כח ‖ ἰσχύς).⁶⁸ The Servant appears to have undertaken his commission with the expectation that his work would receive a divine "reward" (פעלה).⁶⁹ This expectation appears to the Servant to have been thwarted.⁷⁰ We see this existential moment of crisis⁷¹ bubble up for a moment in v. 4a, but then quickly pass. For, almost in the same breath, at v. 4b, the Servant reaffirms his trust that God will not fail to reward him for his labor even though it remains ineffective in the present: "yet (אכן ‖ διὰ τοῦτο) my judgment (משפט ‖ κρίσις) is with the Lord, and my recompense/labor (פעלה ‖ πόνος) is before my God" (v. 4b).⁷² In his study of the congruence between the four Servant songs in view of this motif of assured success expressed in the Servant's משפט at 49:4b, Hermisson finds "die Gewißheit des Erfolgs, des Lohns, der Rechtfertigung des Knechts" to be the "Schlüssel" for unlocking the "innere Zusammenhang" of the four Servant songs.⁷³ Hermisson argues that the two contrasting portrayals in v. 4a and v. 4b must be interpreted in light of each other such that the "recompense" of v. 4b corresponds with and counteracts the "in vain" labor of v. 4a.⁷⁴ And so despite his current experience of rejection and the hardening of the people, the Servant is able to profess faith in YHWH, his commissioner, in v. 5. In doing so he recalls the purpose for which YHWH set him apart from birth, namely, to be the divine instrument for restoring the nation (49:5a), grounded on the dual reality that he is "honored in the

---

findet sich auch schon öfters bei den LXX," listing Job 2:9; 20:18; 39:16; Ps 127:1; Isa 30:5; 49:4; 65:23; Jer 28:58.

⁶⁸ Rosario P. Merendino, "Jes 49,1-6: ein Gottesknechtslied?" ZAW 92 (1980), 236–48, 241, points to the importance of the term כה for Deutero-Isaiah, citing Isa 40:26, 29, 31; 41:1. The linguistic link thus created between Isa 49:4a and 40:26-31 is important in that it depicts the Servant struggling under the same burden as Israel, which will make their differing responses all the more striking (compare 49:4b with 40:27).

⁶⁹ LXX-Isaiah here uses the noun πόνος, presumably in light of the earlier terms from the labor word-field. See the similar expectation of reward by the righteous in Isa 40:10/62:11; 61:8; cf. Ps 58:13; Prov 10:16; Jer 31:16. It is the wicked, alternatively, who are given to expect a failed reward: Isa 65:7; Ps 109:20; Prov 11:18 (פעלת־שקר).

⁷⁰ In the broader context of Isaiah, it is no surprise that the Servant's ministry should appear at times to be ineffective since stubborn Israel consistently rejects God's ministers ("I know that you are obstinate, and your neck is an iron sinew and your forehead brass" [Isa 48:4]; cf. Isa 6:9-10; 29:10; 30:9-11 ["for they are a rebellious people, faithless children"]; 43:22-24; 46:12; 48:1, 8, 18; 56:10-12; 57:4 ["children of transgression, offspring of deceit"], 17; 58:2; 59:3-8; 63:10, 17; 64:5-7; 65:2 ["a rebellious people"], 3, 11). Thus, the ups and downs of the Servant's career (downs in 42:3-4; 49:4; 50:6; 52:14-15; 53:3, 7; ups in 42:6; 49:6-12; 50:7; 52:13; 53:10-12) match the ups and downs of YHWH's own ministry to his unfaithful people, to which they are sometimes receptive and other times not. Note the observation by Lionel J. Windsor, *Paul and the Vocation of Israel: How Paul's Jewish Identity Informs His Apostolic Ministry, with Special Reference to Romans*, BZNW 205 (Berlin: de Gruyter, 2014), 107: "the Servant's authority is affirmed *in the midst of* humility, astonishing rejection and suffering (Isa 49:4, 7; 52:14; 53:1-4, 7-9)."

⁷¹ Westermann, *Isaiah 40–66*, 210, describes this as "the lament of a mediator," comparing the Servant's frustrated ministry with that of Moses, Elijah, and Jeremiah.

⁷² Hermisson, "Lohn," 182, posits that משפט has a common meaning through Deutero-Isaiah with roots in Israel's hymns of lament and trust, in which the "right" of the supplicant is upheld by YHWH against enemies.

⁷³ Hermisson, "Lohn," 178.

⁷⁴ Hermisson, "Lohn," 183. Similarly, Merendino, "Jes 49,1-6," 239, notes that v. 4b signifies "daß die Erfolglosigkeit also keine Ablehnung von seiten Jahwes bedeutet," and that the second half of v. 4 represents the turning point that introduces the second movement in the song. Hence, v. 4b "spricht für seine Bedeutung innerhalb des Ganzen" (p. 241).

sight of the Lord" and that "my God has become my strength" (49:5b).[75] This positive perspective is confirmed by YHWH's subsequent response to the Servant's outburst in which he affirms the Servant's purpose and role "as a light to the nations" (49:6),[76] and promises him help "on a day of salvation" (49:8).[77]

Ekblad's analysis of Isa 49:4 LXX, following Grelot, is that the change from "nevertheless (אכן)" to "consequently (διὰ τοῦτο)" is therefore theologically motivated.[78] As explained by Grelot, the "right" (משׁפט) that the Servant affirms as upheld by God includes the idea that the Servant "deserves" something in return for his "pains" (πόνος) taken on God's behalf, and that it is this right (*le droit*) that he is sure that God will maintain.[79] Two other times in Isaiah (40:10 and 62:11) פעלה appears with שׂכר (reward). In fact, these two verses present the same phrase verbatim: "Behold, his [viz., YHWH's] *reward* (שׂכר) is with him, and his *recompense* (פעלה) before him." This informs our understanding of the word משׁפט (*right*) that 49:4 pairs with פעלה, in that the Servant hopes for YHWH to *judge* him for his faithful service and thereby grant to him the *reward* that is *his rightful due*.[80]

The significance of the term פעלה in 49:4b is evident in light of its sparse representation in the Hebrew Bible,[81] which is reflected in the LXX, where the translator has idiosyncratically chosen to translate פעלה with πόνος (reflected nowhere else in the LXX).[82] Ekblad again sees in the LXX rendering of פעלה with πόνος an intentional move by the translator, connecting the Servant's labor here in the second song with the Servant's ministry later in the fourth song, at 53:4 and 53:11, where again the Servant's ministry involves "pain" (πόνος).[83] Significant for our present study is the tantalizing

---

[75] Merendino, "Jes 49,1-6," 241, paraphrases the vocational aspect of the Servant's משׁפט in v. 4b as follows: "Die göttliche Bestimmung, die mich zum Knecht gemacht hat, beliebt bei Jahwe bestehen."
[76] Note the use of the grammatical pattern of honorific installation (verb of installation [נתן || τίθημι] followed by direct object and honorific role [לאור || εἰς φῶς]) and the LXX's addition of the idea of the Servant being installed not just into the role of "light" but also into that of a "covenant to nations" (εἰς διαθήκην γένους, a description which does not occur in the MT until v. 8).
[77] Landy, "Construction of the Subject," 65, describes how vv. 4b-6 represent God's response to the Servant's lament in 4a: "In some strange way it does seem to be a response—not only suggesting the absolute value YHWH places on the prophet, but some connection between success and failure, some sense that the prophet's exhaustion and despair are necessary for the further mission." Mark Gignilliat, *Paul and Isaiah's Servants: Paul's Theological Reading of Isaiah 40–66 in 2 Corinthians 5.14–6.10*, LNTS 330 (London: T&T Clark, 2007), 60, views Isa 49:8 as looking ahead to "the climax of God's salvific eschatological work," a time that remains in the future for the Servant but for Paul is in the present.
[78] Eugene R. Ekblad, Jr., *Isaiah's Servant Poems According to the Septuagint: An Exegetical and Theological Study*, BET 23 (Leuven: Peeters, 1999), 101–2.
[79] Pierre Grelot, *Les poèmes du serviteur*, LD 103 (Paris: Cerf, 1981), 91.
[80] Hermisson, "Lohn," 183, defines משׁפט in 49:4b as the Servant's "Recht auf Lohn."
[81] The Hebrew term פעלה (recompense) is rare (only fourteen times in the Hebrew Bible) and occurs four other times in Isaiah (40:10; 49:4; 61:8; 62:11; 65:7). Twice the term is used in the context of divine (eschatological?) recompense (in Isa 61:8 it is used for positive recompense [reward]; in 65:7 for negative recompense [punishment]).
[82] The term πόνος matches the earlier terms from the labor word-field. Evangelia Dafni, "Die sogenannten 'Ebed-Jahwe-Leider in der Septuaginta," in *XII Congress of the International Organization for SCS*, ed. Peters, SCS 54 (Leiden: Brill, 2006), 187–200, 197, describes the connotation of πόνος here as "'Schmerz' bzw. 'Leiden.'"
[83] Ekblad, *Servant Poems*, 103. Arie Van der Kooij, "'The Servant of the Lord': A Particular Group of Jews in Egypt According to the Old Greek of Isaiah, Some Comments on LXX Isa 49,1-6 and Related Passages," in *Studies in the Book of Isaiah*, ed. Jacques van Ruiten and Marc Vervenne, BETL 132

but brief connection that Ekblad makes between the πόνος of the Servant in 49:4 and the "works of their labors" (τὰ ἔργα τῶν πόνων αὐτῶν) enjoyed eschatologically by God's servants in Isa 65:22, to whom it is promised, in contrast to the Servant, that "they shall *not* labor in vain" in the time of their restoration (65:23).

This affirmation by the Servant that his reward is assured is representative of his uniqueness within the context of Isa 40–66, since his trusting faithfulness in the present, despite Israel's rejection of his ministry, sets him apart from a nontrusting Israel. This contrast is evident when comparing Isa 49:4b with Isa 40:27, where Israel is called to account for its faithless declaration that, "My way is hidden from YHWH, and *my right* (משפט || κρίσις) is *disregarded* by my God."[84] The Servant, on the other hand, rather than accusing YHWH of disregarding his משפט, trusts that YHWH will uphold it.[85] The result from this faithfulness on the part of the Servant is that he is taken up into a relationship of reciprocal honor with YHWH. Raurell, commenting on the glory language associated with the Servant in Isa 49:3 and 5, consequently describes this mutuality of honor between the Servant and YHWH in this way: "The 'glorification' of God becomes the 'glorification' of the Servant, and vice versa."[86]

Futility Overturned in Isaiah 65:23

In describing the eschatological community, Isa 65:23 mirrors the Servant's confidence from 49:4b, though drawing its language from 49:4a, when it declares that they will *not* "labor in vain." To this is added the parallel in 65:23: "or bear children *for calamity*," where the MT employs the rare term בהלה that occurs only three other times in the MT, one of which is in Lev 26:16 in the context of the covenant curses. The allusion to the covenantal context of Lev 26 through the use of בהלה ("calamity") in Isa 65:23 imparts confidence to the beleaguered community that they will no longer suffer from the negative repercussions of covenant disobedience. Instead, they are promised the covenant blessings,[87] represented for the Servant in Isa 49:4 as פעלה in the sense of reward. Isaiah, thus, clearly designates a "reward" or positive evaluation and recompense from YHWH for both the Servant and for restored Israel.

This association between Isa 49:4 and Isa 65:23 is part of a recognizable trajectory running through Isa 40–66 involving the sure reward from God that can be expected by

---

(Leuven: University Press, 1997), 383–96, 387, similarly points to the connection between πόνος in Isa 49:4 and in 53:4, 11.

[84] Hermisson, "Lohn," 182: "dem Klagesatz Israels [in Isa 40:27] ... hier das Bekenntnis gewissen Vertrauens entspricht ...: der Knecht lebt im Vertrauen, Israel nicht." This contrast between the faithful Servant and faithless Israel is also apparent in Isa 49:14, where Zion complains, "The Lord has forsaken me."

[85] Peter Wilcox and David Paton-Williams, "The Servant Songs in Deutero-Isaiah," *JSOT* 42 (1988), 79–102, 92, point out that the Servant's faithfulness where Israel was unfaithful entails that he "has become [the true] Israel."

[86] Frederic Raurell, *'Doxa' en la teologia I: Antropologia dels LXX*, CSP 59 (Barcelona: Editorial Herder, 1996), 386 (my translation). Similarly, Rainer Schwind, *Gesichte der Herrlichkeit: Eine exegetisch-traditionsgeschichtliche Studie zur paulinischen und johanneischen Christologie*, HBS 50 (Freiburg: Herder, 2007), 77, writes, "Die Doxa Gottes und seines Knechtes sind eins."

[87] Cf. Isa 65:23b, which speaks of the "blessings of YHWH."

his servants as a result of their faithful labors, which is exemplified most prominently by the Servant himself. In 40:10, the Lord is depicted as a victorious conqueror, coming to his people with strength and bearing the spoils of victory: "his reward (שׂכר || μισθός) is with him, and his recompense/work (פעלה || ἔργον) before him." Although in 40:10 the "reward" could either be the *people* that God has won for himself,[88] or the *spoils* that he bestows on his people,[89] 61:8 clarifies that God's servants are the ones receiving the reward.[90] In the final Servant song, the LXX translator presents the Servant's κρίσις (*right*) as being initially "taken away" (53:8), but then later, when he is released from the "labor" (τοῦ πόνου) of his soul (53:11), the Servant is promised the "spoils with the great" (53:12). Then in 61:8, once again in reference to the eschatologically redeemed servants, the Lord guarantees that he will give to the "just" their "reward/labors" (פעלה || μόχθος), which will be a sign to the nations of God's eschatological, restorative work.

The climax of this trajectory of divinely given eschatological reward for restored Israel's faithful labors is found in Isa 62. We discussed above God's eschatological promise given in 62:7 to make Jerusalem "the praise (תהלה || γαυρίαμα) of the whole earth," which Theodotion and Symachus both render with καύχημα, thereby providing a clear linguistic link back to Israel's covenant promise of exaltation in Deut 26:19 LXX. What might it mean, however, for restored Israel to be a καύχημα in the earth? When viewed from one angle, it means, according to 62:8, that others will no longer reap the produce over which Israel has "labored" (יגע || μοχθέω).[91] In contrast, and repeating verbatim what was said in 40:10, Israel's Savior will come to them, "having his reward (שׂכר || μισθός) with him, and his recompense/work (פעלה || ἔργον) before him" (62:11). Indeed, as chapter 65 reveals, an eschatologically restored Israel will finally be able to enjoy their own "fruit" (65:21),[92] to enjoy fully "the work of their labors" (65:22), thereby experiencing the eschatological blessing of not laboring "in vain" (65:23).

Trifold Mutuality of Glory in Isaiah

Isaiah has thus added to the picture of mutual honor that we developed from our discussion of Deuteronomy. There, we saw YHWH drawing Israel into a relationship

---

[88] Martin Brändl, *Der Agon bei Paulus: Herkunft und Profil paulinischer Agonmetaphorik*, WUNT 222 (Tübingen: Mohr Siebeck, 2006), 256, opts for the former, positing that, in appropriating this for himself, Paul sees his converts themselves as the reward given to him by God. Cf. Motyer, *Isaiah*, 508, on Isa 62:11: "[YHWH's] saved people are both what he has earned and what he has accomplished."
[89] Hermisson, "Israel," 218, argues from Isa 53:12 that the "spoils" given to the Servant are first YHWH's spoils, which he then distributes to his Servant. Hermisson, "Israel," 219: "Der Lohn des Knechts ist also, daß er mit Israel Anteil bekommt an der 'Beute Gottes': der Heilswende für die Welt, und auf diese Weise zuletzt doch Erfolg hat."
[90] W. A. M. Beuken, "Servant and Herald of Good Tidings," in *The Book of Isaiah*, ed. Jacques Vermeylen, BETL 81 (Leuven: University Press, 1989), 411–42, 431: "As the 'justice/recompense' of the Servant were safe with YHWH [49:4], so he ... will grant to the afflicted and to those who mourn 'their recompense' [61:8]."
[91] Beuken, "Herald," 431, unpacks another way in which Israel's glorious restoration can be understood: Israel's eschatological fame entails "that the nations recognize God's work in favour of Israel," which in turn Beuken argues represents a "broader scheme" within Isa 40–66.
[92] Although the language is different, conceptually Paul too envisions fruitfulness as the experience of himself and the Philippians (cf. Phil 1:22; 4:17).

of mutual honor with himself through their acceptance of the covenant agreement. As long as they maintain covenant faithfulness and obedience, YHWH promises to bestow honor upon them (in Deut 26:19 LXX this is described as being made into a καύχημα), an honor that would apply to both Israel and YHWH himself. But, whereas previously it was only YHWH and Israel who enjoyed this reciprocal honor, Isaiah incorporates a third mediating party, with the result that the reciprocation of honor flows now in three ways. YHWH both honors Israel *as well as* the Servant; the Servant honors YHWH and facilitates the honor of Israel; and Israel honors YHWH and enhances the Servant's honor in their faithful reception of his ministry. The following diagram depicts this three-way flow of honor:

Trifold Mutuality of Glory in Isaiah

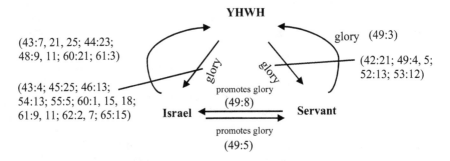

Conclusion

In this chapter, we have demonstrated that Isaiah presents in a new and expanded way the notion we saw in Deuteronomy of mutual honor shared between YHWH and Israel resulting from their covenantal relationship. Despite the present experience of exilic shame, Isaiah promises to Israel the hope of future glorification, when YHWH will empower them through his Spirit to walk in obedience and will then restore them to their place of honor in the world, which the later Greek versions of the Scriptures, like Deut 26:19 LXX, render as Israel's καύχημα. A key means through which YHWH will accomplish this glorious restoration for Israel is through the ministry of the Servant. The Servant is tasked with "gathering" Israel so as to facilitate their glorious restoration and thereby glorify YHWH as well. At the same time, the Servant himself is promised a share in the glory arising from YHWH's exaltation of Israel. The ensuing threefold flow of honor between the Servant, Israel, and YHWH serves as an important backdrop to our development of the similar idea of a three-way flow of honor recognizable in Paul's letter to the Philippians.

Part 2

Mutual Honor in Roman Antiquity

Farewell, then, my joy, my refuge, happiness, glory.
Farewell, and love me, I beseech you,
every way in jest as in earnest.

Fronto, *Ad M. Caes.* 1.8.7[1]

Gird up your loins then!
Do your best to make us
universally both lauded and loved.

Cicero, *Att.* 1.15.2

In the ancient Roman world, honor was the stuff of dreams.[2] It ran cities,[3] ruined fortunes,[4] and instigated wars.[5] It was the common currency in which the culture traded,[6] from the heights of the Roman emperor to the depths of the household

---

[1] All references to classical texts and their English translations are from the LCL unless otherwise noted.
[2] Cf. Cicero, *Tusc.* 2.24.58: "Nature has made us ... enthusiastic seekers after honour, and once we have caught, as it were, some glimpse of its radiance, there is nothing we are not prepared to bear and go through in order to secure it."
[3] On the use of honor as a means to control government and cities, see J. E. Lendon, *Empire of Honour: The Art of Government in the Roman World* (Oxford: Oxford University Press, 1997). Cf. Horst Hutter, *Politics as Friendship* (Waterloo: Wilfrid Laurier University Press, 1978), 138–9, "Roman politics was in the main a system of competition for public office between members of noble families. ... This competition, which was at once fierce and extensive, was fueled by the fires of a peculiarly Roman ambition, that is, the ambition to perform great deeds on behalf of the state in order to win glory for oneself and for one's descendants."
[4] Elite individuals in Roman society were obligated to provide banquets and games out of their own financial resources for the common people. See Paul Veyne, *Bread and Circuses*, trans. Brian Pearce (London: Penguin Press, 1990). Cf. Lendon, *Empire*, 86: "It was in honour terms that the rich man's motivation, involving so much trouble and expense, was understood."
[5] Cicero claimed (*Fam.* 12.23.2) that Julius Caesar started the civil war due to an affront to his *dignitas*. Cf. the comment by P. A. Brunt, "*Amicitia*," in *The Fall of the Roman Republic and Related Essays* (Oxford: Clarendon Press, 1988 [reprint 2004]), 351–81, 380: "At worst it might be said of them [Caesar's assassins] that, like Caesar himself, they set their own *dignitas*, which [Caesar's] 'tyranny' subverted, above the public good." J. P. V. D. Balsdon, "*Auctoritas, Dignitas, Otium*," *CQ* 10 (1960), 43–50, 45, writes that "[Caesar's] *dignitas* ... was something on which he would stake his life," citing *Bell. civ.* 1.9.2.
[6] Note Sallust's comment, *Bell. Jug.* 85.40, "All virtuous men ought to have more fame than riches (*plus gloriae quam divitiarum*)." See Onno van Nijf, "Civic Mirrors: Honorific Inscriptions and the Politics of Prestige," in *Social Status and Prestige in the Graeco-Roman World*, ed. Annika B.

slave.⁷ Honor was the primary matrix for social interaction, governing rules for all types of relations. In the words of John Lendon, "Honour was a filter through which the whole world was viewed, a deep structure of the Graeco-Roman mind, perhaps the ruling metaphor of ancient society."⁸ It is no surprise, then, to find written records of social interaction from the period, whether letters between friends, civic speeches, missives from rulers, and so on, soaked in the language of honor.⁹

Within this larger Greco-Roman cultural phenomenon, this section will investigate how mutual honor could be used for persuasion in the first century. Our goal will be to demonstrate that communicators could and did use the emotional connection of mutual honor with their audiences to persuade them to follow a particular course of action. Before turning to examples of this tactic in Chapter 5, however, Chapter 4 will elucidate two important issues involving honor in the ancient world: first, how honor was used as a form of influence in ancient society, and second, how honor could be shared among individuals in that society. Against this backdrop, the examples of mutual honor used to influence behavior adduced in Chapter 5 will demonstrate the plausibility that Paul presupposed, and in this sense relied upon the mutual honor motif when writing to his thoroughly Romanized converts in Philippi to persuade them to pursue a life worthy of the gospel.

A brief note on the kinds of sources used in the following section is necessary at this point. Although Paul was writing to converts living in a Macedonian city, with deep roots in the Hellenistic culture, the Roman ties of the colony have been well-documented by numerous scholars.¹⁰ Thus, when we turn in Chapter 5 to certain

---

Kuhn (Stuttgart: Franz Steiner Verlag, 2015), 233–45, 235, who describes Roman and Hellenistic epigraphic culture as a way in which these "honorific communities … used the language of honour to control and frame power from below."

[7] Val. Max. 8.14.5: "There is no rank too humble to be affected by the sweetness of glory." Similarly, Horace, *Sat.* 1.6.23-24, "Glory drags along the obscure no less than the nobly-born bound to her shining chariot." Both cited from Joseph H. Hellerman, *Reconstructing Honor in Roman Philippi: Carmen Christi as Cursus Pudorum*, SNTSMS 132 (Cambridge: Cambridge University Press, 2005), 60 and 44.

[8] Lendon, *Empire*, 73. Similarly, Hans Drexler, "*Dignitas*," in *Das Staatsdenken der Römer*, ed. Richard Klein, WF 46 (Darmstadt: Wiss. Buchges., 1966), 231–54, 232, "*Dignitas* ist einer der zentralen, ja vielleicht der zentralste Begriff der politischen und sozialen Sphäre in Rom."

[9] As with New Testament sources, Roman and Hellenistic texts deploy an array of terms to convey the semantic range of honor. Common Latin terms for honor include, e.g., *gloria, dignitas, laus, fama, honos, auctoritas*; Greek terms include, e.g., τιμή, δόξα, ἀξίωμα, σεμνός, κλέος. Again, in the present study I am not seeking to press the differences between each of these distinct terms, but rather to capitalize on their commonality in similarly referring to value and worth recognized by others. For a similar listing of honor terminology, see Lendon, *Honour*, 272–9. Cf. also Joseph Hellegouarc'h, *Le Vocabulaire latin des relations et des partis politiques sous la République*, FLSHUL 11 (Paris: Les Belles Lettres, 1963), 364–414; and A. D. Leeman, *Gloria: Cicero's waardering van de roem en haar achtergrond in de Hellenistische Wijsbegeerte en de Romeinse samenleving* (Rotterdam: N. V. Drukkerij M. Wyt & Zonen, 1949), 186, who discusses this in an appended English summary (177–90). The comments by Annika B. Kuhn, "The Dynamics of Social Status and Prestige in Pliny, Juvevnal and Martial," in Kuhn, *Status and Prestige*, 9–28, 9, are helpful: "Among the expressions that circumscribe the semantic field of prestige—such as *dignitas, honor, fama, auctoritas, maiestas, gloria, existimatio*—the first two terms, *dignitas* and *honor*, reflect particularly well this close link between status, prestige, rank and office."

[10] Cédric Brélaz, "Entre Philippe II, Auguste et Paul: la commémoration des origines dans la colonie romaine de Philippes," in *Une mémoire en acts: Espaces, figures et discours dans le monde romain*,

Roman authors to illumine how mutual honor was employed rhetorically to motivate appropriate responses, the influence of such writers on Philippian culture is warranted, especially on the elite within Philippian society who were attempting to mimic social trends in Rome. The lower classes in Philippi, therefore, who would most likely have made up the majority of Paul's auditors in the letter,[11] were also known to mimic the upper classes of society,[12] thereby allowing for the recognition of such a rhetorical technique taking place in the elite writers in Rome by the lower classes in the Philippian colony.

---

ed. Stéphane Benoist, Anne Daguet-Gagey, and Christine Hoët-van Cauwenberghe (Lille: Presses Universitaires du Septentrion, 2016), 119–38, discusses first Antony's transformation of the Philippian city, which was previously founded in the fourth century BCE by the Hellenistic Alexander the Great, into a Roman colony in 42 BCE, and then Augustus's subsequent strategy to "refound" the colony after his military victory over that rival to imperial ascendancy, thereby reestablishing yet again Philippi's *Romanitas* in a recognizably imperial sense.

[11] Richard S. Ascough, *Paul's Macedonian Associations: The Social Context of Philippians and 1 Thessalonians*, WUNT 2.161 (Tübingen: Mohr Siebeck, 2003), 122–9, points to prosopological evidence from the letter showing that Paul's auditors were not high-status members of the *polis*.

[12] See Hellerman, *Reconstructing Honor*, 100: "Throughout the empire, non-elite voluntary associations and cult groups tended to replicate in their own social contexts the verticality of elite society."

4

The Influence and Mutuality of Honor in the Hellenistic and Roman World

Because honor was so valued in the Hellenistic and Roman world, it was commonly held forth as a reward for proper conduct.[1] Most honor in this world consisted of inherited honor, based solely on birth (or, by extension, adoption).[2] Still, for those lacking such a glorious ancestry (indeed, for the noble-born as well) there remained the prospect of acquired honor, which often was considered even more important,[3] and it was the universal desire for this type of honor that society relied on to motivate virtuous behavior among its citizens.[4]

Honor as Influence in the Hellenistic and Roman World

This strategy to use honor as motivation was common in civic discourse, both in Roman provinces and in the outlying districts. For instance, one city in the Greek East publicly advertised such an offer of honor in an inscription from 71 BCE honoring two Roman benefactors.

> Since Numerius and Marcus Cloatius ..., *proxenoi* and benefactors of our city, from the very beginning have continued to act justly both toward our city ..., omitting nothing of zeal and ardor, because of which at appropriate times the city

---

[1] Eleanor Leach, "*An gravius aliquid scribam*: Roman *seniores* write to *iuvenes*," TAPA 136 (2006), 247–67, 261, speaks of *gloria* as the "carrot of compliance."
[2] Peter Anderson, "'Fame is the Spur': *Memoria, Gloria*, and Poetry among the Elite in Flavian Rome" (PhD diss., University of Cincinnati, 2002), 88, describes the obligations raised by the *gloria* of previous generations: "The pseudo-existence of *gloria* meant that it could have direct repercussions on the *gloria* of following generations, and that it came with certain inherent obligations for family members."
[3] Bruce J. Malina, *New Testament World: Insights from Cultural Anthropology* (London: SCM Press, 1983), 29.
[4] Julian A. Pitt-Rivers, "Honour and Social Status," in *Honour and Shame: The Values of Mediterranean Society*, ed. John G. Peristiany (Chicago, IL: University of Chicago Press, 1966), 19–77, 22: "The sentiment of honour inspires conduct which is honourable, the conduct receives recognition and establishes reputation, and reputation is finally sanctified by the bestowal of honours. Honour felt becomes honour claimed and honour claimed becomes honour paid."

gratefully made public mention and voted suitable honors (ἐκόσμησεν τιμαῖς) for them ... In consideration of the aforementioned, it was decreed by the People ... to praise Numerius and Marcus Cloatius ... for the goodwill that they have continued to exercise, toward our city; they shall have all the honors and privileges that belong to the other *proxenoi* and benefactors of our city ... *so that it may be clear to all that our city honors worthy men.* (*SIG* 748, italics added)[5]

Thus, in the assembly's voting of honors for these benefactors, the city thereby promotes further benefaction. The city perpetuates the system of benefaction by publicly advertising the honors decreed on inscriptions, thereby prodding others to carry out similar benefactions by promising further praise.[6]

Honor as Influence in Roman Letter Writing

An individual who possessed great honor, whether inherited, acquired, or a combination of the two, could then use it to influence others, to flex their so-called honorific muscles.[7] Such influence extended throughout ancient Roman society, from households to governments, from friendships to business deals. For the purposes of this study, however, we will focus on how such "honour-based forms of influence"[8] appear in communicative mediums such as letters and orations that were based on already-established relationships.

One way in which individuals wielded their *auctoritas* was through letters of introduction or recommendation. As one classicist declares, "Recommendations were a major means by which members of the Roman elite protected and extended

---

[5] Translated by Robert K. Sherk, *Rome and the Greek East to the death of Augustus* (New York: Cambridge University Press, 1984), 93–4. Cf. *SIG* 762 (Sherk, §78), an inscription from 49/48 BCE, in which the city of Dionysopolis honors its citizen Akornion:

> He exhibited the greatest zeal for the safety of his native city: *in order therefore that the People also might be seen honoring fine and good men and those who benefit them*, it is decreed by the Boule and the People for these services to praise Akornion and to present to him at the Games of Dionysos a gold crown. (emphasis added)

[6] See Margareta Benner, "The Emperor Says: Studies in the Rhetorical Style in Edicts of the Early Empire" (PhD diss., Acta Universitas Gothoburgensis [Sweden], 1975), 11, who notes that Hellenistic honorary decrees often include either an ἐπειδή-clause or a ὅπως-clause, which can serve as "an exhortation to others to follow the example." Cf. the discussions of the recurring ἐπειδή-clause in inscriptions by Pierre Charneux, "En relisant les décrets argiens II," *BCH* 115 (1991), 297–323 (319–21) and Maurice Holleaux, "Une inscription de Séleucie-de-Piérie," *BCH* 57 (1933), 6–67 (48–52). Onno van Nijf, "Civic Mirrors: Honorific Inscriptions and the Politics of Prestige," in *Social Status and Prestige in the Graeco-Roman World*, ed. Annika B. Kuhn (Stuttgart: Franz Steiner Verlag, 2015), 233–45, 237, describing civic life within the Greek *polis*, notes how "honorific practices provided the Greek cities ... with an impressive and effective mechanism for the public renewal of the social contract between the *demos* and the elite."

[7] Benner, "Emperor Says," 14, defines *auctoritas* as "a concept which is affined [*sic*] to the idea of the force of persuasion: it denotes a moral prestige which others acknowledge of their own free will, and which makes them consent voluntarily to the opinions and wishes of the person possessed of *auctoritas*."

[8] J. E. Lendon, *Empire of Honour: The Art of Government in the Roman World* (Oxford: Oxford University Press, 1997), 80–1.

their reputation and influence."[9] The phenomenon, according to an avid writer of recommendations from the second century CE,[10] originally sprang from the friendly desire to establish a relationship between two of one's intimates previously unfamiliar with one another. The practice quickly deteriorated, however, into a business-like transaction, as some might describe Cicero's *Ad familiares* book 13, which consists entirely of such letters.[11] Even in extreme cases of formality, though, commendations cannot be wholly detached from their relational roots. Rather, commendation letters exhibit elements along a spectrum of formality within Roman friendship.[12]

Recommendation letters often reflect the great ambition of those striving to climb the social ladder in Roman society, who attempt to enlist the help of more prominent friends to promote their reputation by asking them to write such a letter on their behalf. They are thus eliciting a favor from such a friend, asking him to place his own reputation on the line for their sake.[13] The older statesmen were happy to do so because they too benefited from the interaction.[14] It was a boon to the writer's own reputation in that it established him within the coveted role of patron over an ever-widening web of social networks.[15]

The Mutuality of Honor in the Hellenistic and Roman World

The second idea important to understanding how shared honor could be used for persuasion is the simple fact that in Greco-Roman antiquity honor could be *shared*. To some the Greco-Roman honor-culture had no place for mutuality of honor.[16]

---

[9] Amanda Wilcox, *The Gift of Correspondence in Classical Rome* (Madison: University of Wisconsin Press, 2012), 79.
[10] M. Fronto, *Ad Amicos* 1.1.1: "The custom of recommendation is said in the first instance to have sprung from good will, when every man wished to have his own friend made known to another friend and rendered intimate with him."
[11] See Roger Rees, "Letters of Recommendation and the Rhetoric of Praise," in *Ancient Letters*, ed. Ruth Morello and A. D. Morrison (Oxford: Oxford University Press, 2007), 149–68.
[12] On friendship in the Roman period, see the discussion below, as well as P. A. Brunt, "*Amicitia* in the Late Roman Republic," in *The Fall of the Roman Republic and Related Essays* (Oxford: Oxford University Press, 1988 [reprint 2004]), 351–81.
[13] For instance, see Pliny, *Ep.* 2.9.1, on which Ramsay MacMullen, "Personal Power in the Roman Empire," *AJP* 107 (1986), 512–24, 517, remarks: Pliny's distressed note "is over a matter of career-advancement ... and [it is] not even his own career at stake but a young protégé's."
[14] Efrain Agosto, "Paul's Use of Greco-Roman Conventions of Commendations" (PhD diss., Boston University, 1996), 83: "A commendation letter often proves to be as strategic for the leadership position of the writer as for the subject of the commendation."
[15] Wilcox, *Gift*, 96: "Relationships recorded and performed by a series of epistolary requests could extend an individual's social network, not simply through a 'chain of *officia*,' but also through a chain of interlocked people." Cf. Horst Hutter, *Politics as Friendship* (Waterloo: Wilfrid Laurier University Press, 1978), 144: "The stature of a Roman could be measured by the quality and quantity of his ... friends."
[16] Pitt-Rivers, "Honour," 24, discusses such competition: "Where honour is established through the bestowal of honours, there must needs be competition for them ... The victor in any competition for honour finds his reputation enhanced by the humiliation of the vanquished." Cf. G. B. Davis, "True and False Boasting in 2 Cor 10–13" (PhD diss., University of Cambridge, 1999), 24, who notes that "in a competitive environment where honour was limited, ambition function as a catalyst for

Rather, anthropologists of Mediterranean culture present honor as a "limited good" for which individuals within society compete.[17] For instance, in his comparison between Demosthenes and Cicero, Plutarch criticizes Cicero because "he praises not only his deeds and actions, but also his speeches ..., *as if he were impetuously vying with*" others.[18] In Cicero's orations, then, self-praise seems to manifest the competition in which Roman statesmen were engaged for the limited good of honor within Roman society.[19] Similarly, Lucretius, in a section of anthropological musings within his great poem on natural law, describes the fierce, characteristically Roman contest for honor in drastic terms: "Leave them then to be weary to no purpose, and to sweat blood in struggling along the narrow path of ambition."[20]

How, then, could such an environment of fierce competition allow room for any sharing or mutuality of honor? Though often overlooked in treatments of the Hellenistic and Roman honor culture, the answer is to be found in the way that individuals in antiquity experienced group solidarity through family and, by extension, through friendship.[21] The following discussion will thus present various examples from Greco-Roman antiquity[22] in which one individual, whether family member or friend, could participate in the honor of another. Only rarely, however, did such co-participation in honor go both ways, reaching actual mutuality in the sense that both parties gained honor and both participated in the other's honor. Even the cases where the participation in honor was merely one-directional, though, are sufficient to demonstrate the reality

---

achievement and manifested and reinforced the importance of recognition in the Graeco-Roman world."

[17] Malina, *World*, 29. Carlin A. Barton, *Roman Honor: The Fire in their Bones* (Berkeley: University of California Press, 2001), 43, speaks of the "Roman contest culture." Lendon, *Empire*, 93, similarly speaks of "the whole proud, competitive, jostling ethos of the ancient city."

[18] *Comp. Dem. Cic.* 2.2 (emphasis added).

[19] Plutarch similarly critiques the practice of self-praise in his treatise *de laude ipsius*: "Now the praise is frivolous (κενός) which men are felt to bestow upon themselves merely to receive it; and it is held in the greatest contempt, as it appears to aim at gratifying ambition (φιλοτιμίας) and an unseasonable appetite for fame (δόξης ἀκαίρου)" (*Mor.* 540A). On self-praise in Cicero's writings, see *Fam.* 5.12: "I have a burning desire, of a strength you will hardly credit but ought not, I think, to blame, that my name should gain lustre and celebrity." For discussion of this letter, see Niall Rudd, "Stratagems of Vanity," in *Author and Audience in Latin Literature*, ed. Anthony John Woodman and Jonathan Powell (Cambridge: Cambridge University Press, 1992), 18–32, 22, who comments, "Given traditional upper-class ideas about *laus, fama,* and *gloria,* Cicero's desire was unusual only in its intensity." Cicero himself recognizes the pitfalls of self-praise in this same letter: "This genre [i.e., *periautologia*] has certain disadvantages" (*Fam.* 5.12.8).

[20] *De Rerum Natura* 5.1120-1130. The fact that Lucretius is here criticizing such a contest does not negate but rather attests to the widespread reality of competition for honor within Roman society.

[21] Malina, *World*, 38, speaks of social groups, like individuals, possessing a "collective honor." Nicole Chibici-Revneanu, *Die Herrlichkeit des Verherrlichten: Das Verständnis der δόξα im Johannesevangelium*, WUNT 2.231 (Tübingen: Mohr Siebeck, 2007), 341, describes the mutuality of glory that pertained between the ancient Greek *polis* and its citizens: "Die δόξα einer Polis und die δόξα von Menschen können dabei aufeinander hingeordnet sein."

[22] In this section, we attempt to build a holistic picture of how friendship would have been perceived throughout the Roman Empire at the time of Paul. This holistic picture draws on writers of various time periods from the Homeric writings of ancient Greece through the Greek philosophers and into the Roman writers from both the Republican period and into the Julio-Claudian Empire. While we recognize that each writer can be distinguished from others in culture, language, and perspective, we aim in this study for a synthesis that presents a view of friendship that would have been broadly understood and accepted.

that honor could be shared in antiquity, allowing for the possibility of mutual honor in certain rare instances.

Mutuality of Honor within the Family

In antiquity, glory constituted "un capital familial,"[23] allowing for the glorious deeds of previous generations to be applied to their posterity. Such a transmission of honor was not necessarily a benefit, however, since it could also function as a burden on the new generation, obligating them to match, if not exceed, the honor acquired by their ancestors.[24] Still, apart from the accompanying burden, the sharing of honor among family members caused individuals to behave differently toward family than toward others.[25] Rather than competing for honor, with family one sought to augment one another's honor.[26]

The concept of brothers sharing honor is presented in Plutarch's philosophical treatise on the subject of brotherly love (*de fraterno amore*).[27] Plutarch declares that if one has a brother who is highly esteemed, then "most of his influence is [the brother's] to share" (*Mor.* 486E). He points to the example of Apollonius the Peripatetic, who "by making Sotion, his younger brother, more famous than himself, refuted the man who asserted that fame (δόξαν) could not be shared

---

[23] Auguste Haury, "Cicéron et la gloire," in *Mélanges offerts à Pierre Boyancé* (Rome: École Française de Rome, 1974), 401–17, 404. See also Malina, *World*, 29, who speaks of the ancient family as "the repository of honor."

[24] See Marius's critique of the people of Latium in Sallust's *Bell. Jug.* 85.23: "The glory of ancestors (*gloria posteris*) is … a light shining upon their posterity." Haury, "Cicéron," 404, argues that such family glory is "un héritage, un patrimoine, dont la conservation et l'accroissement exigent un effort soutenu."

[25] Robert A. Kaster, "The Shame of the Romans," *TAPA* 127 (1997), 1–19, 15, alternately, describes how Roman friends implicated one another in the other's shame: "An *amicus* … was someone whose sense of *pudor* it was in your interest to shield, not only because he was your *amicus*, bound to you by sentiment and mutual obligation, but because the revelation that a friend was ethically deficient implied that you had misplaced your friendship—and that would be a cause of *pudor* to yourself. … This impulse toward self-protection applied *a fortiori* to dealings with the members of your own household, whose exposure to *pudor* implicated you in still more intimate ways."

[26] Philip F. Esler, "Family Imagery and Christian Identity in Gal 5:13 to 6:10," in *Constructing Early Christian Families*, ed. Halvor Moxnes (London: Routledge, 2002), 121–49, 124, notes about Mediterranean culture broadly that "Honour is not only possessed by individuals"; rather, "groups are the carriers of honour and this is particularly the case with the most important group of all, the family." He goes on, "Few aspects of Mediterranean culture are more pervasive or central than family honour. Outside the family the battle for the acquisition of honour goes on, but inside it the family members work to maintain and extend their collective honour." Elsewhere, Philip F. Esler, "Group Boundaries and Intergroup Conflict in Galatians," in *Ethnicity and the Bible*, ed. Mark Brett, BIS 19 (Leiden: E. J. Brill, 1996), 215–40, 236, argues that, ideally, members within a family did not compete with one another for honor, but rather "[defended] one another's honour." Similarly, Joseph H. Hellerman, "Brothers and Friends in Philippi: Family Honor in the Roman World and in Paul's Letter to the Philippians," *BTB* 39 (2009), 15–25, 20, argues that the social context of family "had the potential … to create a community in which individuals preferred one another in honor."

[27] Plutarch, *Mor.* 478B–492D. See Hans Dieter Betz, "*De fraterno amore*," in *Plutarch's Ethical Writings and Early Christian Literature*, ed. Hans Dieter Betz, SCHNT 4 (Leiden: Brill, 1978), 231–63.

(ἀκοινώνητον)" (487D). Even more to the point is the advice that Plutarch gives to brothers earlier in the treatise:

> One would therefore advise (παραινέσειεν) a brother, in the first place, to make his brothers *partners* (κοινὰ ποιεῖν) in those respects in which he is considered to be superior, *adorning them with a portion of his repute* (συνεπικοσμοῦντα τῇ δόξῃ) and adopting them into his friendships, and if he is a cleverer speaker than they, to make his eloquence available for their use *as though it were no less theirs than his*. (484D, emphasis added)

The vision that Plutarch here espouses is an ideal one in which brothers do not work against each other, but rather contribute to each other's success and repute (δόξα). He goes on in the treatise attempting to undermine those who might argue (as do, e.g., Epictetus[28] and Fronto)[29] that by contributing to a brother's honor one is actually diminishing one's own. Assuming the voice of one arguing against those who say that sharing honors with brothers is harmful, Plutarch writes,

> "But you, fortunate man," one might say, "are so situated that, without in the least diminishing your present blessings, you can make another (ἀδελφόν) an equal sharer (συνεξομοιοῦν) in them and give him a portion of your adornment (συνεπικοσμεῖν) so that he may enjoy the radiance, as it were, of your reputation (δόξης) or excellence (ἀρετῆς) or prosperity (εὐτυχίας)." (484E)

Plutarch posits that brothers are in the "fortunate" position of having others ("brothers") who can enjoy the radiance of their glory without at all diminishing their own honor. Far from brothers having to compete with one another for honor, Plutarch argues that the advancement of one is the advancement of the other:

> He that permits his brother to be left out of no task that is worthy of notice and would bring honour (τιμήν), but makes him a sharer (κοινωνόν) in all honourable (καλῶν) enterprises ... he deprives (παραιρούμενος) himself of nothing, but adds a great deal to his brother. (485C)

---

[28] Cf. Epictetus, *Diatr.* 2.22, who comments that if "glory" (δοξάριον) were to come between friends or family members then their sense of solidarity would be overturned, and then notes,

> It is a general rule—be not deceived—that every living thing is to nothing so devoted as to its own interest (τῷ ἰδίῳ συμφέροντι). Whatever then appears to it to stand in the way of this interest, be it a brother, or father, or child ... the being hates, accuses, and curses it. For its nature is to love nothing so much as its own interest (τὸ αὑτοῦ συμφέρου).

[29] Cf. Fronto's philosophical musings in two Greek letters:

> He that does another honour, manifestly does himself dishonour (ἐν αἷς ὁ τιμῶν ἕτρον δῆλός ἐστιν αὐτὸς αὐτὸν ἀτιμάζων), and sets him whom he has honoured above himself (καὶ ἐν δευτέρῳ τιθεὶς τοῦ προτετιμημένου) ... For each man is his own nearer concern (οἰκειότερος γὰρ αὐτὸς ἕκαστος αὑτῷ) and more deserving of honour at his own hands (καὶ προτιμᾶσθαι πρὸς αὑτοῦ δικαιότερος). (*Epist. Graec.* 5.4)

> And again, "A man acts unjustly if he so acquire praise for himself as to rob another of his (ἔτι τις ἑαυτῷ μὲν ἔπαινον παρασκευάζοι ἕτερον δὲ ἐπαίνου ἀποστεροίη, οὐ δίκαιος)" (5.8).

Thus, as Aasgaard notes from his study of role expectations for brothers in antiquity emerging from Plutarch's treatise, "one important task of siblings was to maintain their own honour and that of the family."[30]

Valerius Maximus also envisions the relationship between brothers as one in which both sides forego their own honor to magnify the other's. In his essay on brotherly love, Maximus first recounts the story of Scipio Africanus, who, though he was "considerably greater in service than his brother," after winning two great victories, "took the glory of the one triumph," but then "handed over that of the other" to his brother.[31] Later in the essay Maximus extols the strength of filial love by relating the story of M. Fabius, who, after winning a glorious victory, refused the honor of the accompanying triumph because his brother had died in the battle:

> What piety of fraternal affection (*pietatem fraternae caritatis*) must we think dwelt in his [viz., M. Fabius's] breast that on account of it such lustre of the highest of honours (*amplissimi honoris fulgor*) could be extinguished. (Val. Max. 5.5.2)

The point that Maximus draws out is that brotherly love counteracts the natural ambition for personal honor, replacing it with a desire to see a brother's honor magnified above one's own.

Mutual Honor in the Parent–Child Relationship

Such a notion of boasting in another's successes and accomplishments was also experienced within the father–child relationship. As far back as Homer, we see the father's desire to be surpassed in glory by his son. Thus, Hector prays for his son, Astyanax:

> Zeus …, grant that this my child may likewise prove, just like me, pre-eminent among the Trojans, and as good in strength … And some day may some man say of him…: "This one is better far than his father." (*Il.* 6.476–79)

Such parental concern for one's child is echoed in the Roman context by the moralist philosopher, Seneca, who observes that "a father's power … is most forbearing in its care for the interests of his children and subordinates his own to theirs."[32] In the eyes of society, however, the idea is reversed so that instead of the child benefitting from the parent's glory, it is rather the parent who shares in the glory of the child, as can be seen in Valerius Maximus's depiction of Fabius Gurges's triumph. In the procession, the conquering general is trailed by his father, who "was not watched as an adjunct to that glorious procession but as its author."[33]

---

[30] Reider Aasgaard, "Role Ethics in Paul: The Significance of the Sibling Role for Paul's Ethical Thinking," *NTS* 48 (2002), 513–30, 519.
[31] Val. Max. 5.5.1.
[32] *Clem.* 1.14.2.
[33] Val. Max. 5.7.

Different than the relation between siblings, therefore, the father–child relation allowed the father to share in the victories and accomplishments of his child because he is the source of the other's abilities. Whereas the friend–friend relation is ideally characterized by equality,[34] the father–son relation is uneven. That is, friends share equally in each other's success, but the father always maintains the position of preeminence above his child. This is because, while both father and child seek to bestow benefactions upon the other, the child will always come away second in prestige, since every gift given by child to father bestows honor not on the son as benefactor but on the father as the ultimate source undergirding the benefaction.[35] Seneca points to this fact in his treatise on benefaction:

> What a son gives to a father is ... less, because he owes to his father this very power of giving. So a father is never surpassed in the matter of a benefit (*numquam beneficio vincitur*), for *the very benefit in which he is surpassed is really his own*. (*Ben.* 3.29.3, emphasis added)[36]

Seneca goes on to discuss the great source of joy and satisfaction for parents when they can boast in the success of their children, even when such success surpasses their own:

> How else comes to parents a happiness so great (*tantam felicitatem*) that, in the matter of benefits, they acknowledge themselves to be no match for their children? ... The fathers themselves will be willing and glad to have it happen ... What can be more fortunate than the old man who, to all ears and in all places, will declare that in benefits he has been surpassed (*beneficiis vincerer*) by his son? (*Ben.* 3.36.2; 38.2)

Therefore, just as friends in the Greco-Roman world could take joy and pride in the accomplishments and success of each other, so too could parents take joy in the good deeds and virtue of their children.[37]

---

[34] Seneca, *Ben.* 2.15.1: "Since the sum total of friendship consists in putting a friend on an equality with ourselves, consideration must be given at the same time to the interests of both."

[35] Note this same idea reflected in the Jewish writings of the Second Temple period, cf. Sir 7:28, "Remember that you were begotten by [your parents], and how can you recompense them the things that they have done for you?"

[36] Cf. also 3.34. Cf. Aristotle, *Eth. nic.* 1161b: "Parents love their children as part of themselves, whereas children love their parents as the source of their being." Lorraine Smith Pangle, *Aristotle and the Philosophy of Friendship* (Cambridge: Cambridge University Press, 2003), 62, observes, "In the archetypical unequal friendship [i.e. that between parent and child] ... *there is no equalization*" (emphasis added).

[37] T. R. Stevenson, "Ideal Benefactor and the Father Analogy in Greek and Roman Thought," CQ 42 (1992), 421–36, 427, discusses the tension involved in parents both supporting, but also hoping to share in the success of their children: "There is a strong belief [in Plutarch] that parental care is demeaned when motivated by expectation of financial or other return. On the other hand, it seems to be Plutarch's view that the expectation of such return is not unnatural in itself because ... he subscribes to the concept of creditor-debtor relationship in parent-child love." James R. Harrison, "Paul the 'Paradoxical' Parent," in *Theologizing in the Corinthian Conflict*, ed. Reimund Bieringer et al., BTS 16 (Leuven: Peeters, 2013), 399–426, 409, argues with reference to Plutarch: "While the majority of the ancient evidence focuses on the importance of the requital of parental beneficence, there is evidence that highlights the beneficence of parents independent of the demands of the

Mutual Honor within Friendship

At the heart of ancient friendship is the practice of sharing: friends shared everything. They shared resources with each other,[38] they shared time together,[39] they shared purposes and goals,[40] pleasures and pains,[41] it could almost be said that they shared one identity and soul.[42] Friends were so united that one could speak of a friend as "another self."[43] Ideally, this then meant that when one was striving for the benefit of a friend, whatever gains the friend received could actually be counted as one's own, since friends shared their victories so that success for a friend meant success for oneself.[44] Among Greco-Roman philosophers, this perspective motivated individuals to put aside their own interests in order to seek the interests of others.[45] A few of the ancient philosophers attempted to expand this principle so as to include all of humanity, thus presenting a benefit for the greater society as a benefit for the individual.[46] But on the whole, this

---

reciprocity system. However, we have to be careful here, because often reciprocity lurks beneath the surface of our literature and documents."

[38] Plutarch, *Amic. mult.*: "Friendship draws persons together and unites them and keeps them united in a close fellowship by means of continual association and mutual acts of kindness" (*Mor.* 95A); Seneca, *Ben.* 2.32.2, describes that friendship requires "reciprocal volleys and returns."

[39] Cicero, *Off.* 1.58: "Intimate relationship of life and living ... [flourishes] best in friendships"; Aristotle, *Eth. nic.* 1158a, 1159b: "A shared life and shared living, counsel and conversation, encouragement, comfort, and sometimes even reproofs, flourish most of all in friendships ... *The goods of friends are common* (κοινὰ τὰ φίλων), since friendship rests upon communion."

[40] Aristotle, *Eth. nic.* 1167a: "Unity of sentiment ... is plainly connected with friendship"; Cicero, *Amic.* 20: "Friendship is nothing else than an accord (*contracta*) in all things ... conjoined with mutual goodwill and affection (*cum benevolentia et caritate consensio*)"; Xenophon, *Mem.* 2.6.26: "It is a benefit ... to see in [friends] partners and fellow-workers (κοινωνοῖς καὶ συνεργοῖς) in a common cause."

[41] Aristotle, *Eth. eud.* 7.6.9 (1240a): "A friend wishes most of all that he might not feel pain when his friend is in pain, but feel actually the same pain ... if this were possible, and if not, as nearly the same as may be"; *Eth. eud.* 7.12.19 (1245b), "It seems to be characteristic ... of the person for whom affection is felt to wish to share [their troubles]"; Homer, *Il.* xvi: "Speak those sorrows which a friend would share" (translation from Alexander Pope, The Iliad [London: Penguin Classics, 1996, reprint, original 1773]). W. F. R. Hardie, *Aristotle's Ethical Theory* (Oxford: Clarendon Press, 1968), 324–5, correctly notes, however, that the sharing of sorrows among friends is limited in that they do not feel the same pain but rather feel "sympathy and pity." Pangle, *Aristotle*, 228 n. 4, concurs, "We can never precisely feel another's pain, or 'sympathize' with our own."

[42] Plutarch, *Amic. mult.* (*Mor.* 96F), notes that, in friendship, "It must be as if one soul were apportioned among two or more bodies." Cf. Lucian, *Tox.* 53: "Stop making me a different person than yourself."

[43] Aristotle, *Eth. nic.* 1166a: "The good man ... feels towards his friend in the same way as towards himself (for a friend is another self)." On the friend as another self in Aristotle, see Pangle, *Aristotle*, 142–54.

[44] Cicero, *Amic.* 22: "[A friend is] someone whose joy in [your prosperity] would be equal to your own ... and to whom the burden [of your adversity] would be heavier even than to yourself"; Seneca, *Ben.* 2.22.1: "It is a legitimate source of happiness to see a friend happy." This idea is applied to the system of Roman patronage by Richard P. Saller, *Personal Patronage under the Early Empire* (Cambridge: Cambridge University Press, 1982), 123, who observes that "the honor of a man's kin, friends and dependents reflects on his own standing."

[45] Cicero, *Amic.* 57: "There are numerous occasions when good men forgo, or permit themselves to be deprived of, many conveniences in order that their friends rather than themselves may enjoy them"; Aristotle, *Eth. nic.* 1155b, "We are told that we ought to wish our friend well for his own sake."

[46] Cicero, *Off.* 3.24: "It requires a great and lofty spirit to despise these [viz., pleasures, life, riches, etc.] and count them as naught, when one weighs them over against the common weal (*utilitate communi*)"; *Off.* 3.52, "It is your duty to consider the interests of your fellow-men and to serve society ... Your interest (*utilitas tua*) shall be the interest of the community (*communis utilitas*) and

principle of seeking another's interests above one's own was primarily tethered within the bounds of friendship, that is, one was obliged to sacrifice or diminish one's own interests only to promote the interests of a friend.[47]

When it came to everyday living, this principle of friendship acquired more utilitarian ends in that an individual would spend resources to benefit a friend with the assumption that such a gift would be reciprocated.[48] This principle of reciprocity thus becomes the backbone of the benefaction system that played such a major role in sustaining the ancient economy.[49] It must be kept in mind, however, that philosophers of the period attempted to diminish this utilitarian motivation for friendship and sought a return to a more altruistic ideal of sharing within friendship that was motivated by the goodwill that friends felt for each other, not by the goods and services that might accrue through the friendship.[50]

Part of the discussion that arose out of this corrective thrust against utilitarianism in the friendship debate was the concept that it was appropriate for individuals to take joy in their friends' progress toward virtue. As mentioned above, seeing a friend as "another self" meant that the friend's progress toward virtue was also one's own progress toward virtue,[51] and since virtue was the common goal toward which mankind was striving,[52] progress in this direction (i.e., moral growth) was something in which to take pride and joy. For instance, Xenophon relates a conversation between

conversely ... the interest of the community shall be your interest as well." Cf. Plato's advice to rulers as related by Cicero, *Off.* 1.85: "to keep the good of the people (*utilitatem civium*) so clearly in view that regardless of their own interests they will make their every action conform to that."

[47] Aristotle, *Eth. nic.* 1168a: "A good man acts from a sense of what is noble ... and he considers his friend's interest, disregarding his own." Lucian, *Tox.* 6, describes the person in battle who "[counts] it nothing to die if he saves his friend and intercepts with his own body the stroke that is being directed at the other."

[48] Cicero, *Off.* 1.56: "A strong bond of fellowship is effected (*Magna etiam illa communitas est*) by mutual interchange of kind services; and as long as these kindnesses are mutual (*mutua*) and acceptable, those between whom they are interchanged are united by the ties of an enduring intimacy." Cf. Richard Seaford, *Reciprocity and Ritual: Homer and Tragedy in the Developing City-State* (Oxford: Clarendon Press, 1994), 25, who describes how reciprocal gift-giving established bonds in ancient Greece: "They both [i.e. friendships and enmities] may create ... a well-defined socially important network of relations between households or kinship groups."

[49] Saller, *Personal Patronage*, 13: "*Amicitia* was expected basically to entail reciprocal exchange of *officia* and *beneficia*." Elsewhere, Richard P. Saller, "Patronage and Friendship in Early Imperial Rome," in *Patronage in Ancient Society*, ed. Andrew Wallace-Hadrill (London: Routledge, 1989), 49–62, 61, argues that the lines between benefaction and friendship were blurred within the classical Roman literature, entailing "the ambiguity and overlap in Latin of *amicitia* and *clientela*." Terry Johnson and Christopher Dandeker, "Patronage: Relation and System," in Wallace-Hadrill, *Patronage in Ancient Society*, 219–41, 221, further describe the similarity between friendship and benefaction in the Roman context, writing that patronage is "a durable, two-way relationship of 'lop-sided' or 'vertical' friendship."

[50] E.g., Seneca, *Ben.* 3.17.3: "He who is happy in having received a benefit ... rejoices (*gaudet*) in viewing, not the gift, but the intention of him from whom he received it." Similarly, Cicero, *Amic.* 31, comments that "friendship is desirable, not because we are influenced by hope of gain, but because its entire profit is in the love itself."

[51] Pangle, *Aristotle*, 55, comments on Aristotle's view of friendship that "the more one shares and enjoys sharing one's life with another, the more the other then becomes one's own, and *his good becomes a part of one's own good*" (emphasis mine).

[52] Aristotle, *Eth. eud.* 7.12.15 (1245b), describes this mutual encouragement to pursue the virtuous end: "Each really wishes to share with his friends the End that he is capable of attaining, or failing this, men choose most of all to benefit their friends and to be benefited by them."

Socrates and Cristobulus in which the philosopher describes to his interlocutor that within friendship, "You take as much pride (ἀγάλλῃ) in your friends' fair achievements as in your own, and as much pleasure (χαίρεις) in your friends' good as in your own" (*Mem.* 2.6.35). Cicero, writing a few centuries later, echoes this Socratic ideal within the Roman context: "For when two people have the same ideals and the same tastes, it is a natural consequence that each is as much *delighted* (*delectetur*) *with the other as he is with himself.*"[53] Seneca, as well, expresses this same mentality of rejoicing in a friend's moral advancement. Discussing the benefits of cultivating relationships with the wise, he asserts, "It is in accordance with Nature to show affection for our friends, and to rejoice (*laetari*) in their advancement (*auctu*) *as if it were absolutely our own* (*suo proprioque*)."[54]

Thus, within the ancient adage that friends share all things is firmly entrenched the notion of a mutual delight and joy shared between friends when it came to victories won and successes accomplished.[55] On the one hand, this was experienced by way of an amicable competition among friends in which each strove to surpass the other in virtuous deeds.[56] Yet still the final outcome was that the friends could take joy in whatever successes had been accomplished, no matter which friend had actually accomplished the feat.[57] Viewing the friends as a single unit, a victory for one entails a victory for all, something about which the entire group could boast.

Mutual Honor in the Teacher–Pupil Relationship

One further way in which honor was shared was in the teacher–pupil relationship. This can be clearly seen in the eulogy written by Aelius Aristides for his mentor and teacher, Alexander of Cotiaeum.[58] In the speech, Aristides praises his teacher and consoles Alexander's hometown regarding his recent death.[59] A recurring theme throughout the lengthy address is the sense of pride (φιλοτιμία) and glory (δόξα) that Alexander's life and career brought to those around him, especially to his students and his city. Describing the way in which the city could share in Alexander's glory, Aristides writes,

---

[53] Cicero, *Off.* 1.56 (italics added). Cf. Aristotle, *Eth. eud.* 7.6.9: "It is characteristic of a friend to rejoice (χαίρειν) for no other reason than because the other is rejoicing."

[54] Seneca, *Ep.* 109.15 (italics added).

[55] Additionally, cf. Cicero, *Amic.* 22, who describes a friend as "someone whose joy in [your prosperity] would be equal to your own."

[56] Xenophon, *Mem.* 2.6.35: "A man's excellence consists in outdoing his friends in kindness." Similarly, Cicero, *Fam.* 7.31: "We now have only to vie with one another in acts of friendship, a contest in which the victory of either will leave me equally content."

[57] Lucian's portrayal, *Tox.* 53, of the close connection between two friends shows this well: "Having fused ourselves together ... and united, as far as we could, into a single person (εἰς ἕνα συνελθόντες), it would be ridiculous if ... we should continue to think it a great thing if this or that part of us has done something useful in behalf of the whole body; for it was working in its own behalf as a part of the whole organism to which the good was being done."

[58] Discourse 32: "Funeral Address in honor of Alexander." English translation from C. Behr, *Aelius Aristides: Complete Works* (Leiden: E. J. Brill, 1981), 158–65. Greek text from Jean-Luc Vix, *Les Discours 30 à 34 d'Aelius Aristide* (Turnhout: Brepols, 2010), 442–57.

[59] For contextual comments, see Behr, 394 n. 1. Due to ill health Aristides was unable to deliver the speech in person, and thus sends the eulogy as a letter.

> [Alexander's] position among the Greeks ... would give you a sense of pride (φιλοτιμία). For his glory is shared by the city (ἡ γὰρ ἐκείνου δόξα κοινὴ τῆς πόλεως γεγένηται). (§20)

Earlier in the address Aristides described Alexander's work as providing the city of Cotiaeum, along with the entire Greek race, a source of boasting:

> [Alexander] has caused both the city and the entire race to take pride in him (τὴν φιλοτιμίαν αὐτοῦ), and for all of you it is no little boast (οὐ μικρὸν καύχημα) to the Greeks to be his fellow citizens. (§5)

This sense of pride is felt even more strongly by Alexander's students. As Aristides comments, "For the students of oratory it was a matter of pride (φιλοτιμία) to have studied with him" (§12). Aristides, however, reserves the most poignant language of mutual honor for his own relationship with Alexander, which, though it began as a teacher-student relationship, had blossomed into a fruitful friendship,[60] in which their individual glories coincided. Hence, in his opening words of the eulogy, Aristides exclaims,

> The greatest bond between us was that we could be equally proud of one another (ἴσον φρονῆσαι ἐπ᾽ ἀλλήλοις εἴχομεν). I felt self-esteem (φιλοτιμούμενος) to have had him as a teacher and he counted my career as part of his own glory (ὁ δ᾽ ἐν οἰκείας δόξης μέρει τὸ καθ᾽ ἡμᾶς τιθέμενος). (§12)

Therefore, Aristides refers to his relationship with his once teacher/now friend using the language of mutual honor.[61] Aristides can be proud of Alexander because he could claim connection with so great a teacher, while Alexander was able to be proud of Aristides because his student's later glorious career could be set down (τίθημι) as his own glory. And this entire discussion originates from the *student*, who is glad to share his glory with his teacher if it might add to his reputation now that he has passed away.

Conclusion

Overall, it is evident that the glory that arises from virtue is not only accessible to the virtuous individual but also becomes available to others associated to that individual

---

[60] "I got a rich harvest back from the friendship which I felt toward him" (§39).
[61] Though on the possible mixed motives of Aristides for contributing to his own self-praise in his discourses, see Dana Fields, "Aristides and Plutarch on Self-Praise," in *Aelius Aristides between Greece, Rome, and the Gods*, ed. W. V. Harris and Brooke Holmes (Leiden: Brill, 2008), 151–73, in which Fields compares Aristides's thinking to that of Plutarch, pointing to *Discourse* 28, "Concerning a Remark in Passing," where Aristides elaborates at length on the subject of *periautologia*. Fields, 170 n. 68, comments on Aristides's use of the key phrase φιλοτιμία: "Benefaction [is just] another form of self-aggrandizement (hence often denoted by the word φιλοτιμία)." For further discussion of Aristides's self-praise, see Laurent Pernot, "Periautologia: Problèmes et méthodes de l'éloge de soi-même," *REG* 111 (1998), 101–24, 118–19: "La fierté apparaît comme un trait constitutif de l'esprit grec, l'éloge de soi-même comme une tradition nationale." Cf. also Peter Brown, *The Making of Late Antiquity* (Cambridge: Harvard University Press, 1978), 61, who describes φιλοτιμία with the comment: "No word understood to its depths goes further to explain the Greco-Roman achievement."

through various networks of relationships, whether among friends, families, or teacher-pupils. The idea that glory or fame was somehow mutually exclusive and could only be possessed on an individual basis is untrue of the intimate connection between friends, between fathers and sons, and between teachers and students. The glory that arose from success was simply one possession among many that was intended to be shared among one's network of relationships.

5

Mutual Honor as Motivation in the Hellenistic and Roman World

In antiquity, the concept that honor could be shared was combined with the reality that the concern for honor could control behavior, thereby creating a rhetorical strategy within interpersonal communication wherein a relationship of mutual honor was used to persuade or influence others. This is seen most clearly in the ancient communication form of letter writing, which was commonly used to exhort or give advice to one's correspondent.[1]

Mutual Honor as Rhetorical Strategy in Ancient Letter Writing

Scholars agree that one of the main purposes of ancient letters was to maintain relationships.[2] Thus, there was a strong connection between the social phenomenon of friendship and the use of letter writing.[3] Since, as shown above, ancient conceptions of friendship envisioned friends sharing honor with one another, it is not surprising to find the notion of shared honor emerging within ancient letters. What is interesting for this investigation, however, is the way in which such notions of shared honor could function within the persuasive rhetoric of a letter between friends. We will examine, first, the way in which mutual honor was employed in the nonliterary Greek papyri, and then move on to the more robust development of shared honor as a persuasive technique in literary letter collections handed down from antiquity.

---

[1] On persuasive strategies in letters, see Michael Trapp, *Greek and Latin Letters: An Anthology with Translation* (Cambridge: Cambridge University Press, 2003), 41: "Letters exist in order to establish and conduct relationships between senders and recipients. In this role they are constantly liable to become involved in games of etiquette and power."

[2] Trapp, *Letters*, 40: "Letters have an important role to play in creating and sustaining friendships, whether between private individuals, or in contexts in which friendship has some larger public or organizational importance."

[3] Cf. Stanley K. Stowers, *Letter Writing in Greco-Roman Antiquity*, LEC 5 (Philadelphia, PA: Westminster, 1986), 29: "The ideals of Greek male friendship greatly influenced ancient epistolography."

Mutual Consideration as Persuasive Strategy in Papyrus Letters

In his foundational study of Greek papyrus letters, John L. White has demonstrated that these nonliterary letters discovered in Egypt exhibit various common features. One of these features is "the sender's statement near the close of the letter, that the sender would be 'favored' if the recipient attended to something the sender wanted," which "could convey either the sender's wish for the recipient's welfare (health wish) or as a body-concluding formula for 'nailing down' a request that the sender had made earlier in the body."[4] Since the papyrus letters generally reflect correspondence among the nonelite, this convention, while aiming at persuasion,[5] remains at a relatively low level of rhetorical development.[6] Although this convention does not involve an explicit consideration of mutual honor but instead utilizes for persuasion the emotional pull of that which will be beneficial to the sender, it stands as an important link to what becomes an appeal to mutual honor in the more elaborate rhetoric of the literary correspondence.[7]

Some examples of such a persuasive technique among the Greek papyrus letters include comments such as that found in a letter from Ammonius to Apollonius (ca. I/II CE):

> [I] urge you to live at peace and not to give others a handle against you. So try and do this *for my sake too*—a favour to me, which in the interim you'll come to recognize as advantageous (to you as well). (*P. Oxy.* 3057, emphasis added)[8]

Here Ammonius urges a general exhortation to his friend Apollonius (*not to give others a handle against you*) with the motivation coming from the simple fact that it is *for [his] sake* and *a favour to [him]*. Thus, the writer is relying on the fact that the recipient, Apollonius, does in fact want to grant him a favor, that he cares about how his compliance will affect his friend. However, Ammonius adds to this simple motivation the claim that adhering to the command will be *advantageous* for Apollonius himself as well, thereby establishing a level of mutuality within the benefits to come from the friend's positive response.

---

[4] John L. White, *Light from Ancient Letters* (Philadelphia, PA: Fortress Press, 1986), 219.
[5] White, *Light*, 195, speaks of both recommendation letters and petitionary letters that exhibit "a structure by means of which the sender tries to persuade the recipient to do something." He goes on to describe "a spectrum of means whereby, at the close of the body, letter writers pleaded, cajoled, and threatened recipients to attend to some duty earlier specified in the letter" (p. 219).
[6] Stowers, *Letter Writing*, 96, notes, "I have not yet found any good examples [of complex paraenetic letters] among the papyri, although there are simpler exhortations."
[7] G. O. Hutchinson, "Down to the Documents: Criticism and Papyrus Letters," in *Ancient Letters: Classical and Late Antique Epistolography*, ed. Ruth Morello and A. D. Morrison (Oxford: Oxford University Press, 2007), 17–36, 32, discusses "the use of language to persuade" in the papyrus letters and concludes that "even without rhetorical education, a rhetorical impulse is apparent."
[8] Text from Stowers, *Letter Writing*, 98.

Motivating a positive response to a petition by means of appealing to the recipient's goodwill toward the sender can again be seen in a letter of introduction written by a certain Theon to his friend on behalf of his brother: *"You will grant the greatest favor to me if* he [viz., Theon's brother] receives your attention."[9] A letter writer most likely would include such a convention ("you will grant me favor if …") because it presumably would carry motivational power, providing support for whatever petition was to follow. The implied assumption is that the recipient of the letter does indeed desire to grant a favor to the sender, whether because of goodwill toward the sender or merely because such a favor granted will engender a reciprocated favor.

What the rhetorically untrained writers of the papyrus letters attempted persuasively at this humbler level, the sophisticated writers among the Roman elite honed to the level of artistic precision. Thus, we find the same strategy woven throughout various persuasive ploys of the upper echelon of Roman letter writers.

Mutual Honor as Motivational Strategy within Roman Epistolary Corpora

As we turn to the more sophisticated rhetoric found in the epistolary tradition of the Roman elite, this tactic of the sender's appealing to concern for his own honor as a means to spur the addressee to action becomes both more pronounced and more complex.[10] Such tactics were usually found in letters between friends of relatively equal status, since, if the sender was substantially superior, then he could simply rely on his *auctoritas* to bring about the addressee's acquiescence.[11] In such a hierarchically lop-sided case, the appeal to emotion and goodwill inherent within the strategy of presenting the author's benefit as motivation for the request would be unnecessary. On the other hand, if the writer was far inferior socially than the recipient (as in the case of, e.g., petitionary letters to officials), then the tactic would similarly misfire because the addressee would have no reason to heed the *dignitas* of the sender.

Thus, the use of mutual honor for motivation was at home in the delicate realm of the back and forth jostling (challenge and riposte) within relationships among the Roman upper classes, where friendships represented a powerful asset in the

---

[9] White, §79, emphasis added. Cf. Trapp, §12, §22; White, §24, "You would do me a favor by … for by doing so I will have a better (supply) of the necessities."

[10] Cf. G. O. Hutchinson, *Cicero's Correspondence* (Oxford: Clarendon Press, 1998), 21:

> Persuasion plays a very large part in the corpus [of Cicero's letters], much larger than might at first appear … Even where letters seem at a superficial glance to be simply expressing the writer's feelings, or conveying news, or merely joking, closer consideration of the context … shows again and again that the writing is infused with persuasion, with the attempt to make the addressee believe or feel in a particular way, most commonly about the author.

[11] However, Margereta Benner, "The Emperor Says" (PhD diss., Acta Universitas Gothoburgensis [Sweden], 1975), 8, shows how even the emperor chose persuasion to command obedience, so as not to humiliate his subjects through force.

competition for advancement. This tactic of appealing to a friend's concern for one's own honor, then, was a polite way to garner support when seeking help in achieving one's goals. The goals were as varied as the peculiar interests of each letter writer, but the rhetorical strategy was the same: draw on the recipient's concern for oneself to influence their behavior.

Mutual Honor as Motivation in Cicero's Letters

The first place we turn to see this tactic among the Roman upper classes is in the substantial corpus of letters extant from M. Tullius Cicero.[12] In many ways, the 931 letters left by Cicero between 68 and 43 BCE provided the paradigm for every Latin letter writer to follow. Hence, it is not surprising that whatever rhetorical strategies and devices he employs reappear in other letters of the period. In order to see Cicero's use of the appeal to his own *dignitas* for the purpose of persuading his addressees,[13] we will focus on Cicero's political correspondence, that is, letters that specifically deal with matters of state.[14] It is in these letters[15] that the great orator turns his sights on swaying his peers toward actions that will serve to promote the safety and restoration of the Republic.[16] In doing so Cicero deftly merges his own *dignitas* with the interests of the state in order to redirect the support that his friends would gladly have given to him toward the benefit of the Republic.[17]

---

[12] A. D. Leeman, *Gloria: Cicero's waardering* (Rotterdam: N. V. Drukkerij M. Wyt & Zonen, 1949), in his English appendix, declares that Cicero's "own glory ... plays an important part in his works, especially in his letters" (p. 189). Leeman summarily declares that "[Cicero's] life may be regarded as the embodiment of the idea of glory" (p. 177).

[13] Hutchinson, *Cicero's Correspondence*, 19: "Concern with their *dignitas* is so often voiced by other correspondents, and both they and Cicero are so clearly alert to the standing and susceptibilities of their addressees."

[14] Catherine E. W. Steel, *Reading Cicero* (London: Duckworth, 2004), 103, notes that "three of the sixteen volumes of *Letters to Friends* (10–12) fall into this category," i.e., correspondence with men through whom Cicero attempts to orchestrate the opposition to Marcus Antonius. Steel continues, "Cicero's main purpose in [*Fam*. books 10–12] is hortatory: his correspondents must continue their struggle against Marcus Antonius, and are encouraged to do so by an appeal to the reputation which they will acquire should they so act" (p. 104).

[15] Amanda Wilcox, *The Gift of Correspondence in Classical Rome* (Madison: University of Wisconsin Press, 2012), 85, makes a similar claim about Cicero's numerous letters of introduction in *Fam*. book 13: "Cicero frequently presents the performance of the request in a letter of recommendation *as a test of the addressee's regard for him*" (italics added).

[16] Peter White, *Cicero in Letters* (Oxford: Oxford University Press, 2010), 164, remarks on these more political of Cicero's letters: "Cicero's rhetorical objective ... in [wartime correspondence] letters ... was to engage the addressee in a way that would spur him to action." White goes on to note that, in line with this purpose, what Cicero dwells on in these letters is "personal connections attesting shared commitments in public life ... and the craving for prestige."

[17] Francis A. Sullivan, "Cicero and Gloria," *TAPA* 72 (1941), 382–91, 390–1, shows that Cicero's mature reflections about *gloria* reveal its close connection to "unselfish devotion to the State." Cicero's interweaving of his own interests within those of the state to motivate his readers to action mirrors Paul's interweaving of his own interests within those of the gospel (in Phil 1:12–26) to motivate the Philippians to behave worthily of the gospel (1:27) so that his own honor may benefit from their virtuous behavior (2:16).

Cicero's Correspondence with Quintus

We begin with an example in which Cicero appeals to the mutual honor that he shares with his brother Quintus. The letter (*Quint. fratr.* 1.1) comes early in the sequence of Cicero's letters (most likely 62 BCE).[18] In the letter, Cicero employs his own honor to put pressure on his brother to be cautious in his behavior in office. Cicero admonishes Quintus:

> Your third year [as Consul] ought to be so free from blemish that nobody could possibly find the slightest fault with it. And here I no longer plead with you by exhortation and precept, but by beseeching you in brotherly fashion to devote all your mind to the winning of praise from every man's lips in every quarter ... if we fail to secure the highest praise for the administration of your province, it seems hardly possible *for us to escape the bitterest vituperation*. Remember, you are not seeking *glory* (*gloriam*) for yourself alone ... but *you have to share it with me* (*communicanda mecum*), and hand it down to our children. (*Quint. fratr.* 1.1.40–44, emphasis added)

While Cicero's admonition is vague, the persuasive motivation is clear: "if *you* fail, *we* fail, and we *both* face shame!" Cicero's emphasis appears in his repetition of the first-person plural at the close (*we*, *us*),[19] and by tethering himself to the outcome of his brother's success or failure, he intends to motivate his brother to heed his advice.

Cicero's Correspondence with Cassius

This same tactic appears again in a later set of Cicero's letters, this time outside the family, at a much tenser time for the Republic, and to a recipient of far higher status than Quintus ever held, that is, Gaius Cassius Parmensis. Since Cicero's letter corpus contains a series of letters written back and forth between himself and Cassius, it shows how both friends employ the same tactic of appeal to the other's dignity to add weight to their respective petitions.[20] At the outset, both friends make it apparent throughout their correspondence how devoted they are to the other's honor. Thus, Cassius writes to Cicero after the latter's recent restoration from exile: "I am rejoicing not only at the

---

[18] Timothy P. Wiseman, "The Ambitions of Quintus Cicero," in *Studies on Cicero*, ed. John Ferguson (Roma: Centro di studi Ciceroniani, 1962), 34–41, 36 n. 34, notes that, though the letter is "largely about the preservation of Cicero's own *dignitas*," there are still key moments in the letter that address Quintus's honor, e.g., §43 and §44.

[19] Cf. also §38,

> Since *we* have been brought, not so much by any kind of desire for glory (*cupiditas quaedam gloriae*) as by the mere force of circumstances and by fortune, into such a position of life that men are likely to talk about *us* for all time, let *us* be careful ... to avoid its being said of *us* that *we* had any particularly notorious failing. (italics added)

> There is a similar rhetorical tactic in a letter to Cicero's closest friend, Atticus (*Ad Att.* 1.15.1): "Gird up your loins then! Do your best to make *us* universally both lauded (*laudemur*) and loved."

[20] All the petitions in these letters revolve around the tense moments in the aftermath of Caesar's assassination, in which Cassius (not to be confused with G. Cassius Longinus, who with Brutus murdered Caesar) was involved.

national salvation and victory, but *at the renewal of your glory* (*instauratione tuarum laudum*)" (*Fam.* 12.13.1). Similarly, Cicero writes to reassure Cassius of his ongoing support after Caesar's murder: "How zealously I have defended your position both in the senate and before the people ... I was for the common-wealth, as always, and *for your dignity* (*dignitati*) *and glory* (*gloriae*)" (*Fam.* 12.7.1).

However, both friends use this mutual concern for the other's honor to add motivation for specific petitions. For instance, Cassius, in a letter requesting that Cicero send support to his army in Syria, writes, "May I ask you to regard my *dignitas* (*dignitatem meam*) as entrusted to your care" (*Fam.* 12.12.2).[21] Cicero, too, though characteristically with more panache, writes in a letter seeking Cassius' backing in his current political maneuvering:

> As a boy you drew towards me, and on my side I always believed that I should be proud of you (*ornamento te mihi*) ... In your joint talents and energy I think I have a rich prospect of pleasure and prestige (*dignitatis*); and I earnestly ask you to confirm that opinion by your zeal. (*Fam.* 15.14.6)

In a move that will become apparent in the next two examples as characteristic of Cicero, he positions himself in the letter as the older statesman who has been helping the younger Cassius since he was a boy.[22] Establishing such an epistolary persona then allows him to occupy the patronizingly superior position in which he can be "proud" of Cassius and benefit from Cassius's *dignitas*.[23] More importantly, though, he can then appeal to the fatherly persona he has created as well-deserving of Cassius's "zeal" on his behalf when it comes to the younger individual's military decisions. In plain terms, Cicero is trying to get Cassius to dedicate his substantial political influence toward Cicero's own cause, and in order to persuade Cassius to that end he employs this strategy of appealing to his own (paternal) share in Cassius's *dignitas*.

Cicero's Correspondence with Dolabella

The following two examples continue this rhetorical strategy on Cicero's part, first in the case of his letters to Publius Cornelius Dolabella and then in his correspondence

---

[21] H.-J. Klauck, *Ancient Letters and the New Testament* (Waco, TX: Baylor University Press, 2006), 75, describes how this letter formally entails a recommendation letter, but rather than commending a *person* to Cicero's favor, Cassius commends his *dignitas*.

[22] Eleanor Leach, "*An gravius aliquid scribam*: Roman *seniores* Write to *iuvenes*," *TAPA* 136 (2006), 247–67, 253, describes this tactic in Cicero's letters to junior statesmen: "Cicero underlines his acquaintance with the recipient from boyhood, a claim no doubt true, but nonetheless recognizable as a form of positioning within the network of aristocratic society—a strategic gesture, as we may think it, when we see this paternalistic benevolence functioning as preliminary to some no less paternalistic form of exhortation or request."

[23] Cf. Ruth Morello, "Writer and Addressee in Cicero's Letters," in *The Cambridge Companion to Cicero*, ed. Catherine E. W. Steel (Cambridge: Cambridge University Press, 2013), 196–214, 207, who describes the lengths to which Cicero goes to "construct a favorable epistolary persona for his addressee as well as for himself." Similarly, Leach, "*An gravius*," 249, speaks of Cicero's "persona-creation" or "epistolary construction of self."

with L. Munatius Plancus.[24] In the case of the former, Dolabella had ascended to the status of general in the wake of the coup against Caesar, leaving him with a sizeable army so that he occupied a position that could either be fortuitous or detrimental to Cicero's side in the fight for the Republic.[25] Thus, Cicero attempted to garner his long-standing relationship with the young general in order to bring Dolabella over to his party's side.[26] All of the rhetoric within Cicero's letter to Dolabella in 44 BCE (*Fam.* 9.14) should thus be read in light of this precarious political situation.[27]

The letter begins with Cicero plunging directly into his strategy of claiming his share in Dolabella's monumental success:

> Though I am well content, my dear Dolabella, with the glory (*gloria*) you have won, and though the happiness and pleasure I have derived from it is amply sufficient, still I cannot but admit that my greatest and crowning joy (*cumulari me maximo gaudio*) is that popular opinion writes me down a partner in your praises (*socium me ascribat tuis laudibus*). (*Fam.* 9.14.1)

Cicero goes on in the letter to justify his claim to being Dolabella's "partner" in glory— it is due to his previous role as instructor and advisor to Dolabella:[28]

> I have met none, I say, who, after praising you up to the skies in the most handsome terms, do not go on without pause to express their warmest gratitude to myself, declaring that they have no doubt that it is because you comply with my instructions and advice that you are proving yourself so excellent a citizen and so incomparable a consul. (9.14.2)

Cicero neither completely assents to such praise nor does he deny it, thanks to his own unreasonable ambition for glory:

> Now although I might answer them with perfect truth that whatever you do is done according to your own judgment and on your own initiative, and that you stand in need of no man's advice, still I neither agree absolutely with their assumption, lest I should depreciate your credit, should it appear to be wholly due to my advice,

---

[24] White, *Cicero in Letters*, 153 n. 46, interprets Cicero's letters to both these younger men as "attempts at political reeducation."

[25] For historical details, see White, *Cicero in Letters*, esp. 35, as well as 13, 26. Craig A. Williams, *Reading Roman Friendship* (Cambridge: Cambridge University Press, 2012), 224 n. 93, describes the dramatic swings in Cicero's correspondence with Dolabella, "So quickly can one go from being the object of winning expressions of *amor* to being called *inimicissimus* and the object of *odium*, and back and forth."

[26] Jon Hall, *Politeness and Politics in Cicero's Letters* (Oxford: Oxford University Press, 2009), 184, notes Cicero's "affiliative politeness" in this letter, describing how his praises of Dolabella "[convey] quite emphatically Cicero's support and amenability to political cooperation."

[27] Hall, *Politeness*, 186, observes, however, that "the letter as a whole seems rather poorly conceived, and its effusive eulogy of Dolabella's actions prompted censure from Atticus, who evidently took a rather more cynical view of Dolabella's susceptibility to this kind of courtship."

[28] Hall, *Politeness*, 184, describes the audacity of Cicero's ploy: "The orator also attempts something rather ambitious, trying to maneuver himself into a position of adviser to the new consul."

nor do I emphatically deny it; *for I am more greedy of glory than is even reasonable* (*Sum enim avidior etiam, quam satis est, gloriae*). (9.14.3)

Cicero compares his relationship to Dolabella with that between King Agamemnon and the wise old Nestor, further explicating Cicero's role as advisor to the young general:

> And after all, what was no discredit to that king of kings, Agamemnon himself—the having some Nestor at hand when he formed his plans—is not inconsistent with your own dignity (*tua dignitate*), while to me it is something to boast about (*mihi vero gloriosum*) that you, a pupil, so to speak, of my own training, should win such fame (*florere laudibus*) as consul while still a youth. (9.14.4)

Thus, in the letter Cicero attempts, once again, to establish himself in the role of patron, that is, the benevolent teacher who has wisely educated his pupil. In light of this, any glory attained by Dolabella's success redounds back to the glory of Cicero as his teacher. Cicero has attempted[29] this insertion of himself into the role of the successful general's mentor for the purpose of setting up his final exhortation to Dolabella at the end of the letter, where Cicero insinuates his petition with the statement:

> You should understand that the commonwealth rests on your shoulders, and that those men from whose initiative freedom has sprung are deserving not only of your protection, but of your favour. (9.14.8)

How, then, should Cicero's earlier comments about his being the teacher who shares in the glory of the pupil relate to the final petition? Probably the best way to understand the rhetoric is to see Cicero positioning himself as a teacher who is then able to give advice. Cicero admits that his hyperbole has only been in jest, but his intent has still been to bring about the desired result, soliciting Dolabella's favor, and so all the rhetoric, including that involving mutual glory between the two, has sought that end.

Cicero's Correspondence with Plancus

What can be seen only in part in the Dolabella letter shines out much more fully in the next and final example from Cicero's letters, his correspondence with L. Munatius Plancus,[30] all the more so because, like the Cassius correspondence above, we see how Cicero's tactics were received through letters of response.[31] During the politically tense situation following Caesar's assassination Cicero carried on a substantial

---

[29] Hall, *Politeness*, 186, is skeptical that Cicero was effective, taking his cue from the lack of response from Dolabella within Cicero's collection of letters.
[30] For general details about Plancus, see Thomas H. Watkins, *L. Munatius Plancus: Serving and Surviving in the Roman Revolution*, ICSSup 7 (Chicago, IL: Scholars Press, 1997).
[31] Hall, *Politeness*, 178, describes the uniqueness of the Plancus correspondence: "These letters are particularly valuable because they regularly preserve *both* sides of the various diplomatic gambits that the two men undertook. Indeed, Plancus's twelve letters provide our most extensive sample of formal correspondence outside that written by Cicero himself."

correspondence with Plancus, a younger statesman who occupied a very similar position of influence to that of Dolabella, indeed, perhaps of even greater influence insofar as Cicero is concerned.[32] In the course of their extended correspondence, which takes up almost the entirety of book 10 in *Ad familiares*, we hear the entire history of Plancus's relationship with Cicero, beginning from Plancus's youth (since Cicero was friends with the boy's parents) on into his career as a statesman. For instance, in one letter, Cicero describes the history of their friendship thus:

> My friendly connection with your family, my dear Plancus, came into being some time before you were born. My affection towards yourself dates from your early childhood ... For these reasons I take the most lively interest in your standing (*dignitati*) in the world, *which I hold to be mine also* (*quam mihi tecum statuo debere esse communem*). (*Fam.* 10.3.2; emphasis added)

Such a warm and affectionate comment, as it stands, would merely be evidence that Cicero sees himself connected to the successes of his younger friend, were it not for the passionate appeal that follows:[33]

> In heaven's name, throw your thoughts and solicitude into the channel which will bring you to the highest honour and glory (*summam dignitatem et gloriam*). To glory there is only one path, especially now, when the body politic has so many years been torn asunder: good statesmanship. (10.3.3)

In a passage reminiscent of his advice to his brother,[34] Cicero urges Plancus to pursue glory, but then quickly defines what he means by that, namely, to be a good statesman, which means promoting the Republic.[35] But the appeal cannot be read apart from the earlier context, in which Plancus's standing is presented as shared by Cicero. Thus, the motivation is not just for Plancus's glory alone but also for that of his older friend Cicero.

Thus far, the Plancus material is in line with the other examples we have looked at from Cicero—it too shares a key strategy Cicero uses for persuasion: his appeal to his own honor's maintenance at the hands of his correspondents. One of the interesting things that arises uniquely from the Plancus correspondence, however, is a number of return letters from Plancus in which he specifically responds to and engages with this

---

[32] This was due to the strategic location of Plancus's army in the province of Gaul during the fall of 44 BCE. For the historical circumstances surrounding the Plancus correspondence, see White, *Cicero in Letters*, 150–8. White, *Cicero in Letters*, 153, summarizes Cicero's aim in these letters: "He wants Plancus to renounce the politics of the Caesarian era and to conform again to the spirit of Republican government." Leach, "*An gravius*," 260, writes that "of all Cicero's cross-generational correspondences that with Plancus is the most politically exigent."

[33] Similar to the attempt with Dolabella, Cicero seeks to position himself as the superior in the relationship. Hall, *Politeness*, 180, notes that, despite acknowledging Plancus's own abilities, "the accompanying exhortation defines Cicero as the more experienced partner in their relationship, who assumes an authority to dispense advice regarding the correct path to *dignitas* and *gloria*."

[34] *Quint. fratr.* 1.1.

[35] Leach, "*An gravius*," 261: "Cicero enforces his exhortations [to Plancus] with pointed reference to the definition of glory in philosophical terms."

Ciceronian tactic.[36] For instance, in his reply to Cicero's above quoted letter, Plancus writes,

> My dear Cicero, be assured that (as our respective ages allow) in cultivating your friendship I have invested you, and only you, with the sacred character of a father ... *I shall take good care not to let any of my actions give you fair ground for censure.* (10.4.2-3)

In these closing words, Plancus goes along with Cicero's epistolary construct by casting himself in the role of a dutiful, obedient son who does everything with the hope of pleasing Cicero and keeping him from censure. Either Cicero's strategy has worked to perfection, or, more likely, Plancus has, for whatever motives of his own, decided to play along.[37]

This first bout of success, though, prompts Cicero to press on, continuing this winning tactic in future letters. In his next letter to Plancus, Cicero writes,

> I urge you, my dear Plancus, nay more, I beg you ... to bend all your thoughts and mental energy upon public affairs. There is nothing that can so richly reward you or so redound to your glory (*nihil est quod tibi maiori fructui gloriaeque esse possit*) ... than service to the commonwealth. (10.5.2-3)

Cicero then rounds off his exhortation with the addition: "I admonish you as a son, *I hope for you as for myself.*" Just as he has done with Quintus and with Cassius, Cicero urges Plancus to pursue the type of glory for himself that comes only from good service to the commonwealth. And he adds to the motivation by reminding Plancus that the young man's actions also reflect back upon Cicero, his pseudo-father.

In line with this emphasis on the mutuality of glory, there are references to shared honor all through the numerous letters exchanged between these two: "A great part of my happiness is in your *dignitas*" (10.12.1); "support my public standing" (10.7.2); "I shall most zealously ... attend to any matters which ... bear upon your personal standing" (10.3.4); "my effort and industry are entirely devoted to your advancement" (10.1.3); "my zeal ... for your glory" (10.19.2).[38] All the way through to the last two letters in the sequence, Plancus upholds this aspect of Cicero's involvement in his life and career so that Cicero benefits through his advancement:

> I pray that I may be able in person to add by my devoted services to the pleasure you take in your benefactions. (10.23.7)

---

[36] White, *Cicero in Letters*, 158, describes how Plancus uses "Ciceronian camouflage" back to Cicero. Similarly, Hall, *Politeness*, 169: "In Munatius Plancus we find a correspondent who employs with the greatest finesse virtually all of the conventionalized strategies of politeness that we have identified [in Cicero's letter writing]."

[37] Hall, *Politeness*, 181, highlights the manipulative nature of Plancus's replies: "[Plancus's] enthusiastic complacency begins to take on the appearance of a manipulative gambit. Plancus flatters Cicero by playing the part that he thinks Cicero wants him to play."

[38] Cf. Leach, "*An gravius*," 261.

Overall, we see in the epistolary world established by Cicero's *wechselseitig* letters with Plancus that Cicero's rhetorical strategy had just the effect that he desired. Plancus's responses reveal that just as Cicero is working for Plancus's glory, so, too, Plancus is bearing Cicero's honor in mind as he determines his actions, attempting to follow his instructor's advice whenever possible.

Cicero's vast corpus of letters has thus brought to the surface numerous examples that set the pattern for the epistolary strategy in which the letter sender appeals to his own dignity and honor to motivate the addressee to follow his advice and act in a particular way. This same strategy resurfaces again in other epistles of the Roman elite, as seen in the moral epistles of L. Annaeus Seneca and the royal correspondence of M. Cornelius Fronto.

Mutual Honor as Motivation in Seneca's Moral Epistles

Seneca's *Epistulae Morales ad Lucilium* (ca. 63–65 CE) stand apart from the letters of Cicero because, in being written entirely to one individual, they appear to be a philosophical compendium of insights rather than representing correspondence with an actual friend.[39] However, despite their differences, Seneca's letters reflect in some degree a similar rhetorical ploy to that found above in Cicero's letters.[40] The two letters of Seneca that most reflect the tactic of using shared honor toward persuasive ends come one after the other in the collection. The first is a letter that Seneca writes to a young pupil regarding his prospects in following Seneca's philosophy.[41] After praising the pupil for great advancement made toward this end,[42] Seneca adds,

> I claim you for myself (*Adsero te mihi*), you are my handiwork (*meum opus es*); when I saw your abilities, I laid my hand upon you, I exhorted you, I applied the goad and did not permit you to march lazily, but roused you continually. And now I do the same; but by this time I am cheering on one who is in the race and so in turn cheers me on (*iam currentem hortor et invicem hortantem*). (*Ep.* 34)[43]

---

[39] Cf. H.-J. Klauck, "Letters in Cicero's Correspondence," in *Early Christianity and Classical Culture*, ed. John T. Fitzgerald, Thomas H. Olbricht, and L. Michael White, NovTSup 110 (Leiden: Brill, 2003), 131–55, 133–4: "Probably [Seneca] consciously chose the letter form to give a more dialogical frame to his philosophical and ethical reasoning."

[40] Brad Inwood, "Form in Seneca's Letters," in Morello and Morrison, *Ancient Letters*, 133–48, 136, speaks of Cicero's correspondence as Seneca's "obvious target for emulation" in his letter collection.

[41] This letter (*Ep.* 34) is discussed in connection with Phil 2:16 by Russel Sisson, "A Common Agōn: Ideology and Rhetorical Intertexture in Philippians," in *Fabrics of Discourse*, ed. David B. Gowler, L. Gregory Bloomquist, and Duane F. Watson (Harrisburg: Trinity Press International, 2003), 242–63, 260–1. Abraham J. Malherbe, *The Letters to the Thessalonians*, AB 32b (Yale: Yale University Press, 2000), 186, also brings in Seneca's epistles (*Ep.* 20.1) to illumine Paul's comment that the Thessalonians are his joy and his crown in 1 Thess 2:20, noting that "Lucilius will be Seneca's glory if Seneca succeeds in nourishing him philosophically."

[42] Catharine Edwards, *Seneca: Selected Letters*, CGLC (Cambridge: Cambridge University Press, 2019), 170, speaks of "the warmth and excitement of *Ep.* 34," which is "in part an effect of the sixteen first person singular verbs." Seneca's focus on himself in this letter parallels Paul's striking use of the first-person singular throughout Philippians.

[43] Catharine Edwards, "Absent Presence in Seneca's *Epistles*: Philosophy and Friendship," in *The Cambridge Companion to Seneca*, ed. Shadi Bartsch and Alessandro Schiesaro

Thus, Seneca describes the way in which he, as the student's teacher, can share in the other's success,[44] and even envisions a situation of mutual benefit (*I am cheering on one who ... in turn cheers me on*). As Wilcox observes, Seneca's presentation of the relationship between himself and his correspondent entails that "the well-being of the two partners is interconnected, and strikingly so," as the letter moves back and forth between emphasizing "Seneca's reliance on his partner" and Seneca's "own authoritative position."[45] But, just as we saw in Cicero's letters, Seneca does not stop at the mere mention of such sharing but goes on to capitalize on the mutual relationship of honor by way of adding an exhortation: "I see such a person [viz., complete] in you, *if only you go steadily on* (*si perseveraveris*) and bend to your task."[46] Thus, Seneca employs the goal of sharing a mutual benefit in order to motivate virtuous perseverance in the life and actions of his pupil.[47]

Seneca then goes on to follow a similar tack in the next epistle in the sequence, this one in praise of the friendship of kindred minds. In the letter, Seneca appeals to his own desires as the grounds for the addressee to cultivate maturity:

> When I urge you so strongly to your studies, *it is my own interest which I am consulting* (*meum negotium ago*); I want your friendship, and it cannot fall to my lot unless you proceed, as you have begun, with the task of developing yourself (*nisi pergis ut coepisti excolere te*). (*Ep.* 35)

Seneca follows this statement with a further admonishment, again referring to the mutual benefits that he and the addressee will receive from one another:

> Hasten ... in order that, while thus perfecting yourself *for my benefit* (*mihi proficis*), you may not have learned perfection for the benefit of another (*alteri*). To be sure, I am already deriving some profit by imagining that we two shall be of one mind, and that whatever portion of my strength has yielded to age will return to me from your strength.

(Cambridge: Cambridge University Press, 2015), 41–53, 45, speaks of Seneca's exclamation here as both "arresting" and "disconcerting," in that, "insofar as [Lucilius] has progressed as a *proficiens*, a would-be wise man, [he] is Seneca's creation."

[44] Catharine Edwards, "Self-Scrutiny and Self-Transformation in Seneca's Letters," in *Oxford Readings in Seneca*, ed. John G. Fitch, ORCS (Oxford: Oxford University Press, 2008), 84–101, 93, describes how Seneca here "claims some credit for Lucilius' spiritual transformation."

[45] Wilcox, *Gift of Correspondence*, 144. Miriam T. Griffin, *Seneca: A Philosopher in Politics* (Oxford: Clarendon Press, 2003), 417, views Seneca's wavering in this letter between a "patronizing tone" and that of "a teacher who is himself learning" as proof of "faulty simulation" in the Stoic's epistolary rhetoric.

[46] Edwards, *Seneca*, 172, describes the "urgency" expressed by the metaphors here as Seneca goads Lucilius toward "philosophical development."

[47] A similar example of mutuality in Seneca's epistles can be found in *Ep.* 109.1, 4–6: "Good men are mutually helpful (*Prosunt inter se boni*) ... a good man will help another good man ... because he will bring joy to the other, he will strengthen his faith, and from the contemplation of their mutual (*mutuae*) tranquility the delight of both will be increased ... even one who is running well is helped by one who cheers him on." Wilcox, *Gift of Correspondence*, 146, astutely comments on the connection between *Ep.* 34 and 109 that while "neither runner depends on the other. Yet their relationship continues, and continues to be mutually beneficial."

Wilcox rightly argues from this exhortation that "although Seneca frankly admits that his own well-being profits from Lucilius's progress, he also emphasizes that Lucilius must continue to progress for his own sake."[48] Hence, Seneca is able to hold together both the Stoic goal of individual progress in virtue and the shared good of friendship, with the outcome that both parties mutually benefit from the respective endeavors toward virtue of each.

Even though the strategy emerges explicitly in only two out of Seneca's numerous moral epistles, where it does occur it appears to function in a similar way to its use by Cicero in that Seneca too brings up mutuality between himself and his addressee to prompt appropriate behavior. And whereas Cicero employed the rhetorical strategy of appealing to mutual honor for the purpose of promoting political goals, Seneca did so to promote the philosophical goal of progress in virtue for both himself and his correspondent.

Mutual Honor as Motivation in Fronto's Royal Correspondence

Our final example of this motif will be in the letters of Fronto,[49] who was tutor to the emperor Marcus Aurelius and his adoptive brother, Lucius Vero, writing in the mid-second century CE.[50] Fronto intentionally sought to mimic the writing of Cicero.[51] Therefore, similarly in his correspondence, there arises the tactic of an appeal to shared honor for the purpose of persuasion. Throughout Fronto's correspondence with Marcus Aurelius, his pupil, both before, during, and after his reign as emperor, there is an abundance of warmth and intimacy of language.[52] Both writers repeatedly refer to one another in the vocative[53] as "my joy (*meum gaudium*)" and "my glory (*gloria mea*)" (Fronto to Marcus: *Ad M. Caes.* 1.5.4,[54] 1.8.7;[55] Marcus to Fronto: *Ep. Graec.* 7.2;[56] *Ad*

---

[48] Wilcox, *Gift of Correspondence*, 148.
[49] All citations and translations for Fronto's correspondences are from C. R. Haines, *Marcus Cornelius Fronto*, Loeb, 2 Vols (London: G. P. Putnam's, 1919).
[50] For Fronto's influence on Roman culture, see Williams, *Roman Friendship*, 238. Although Fronto did not write until after the time of Paul, his letters reflect common rhetorical practices that were active already in the apostle's period, as the previous letters from Cicero and Seneca attest. Cf. David E. Fredrickson, *Eros and the Christ: Longing and Envy in Paul's Christology* (Minneapolis, MN: Fortress Press, 2013), 16, who argues that "in Philippians, Paul anticipates the epistolary habits of the fourth century."
[51] Fronto uses Cicero as the example to which he urges his pupils in their oratory (*Ad Verum Imp.* 2.1.13).
[52] Edward Champlin, *Fronto and Antonine Rome* (London: Harvard University Press, 1980), 4, observes that "two passions run through and unify Fronto's life as they do his letters: an obsession with rhetorical culture and a love for Marcus Aurelius." Cf. Fredrickson, *Eros and the Christ*, 25, who calls attention to the "affectionate forms of address" that abound in the correspondence between Marcus and Fronto, comparing their *pothos*-revealing epithets with those used by the apostle Paul in Phil 4:1.
[53] Williams, *Roman Friendship*, 240: "The closing sentences of these letters attract accumulations of formulaic vocatives expressing respect, affection, or both."
[54] Haines, *Fronto*, 1.98.
[55] Haines, *Fronto*, 1.124. Here Fronto piles on the vocatives: "Farewell, my joy, my security, happiness, glory (*meum gaudium, mea securitas, hilaritas, gloria*)."
[56] Haines, *Fronto*, 1.32.

M. Caes. 5.59⁵⁷). They both speak with pride of the other's achievements.⁵⁸ Thus, Fronto writes to Marcus, "Rightly have I devoted myself to you, rightly invested in you and your father all the gains of my life" (*Ad M. Caes.* 3.3⁵⁹), and again,

> O Antoninus, sweetest joy of my heart: whom, since I have known you and given myself up to you, I have ever held sweeter than all things ... Just as it is with parents, when in their children's faces they discern their own lineaments, so it is with me when in the speeches of either of you [Marcus and his brother Pius] I detect marks of my school—"*and glad in her heart was Latona*." (*Ad Antoninum Imp.* 1.2.1-2⁶⁰)

Similarly, Marcus writes to Fronto his tutor:

> For I am in love and, after all, I do believe lovers ought to be allowed to rejoice (*gauderent*) all the more in the victories (*victoriis*) achieved by their *eromenoi* ... All my best to you ... my pride and joy (*gloria mea*). (*Ep. Graec.* 7.2-4⁶¹)

This effluence of affectionate language is paired with similar tones in Fronto's correspondence with Marcus's brother, Lucius Verus, who was to succeed him as emperor. Lucius can speak to Fronto of inviting him "to share in [his] joy (*ad gaudii societatem vocare*)" (*Ad Verum Imp.* 2.2⁶²). But the more elaborate language comes on the side of Fronto, where, in a congratulatory letter to Lucius in the wake of a great military triumph won in Syria, he too employs an appeal to mutual honor as a way to urge both Lucius and his brother, Marcus, to continue their pursuit of eloquence. The letter begins with a description of the prerogative that Fronto can claim over Lucius's success in eloquence: "In the case of your eloquence, of which you gave such plain evidence in your dispatch to the Senate, *it is I who triumph indeed*" (*Ad Verum Imp.* 2.1⁶³). He goes on to speak of both Marcus's and Lucius's success in oratory as contributing to his lasting fame:

> I have received, and I have and hold a full return from you in like measure heaped high: I can now depart this life with a joyous heart, richly recompensed for my labours and *leaving behind me a mighty monument to my lasting fame* (*aeternam gloriam*). That I was your master all men either know or suppose or believe from your lips: indeed, I should be shy of claiming this honour for myself did you not yourselves both proclaim it: since you do proclaim it, it is not for me to deny it. (§2)

---

⁵⁷ Haines, *Fronto*, 1.54. Marcus here calls Fronto his "chief joy (*praecipuum meum gaudium*)."
⁵⁸ Ryan Wei, "Fronto and the Rhetoric of Friendship," *CEA* (2013), 67–93, 90, notes how "the language and articulation of *amicitia* serves to foster 'a community of addressees' whose inclusion in the immediate circle of friendships is indicated by the repeated confirmation of affection."
⁵⁹ Haines, *Fronto*, 1.63.
⁶⁰ Haines, *Fronto*, 2.37.
⁶¹ Haines, *Fronto*, 1.32.
⁶² Haines, *Fronto*, 2.117.
⁶³ Haines, *Fronto*, 2.131.

But after all of this extravagant description of Fronto's sharing in the brothers' glory, Fronto comes to the point of admonition. At two points in the letter he pushes the brothers to even more glorious oratorical endeavors: "In fine, *I challenge [you] boldly* ... [not to] give up eloquence" since it "will be as regards fame more ennobling" (§5[64]), which is continued later by the exhortation: "Both of you, aspiring to the charm of either [Cato or Cicero], *go the way I guide you*" (§15[65]). He then follows this with a letter pleading with emotion that, despite his ill health,[66] Lucius would ensure that his life will not have been lived in vain:

> Although for a long while past with this ill-health of mine it has been pain and grief for me to live on, yet when I see you return with such great glory gained by your valour, *I shall not have lived in vain (incassum)*, nor shall I be loth to live, whatever span of life remains to me. (*Ad Verum Imp.* 2.4)[67]

In all of this, we see Fronto utilizing the affection that his pupils feel toward himself as a way to garner further support for his admonitions that they carry on in the path to which he has set them. Freisenbruch speaks of an "epistolary contract" between Fronto and Marcus in which the teacher's love is "conditional" on the protégé's *eloquentia*, with frequent claims by Fronto "to the effect that all aspects of his own well-being are intricately tied up with that of his pupil."[68] Often the exhortations given are merely general in nature, but they tap into a holistic body of instruction that Fronto spent his life pouring into these pupils.[69] He knows how strongly they feel for him (indeed, they have said as much in their letters to him), and so he lets them know how much it means to him if they continue on in the way he has guided them, trusting that their concern for him will be reason enough for them to heed the advice given.[70]

---

[64] Haines, *Fronto*, 2.137.
[65] Haines, *Fronto*, 2.145.
[66] Annelise Freisenbruch, "Back to Fronto: Doctor and Patient in His Correspondence with an Emperor," in Morello and Morrison, *Ancient Letters*, 235–56, 237, notes the way in which Fronto attempts to persuade his pupils through his letters, describing how Fronto's references to his own sickness and health "is in fact intimately bound into the teacher's discourse of authority over his pupil."
[67] Haines, *Fronto*, 2.236. Freisenbruch, "Back to Fronto," 237, argues that "Fronto's pedagogical prerogative lingers over *all* areas of his discourse with his royal pupil(s)."
[68] Freisenbruch, "Back to Fronto," 241. She also speaks of the "co-dependency" presented by both Fronto and Marcus in their respective epistolary persona (p. 242).
[69] Freisenbruch, "Back to Fronto," 247:

> Fronto has a very special investment in having Marcus Aurelius (and his other royal pupil, Lucius Verus) play along with him in their own game ... The message that Marcus Aurelius is Fronto's legacy to the world, and that his state of health is invested not just in his pupil's *amicitia* and *amor*, but also in that pupil's *eloquentia*, is reiterated on several occasions.

> As we will see, this "special investment" by Fronto in the lives of his students is equivalent to Paul's special investment in his churches, on behalf of which he, too, has poured out his life and energies. Both individuals, Paul and Fronto, use the image of the possibility that their own life's efforts might have been "in vain" (*incassum* || εἰς κένος) as a rhetorical tool to spur on their readers to continue following their instructions.

[70] To these examples of letter writers deploying mutual honor to motivate their correspondents could be added the use of the same motif in civic orations. Dio Chrysostom regularly appeals to honor for persuasion (e.g., 31.159), but see especially Aelius Aristides, who exhorts the Rhodians: "Control

Conclusion

Overall, we have seen that ancient letter writers appealed to the mutuality of honor shared between themselves and their correspondents as a tool to motivate particular behavior. Oftentimes the injunctions given were of a general nature, but the tactic was evident: the writer sought to spur others on to some type of virtuous action by highlighting the mutuality of honor shared between themselves.

---

yourselves, *so that we may take pride* (φιλοτιμώμεθα) *in you* as our good comrades *and you in us* as having the power of persuading whatever the occasion requires" (24.59, my emphasis).

Part 3

Mutual Honor in Philippians

Fame is the spur ... of noble mind.

John Milton

Due Praise, that is the spur of dooing well.

Edmund Spenser

Now we are made each other's glory.

Charles Williams

In the Introduction, we highlighted the prominence of the theme of honor in Philippians as a whole and showed how this theme comes to the fore in Paul's use of the καυχ- lexeme in Phil 1:26 and 2:16 (cf. 3:3). Moreover, when read in tandem, these two pivotal texts make it clear that, for Paul, such honor is always a mutually shared reality between Paul, the Philippians, and God/Christ. These texts also make clear that Paul's development of the theme of mutual honor in Phil 1:26 and 2:14–16 took place within a specific Scriptural context and cultural milieu, to which we then turned our attention.

In Part 1, we traced the theme of mutual honor in the Scriptural material by first examining the link between Deut 26:19 and Deut 10:21, as signaled by Paul's allusion to Deut 32:5 in Phil 2:15, to show how YHWH and Israel participated in a mutuality of boasting as an expression of their covenant relationship. We then examined this same mutuality of honor as found in the dual perspective gained from Isa 60:19 and Isa 62:3, which are the natural corollary to the themes introduced by Paul's allusion to Isa 49:4 in Phil 2:16.[1] Part 2 elucidated the way in which, as a central aspect of Hellenistic and

---

[1] As we have seen, the mutuality of boasting apparent in the MT for these two Isaianic texts (via the noun תפארת) reappears (via the noun καύχημα) in the Hexaplaric translations (the LXX employs the δόξα and κάλλος roots in Isa 60:19 and 62:3, respectively). While these Hexaplaric translations did not appear until much later, their linguistic choice for rendering both verses with the καυχ- root supports the plausibility that Paul could have seen in these two texts the idea of καύχημα, and, indeed, a mutual καύχημα when viewed together, just as he would have in the two verses from Deuteronomy LXX (cf. Deut 10:21 and 26:19). On the validity of appealing to the Hexaplaric

Roman culture, a mutuality of honor existed and could be augmented within families, among friends, and between mentors and disciples. It was subsequently shown how, culturally and rhetorically, this mutual honor could motivate paraenesis. Drawing on this Greco-Roman material, we will argue in Part 3 that the mutuality of honor enjoyed between Paul and the Philippians not only derives from this Scriptural backdrop but also correlates with the Philippians' cultural understanding of the sharing of honor evinced among friends and family.

Part 3 thus draws together the twin threads of Paul's Scriptural and Greco-Roman contexts to illumine his own use of the mutual boasting theme in Philippians. While Paul's utilization of both the Scriptural and the cultural paradigms proves distinct from them, in that the apostle's understanding of Jesus has radically reshaped what it means to be the people of God and what true honor entails, yet this twin backdrop remains fruitful for exploring his unique presentation of mutual boasting in Philippians. Chapter 6 will situate Phil 1:25–26 within its broader context (1:12–26), demonstrating that Paul's self-sacrificial decision to return to the Philippians furthers the mutual honor that exists between Paul and his "siblings in the faith" in Philippi in that Paul himself is held forth as a model worthy of imitation and honor, who contributes to the Philippians' abundant boasting. The mutuality of honor reflected in this passage, however, encompasses not two but three parties, since the Philippians' boast, as will be shown, involves both Paul and Christ, so that, as in the tripartite boast portrayed in Isaiah, the honor of all three parties is mutually involved in the others.

Chapter 7 will then treat Phil 2:14–16, which offers the corresponding idea to that found in 1:26: now it is the Philippians' spotless behavior that garners honorable recognition for themselves and boasting for Paul. Here, too, the mutual honor is threefold in that God stands behind the Philippians' actions as the ultimate benefactor who works in the Philippians for his own good pleasure (2:13) and receives the glory from his benefactions (1:11; 4:20). Drawing again from our presentation of the Scriptural background in Part 1, we will argue that Paul's allusion to Pentateuchal material in 2:14–15 directs us to see his use of καύχημα in 2:16 as constituting the eschatological fulfillment of the covenant blessing offered to Israel as a reward for covenant obedience in Deut 26:19. But Paul's surprising appropriation *to himself* of the honor accruing originally in Deuteronomy to God from his people's obedience (Deut 26:19; cf. Jer 13:11) can only be understood within the purview of Isa 40–66, which the apostle presupposes in 2:16 as the larger context of his allusion to Isa 49:4. Picking up the prominent theme in Isa 40–66 of the Servant's reward for his faithful (though unsuccessful) ministry to Israel, Paul depicts himself as the Servant whose prerogative it is to receive a reward, an honor that places him within the matrix of mutual honor enjoyed between God and his people.

Finally, Chapter 8 will conclude our study by explaining how this Scriptural warrant for mutual honor in the passage allows Paul to motivate the Philippians culturally and

---

versions for interpreting Paul, see Otto Michel, "Zur Exegese von Phil 2,5-11," in *Theologie als Glaubenswagnis*, eds. K. Elliger, A. Weiser, E. Würthwein, and O. Bauernfeind (Hamburg: Furche-Verlag, 1954), 79–95, 92; Lucien Cerfaux, *Christ in the Theology of St. Paul*, trans. Geoffrey Webb and Adrian Walker (New York: Herder and Herder, 1959), 386: "Paul's quotations agree with Aquila" *against* the LXX on numerous occasions.

rhetorically so that they might respond appropriately to his exhortations by drawing on the pathos that such a mutual honor would have engendered in his audience. Although Paul diverges from the accepted Roman perspective in his radically different understanding of what types of behavior bestow honor, his approach is similar to theirs insofar as he deploys mutual honor for the purpose of motivation. Much as the Greco-Roman letter writers employed the notion of a mutual honor shared with their correspondents as family and friends for the purpose of persuasion, so too Paul uses the theological reality of a shared honor with the Philippians as his family and friends to persuade his audience to maintain unity in the face of opposition. For in "working out their own salvation in fear and trembling" (Phil 2:12), the honor of God, the honor of Paul, and the honor of the Philippians themselves are all at stake.

6

Mutual Honor in Philippians 1:25–26

In Phil 1:25–26 Paul states that surviving his imprisonment and returning to the Philippians will be for their "progress and joy in the faith," with the result that their "boasting may abound in Christ Jesus, in [Paul], through [his] coming again" to them.[1] Paul's contribution to the Philippians' boasting as outlined in this text occurs as the first move in a two-step presentation of mutual boasting in the letter, with the Philippians' contribution to Paul's boasting presented in Phil 2:16 as its counterpart. It is necessary to hold both passages in conjunction, since otherwise the picture of honor in Paul's relationship with the Philippians would lose its mutuality and become lopsided. Paul's is not the only honor in view;[2] neither are the Philippians the sole repositories of honor in the letter. Rather, the honor of the one simultaneously contributes to the honor of the other, and, hence, their honor is mutual. Were this not the case, then those scholars who claim Paul to be self-absorbed and arrogant on the one hand, or manipulative on the other, would be justified.[3] The reality, however, is that Paul holds forth the same hope for his converts as he does for himself. As he looks forward to his καύχημα on that final day (2:16), he also envisions the Philippians having a καύχημα as well (1:26). In fact, the mutual reality of a καύχημα for Paul and a καύχημα for the Philippians structures the epistle's opening chapters, providing a balanced reciprocity between apostle and community, which in turn affords the foundation for Paul's paraenesis.

Mutual Καύχημα in the Structure of Philippians 1–2

Once Paul moves out of the introductory thanksgiving and prayer for the Philippians (1:3–11), the letter's first two epistolary sections broadly entail (1) a report on Paul's

---

[1] All translations of the Greek New Testament are my own unless otherwise noted.
[2] *Pace* Russel B. Sisson, "A Common Agōn,: Ideology and Rhetorical Intertexture in Philippians," in *Fabrics of Discourse*, ed. David B. Gowler, L. Gregory Bloomquist, and Duane F. Watson (Harrisburg, PA: Trinity Press International, 2003), 242–63, 256: "In the end … the focus is on Paul's desire to secure his own prize and honor."
[3] On Paul as egocentric, see Robert T. Fortna, "Paul's Most Egocentric Letter," in *The Conversation Continues*, ed. Robert T. Fortna and Beverly R. Gaventa (Nashville, TN: Abingdon, 1990), 220–34; on Paul as manipulative, see Joseph A. Marchal, *Hierarchy, Unity, and Imitation*, SBLAB 24 (Leiden: Brill, 2006), 204, who argues that Philippians is "Paul's attempt to establish a kyriarchal relationship between the Philippian community and himself."

prison circumstances relating to his gospel ministry (1:12-26)[4] and (2) an exhortation regarding the Philippian community's circumstances in view of Paul's gospel ministry (1:27-2:18). These two sections also display a structural patterning that reflects mutuality.[5] Philippians 1:12-26 is introduced as a discussion of Paul's affairs (τὰ κατ' ἐμέ, 1:12; cf. 1:27: τὰ περὶ ὑμῶν), similar to that found in many ancient letters of the friendly, or familial, type, which often begin with a presentation of the writer's situation and well-being.[6] One striking element of Paul's presentation of his own circumstances, however, is that he speaks less about what has happened to himself and more about what has happened to the spread of the gospel. He has intertwined his own interests with the advance of the gospel, presumably with the intention of directing the Philippians' gaze *away from* the negative circumstances of his imprisonment and *toward* the progress of the gospel (cf. 1:12). In doing so, Paul's strategy is comparable to that which we adduced in Cicero's political correspondence with his friends.[7] We saw that Cicero depicted his own *dignitas* as merged with that of the State so that he could redirect the goodwill that his friends felt toward himself to the benefit of the State.[8] Here Paul makes a similar move. Presupposing the goodwill that the Philippians feel toward himself and their concern in his own situation, he merges his fate with the fate of the gospel, thereby directing any efforts that they would have undertaken to support him toward a further backing of the progress of the gospel. Of course, to support the gospel, the Philippians must support Paul (hence, their financial support described in Phil 4). Indeed, they have maintained support for the gospel in both Paul's "presence" and now in his "absence" (1:27; 2:12). Hence, the report section from 1:12-26 demonstrates the close connection between the sender and recipients of the letter specifically because it focuses on the gospel endeavor around which they have united.

---

[4] Hans Dieter Betz, *Studies in Philippians*, WUNT 343 (Tübingen: Mohr Siebeck, 2015), 125, argues that not only this preliminary section but the entire letter deals with Paul's "evaluation of his own situation" since he is responding to their request for information.

[5] Gordon D. Fee, *Paul's Letter to the Philippians*, NICNT 46 (Grand Rapids, MI: Eerdmans, 1995), 156, comments on the "formal similarity" between 1:12-26 and 1:27-2:18: "Each begins on the same note: 'my affairs/your affairs.' First person pronouns and verbs dominated 1:12-26; second plural pronouns and verbs ... dominate [1:27-2:18]. 'His affairs' concluded in a transitional way by focusing on them (vv. 24-26); this section concludes by focusing on Paul (2:16-18), also in a transitional way."

[6] Loveday Alexander, "Hellenistic Letter Forms and the Structure of Philippians," *JSNT* 37 (1989), 87-101, 92, writes about "family letters" that the formal section following the salutation and prayer wish deals with *reassurance about the sender* in which "a general reassurance about their own 'welfare' (σωτηρία)" is central to the writers' interest. See John L. White, *Light from Ancient Letters* (Minneapolis, MN: Fortress, 1986), 197, who presents as typical within the "friendly hortatory letter" (his classification for Philippians) the exchange of information that is prompted by "the correspondents' interest in each others welfare."

[7] See Chapter 5. For a similar comparison between Paul's letter to the Philippians and Cicero's letters to his friends, cf. Luc Pialoux, *L'épître aux Philippiens: L'Évangile du don et de l'amitié*, ET 75 (Leuven: Peeters, 2017), 196-7.

[8] Francis A. Sullivan, "Cicero and *Gloria*," *TAPA* 72 (1941), 382-91, 390, describes how Cicero sought to recapture the old ideal of glory as "unselfish devotion to the State." See also Cicero, *Pro Sestio* 38, in which Cicero describes how he acted "to promote not my own single glory, but the common safety of all the citizens." Cf. Joseph Hellegouarc'h, *Le Vocabulaire latin des relations et des partis politiques sous la République*, FLSHUL 11 (Paris: Les Belles Lettres, 1963), 381, who describes that, for Cicero, those who are truly virtuous "font l'intérêt commun avant leurs avantages personnels et veulent uniquement server leurs concitoyens."

Then, at 1:27, Paul begins to address the circumstances facing his readers (τὰ περὶ ὑμῶν), to which circumstances most, if not all, of his exhortations are addressed. This focus on the situation of the Philippians pervades the section of 1:27-2:30 (cf. the repetition of τὰ περὶ ὑμῶν in 2:19 and 20, thereby forming a chiasm with 1:27). The link between the two sections, first regarding Paul and then the Philippians, comes to the fore, however, in the travelogue section in 2:19-30 discussing the interchange of emissaries between apostle and community, which takes up once again the reference to Paul's circumstances (cf. τὰ περὶ ἐμέ, 2:23, forming an even larger chiasm with 1:12). This *inclusio* encompassing the situation of both Paul and the Philippians, together with the parallel structure of 1:12-26 and 1:27-2:18, highlights the mutuality between the writer and his auditors in these first two chapters.

Both sections also touch on the relative well-being of each party, with Paul's σωτηρία coming into view in the first section at 1:19,[9] and the σωτηρία of the Philippian community in the second section at both 1:28 and 2:12.[10] In Paul's case, the Philippians play an integral role in safeguarding his σωτηρία: it comes about "through [their] prayers" (1:19).[11] This emphasis on the believers' beneficial activity on behalf of their apostle is not surprising in light of the numerous references in the letter to the community's enthusiastic support of Paul's ministry (1:5, 7, 30; 2:25, 30; 4:2, 10, 14-18). In the reverse direction, Paul too seems integrally involved in the progress of these believers as a teacher and a model (4:9), both in his presence and in his absence (1:27, 30; 2:2, 12).

Moreover, the theme of mutuality between apostle and community reaches a crescendo in each respective unit when Paul introduces the language of boasting (καύχημα) in 1:26 and 2:16.[12] Moreover, this mutuality of boasting draws Christ/God

---

[9] Lukas Bormann, *Philippi: Stadt und Christengemeinde*, NovTSup 78 (Leiden: Brill, 1995), 212, argues, in light of his understanding of Paul's relationship with the Philippians as that between patron and client, that Paul's success at the trial reflects back upon the Philippians: "Dieser Prozeß ist … nicht seine Privatsache, sondern wird von den Philippern als seine ihre Zusammengehörigkeit betreffende Angelegenheit verstanden."

[10] Scholars debate about whether these uses of σωτηρία in the letter refer to sociological realities (i.e., bodily health, well-being, safety; cf. Moulton and Milligan, *Vocabulary* [London: Hodder and Stoughton, 1914-29], 622, who note that such usage is "common in the papyri") or eschatological realities (i.e., eternal destiny; cf. Moises Silva, *Philippians* [Grand Rapids, MI: Baker, 2005], 70). This study favors the latter approach in light of the importance of eschatology for Paul's thinking in the letter, though the two need not be mutually exclusive. For a detailed analysis of the issue, see Paul S. Cable, "'We Await a Savior': 'Salvation' in Philippians," Wheaton College Diss., 2017.

[11] Stefan Schapdick, *Eschatisches Heil mit eschatischer Anerkennung: Exegetische Untersuchungen zu Funktion und Sachgehalt der paulinischen Verkündigung vom eigenen Endgeschick im Rahmen seiner Korrespondenz an die Thessalonicher, Korinther und Philipper*, BBB 164 (Göttingen: Vandenhoeck & Ruprecht, 2011), 188, notes the connection between the Philippians' efforts (via prayer) to bring about their apostle's σωτηρία in 1:19 and their continued efforts (via obedience) to bring about his καύχημα in 2:14-16, though Schapdick argues, in p. 188 n. 303, for a distinction between the "eschatische Heil als solches" depicted in 1:19 and the "eschatischer Anerkennung" represented in 2:16. This study follows Schapdick in viewing Paul's καύχημα in 2:16 as representing affirmation from God for the apostle's work rather than Paul's eternal destiny.

[12] See Mark. A. Jennings, *The Price of Partnership in the Letter of Paul to the Philippians: "Make My Joy Complete"*, LNTS 578 (London: Bloomsbury T&T Clark, 2018), 118, who notes the coherence between 1:26 and 2:16 such that when the two verses are read in tandem we see how "Paul's and the Philippians' labors for one another contribute to each other's eschatological blessing in Christ. Philippians 2:16b complements Paul's desire … in 1:26."

into the matrix already established between Paul and the Philippians, thereby depicting a threefold interrelationship that includes all three parties. Bouttier describes well this tripartite mutuality of honor reflected in Phil 1:26:

> What unites [Paul] with the Philippians unites him with Christ. Paul's only "boasting" *in Christo* is expressed in the fact that henceforth, and equally, the members of Christ have become with him what he has become for the others. Consequently, *this mutual "glorification"* does not arise from any mutual complacence ... The glory that they receive from each other comes not from any success, but from Christ alone, from Christ in them as in him.[13]

We will see in 2:16 that the section discussing "the things regarding" the *Philippians* (τὰ περὶ ὑμῶν) culminates in an appeal that they would bring about *Paul's* καύχημα.[14] In 1:26, alternately, the discussion about "the things regarding" *Paul* (τὰ κατ' ἐμέ) climaxes with the assurance of abundant boasting for the *Philippian* community.[15]

The Philippians' Καύχημα Resulting from Paul's *Syncrisis*

In light of Paul's conviction that his physical presence is necessary for the Philippians to thrive (1:24–26), Paul concludes both his *syncrisis* from 1:21–24[16] and his entire section focused on τὰ κατ' ἐμέ in 1:12–26[17] by laying out his projected visit (παρουσία) in vv. 25–26. Such references to the apostolic presence or "travel notes" often form components of Paul's letters,[18] but their function goes beyond merely presenting an anticipated itinerary; as Funk notes, they often treat apostolic status and eschatology.[19] In Philippians, Paul's conviction about his future visit (cf. 1:25a: τοῦτο πεποιθώς) emerges ultimately out of a conviction that living for Christ requires putting aside

---

[13] Michel Bouttier, *Christianity According to Paul*, trans. Frank Clarke (London: SCM Press, 1966), 62–3 (emphasis added).
[14] Ernst Synofzik, *Die Gerichts- und Vergeltungsaussagen bei Paulus*, GTA 8 (Göttingen: Vandenhoeck & Ruprecht, 1977), 23, points to Paul's "Versicherung der bis ins Eschaton geltenden Zusammengehörigkeit von Apostel und Gemeinde," evident in such texts as 2 Cor 1:14 and 1 Thess 2:19–20.
[15] Cf. Fee, *Philippians*, 249.
[16] Lukas Bormann, "Reflexionen über Sterben und Tod bei Paulus," in *Das Ende des Paulus: Historische, theologische und literaturgeschichtliche Aspekte*, ed. F. W. Horn, BZNW 106 (Berlin: de Gruyter, 2001), 307–30, 320, describes how Paul reevaluates life and death in light of his existence in Christ, drawing attention to the *two-way amplification of boasting* experienced by apostle and community: "Leben und Sterben sind keine Werte an sich, sondern ihre Bedeutsamkeit mißt sich an der Einbindung in den Prozeß der gegenseitigen Mehrung des καύχημα, des eschatologischen Ruhms."
[17] The *inclusio* formed by προκοπή in 1:12 and 1:25 support taking vv. 25–26 as the climax to 1:12–26.
[18] See Terence Mullins, "Visit Talk in the New Testament Letters," *CBQ* 35 (1973), 350–8.
[19] Robert W. Funk, *Language, Hermeneutic and Word of God* (New York: Harper & Row, 1966), 265, argues that in Philippians "the travelogue forms a distinct but closely related unit, which appears to permit, or even to demand, a conclusion that embraces an eschatological motif." Cf. Robert W. Funk, "The Apostolic Parousia: Its Form and Significance," in *Christian History and Interpretation*, ed. W. R. Farmer (Cambridge: Cambridge University Press, 1967), 249–68, 265: "Paul must have thought of his presence as the bearer of charismatic, one might even say, eschatological, power."

one's own desires for the sake of serving the gospel and benefiting others.[20] In fact, the conclusion in vv. 25-26 bolsters Paul's overall argument in the letter that the needs of fellow believers should stand above one's own (2:4, 17, 20, 25; 4:14-16), though he presents this by way of self-disclosure for the purpose of modeling self-sacrificial service (cf. 3:17 and 4:9).[21]

Grammatical Analysis of Philippians 1:25-26

The text of Phil 1:25-26 can be divided logically as follows:

25a Καὶ τοῦτο πεποιθὼς
25b οἶδα ὅτι μενῶ
25c καὶ παραμενῶ πᾶσιν ὑμῖν
25d εἰς τὴ ὑμῶν προκοπὴν καὶ χαρὰν τῆς πίστεως,
26a ἵνα τὸ καύχημα ὑμῶν περισσεύῃ
26b ἐν Χριστῷ Ἰησοῦ
26c ἐν ἐμοί
26d διὰ τῆς ἐμῆς παρουσίας πάλιν πρὸς ὑμᾶς.

25a And being confident of this
25b I know that I will remain
25c and I will stand fast with all of you
25d for the goal of (εἰς) your progress and of (your) faith,
26a in order that your claim to honor might abound
26b in the sphere of (ἐν) Christ Jesus
26c in the sphere of (ἐν) me
26d by means of my presence again with you.

It is clear in this passage that Paul wants the Philippians to enjoy an abundant καύχημα; indeed, he has forgone his own preference to bring this about. What remains unclear is how the three prepositions following περισσεύῃ in v. 26b-d correlate.[22] It is best to

---

[20] Georges Didier, *Désintéressement du Chrétien: La rétribution dans la morale de saint Paul*, Théo 32 (Paris: Aubier, 1955), 170: "Le bonheur personnel d'être avec le Christ se trouve donc sacrifié aux besoins apostoliques." Joseph A. Marchal, "Mutuality Rhetorics and Feminist Interpretation," *BCT* 1.3 (2005), 1-17, 2, notes that Paul displays in Phil 1:21-24 "how his actions ... are primarily oriented toward the benefit of the community," illustrating a dissociation "between self-benefit and community-benefit," and thereby presenting "unity and communal benefit as guiding values" for the Philippians. Marchal further notes, in p. 3, that "three more times ... Paul extols his own model through his apparent concern with the benefit of the community (2:17; 3:1; and 4:17)." Peter-Ben Smit, *Paradigms of Being in Christ*, LNTS 476 (London: T&T Clark, 2013), 65, argues that Phil 1:19-26 reflects "the orientation of Paul away from his own interests towards the interests of the Philippians in the midst of his suffering."

[21] Troels Engberg-Pedersen, *Paul and the Stoics* (Edinburgh: T&T Clark, 2000), 129: "In 1:12-30 [Paul] plays out, even *acts*, his own bending down to the Philippians, thus self-description constitutes a model for his converts. Stefano Bittasi, "La prigionia di Paolo nella lettera ai Filippesi e il problema di una sua morte possibile. 1," *RdT* 45 (2004), 19-34, 23, labels 1:12-26 as "une *periautologia*," since Paul speaks about himself for the purpose of modeling ethical behavior for his readers.

[22] Carolyn Osiek, *Philippians, Philemon* (Nashville, TN: Abingdon, 2000), 45, describes v. 26 as a "syntactical jumble." Cf. I-Jin Louw and Eugene Nida, *A Translator's Handbook on Paul's Letter to the*

interpret all three prepositional phrases adverbially as modifying, in respective ways, the verb περισσεύῃ.²³ Hence, both ἐν Χριστῷ²⁴ and ἐν ἐμοί provide the *sphere* in which the Philippians' boasting abounds, while διὰ τῆς παρουσίας provides the *means* by which it abounds: "in order that your boast might abound in the sphere of Christ Jesus, in the sphere of me, by means of my presence again with you."²⁵ The parallel positioning of ἐν Χριστῷ with ἐν ἐμοί²⁶ favors viewing the Philippians' boast, or claim to honor, as abounding both in Christ Jesus and in Paul,²⁷ thereby including Paul within the gamut of honor associated with the Philippians' boasting.²⁸ Rather than merely serving as the means through which the Philippians' boast emerges, Paul joins with Christ as the sphere in which the Philippians' boast abounds. Hence, the Philippians acquire a claim to honor that is amplified by taking place within the realm of Christ's honor, while at the same time being amplified by taking place within the realm of Paul's honor.

Paul's Honorable Self-Sacrifice in Philippians 1:21–26

The reason that the Philippians' boast gains from abounding in the sphere of Paul in addition to abounding in the sphere of Christ is due to Paul's honorable behavior vis-à-vis them as depicted in 1:21–26. This honorable behavior begins with Paul's unique

---

Philippians (New York: UBS, 1977), 36: the grammar is "somewhat obscure"; Fee, *Philippians*, 154: it is "a bit strained in its expression"; and Betz, *Philippians*, 138: it is a "contorted sentence."

[23] See the discussion by Ragnar Asting, "*Kauchesis*. Et bidrag til forståelsen av den religiøse selvfølelse hos Paulus," *NTT* 26 (1925), 129–204, 141, who draws on Adolf Deissman (*Die neutestamentliche Formel 'in Christo Jesu'* [Marburg: N. G. Elwertsche Verlagsbuchhandlung, 1892], 57–8, 64–5): "When ἐν occurs with καυχᾶσθαι it describes *the area where boasting (or rejoicing) has its source and within which the laudatory statements about oneself (or out-breaking of cheers) move*" (my translation of Asting, emphasis original).

[24] Lyder Brun, "Zur Formel 'In Christus' im Brief des Paulus an die Philipper," *SO* 1 (1922), 19–37, 33–4, argues that "the stuff of boasting (*Ruhmesstoff*) for the Philippians, that is, the results/produce (*Ertrag*) which they would have from the *parousia* of Paul and in which they would boast, will abound 'in Christ Jesus,' that is, in the realm of activity ruled by him" (my translation). Florian Wilk, "Ruhm *coram Deo* bei Paulus?" *ZNW* 101 (2010), 55–77, 58 n. 25, argues that ἐν Χριστῷ provides the "Bezugsrahmen (und nicht den Gegenstand) des Rühmens" of the Philippians in 1:26.

[25] J. B. Lightfoot, *Saint Paul's Epistle to the Philippians: A Revised Text with Introduction, Notes, and Dissertations* (London: MacMillan, 1908), 94, interprets the first ἐν denoting "the sphere in which their pride lives," and the second "the object on which it rests." Similarly, Louw and Nida, *Philippians*, 37, "The Philippian Christians' pride in Paul is developed in the sphere of Christ Jesus."

[26] John H. P. Reumann, *Philippians: A New Translation with Introduction and Commentary*, AB 33B (New Haven, CT: Yale University Press, 2008), 230, notes a textual variant, however, that emphasizes Paul in the sentence, by placing ἐν ἐμοί *before* ἐν Χριστῷ (F G f g).

[27] Davorlin Peterlin, *Paul's Letter to the Philippians in the Light of Disunity in the Church*, NovTSup 79 (Leiden: Brill, 1995), 46, argues that ἐν ἐμοι should be viewed in conjunction with ἐν Χριστῷ Ἰησοῦ, though he interprets both phrases as providing the object of the noun καύχημα, whereas I see them modifying the verb. See also Alexander N. Kirk, *Departure of an Apostle: Paul's Death Anticipated and Remembered*, WUNT 2.406 (Tübingen: Mohr Siebeck, 2015), 203, who similarly finds no problem with Paul contributing toward the Philippians' abundant boasting: "It is no contradiction to claim that the Philippians could boast in Paul while boasting only in Christ Jesus."

[28] Reumann, *Philippians*, 230, notes that the emphatic form of the pronoun (ἐμοί) is "expected after the prep[osition]," citing BDF §279. Paul's use of the first-person pronoun (fifty-two times in the letter) is a recognizable aspect of his intimate communication with the Philippians. Cf. Brian J. Dodd, *Paul's Paradigmatic "I": Personal Example as Literary Strategy*, LNTS 177 (Sheffield: Sheffield Academic Press, 1999), 171.

perspective on life and death presented in 1:21. The maxim "to live is Christ; to die is gain"[29] represents the apostle's Christological response to the upcoming Roman trial that will decide his earthly fate.[30] It poses two alternatives, life or death, reinterpreting them through an inversion brought about by his experience of conformity with Christ so that death no longer represents an evil but is rather a good, because it means immediate access to Christ (σὺν Χριστῷ εἶναι, v. 23).[31] Similarly transformed, however, is Paul's view of life, which now also entails Christ insofar as it provides a continued experience of empowerment from Christ (4:13, cf. 2:13) to labor for the gospel about Christ (1:5–7, 12–13, 16; 2:22; 3:20–21; 4:3). This is clear from the fact that Paul's "fruitful labor" (1:22) involves a continuation of his efforts on behalf of the gospel to produce fruit (4:17), much like the Philippians' own conduct was to produce "the fruit of righteousness," which came only *through Jesus Christ* (1:11). Both options, life and death, thus intimately involve Christ. Accordingly, Paul makes it clear which option he prefers, and which he chooses despite this preference,[32] manifesting that he has sacrificed his own ἐπιθυμία (1:23) for the sake of the Philippians (cf. ἀναγκαιότερον in 1:24) and thereby modeling the type of moral discernment for which he prays on their behalf (1:9).[33]

Frederick Danker proposes that in Phil 1:12–26 Paul casts himself in the honorific role of the "endangered benefactor," that is, someone who willingly undertakes dangerous situations for the service of others.[34] Paul's use of this theme involves a major variation, however, because Paul here undertakes the *avoidance* of physical death to pursue life, though it is a life lived in service to others. Ironically, then, the danger is that Paul voluntarily reenters the battlefield of ministry (via life!), rather than retiring to the safety of being with Christ (via death!). He chooses to "remain," and this choice is honorable insofar as it involves taking up again the ἀγών of the gospel (1:30).

Lohmeyer's insight that the verb παραμενῶ in 1:25 could be used in contexts of slavery[35] corroborates the idea that the life which Paul takes up again is one of service

---

[29] Cf. Betz, *Philippians*, 24.
[30] For a discussion of Paul's *syncrisis* in this passage, see Samuel Vollenweider, "Die Waagschalen von Leben und Tod: Zum Antiken Hintergrund von Phil 1,21-26," *ZNW* 85 (1994), 93–115, who places Paul's discussion in conjunction with Greco-Roman comparisons between life and death. Cf. Paul A. Holloway, "Deliberating Life and Death: Paul's Tragic *Dubitatio* in Philippians 1:22–26," *HTR* 111 (2018), 174–9, who alternately labels this section as an instance of *dubitatio*, a monologue in which speakers reveal their decision-making process, and offers Greco-Roman parallels.
[31] For a classic discussion of this passage, see Jacques Dupont's section in ΣΥΝ ΧΡΙΣΤΩΙ: *L'union avec le Christ suivant Saint Paul* (Paris: Desclée, 1952), "Art. III: 'Dissolvi et esse cum Christo,'" 171–87.
[32] Scholars debate whether Paul had the power to bring about his decision to "remain." For some, Paul's "choice" (αἱρέομαι, 1:22) means that he could implicate himself at the trial and thereby ensure his execution, yet Paul's conviction that the Philippians require his presence leads him to forego this pseudo-suicidal option. See A. J. Droge, "*Mori Lucrum*: Paul and Ancient Theories of Suicide," *NovT* 30 (1988), 263–86. The reality of the choice is in some ways a moot point, since in the rhetoric of the letter he presents it as in his power and develops his self-sacrificial epistolary persona on that basis.
[33] Cf. Pialoux, *Philippiens*, 186, who describes how the apostle orients the elements of his *narratio* in 1:18-26: "d'une manière particulière et intentionnelle, qui reflète et illustre un point déjà annoncé en 1,9: le souhait de perfection morale."
[34] Frederick W. Danker, *Benefactor: An Epigraphic Study* (St. Louis, MO: Clayton, 1982), 425. Paul employs the endangered benefactor motif again in Philippians when characterizing Epaphroditus, who has "drawn near to the point of death" on behalf of the Philippian believers (2:30).
[35] Ernst Lohmeyer, *Die Briefe an die Philipper, Kolosser und an Philemon*, KEK (Göttingen: Vandenhoeck & Ruprecht, 1954), 67 n. 3. Cf. Hauck, "παραμενῶ," *TDNT* 4.577: "To remain in a place or spot," [opposite] to run away, [especially] of a slave," citing Plato, *Men.* 97e.

(cf. δοῦλοι in 1:1), whereas the death that he forsakes would have entailed a victorious, and therefore less strenuous, reunion with his Lord. Paul's insistence throughout the letter on presenting such slavery to the needs of others as honorable (cf. 1:1; 2:7, 22) allows us to connect Danker's notion of Paul's honorable status as an "endangered benefactor" with Lohmeyer's idea of Paul as returning to a post of slave-like service among the Philippians. Hence, while Paul presents himself as constricted by, and, in a way, "enslaved" to the needs of the Philippians,[36] this self-willed lowering in status by the apostle reflects the self-sacrifice that Christ's vindication in the hymn now makes honorable. That is, Paul's choice to remain with the Philippians in 1:25 is essentially an act that should bring *Paul* honor, but what we find in v. 26 is that it is *the Philippians* who also acquire the abundant boast resulting from Paul's choice. This sharing of honor rests, as will be argued below, on the metaphorical kinship relation shared between Paul and his readers, which at the same time is expressed in a letter style associated with friends.

Paul's Honor Abounding to the Philippians

In Phil 1:25–26 there are ultimately two distinct, though associated, goals for Paul's divine reassignment to ministry in Philippi.[37] First, his return to the Philippians is meant to facilitate their "advance" (προκοπή) and "joy in the faith" (1:25). The military metaphor evinced throughout this section (cf. προκοπή in 1:25,[38] followed by στήκω in 1:27 [cf. 4:1], both of which are well-represented in ancient military parlance)[39] illumines the idea of Paul's return. As Krentz adduces, "A general should not be absent from battle, but should exhort the troops and lead them into war."[40] Paul's characterization of the Philippians' success as their προκοπή could additionally bear honorific implications. For instance, a later honorific epitaph (ca. 300 CE) refers to the

---

[36] Paul A. Holloway, *Philippians: A Commentary*, Hermeneia (Minneapolis, MN: Fortress Press, 2017), 96, recognizes this aspect in which Paul depicts the Philippians as hindering him as a result of their lack of maturity, though Holloway needlessly presents this as burdensome to the apostle ("the constraints their failings are placing on him"), which contradicts the apostle's own self-presentation in which he sacrifices his desires willingly and joyfully.

[37] Mark J. Keown, *Philippians 1:1–2:18*, EEC (Bellingham, WA: Lexham Press, 2017), 186, notes the military overtones of Paul's statement in 1:16 that he has been "stationed" (κεῖμαι) where he is for the defense of the gospel. Cf. Keown, *Philippians*, 177, where Keown previews that "arguably κεῖμαι, 'appoint'" represents military language; Paul is "an appointed general" (p. 291).

[38] The military overtones of the term προκοπή have been adduced by numerous scholars; see Johan S. Vos, *Die Kunst der Argumentation bei Paulus: Studien zur antiken Rhetorik*, WUNT 149 (Tübingen: Mohr Siebeck, 2002), 142; Edgar Krentz, "Paul, Games, and the Military," in *Paul in the Greco-Roman World*, ed. J. Paul Sampley (Harrisburg, PA: Trinity Press International, 2003), 344–83, 361.

[39] Mikael Tellbe, *Paul between Synagogue and State: Christians, Jews, and Civic Authorities in 1 Thessalonians, Romans, and Philippians*, CB 34 (Stockholm: Almqvist & Wiksell, 2001), 248. Other instances of military language in Philippians include Paul's reference to Epaphroditus as his "fellow-soldier" (2:25) and to his coworkers as "fellow-athletes in the struggle" for the gospel (1:27; 4:3). Cf. Gordon Mark Zerbe, *Philippians*, Believers Church Bible Commentary (Waterloo: Herald Press, 2016), 178; Gordon Mark Zerbe, *Citizenship: Paul on Peace and Politics* (Winnipeg: CMU Press, 2012), 131–2.

[40] Krentz, "Games," 360.

προκοπή of a certain Rufinus, most likely alluding to "the advancement of Rufinus' career."[41] The combination of these various settings in which the term προκοπή would have been used in ancient Philippi, all of which are positive instances of success, prepares the way for the overtly honorific term καύχημα in 1:26.[42]

This goal of the Philippians' advancement and joy with respect to their faith culminates in a yet more far-reaching effect, namely, that the Philippians' καύχημα would abound (1:26).[43] Though not typically connected to the field of military metaphors in Paul's usage,[44] καύχημα fits well as the crescendo of the preceding martial dialogue.[45] Thus, in 1:26, once the Philippians receive their captain back, they press forward in a final and successful assault that results in rejoicing (χαρά) and an effulgence of boasting in the realm of the Savior who empowered their victory (ἐν Χριστῷ Ἰησοῦ) and in the realm of Paul who spearheaded the attack (ἐν ἐμοί).[46] Paul's presentation of himself, a prisoner, as a returning victorious leader represents a "massive paradigm shift" for the Philippians.[47] In a foreshadowing of the radical reorientation that will occur in the Christ-event narrated in Phil 2:9–11, where a crucified rebel-slave is ultimately acclaimed as the glorious Lord, Paul presents in 1:26 an "alternate 'court of reputation'"[48] for the Philippians, since their boasting is tied to the slaves, Jesus (2:7) and Paul (1:1).

---

[41] *IG* XIV 1976, cited in G. H. R. Horsley, "10. A Judicial Career Cut Short," *New Docs* 4 (1979), 35–6. Cf. also the prominent Stoic usage of προκοπή to affirm individuals who advance in wisdom and virtue, as noted by Engberg-Pedersen, *Paul and the Stoics*, 70–2.

[42] Stephen E. Fowl, *Philippians*, THNTC (Grand Rapids, MI: Eerdmans, 2005), 54: "In the Greco-Roman world, boasting is quite compatible with a cultural system based on honor and shame. It is a way of rightly locating honor."

[43] Timothy C. Geoffrion, *The Rhetorical Purpose and the Political and Military Character of Philippians* (Lampeter: Mellen Biblical Press, 1993), 176: "As much as Paul is affirming his devotion to the Philippians, it is equally clear that the goal of his devotion is the status of their faith and 'boast in Christ Jesus.'"

[44] Within Greco-Roman literature, the καυχ- word-group (including the similar αὐχ- stem) appears conspicuously in the athletic word field (which is closely linked with the military word field). Note its usage by Pindar: *I.* 5.51: "drench your boast (καύχαμα) in a reign of silence" (here referring to the "celebration of the military victories of [Pindar's] fatherland," as noted by Silvia Montiglio, *Silence in the Land of Logos* [Princeton, NJ: Princeton University Press, 2010], 112); *O.* 9.38: "to revile the Gods is an odious art, and to boast [καυχᾶσθαι] beyond measure"; *N.* 9.7: "hide not on the ground in silence a noble thing [καύχας] done," celebrating athletic victories. Louis Robert, *Les gladiateurs dans l'Orient grec* (Amsterdam: Adolf M. Hakkert, 1971), 302–3, calls attention to the use of the verb καυχᾶσθαι in gladiatorial epitaphs, where "le sentiment de la gloire" looms large; cf. §34 (pp. 94–5) and §107 (p. 146–7). See also the militaristic use of the noun καύχημα as an honorific epithet for Judith after she strikes down Olofornes (Judith 15:9: σὺ καύχημα μέγα τοῦ γένους ἡμῶν).

[45] Johan S. Vos, "Philippians 1:12–26 and the Rhetoric of Success," in *Rhetoric, Ethic, and Moral Persuasion in Biblical Discourse: Essays from the 2002 Heidelberg Conference*, ed. Thomas Olbricht and Anders Eriksson, ESEC 11 (London: T&T Clark International, 2005), 274–83, 283, argues that in this passage Paul is using "a rhetorical strategy very similar to one featured in ancient military handbooks" (p. 277), and points to the culmination of success as characterized by the boasting of both the Philippians and Paul. Gerald F. Hawthorne and Ralph P. Martin, *Philippians*, WBC 43 (Milton Keynes: Word Books, 2004), 147, note regarding Paul's καύχημα in 2:16 that this "prize is like a military victory."

[46] Schapdick, *Heil*, 177, recognizes about 1:26 that the Philippians' καύχημα is first "verortet und legitimiert" by Christ, yet still "der Fokus wendet sich wieder dem Apostel zu."

[47] Tellbe, *Synagogue and State*, 269.

[48] Tellbe, *Synagogue and State*, 269.

Paul uses the term καύχημα in 1:26 to designate the honorific, oftentimes, eschatological outcome that emerges from his relationship with his churches.⁴⁹ The eschatological element⁵⁰ emerges from the rare combination of καύχημα with the verb περισσεύω. This is the only time Paul uses a noun from the καυχ- word group with περισσεύω, a verb that he used earlier when describing the community's eschatological goal of purity on the day of Christ (1:9–10).⁵¹ A final, climactic outflow of boasting for himself, for his communities, and for Christ is something that the apostle envisions as taking place on the day of Christ.

This depiction of mutual honor for Paul and the Philippians in 1:26 is not meant to diminish the central role that Jesus holds in this experience of honor. The Philippians' boasting, which Paul's return will bring about, abounds first and foremost "in the realm of Christ Jesus." As the pious one of Sir 9:16 finds his claim to honor (καύχημα) "in (ἐν) the realm of the fear of the Lord," that is, fear of YHWH represents the primary framework for this individual's claim to honor, so too in 1:26 the Philippians can hope to acquire in the realm of Christ their eschatological honor, just as Paul himself does (cf. Rom 15:17). Their eschatological claim to honor will abound in the realm of Christ's lordship and in the realm of Paul's ministry as well. Paul's mediatorial role in bringing about honor for his community is evident in this verse. Hence, scholars can speak of a "hierarchy of agency and honor" moving from Christ to Paul to the Philippians.⁵² This chain represents no one-directional hierarchy, however, since the honor clearly flows in the reciprocal direction in 2:16, as we will see in the following chapter. In 1:26, Christ's honor provides the fund from which the Philippians' honor is drawn. Their honor is therefore linked with that of Christ as well as with that of Paul. Paul's presence with them will provide the basis for this abundant boasting, but, more foundationally, Christ himself will provide its basis, since he supplies the power undergirding Paul's own ministry (Phil 1:21; 4:13).

---

⁴⁹ For a similar eschatological interpretation of the boast in 1:26, see Wolfgang Schenk, *Die Philipperbriefe des Paulus: Kommentar* (Stuttgart: Kohlhammer, 1984), 162, who argues that ἐν Χριστῷ Ἰησοῦ is a shortened form of the full, eschatologically anchored phrase ἐν ἡμέρα Χριστοῦ Ἰησοῦ. Pace Schapdick, *Heil*, 177, who sees this use of καύχημα as "rein innerweltliche." Betz, *Philippians*, 138, argues that Paul's return to Philippi would lead "ultimately to their eschatological success (καύχημα) on the Day of Christ." See too David E. Briones, *Paul's Financial Policy*, LNTS 494 (London: T&T Clark, 2013), 91: "When placing their καύχημα in conjunction with Paul's in 2.16, we discover that their boast will not only occur when their apostle arrives into Philippi but also on the day of Christ."

⁵⁰ Lohmeyer, *Philipper*, 69, speaks of Paul's contribution, alongside that of Christ, to the Philippians' boast being "eschatologically determined" via the ἐν ἐμοί phrase, just as it is "historically determined" via the διὰ τῆς παρουσίας μου phrase. Betz, *Philippians*, 16, points to 1:26 as having "an eschatological epilogue" in which Paul unveils, as he does elsewhere in the letter, his "eschatological hope" of καύχημα. See also Jennings, *Partnership*, 118: "In 1:26, Paul says that the Philippians will have a reason for eschatological boasting because of his actions toward them."

⁵¹ Reumann, *Philippians*, 257, accordingly characterizes περισσεύω "as an eschatological term."

⁵² Sisson, "Agōn," 254. Cf. Sisson, "Agōn," 253:

> Paul here speaks of a "ground of boasting" (καύχημα) that he and the Philippians will share, but Paul puts particular emphasis on how his presence among the Philippians is essential to helping them secure this eschatological honor … Paul's words evoke the idea of a hierarchical chain of agents responsible for helping the Philippians secure their salvation. Paul is the immediate agent, but above him is Christ whom he models for the Philippians.

Sisson here draws on Engberg-Pedersen, *Paul and the Stoics*, 127.

Some interpret Paul's reference to καύχημα in 1:26 within the framework of the patron-client relationship. Bormann asserts that in 1:26 Paul formulates an idea that is anchored "im Patronatsdenken."[53] In Bormann's analysis, Paul depicts himself in 1:18–26 as fulfilling his side of the patron–client relationship that he experiences with the Philippians, namely, his faithful proclamation of the gospel and his periodic presence (παρουσία) with this community.[54] Hence, the Philippian believers participate in the honor (i.e., they receive an abundant boast) that accrues from their patron's faithful upholding of his patronal duties. This is seconded by Schmeller, who describes the situation in this passage as one in which "das Prestige eines Patrons färbt gleichsam auf die Klienten ab."[55] The patron-client model, however, is not sufficient to explicate fully the relational dynamics shared between Paul and his community.[56] Still, it will be shown below that this element of the patron's honor attaching itself to clients bears similarities to the group honor in which the family participates. And since Paul clearly presents himself as the superior family member, it would have been recognizable to his Romanized audience that they could expect to participate in Paul's honor much like clients expected to participate in their patron's honor.[57]

Paul's παρουσία, referred to in 1:26 and alluded to again in 1:27 and 2:12, 24, along with signifying presence, can also convey honorific implications. This term was used to describe the arrival of a prominent individual into a city. As Beare describes, Paul's return will be like "the ceremonious entry of a king or governor into a city, with all the manifestations of joy which attended it," at which time Paul "will receive a king's welcome from them."[58] Beare probably overstates his case, but it remains true that Paul's παρουσία would have provided the prospect of an honorable entrance for Paul, which will more importantly establish honor for the Philippians themselves. Oepke thus speaks of the many honors paid when a district was "favoured by the *parousia* of the king or his ministers," with such a παρουσία at times representing "a ray of hope for those in trouble" and therefore sought after.[59] So when Paul uses the term to refer to his own arrival here in 1:26, it appears that his coming as God's minister brings with it honors for those receiving him, which is why their boasting abounds.[60] The

---

[53] Bormann, *Philippi*, 215.
[54] Bormann, *Philippi*, 214.
[55] Thomas Schmeller, *Hierarchie und Egalität: Eine sozialgeschichtliche Untersuchung paulinischer Gemeinden und griechisch-römischer Vereine*, SB 162 (Stuttgart: GmbH, 1995), 57.
[56] For a helpful critique of Bormann's model, see Briones, *Paul's Financial Policy*, 76–7, who argues that the unequal relationship between Paul and his Philippian converts espoused by Bormann downplays God's presence in the relationship, since the letter evinces "a three-way bond" that includes God.
[57] Cf. the comment by Pheme Perkins, "Philippians: Theology for the Heavenly Politeuma," in *Pauline Theology Vol. I*, ed. J. Bassler (Minneapolis, MN: Fortress Press, 1991), 89–104, 100: "When Paul equates his own success with that of his churches (2:16), he could also be referring to such [athletic] images, for the patron of a runner, who has provided material support for his training, could be described as being crowned when his protégé became victorious" (referring to White, *Letters*, 38).
[58] F. W. Beare, *A Commentary on the Epistle to the Philippians*, 3rd ed., BNTC (London: Adam & Charles Black, 1969), 63. Cf. Kirk, *Departure*, 203: "To boast in Paul at his coming would be to receive him with joy and honor him appropriately (cf. 2:29)."
[59] A. Oepke, "παρουσία," *TDNT* 5.860.
[60] The apostle's return would also represent Paul's vindication in his upcoming Roman trial, similar to the vindication that Jesus experiences following his crucifixion at the hands of the Roman government as narrated in 2:9–10.

Philippians participate in the honor of their returning apostle so that it is *their* boasting that abounds as a result of *his* activity as described in 1:18–26. As the letter progresses, however, Paul places the ball in the court of the Philippians, invoking them to fulfill *their* side of the relationship, preserving the group's honor by maintaining unity and persevering for the gospel (2:2, 16; 4:1).

The Mutual Honor of Friends and Family in Philippians 1:26

Although Paul's honor is portrayed in the images of a military campaign and the arrival of a prominent political figure, not to mention its reference back to the link between Paul's faithfulness and the faithfulness of Christ, the way in which Paul's honor in this passage contributes to the honor of the Philippians would have been understood *culturally* within the dual paradigms of shared family honor and shared honor among friends as set forth in Part 2 of our study. As we have noted, scholars have observed that Paul's relay of information regarding his own endangered situation in 1:12–26 correlates with the typical aim of letters designed to convey personal news to someone with whom one shares an intimate relationship.[61]

The Mutual Honor of Friends in Philippians 1:26

One such relationship of intimacy is that between friends, and numerous scholars have pointed to friendship terminology present in Philippians.[62] For example, in antiquity it was expected that friends would be emotionally invested in one another,[63] and Paul effusively displays his emotional connection with the Philippians throughout the letter (see 1:7, 8; 2:2, 12, 17, 18, 19, 28; 4:1, 10).[64] Moreover, the recurrence of the κοιν- word group, especially prominent in Paul's depictions of his own relationship with the Philippians (1:5; 4:14), reflects the well-known adage: κοινὰ τὰ φίλων.[65] Similarly, the

---

[61] Cf. Alexander, "Letter Forms," 92.
[62] See especially L. Michael White, "Morality between Two Worlds," in *Greeks, Romans, and Christians*, ed. David L. Balch, E. Ferguson, and Wayne A. Meeks (Minneapolis, MN: Fortress Press, 1990), 201–15; cf. *Friendship, Flattery and Frankness*, ed. John T. Fitzgerald, NovTSup 82 (New York: E. J. Brill, 1996). The following paragraph draws on John T. Fitzgerald, "Philippians in the Light of Friendship," in *Friendship, Flattery and Frankness*, ed. John T. Fitzgerald, 141–60, 144–7. See also Rainer Metzner, "In aller Freundschaft," *NTS* 48 (2002), 111–31, 119, who argues that "Der freundschaftliche Grundton des Philipperbriefes ist für das Schreiben prägend."
[63] See Seneca, *Ep.* 109.15; Aristotle, *Eth. nic.* 1167a; Cicero, *Amic.* 20. Cf. Stanley K. Stowers, "Friends and Enemies in the Politics of Heaven," in *Pauline Theology*, ed. Jouette Bassler (Minneapolis, MN: Fortress, 1991), 105–21, 109: "Expressions of affection and longing to be with one's friends were considered appropriate for letters of friendship."
[64] This emotional component of Paul's correspondence with the Philippian believers anticipates that of the later second-century letter writer, Fronto, whose correspondence is soaked with emotion; see David E. Fredrickson, *Eros and the Christ: Longing and Envy in Paul's Christology* (Minneapolis, MN: Fortress Press, 2013), 11–34.
[65] Aristotle, *Eth. nic.* 1168b; Plat, *Lys.* 207C; Diogenes Laertius 8.10; 10.11. Cf. Aristotle, *Eth. nic.* 1161b: "All friendship ... involves community" (ἐν κοινωνίᾳ μὲν οὖν πᾶσα φιλία ἐστίν). See Martin Ebner, *Leidenslisten und Apostelbrief: Untersuchungen zu Form, Motivik und Funktion der Peristasenkataloge bei Paulus*, FB 66 (Würzburg: Echter Verlag, 1991), 358: "Damit stehen

abundance of the σύν preposition reflects the close connection between Paul and this community (1:7; 2:17–18; 3:17; 4:14), along with his description that they participate in "the same" (τὸν αὐτόν) struggle in which he is engaged (1:30). The presence and absence motif that Paul uses (1:26, 27; 2:12) was also prominent within friendship letters in antiquity, creating the accompanying longing for each other felt by friends.[66]

The presence of such friendship terminology reflects the close intimacy shared between Paul and the Philippians, a relationship that bore accompanying expectations. One important outcome from the friendship relationship, as we saw in Chapter 4, was that friends participated in a mutual relationship of honor.[67] That is, the virtuous actions of one friend contributed toward the honor of the other, with the expectation that true friends acted to bring about honor for each other. As Cicero affirmed, an individual should seek to "[enhance] (*ampliores*) the dignity of all his friends" and to "be the source of honour and influence (*eorum augeant opes eisque honori sint et dignitati*)" for them.[68] This is precisely how Paul presents his own decision in Phil 1:21–26. The apostle shows that his actions are determined not by his own preference but by that which is more beneficial for the Philippians,[69] that which will ultimately lead to the amplification of their honor.

The Mutual Honor of Siblings in Philippians 1:26

In addition to the literary evidence surveyed in Chapter 4, Hellerman has demonstrated from the honorific inscriptions of first-century Philippi the pervasive reality of the concept of mutual honor among family members that forms an essential aspect of the cultural context of Paul's letter. He observes that "the great majority of more than seven hundred inscriptions unearthed in [Philippi] portray one family member honoring another and thereby securing public recognition for the broader kinship unit."[70] Against this backdrop, it would make intuitive cultural sense to the Philippians that in addition to their being his "friends," Paul could also speak of his actions contributing to their honor as his "siblings" (ἀδελφοί), since together they participated in the honor possessed by the family group. This is precisely how family

---

die Konnotationen von (συγ-)κοινωνεῖν in Phil 4,14 und 4,15 völlig parallel zu den aufgezeigten wesentlichen Komponenten der Koinonia in der Freundschaftsethik."

[66] Metzner, "Freundschaft," 120, notes that despite bodily absence friends are "geistig miteinander in Konstanz und Loyalität verbunden," citing Ps. Libanius, *Epist. Char.* 58.
[67] Cf. Xenophon, *Mem.* 2.6.35: "You take as much pride (ἀγάλλῃ) in your friends' fair achievements as in your own."
[68] *Amic.* 69–70. See Lyons and Malas Jr., "Paul and His Friends within the Greco-Roman Context," *WTJ* 42.1 (2007), 50–69, 56, who apply this passage from Cicero to Christ's voluntary humility in Phil 2.
[69] Cf. Cicero, *Amic.* 57: "There are numerous occasions when good men forgo, or permit themselves to be deprived of, many conveniences in order that their friends rather than themselves may enjoy them"; Aristotle, *Eth. nic.* 1168a: "The good man acts from a sense of honour … and for his friend's sake, and is careless of his own interest."
[70] Joseph H. Hellerman, "Brothers and Friends in Philippi: Family Honor in the Roman World and in Paul's Letter to the Philippians," *BTB* 39 (2009), 15–25, 17, where he draws on Peter Pilhofer, *Philippi. Band II: Katalog der Inschriften von Philippi*, WUNT 119 (Tübingen: Mohr Siebeck, 2000).

honor functioned in antiquity, as manifested in the archeological remains from the colony at Philippi.[71]

Hence, even more explicit than the friendship paradigm[72] (especially since the key term φιλία is absent from this letter, indeed, from all of Paul's letters) is the familial relationship that Paul shares with the Philippians.[73] In the prescript, Paul sends greetings "from God *our Father*" (1:2), establishing from the outset the relation of kinship that he shares with the Philippians based on their common link to God their Father.[74] Alexander consequently argues that the entire epistle should be read as a family letter, equivalent to common letters in antiquity, in which one family member reassures another regarding health and safety.[75] Indeed, Paul first refers to them as his "siblings" at 1:12, where he begins the relay of information about his circumstances. Paul then capitalizes on this familial bound through recourse to the kinship relation (ἀδελφοί) existing between them, consistently referring throughout the letter to the Philippians as "(my) siblings," especially when giving instructions.[76] Thus, he commands his "siblings" to rejoice (3:1), to imitate him (3:17), to stand firm (4:1), and to consider that which is virtuous and to put it into practice (4:8). In 2:12, Paul also uses the related term ἀγαπητοί ("my beloved") to preface his central exhortation to work out their salvation with fear and trembling, which in reflecting the concept of their election as God's "children" is closely linked with the idea of kinship (cf. 2:15).[77]

If it is Paul's friendship with the Philippians that led to their mutual concern for each other's circumstances, with its attendant honor, in all of these cases it is the familial nature of his relationship with the Philippians that allows Paul to issue his commands.[78] Because they are mutually involved with each other as siblings were mutually involved with one another in antiquity,[79] Paul can count on their faithful response to his

---

[71] Hellerman, "Brothers," 20, finds the same sharing of honor among friends in the inscriptions, though to a lesser extent.

[72] John T. Fitzgerald, "Paul and Friendship," in *Paul in the Greco-Roman World*, 2nd ed., 1.331–362, 351, notes that "kinship terms were often used to describe friendship" and that Paul uses friendship terminology "as both a complement and a substitute for kinship language," thereby cautioning against sharply dividing between kinship and friendship models for understanding Paul's relationship with his communities.

[73] Hellerman, "Brothers," 17: "Paul clearly conceives of the Jesus community in Philippi as a surrogate family."

[74] It must be remembered that kinship was the primary relational model for the covenant between YHWH and his people in the Scriptures. Cf. F. M. Cross, "Kinship and Covenant," in *From Epic to Canon: History and Literature in Ancient Israel* (Baltimore, MD: Johns Hopkins Press, 1998), 3–21.

[75] Alexander, "Letter Forms," 90.

[76] See Reider Aasgaard, *"My Brothers and Sisters!": Christian Siblingship in Paul*, JSNTSup 265 (London: T&T Clark, 2004), 273–4.

[77] Cf. Oda Wischmeyer, "Das Adjektiv ΑΓΑΠΗΤΟΙ in den paulinischen Briefen: Eine traditionsgeschichtliche Miszelle," *NTS* 32 (1986), 476–80, 476: "das Adjektive [i.e., ἀγαπητοί] schließlich behält er ganz überwiegend der Charakteristik seiner [i.e., of Paul's] christlichen Brüder vor." See also Keown, *Philippians 1:1–2:18*, 453, who writes that ἀγαπητοί constitutes "the language of family."

[78] Cf. James L. Jaquette, "Life and Death, *Adiaphora*, and Paul's Rhetorical Strategies," *NovT* 38.1 (1996), 30–54, 37, who comments on Paul's deliberations in 1:21–26 that "by creating his own exemplary ethos and eliciting positive pathos, Paul secures his readers' attention, receptivity and goodwill."

[79] Cf. Plutarch's treatise *de fraterno amore* in which he refutes those who assert that "fame could not be shared (ἀκοινώνητον)" (487D), advising siblings to "adorn [each other] with a portion of [their] repute" (484D).

commands (see Chapter 5). It is thus the cultural context of this mutuality of familial honor[80] that makes Paul's reference to the Philippians' boast accruing from his own faithfulness on their behalf (1:26), as well as his boast as a result of their faithfulness (2:16), readily intelligible and rhetorically forceful.[81]

The fact that Christ remains central to Phil 1:26 (ἐν Χριστῷ Ἰησοῦ comes between τὸ καύχημα ὑμῶν and ἐν ἐμοί), however, guards against the criticism that Paul's contribution toward their boast displaces the honor that ultimately accrues to Christ. Rather, for the Philippians' boasting to abound in Paul means that their boast is abounding in *what Christ has done and will do through Paul* (Phil 4:13).[82] This mutuality between the Philippians, Christ, and Paul is evident in the complicated grammar of 1:26, where Paul and Christ are both intricately involved with the boasting of the community.

Conclusion

Thus, in Phil 1:26, after depicting his decision to remain "in the flesh" in order to minister to the Philippians, Paul describes that the honor accruing from his self-sacrificial act serves not only to augment his own glory but also to foster abundant boasting for the Philippian believers.[83] Hence, and what will become important for the broader sweep of the letter, it is *Paul's faithfulness* on behalf of the Philippians that culminates in honor *for them*. Philippians 1:26 thus encompasses one half of the mutual honor depicted in the letter, as the flow of honor moves here from Paul to the Philippians. What remains to be seen is the reciprocal flow of honor, which would be expected given the relationship of mutuality existing between them.[84] And it is precisely this structure of one individual's faithfulness resulting in the other's boasting as an expression of mutual honor that is mirrored in 2:16, where it is the *Philippians' faithfulness* that culminates in *the apostle's honor* as expressed in his boasting.

---

[80] Philip F. Esler, "Keeping it in the Family," in *Families and Family Relations*, ed. Jan Willem van Henten and Athalya Brenner (Leiden: Deo, 2000), 145–84, 154, remarks that "a fundamental aspect of the honour that is vested in a family is that it is only with outsiders that one engages in a competition over honour."

[81] Elsewhere, Philip F. Esler, "Family Imagery in Galatians," in *Constructing Early Christian Families*, ed. Halvor Moxnes (London: Routledge, 2002), 121–49, 124, shows that "honour gained by one member accrues to the family as a whole." Esler's theoretical insights agree with the primary evidence garnered in our previous section demonstrating the mutuality of honor within ancient families.

[82] Fowl, *Philippians*, 127: "In each act of boasting [in both 1:26 and 2:16], the focus is on what God has done."

[83] John Howard Schütz, *Paul and the Anatomy of Apostolic Authority*, SNTSMS 26 (Cambridge: Cambridge University Press, 1975), 234, argues, on the basis that Paul and his communities "together share something which originates beyond themselves," that "Paul's pride can be mutually enjoyed by the church" (citing Phil 1:26 alongside 2 Cor 1:14).

[84] E. G. Gulin, *Die Freude im Neuen Testament*, AASF B 26.2 (Helsinki: Druckerei-A.G., 1932), 185, captures well this notion of mutuality based on shared faithfulness: "Wie die Gemeinde dem Apostel, so ist auch der Apostel der Gemeinde eine Ursache des Ruhmes, vorausgesetzt, dass sie beide sich treu zu dem Herrn halten."

7

Mutual Honor in Philippians 2:14–16

As the previous chapter made clear, in Phil 1:25–26 Paul presented the first half of the theme of mutual honor in the epistle, since there the honor accruing from Paul's self-sacrificial decision to remain with his Philippian converts abounds *for the Philippians*. We turn now to 2:16, where Paul presents the other side of the mutual relationship by depicting the fact that the honorable, virtuous behavior of the Philippians engenders a boast *for himself*. Moreover, while both instances draw on the common cultural script of honor as an appropriate mutual reward for virtuous behavior (see Part 2), the second appearance of the theme is closely tied additionally to the Scriptural backdrop of mutual honor adduced in Part 1 of our study, where it finds its theological rationale. While both 1:25–26 and 2:16 link up closely with the rhetorical strategy of Greco-Roman letter writers who relied on the pathos garnered from the mutual honor shared with their correspondents to help motivate their behavior, it is the Scriptural context Paul alludes to in 2:14–16 that provides this pathos with its basis for those who now find their identity not merely as occupants of Roman Philippi but also as those called to exercise their responsibility as "citizens of heaven" (cf. πολιτεύομαι in 1:27 with πολίτευμα in 3:20).

Paul's Claim to Honor as the Goal of Philippians 2:14–16

The link in Philippians between the theme of mutual honor, which includes the honor of Christ, and Paul's overall exhortation is evident in that the single sentence comprising Phil 2:14–16 provides a summary of the central hortatory portion of the epistle (1:27-2:18). In this section, Paul's paraenesis involves the two key imperatives of πολιτεύεσθε (in 1:27) and κατεργάζεσθε (in 2:12).[1] In terms of the first of these, the general command to "exercise your civic responsibility (as a Christian)" acquires its modal definition in the repeated imperatives of 2:2 and 2:5 to "think the same thing" as exemplified in Christ's pattern of thought. Similarly, the general command to "*work out* your salvation" acquires its modal definition in the imperative of 2:14 to "*do all things* without grumbling or complaining." This second set of commands, by

---

[1] Mark. A. Jennings, *The Price of Partnership in the Letter of Paul to the Philippians: "Make My Joy Complete"*, LNTS 578 (London: Bloomsbury T&T Clark, 2018), 112, argues that Phil 2:15–16a "is the climax of Paul's entire argument since 1:27."

implication, thus clarify the first set (in 1:27 and 2:5) since it attaches specific activity to the call to imitate Christ's servanthood exemplified in the hymn (2:6–11).[2] This second narrowing of focus in v. 14 then brings about a number of outcomes that are given in vv. 15–16. Should the Philippians behave in the manner so prescribed, they would become "blameless, pure, and faultless" (v. 15a), they would maintain their characteristic of "holding fast" the word of life (v. 16a), and, finally, they would engender "a boast" for their apostle on the day of Christ (v. 16b).

Grammatical Analysis of Philippians 2:14–16

The passage can be organized in the following manner:

14   Πάντα ποιεῖτε χωρὶς γογγυσμῶν καὶ διαλογισμῶν,
15a ἵνα γένησθε ἄμεμπτοι καὶ ἀκέραιοι,
15b τέκνα θεοῦ ἄμωμα μέσον γενεᾶς σκολιᾶς καὶ διεστραμμένης,
15c ἐν οἷς φαίνεσθε ὡς φωστῆρες ἐν κόσμῳ,
16a λόγον ζωῆς ἐπέχοντες,
16b εἰς καύχημα ἐμοὶ εἰς ἡμέραν Χριστοῦ,
16c ὅτι οὐκ εἰς κενὸν ἔδραμον οὐδὲ εἰς κενὸν ἐκοπίασα.

14   Do all things in a manner devoid of grumbling and complaining,
15a in order that (ἵνα) you might become blameless and undefiled,
15b [in order that you might become] children of God who are faultless amid a crooked and twisted generation,
15c among whom you are shining as lights in the world,
16a by means of holding fast the word of life,
16b serving the purpose of a claim to honor on my account with a view towards the day of Christ,
16c because (ὅτι) I did not run for futility and neither did I labor for futility.

Verse 15 provides the purpose (ἵνα) for the command in v. 14. This purpose, however, is fourfold in its ends: it incorporates two adjectival modifiers (ἄμεμπος and ἀκέραιος, v. 15a) and the epithet: "God's children," along with a final adjective (ἄμωμος, v. 15b), all of which it then directs toward the ultimate goal of Paul's boast, or claim to honor in v. 16b. A fifth aspect that then sets the Philippians apart from their depraved surroundings is that, as a consequence of their transformed character, they are (presently) "shining as lights in the world" (v. 15c), which luminous role displays visibly their status as God's people. This is because the Philippians' firm grasp of the word of life constitutes the *means* (ἐπέχοντες as adverbial ptcp. in v. 16a) of their "becoming" (γίνομαι) blameless, et al. in v. 15a.[3] Hence, the Philippians' holding fast to the word

---

[2] Mark J. Keown, *Philippians 1:1–2:18*, EEC (Bellingham, WA: Lexham Press, 2017), 464, points to the relationship between the two appeals, arguing that 2:12 "effectively restates the earlier appeal in 1:27–30."
[3] Ulrich B. Müller, *Der Brief des Paulus an die Philipper*, THKNT 11/1 (Leipzig: Evangelische Verlagsanstalt, 1993), 121.

of life will result both in the initial outcome of their blamelessness and in the further outcome of Paul's claim to honor.[4]

As a confirmation of this outcome of their mutual honor, Paul then adduces a second basis (ὅτι) for his καύχημα relying on the grounds provided by the Philippians' own faithfulness, namely, his fruitful efforts on behalf of gospel ministry among the Philippians (2:16c). Finally, Paul stresses that both the Philippians' standing as blameless and his own claim to honor are directed toward the eschatological judgment (v. 16bc). In v. 16b, Paul's boasting as an apostle is explicitly related to the day of Christ, since the Philippians' present obedience in doing all things without grumbling and arguing (v. 14) leads to their becoming "faultless children of God" (v. 15b) in the final judgment, when they will ultimately stand "pure and undamaged for the day of Christ" (1:10), testifying to the fact that Paul has not labored "for futility" (v. 16c).[5]

The Presence of Scripture in Philippians 2:12-18

In making this argument regarding their mutual honor, the abrupt eruption of Scriptural language in Phil 2:12-18 is striking in that, up till now, Scriptural material has been rather minimal in the letter.[6] Fee thus posits that the most noticeable feature of this passage is its "sudden and profuse influx of echoes from the OT, which is unlike anything else in the Pauline corpus."[7] Edart describes the passage as being marked by "un recours massif à l'Ecriture," pointing to the prominence of the Exodus and the prophets in Paul's allusive language.[8] The structure of the allusions is also significant in that Paul presents two allusions to Isaiah, at 2:10-11 and at 2:16c, which frame the one "centerpiece" allusion to Deuteronomy at 2:15.[9] Indeed, Paul is notorious for turning to these two Scriptural corpora in his writings,[10] often with Deuteronomy and Isaiah being mutually interpretative for the apostle.[11]

---

[4] Casey Wayne Davis, *Oral Biblical Criticism: The Influence of the Principles of Orality on the Literary Structure of Philippians*, LNTS 172 (Sheffield: Sheffield Academic Press, 1999), 83, makes the intriguing observation that "outside of three occurrences in ch. 1 [1:10, 26], all purpose clauses in this letter fall between 2.10 and 3.12 [2:10, 13, 15, 16, 19, 27, 28, 30; 3:8, 9, 10, 11, 12]," which he sees as "to be expected" since this section, for him, constitutes the *probatio*, "the rhetorical proof section, where the speakers attempt to show the results of their claims."

[5] Moises Silva, *Philippians* (Grand Rapids, MI: Baker Academic, 2005), 126, similarly points to connections between 2:14-16 and 1:9-11, noting that, despite the present tense verb in 2:15, "even here Paul does not fail to set his sight, and that of his readers, on 'the day of Christ.'"

[6] Recall the comment by L. Michael White, "Morality between Two Worlds," in *Greeks, Romans, and Christians*, ed. David L. Balch, Everett Ferguson, and Wayne A. Meeks (Minneapolis, MN: Fortress, 1990), 201-15, 205, that Philippians has "so little that is Jewish in its content."

[7] Gordon D. Fee, *Paul's Letter to the Philippians*, NICNT 46 (Grand Rapids, MI: Eerdmans, 1995), 242-3. Cf. Jennings, *Partnership*, 112: "Every phrase in Phil 2:15-16a alludes to a Jewish scriptural text."

[8] Jean-Baptiste Edart, *L'épître aux Philippiens: Rhétorique et composition stylistique*, EB 45 (Paris: J. Gabalda, 2002), 194-6.

[9] John H. P. Reumann, *Philippians: A New Translation with Introduction and Commentary*, AB 33B (New Haven, CT: Yale University Press, 2008), 402.

[10] Richard B. Hays, *Conversion of the Imagination: Paul as Interpreter of Israel's Scriptures* (Grand Rapids, MI: Eerdmans, 2005), 37, speaks of Paul's "de facto canon within the canon," which consists of Deut 32 and especially Isa 40-55.

[11] See J. Ross Wagner, "Moses and Isaiah in Concert," in *As Those Who Are Taught: The Interpretation of Isaiah from the LXX to the SBL*, ed. Claire Matthews McGinnis and Patricia K. Tull, SBLSymS 27 (Atlanta, GA: SBL Press, 2006), 87-103.

Deuteronomy in Philippians 2:12–18: Israel's *Unheilsgeschichte*[12] as Anti-Model

Perhaps the most important element of the apostle's exhortation in Phil 2:14–16 is the sustained "story of Israel"[13] that can be detected within it.[14] The most explicit evidence for this is Paul's overt allusion to the Song of Moses (Deut 32:5) in Phil 2:15, but other Pentateuchal material abounds in the passage.[15] The reader is prepared for this Israel narrative in v. 14,[16] where the grumbling (γογγυσμός) that the Philippians are commanded to avoid involves a term firmly anchored in the Septuagintal narratives about the Israelite wilderness generation (cf. Ex 15:24; 16:2, 7 [*bis*], 8 [*ter*], 9, 12; 17:3; Num 11:1; 14:2, 27, 29, 36; 16:11; Deut 1:27). Indeed, the second behavior to which Paul cautions these believers in 2:14, διαλογισμός, has Scriptural roots as well, where "disputing" across the LXX authors characterizes godless individuals in general.[17] The first of these terms, however, applies almost exclusively to a rebellious Israel, so much so that it represents the *sine qua non* of the Israelite wilderness generation.

The Grumbling Motif in Philippians 2:14–16

The LXX translators link γογγυσμός (*grumbling*) exclusively to Israel's complaining attitude in the wilderness wanderings. Prior to the New Testament the word is scarce in extant Greek literature outside the LXX,[18] where it almost universally describes

---

[12] The term is from Reumann, *Philippians*, 403, though Reumann argues against any "story of Israel" running through this passage on the grounds that Paul's audience would not have detected it. For critique, see the discussion of McAuley and Fowl on audience awareness in the Introduction above.

[13] Fee, *Philippians*, 241.

[14] Stephen E. Fowl, *Philippians*, THNTC (Grand Rapids, MI: Eerdmans, 2005), 121–2, proposes that "Paul seems to read the Philippians situation in the light of Israel in the desert." Cf. James P. Ware, *Paul and the Mission of the Church* (Grand Rapids, MI: Baker Academic, 2011), 251: "In Philippians 2:14–15, Paul's paraenesis will employ Jewish traditions to shape the self-understanding of the community at Philippi."

[15] J. Hugh Michael, *Philippians*, MNTC (London: Stodder and Houghton, 1939), 99, asserts that the reference to Deut 32:5 "is not the only point of contact between this paragraph and Deuteronomy." Michael goes on to observe additional points of contact at 1:28 (with Deut 31:6), at 2:12 (with Deut 31:27, 29), at 2:13 (with Deut 31:8), and at 2:17 (with Deut 31:29). A further link occurs in the double admonitions to rejoice found in both appeals (at Deut 32:43 and Phil 2:17–18), as noted by David McAuley, *Paul's Covert Use of Scripture* (Eugene, OR: Pickwick, 2015), 210. Jennings, *Partnership*, 113, points additionally to a possible connection between the importance of knowledge for God's people found in both Deut 32:28–29 and Phil 1:9–10.

[16] G. B. Caird, *Paul's Letters from Prison in the Revised Standard Version*, NCB (Oxford: Oxford University Press, 1987), 126: "It is probable that [Paul] already had the Old Testament parallel in mind" at v. 14.

[17] For negative usage by the LXX, see, e.g., Pss 9:25; 20:11; 34:20; 35:4; 93:11; 118:59; 139:3; Prov 16:30; 17:12; cf. Hanna Stettler, *Heiligung bei Paulus: Ein Beitrag aus biblisch-theologischer Sicht*, WUNT 2.368 (Tübingen: Mohr Siebeck, 2014), 528: "Auch διαλογισμοί kann im Alten Testament eine Haltung der Auflehnung gegen Gott bezeichnen." Schrenk, "διαλογισμός," TDNT 2.97, notes that "in view of the more flexible LXX usage, it is striking that the NT uses διαλογισμός only in the negative sense for evil thoughts." Despite this LXX usage to designate wicked thoughts, however, we agree with Fee, *Philippians*, 243–4, that whereas γογγυσμός "offers a biblical frame of reference," διαλογισμός "puts their 'grumbling' into the Philippian context."

[18] For later (third-century) documentary evidence that demonstrates popular usage of γογγυσμός, see A. L. Connolly, "Minor Philological Notes," *New Docs* (1979), 141–4, §45, who lists examples from the papyri, one of which is a letter from a doctor to his mother admitting his hesitation to take time away from his patients "lest indeed there should be any *murmuring* against us"

Israel's grumbling.[19] Moreover, David Pao argues that there is a definite theological character emerging from the LXX usage of γογγυσμός to describe Israel's behavior: "In the context of murmuring traditions ... *To murmur is to distrust God* and to refuse to acknowledge his Lordship."[20] In this way, within Paul's rhetoric, Israel provides a negative model for the Philippians;[21] they represent those who have willfully disobeyed God's directions.[22] For Rengstorf, therefore, the verb γογγύζειν contrasts with ὑπακούειν (cf. v. 12), with the implication that those who grumble, that is, disobey, are under God's judgment.[23] Rengstorf argues that Paul, in taking up the word γογγυσμός, has taken up "the judgment contained in it," applying the same possible danger of divine judgment to the Philippian believers.[24] For as Schenk has pointed out, Paul's application of this language to the Philippians entails a situation of danger and threat for the community, since such behavior always poses "die stärke Gefahr" to God's people who live ever under the shadow of the final judgment.[25]

Against this Scriptural backdrop, Paul therefore urges his converts to maintain obedience (ὑπακούειν in 2:12) and to avoid grumbling (γογγυσμός in 2:14). By doing so, a contrast is established between the Philippian believers, whom Paul expects to heed his commands, and the grumbling, non-believing Israel of the wilderness,[26] a

---

(μὴ καὶ τι[ς γ]ογγυσμὸς κ[α]θ᾽ ἡμῶν γένηται). Rengstorf, "γογγύζω," *TDNT* 1.729, notes that "even on Greek soil [γογγύζειν] marks one as a ἁμαρτωλός."

[19] Seven times the grumbling is directed against God: Ex 16:7, 8 (*bis*), 9, 12; Num 17:20, 25 (cf. also γόγγυσιν in Num 14:27). See, however, Wis. Sol. 1:10–11, where γογγυσμός describes interpersonal complaining. These occurrences of the substantive are matched by a similarly specialized usage of γογγύζω, though not exclusively (cf. Judg 1:14; Ps 58:16; Isa 29:24; Lam 3:39; Sir 10:25; Jdth 5:22), to describe Israel's activity of murmuring in the wilderness generation: Ex 17:3; Num 11:1; 14:27 (*bis*), 29; 17:6, 20; Ps 105:25 (cf. Isa 30:12). Cf. also the cognate διαγογγύζω: Ex 15:24; 16:2, 7, 8; Num 14:2, 36; 16:11; Deut 1:27; Josh 9:18 (though, see Sir 31:24 for its use interpersonally).

[20] David W. Pao, *Thanksgiving: An Investigation of a Pauline Theme*, NSBT 13 (Downers Grove, IL: InterVarsity Press, 2002), 159 (emphasis added). Nikolaus Walter, "Der Brief an die Philipper," in *Die Briefe an die Philipper, Thessalonicher and an Philemon*, ed. Nikolaus Walter, Eckart Reinmuth, and Peter Lampe (Göttingen: Vandenhoeck & Ruprecht, 1998), 11–101, 66, argues that the second term (διαλογισμός) similarly evinces "diesen Nebenton des Mißtrauens."

[21] Paul himself provides the positive counterpart in that he responds to present suffering undergone for the gospel's sake with joy rather than with grumbling. Cf. Peter-Ben Smit, *Paradigms of Being in Christ*, LNTS 476 (London: Bloomsbury T&T Clark, 2013), 99, who sees here "a very brief negative *exemplum*."

[22] Cf. Simon de Vries, "Origin of the Murmuring Tradition," *JBL* 87 (1968), 51–8, 54: "The phraseology of murmuring, and especially the vocable לון, point beyond mere discontent and grumbling to outright rebellion."

[23] Rengstorf, *TDNT* 1.729–730 (citing Isa 29:24 LXX for evidence). So too Ernst Lohmeyer, *Die Briefe an die Philipper, Kolosser and an Philemon*, KEK (Göttingen: Vandenhoeck & Ruprecht, 1954), 106, and P.-E. Bonnard, *L'Épître de saint Paul aux Philippiens*, CNT (Paris: Delachaux et Niestlé, 1950), 51. Rengstorf, *TDNT* 1.730, further observes that "the right attitude, in contrast to murmuring, is אָמְרָה, i.e., unconditional acceptance (Nu. 14:11) or obedience, hearkening to the voice of God (Nu. 14:22)." Silva, *Philippians*, 125, posits that the phrase from Deut 32:5 ("crooked and perverse generation") in 2:15 "could serve as a powerful reminder of the dangers created by a disobedient life."

[24] Rengstorf, *TDNT* 1.733–734.

[25] Wolfgang Schenk, *Die Philipperbriefe des Paulus: Kommentar* (Stuttgart: Kohlhammer, 1984), 220.

[26] Johannes Schoon-Janssen, *Umstrittene "Apologien" in den Paulusbriefen: Studien zur rhetorischen Situation des 1. Thessalonicherbriefes, des Galaterbriefes und des Philipperbriefes*, GTA 45 (Göttingen: Vandenhoeck & Ruprecht, 1991), 155, states that the allusion to Deut 32:5 in the next verse "erklärt sich" in light of the grumbling-motif. F. W. Beare, *Philippians*, BNTC (London: Adam & Charles Black, 1969), 88–9, recognizes in Moses's lament found in Deuteronomy 32 "the recollection

contrast that demonstrates Paul's eschatological viewpoint in which he anticipates that Jesus, as the resurrected Messiah (cf. 2:9–11), is bringing about the end-time restoration of God's people as evidenced in their transformed lives.[27]

The Philippians as Blameless Children of God in Philippians 2:15

This initial contrast between Paul's audience in the letter, the "saints" (1:2) called to rejoice (2:18; 3:1; 4:4) and be thankful (4:6), and the grumbling wilderness generation is further developed conceptually in the lengthy v. 15. The initial proposed outcome from the Philippians' nongrumbling and nondisputing behavior is that they would become ἄμεμπτοι καὶ ἀκέραιοι ("blameless and undefiled"). In this, the twofold description of their behavior (i.e., the two activities of grumbling and complaining that they willingly forego) balances with the twofold description of its resultant character (i.e., their description as blameless and pure),[28] which outcome strongly resembles Paul's introductory prayer for them (1:9–11).[29] While Paul's prayer explicitly refers to the eschatological day of Christ (1:10), the eschatological climax for 2:15 does not come until 2:16, though this later end-time context must shape the reference to the Philippians' purity mentioned earlier in the sentence.[30] In other words, "[Paul] challenges the church members to be in the present what he hopes they will be on the day of Christ."[31]

Whereas the second adjective in 2:15 (ἀκέραιος) is used rarely by the LXX, the first (ἄμεμπτος) commonly characterizes uprightness before the Lord.[32] Here too, as with the move from γογγυσμός to διαλογισμός in v. 14, Paul moves from a more distinctive

---

of [Israel's] past disobedience" (in Deut 31:27 LXX), which is correspondingly reversed in Paul's recollection of the Philippians' past obedience (in Phil 2:12).

[27] Heiko Wojtkowiak, *Christologie und Ethik im Philipperbrief: Studien zur Handlungsorientierung einer frühchristlichen Gemeinde in paganer Umwelt*, FRLANT 243 (Göttingen: Vandenhoeck & Ruprecht, 2012), 163, describes how Paul transfers the "heilsgeschichtliche Verheißungen für Israel" onto the church.

[28] Stefano Bittasi, *Gli ensempli necessari per discernere: Il significato argomentativo della struttura della lettera di Paolo al Filippesi*, AnBib 153 (Rome: Biblical Institute Press, 2003), 79, perceptively notes how Paul, as he did in 2:3–4, in 2:14–15 balances negative attitudes to be avoided with positive ones to be taken up.

[29] Fee, *Philippians*, 241: "Paul is clearly exhorting what he has been praying."

[30] Müller, *Philipper*, 120: "[Paulus] nimmt die Aussage von 1,10 mit anderen Begriffen auf, wobei der eschatologische Horizont wiederum deutlich ist (V. 16)." Fowl, *Philippians*, 123, also comments on the eschatological dimensions involved in 2:15: "The conjunction of 'blameless,' 'innocent,' and 'without blemish' gives the very clear impression that Paul is describing the final end toward which God is moving the church at Philippi."

[31] James W. Thompson, *Pastoral Ministry According to Paul* (Grand Rapids, MI: Baker Academic, 2006), 49.

[32] This is clear in Job LXX: 11:4; 4:17; 1:1, 8; 2:3 and in Wis. Sol. 10:5. Cf. Job 9:20; 15:14; 22:3; 33:9; Esther 8:12n; Wis. Sol. 10:15; 18:21. Grundmann, "μέμφομαι," *TDNT* 4.571–574, 572, notes the "surprisingly common" use of ἄμεμπτος in Job LXX, which is important for Philippians where Paul earlier compared himself to Job in Phil 1:19 so that Paul now becomes a model for the Philippians to emulate. On the cultic overtones of these terms, see Michael Newton, *The Concept of Purity at Qumran and in the Letters of Paul*, SNTSMS 53 (Cambridge: Cambridge University Press, 1985), 85, and Martin Vahrenhorst, *Kultische Sprache in den Paulusbriefen*, WUNT 230 (Tübingen: Mohr Siebeck, 2008), 234, who speaks of the "opfertheologischer Begrifflichkeit" of the term ἄμωμα in the LXX.

to a less specific designation. The adjective ἄμεμπτος appears regularly throughout Job LXX, where it often joins a host of other adjectives (most often δίκαιος,[33] but also, e.g., καθαρός,[34] ἀληθινός,[35] and ἄκακος[36]) to describe Job's moral purity and that of the righteous more generally.

This representation of laudable virtue by means of adjectives describing purity also finds resonance in the honorific parlance of Roman Philippi. Danker calls attention to an honorific inscription in which ἄμεμπτος describes a citizen's rendering of public service.[37] Additionally, Danker places this word alongside others (ἁγνεία, ὁσίως, δικαίως, ἀνεγκλήτως, καθαρός,[38] etc.) that were commonly used in honorific decrees praising benefactors. For example, Danker points to an honorific epitaph describing the honorand's behavior as σεμνῶς, ὁσίως, and ἀμέμπτως.[39] Paul uses a similar honorific in Phil 1:10, praying that his converts might be εἰλικρινής, on which Danker comments, "St. Paul expresses his hope that the [Philippians] will conduct themselves with unexceptionable sincerity ([ἵνα ἦτε εἰλικρινεῖς καὶ ἀπρόσκοποι, 1:10]) and thus promote the 'reputation and commendation that is properly God's due' ([εἰς δόξαν καὶ ἔπαινον θεοῦ, 1:11])."[40] Grundmann, however, rightly adduces an important distinction between this Greco-Roman honorific usage for ἄμεμπτος and that reflected in the LXX, since what is at issue is not status in the human court but rather being "ἄμεμπτος before God."[41]

Along the lines of the Israel-narrative, Fee sees in Paul's use of ἄμεμπτος in Phil 2:15 a possible allusion to Gen 17:1,[42] where God renews his covenant with Abraham and commands the patriarch: γίνου ἄμεμπτος ("be blameless").[43] God's covenant requirement for Abraham in Gen 17:1 includes a previous element as well, that is, that he εὐαρέστει ἐναντίον ("be pleasing before") God. The faithfulness of Abraham that is pleasing before God thus renders him "blameless" before God. The link between ἄμεμπτος and εὐαρέστει ἐναντίον [θεῷ] in Gen 17:1 thus bears similarities with Paul's description of the Philippians as ἄμεμπτος in 2:15 and his later depiction of

---

[33] Job 1:1; 9:20; 12:4; 15:14; 22:19; cf. Wis. Sol. 10:5.
[34] Job 4:17; 11:4; 33:9.
[35] Job 1:1, 8; 2:3.
[36] Job 2:3.
[37] Frederick W. Danker, *Benefactor: An Epigraphic Study* (St. Louis, MO: Clayton, 1982), 354, referring to *Magnesia* 164.13-14.
[38] Καθαρός appears in a laudatory inscription in *Priene* 19.15-16; see Danker, *Benefactor*, 356.
[39] Danker, *Benefactor*, 387 n. 178. Vahrenhorst, *Kultische Sprache*, 232, notes this term's appearance on gravestones and honorific inscriptions, which praise "die untadelige Lebens- und Amtsführung eines Menschen."
[40] Danker, *Benefactor*, 357, where he points to a letter written by Seleukos II praising the people of Miletos for maintaining a "sincere [εἰλικρινῇ] and firm esteem among their friends" (*OGI* 227.12-13; cf. *OGI* 763.40-41).
[41] Grundmann, *TDNT* 4.572.
[42] Peter Oakes, "Quelle devrait être l'influence des échos intertextuels sur la traduction?" in *Intertextualités: La Bible en échos*, ed. Daniel Marguerat and Adrian Curtis (Geneva: Labor et Fides, 2000), 251–87, 262, notes that ἄμεμπτοι "est évocateur dans le cadre de l'histoire de l'Ancien Testament," referring to Gen 17:1.
[43] Fee, *Philippians*, 242; he supports his assertion, 245 n. 16, by reference to the relative scarcity of Paul's usage of ἄμεμπτος, the wider context of Phil 2:14–16, and the repetition of this idea in the next phrase. See too Vahrenhorst, *Kultische Sprache*, 232: "[ἄμεμπτος] erinnert an biblische Gestalten wie Abraham (Gen 17,1) oder Hiob [Job 1,1]."

the Philippians' monetary gift as a rightful θυσία that is **εὐάρεστον** τῷ θεῷ ("well-pleasing to God") in 4:18. Read against its Scriptural backdrop in the Pentateuch, Paul accordingly envisions the Philippians as fulfilling in the present the divine stipulations given to Abraham in the past that God's people behave in a manner that is both *pleasing* to him and is *blameless* before him, in contrast to Israel's later history of rebellion, beginning with her grumbling and disputing with God in the wilderness.

In Wis. Sol. 10:5 it is Israel, as opposed to Abraham and Job, who are described as ἄμεμπτος and ὅσιος. These two terms inhabit a constellation of LXX terminology denoting the moral conduct appropriate for God's people.[44] Chief among this constellation is the term ἅγιος, describing the holiness that God expects from his chosen people (e.g., Deut 26:19: "for you to be a people ἅγιος to the Lord your God").[45] Paul, too, often employs the central term ἅγιος in conjunction with other descriptors to illustrate the eschatological characteristics that he hopes to foster among his converts.[46] In Philippians, Paul ascribes ἅγιος to his auditors in the opening and the closing of the letter (1:1 and 4:21), thereby bracketing the whole. He also prays on behalf of the Philippians that they would be εἰλικρινεῖς καὶ ἀπρόσκοποι for the eschatological day of Christ (1:10).[47] Thus, Paul's application of language from the semantic field of holiness to the Philippians situates them within the realm of God's eschatological covenant people. In the words of Thielman, ἅγιος is "a term distinctive of Israel's status as the people of God (Ex 19:6)."[48]

In Phil 2:15b, Paul places in apposition to these first two adjectives (ἄμεμπτος and ἀκέραιος) two additional elements, τέκνα θεοῦ and ἄμωμα, both of which are especially

---

[44] Hauck, "ὅσιος," *TDNT* 5.491, notes that "חָסִיד [most often underlying the LXX's ὅσιος] is an ideal, and thus acquires an ethico-religious content. It is parallel to תָּמִים (Ps. 18:26) and close to צַדִּיק," and that ὅσιοι is a *terminus technicus* in the OT to represent the righteous remnant of Israel, which correlates to the early Christians' self-designation as ἅγιοι. Stettler, *Heiligung*, 224 n. 21, argues for "eine gewisse Nähe zwischen תמים (in der *LXX* ... mit ἄμεμπτος ... übersetzt) und קדש," viz., ἅγιος.

[45] James W. Thompson, *Moral Formation According to Paul* (Grand Rapids, MI: Baker Books, 2011), 48, describes how "Paul applies the terms of the holiness code to [his converts], identifying them with ancient Israel." Thompson, *Moral Formation*, 54, develops this thought further: "Election and holiness are closely related. God called Israel to be a 'holy nation' (Exod. 19:6) and chose Israel to be 'a people holy to the Lord' (Deut. 7:6; 14:2)."

[46] The self-presented goal of Paul's ministry and mission is to establish believers who are: ἁγνός (2 Cor 11:2); cf. Eph 4:13 (τέλειον, describing the purpose of all gospel ministers). Note the similar goal of Christ's ministry in Eph 5:27 (ἁγία and ἄμωμος) and Col 1:22 (ἁγίους, ἀμώμους, and ἀνεγκλήτους). Paul additionally prays for such *Vollendungsprädikate* among his churches: 1 Cor 1:8 (ἀνεγκλήτους); Phil 1:10 (εἰλικρινεῖς and ἀπρόσκοποι); 1 Thess 3:13 (ἄμεμπτος); 5:23 (ὁλόκληρον and ἀμέμπτως); so Ernst Synofzik, *Die Gericht- und Vergeltungsaussagen bei Paulus*, GTA 8 (Göttingen: Vandenhoeck & Ruprecht, 1977), 19. Cf. Paul's more general presentation of the end toward which God's grace is working in believers' lives: 1 Cor 5:8 (εἰλικρινείας and ἀληθείας); cf. Eph 1:4 (ἁγίους and ἀμώμους); 2 Pet 3:14 (ἄσπιλοι and ἀμώμητοι); Jude 24 (ἀμώμους).

[47] Stefan Schapdick, *Eschatisches Heil mit eschatischer Anerkennung: Exegetische Untersuchungen zu Funktion und Sachgehalt der paulinischen Verkündigung vom eigenen Endgeschick im Rahmen seiner Korrespondenz an die Thessalonicher, Korinther und Philipper*, BBB 164 (Göttingen: Vandenhoeck & Ruprecht, 2011), 149 n. 81, affirms that both terms convey the notion of perfection (*Vollkommenheit*).

[48] Frank S. Thielman, *Paul and the Law: A Contextual Approach* (Downers Grove, IL: InterVarsity Press, 1994), 158. In Ex 19:6, God declares that Israel "shall be to [Him] ... a *holy nation*" (ἔσεσθέ μοι ... ἔθνος **ἅγιον**), a description mirrored in Deut 26:19 (εἶναί σε λαὸν **ἅγιον** κυρίῳ). Cf. Stettler, *Heiligung*, 621, who argues that "Der Horizont, vor dem die paulinischen Aussagen zur Heiligung zu verstehen sind, ist das *alttestamentlich-jüdische* Heiligkeitsverständnis."

characteristic of Israel in the Scriptures. The first epithet, τέκνα θεοῦ, possesses manifold resonances,[49] the most important of which is its use in the Scriptures to describe God's covenant community. Israel is paradigmatically designated as God's "first-born son" (Ex 4:22), and, as a community, they consequently bear the title "children of God" (e.g., Deut 14:1 [υἱοὶ κυρίου]; Hos 2:1 [υἱοὶ θεοῦ ζῶντος]; cf. Jer 3:19). This is evident in Deut 32:5, to which Paul overtly alludes (see below).[50] Thus, by employing the epithet τέκνα θεοῦ in Phil 2:15, the apostle is effectively declaring that his Philippian converts belong to the elect people of God so that, if they behave in a grumbling- and disputing-free manner, they will fulfill their calling to a covenant-keeping fidelity, which Israel failed to do.[51] Paul's use thus corresponds with Ware's observation that the τέκνα θεοῦ language "takes up imagery frequent in second temple sources to describe the Jewish nation. This language is especially prominent in descriptions of the purified Jewish nation in the eschatological time of restoration."[52]

The fourth characteristic that will result from the community's obediently rejecting the spirit of grumbling and disputing is their status as ἄμωμα ("faultless").[53] While often interpreted in conjunction with the foregoing adjectives, this term has even stronger Scriptural resonances than the first two.[54] Ἄμωμα, often rendering the Hebrew תמים, is regularly used by LXX authors to describe the acceptable sacrifices that God requires

---

[49] For instance, in a Greco-Roman milieu, the Philippians' status as τέκνα θεοῦ could link with their shining "as heavenly lights" to reflect common perceptions of the emperors, also called "sons of the Gods" who after their death ascended to the heavens to become stars. See Suet, *Jul.* 88; Cicero, *Dream of Scipio*, 13; *Rep.* 6.13; *Laelius*, 11–12; on this, see Lukas Bormann, *Philippi: Stadt und Christengemeinde*, NovTSup 78 (Leiden: Brill, 1995), 219 n. 38. Philo, *Spec.* 1.318, takes the Jewish idea of Israel as God's children (from Deut 14:1) and applies it to all those who "do 'what is pleasing' to nature and what is 'good'"; these are the υἱοὶ τοῦ θεοῦ inasmuch as God "will think fit to protect and provide for [them] as though a father (ὡς ἐκ πατρός)." Elsewhere, Philo transfers Israel's status as God's sons to those "who live in the knowledge of the One" (*Conf.* 145). On Philo's presentation of God as father, see Beatrice Wyss, "Vater Gott und seine Kinder und Frauen," in *The Divine Father: Religious and Philosophical Concepts of Divine Parenthood in Antiquity*, ed. Felix Albrecht and Reinhard Feldmeier (Leiden: Brill, 2014), 165–97, who notes Philo's radical transformation of the concept of Israel's *Gottessohnschaft* away from being grounded in Israel's relationship to YHWH and toward a moral category for the soul.

[50] Paul thus employs Deut 32:5 in inverted form for the purpose of establishing the Philippians' community identity; *pace* Sergio Rosell Nebreda, *Christ Identity: A Social-Scientific Reading of Philippians 2.5–11*, FRLANT 242 (Göttingen: Vandenhoeck & Ruprecht, 2011), 60, who argues that "Paul does not seem to use the Old Testament as a way of creating a shared identity based on kinship relations."

[51] Abera M. Mengestu, *God as Father: Kinship Language and Identity Formation in Early Christianity* (Eugene, OR: Pickwick, 2013), 183, notes that Paul's use of the term τέκνα θεοῦ functions "both to create unity ... and to construct boundary." This does not mean that the church replaces Israel, however. See Guy P. Waters, *The End of Deuteronomy in the Epistles of Paul*, WUNT 221 (Tübingen: Mohr Siebeck, 2006), 157: "The integrity of Israel as a nation is simply not a consideration of the apostle's at Phil 2:15." Rather, Paul employs the Israel of the wilderness generation as a negative foil against which he impels his readers to pursue faithfulness.

[52] Ware, *Mission*, 252; see the primary sources Ware cites on 252 nn. 41–42.

[53] Although Deut 32:5 LXX reads μώμητα for the MT's מום, cf. Deut 15:21 LXX, where מום is rendered μῶμος, correlating with Paul's ἄμωμα in Phil 2:15.

[54] Newton, *Purity*, 74, posits that ἄμεμπτος, ἀκέραιος and ἄμωμος are "all cultic terms [that] describe the cultic offering." Schapdick, *Heil*, 187 n. 291, argues that the adjective ἄμωμος || תָּמִים is a "klassischer Terminus" for the faultlessness of sacrificial offerings (e.g., Lev 23:12–13; Num 6:14; 19:2), though he also points to LXX usage where it characterizes human individuals (e.g., Ps 15:2; 18:23; 37:18 LXX).

from his covenant people.⁵⁵ Outside of this distinct cultic usage, however, ἄμωμος also signifies moral purity, often being linked with the quality of righteousness (Ps 15[14]:2; Prov 20:7).⁵⁶ "Faultless" individuals are assured an inheritance (Ps 37[36]:18) and a reward (Wis. Sol. 2:22); they will never be ashamed (Ps 119[118]:80). Of special significance for our study is the fact that the description also bears an honorific sense, since it is the ἄμωμοι who are (προς)δεκτοί (*acceptable*) before the Lord (Prov 11:20; 22:11).⁵⁷ Thus, Paul's use of ἄμωμος in Phil 2:15 could draw on either the cultic or the moral Jewish background for the term, or perhaps both. As an example of the latter, by describing the Philippians' *moral* character as ἄμωμος before God, Paul indicates their role as the *cultic* sacrificial offering that he will bring to God at the day of Christ (cf. this dual use in Phil 4:18 as well).⁵⁸

In addition to this cultic/moral background for ἄμωμα, the term's appearance at Phil 2:15 lines up with the Israel-narrative adduced above. This is evident when the term is read alongside its accompanying prepositional phrase (μέσον γενεᾶς σκολιᾶς καὶ διεστραμμένης), which is recognizably drawn from Deut 32:5 LXX: ἡμάρτοσαν οὐκ αὐτῷ τέκνα μωμητά, γενεὰ σκκολιὰ καὶ διεστραμμένη ("blemished children, not his, have sinned, a generation, crooked and perverse," NETS).⁵⁹ Moreover, the previous epithet, τέκνα θεοῦ, from 2:15 also hearkens back to this same verse in Moses's Song.⁶⁰ Paul's deployment of this Scriptural phraseology is steeped in irony, since the Song in its original context lamented a faith*less* Israel, who were *not* God's children, but instead were fault*y*, indeed, were *crooked and perverse*. For Paul, the Philippian believers, precisely because they succeed (by not grumbling) where Israel failed (by grumbling), will become fault*less*, and in so doing are acknowledged as God's children, while their surrounding (oddly enough, now *pagan*) context is denounced as crooked and depraved.⁶¹

---

⁵⁵ For example, Ex 29:1; Lev 1:3, 10, etc.; Num 28:3, etc.; Ezek 43:23, etc. Outside the Pentateuch, however, it applies more regularly to noncultic, moral settings: e.g., of God in 2 Sam 22:31; Ps 18(17):31; of God's law in Ps 19(18):8; of the upright way in 2 Sam 22:33; Ps 18(17):33; 101(100):2, 6; Prov 11:5; of the righteous individual in 2 Sam 22:24; Ps 15(14):2; 18(17):24; 19(18):14; 36(35):18; 64(63):5; 119(118):1, 80; Prov 11:20; 20:7; 22:11; Ezek 28:15; Dan 1:4; Wis. Sol. 2:22; Sir 31:8; 40:19; and as a requirement for priests: 1 Macc 4:42.

⁵⁶ For Greco-Roman usage, see, e.g., Herodotus 2.177 ("a *perfect* law").

⁵⁷ BDAG, 221, define one meaning of δέχομαι as "to indicate approval or conviction by accepting."

⁵⁸ Cf. Jane Lancaster Patterson, *Keeping the Feast: Metaphors of Sacrifice in 1 Corinthians and Philippians*, ECL 16 (Atlanta, GA: SBL Press, 2015), 114, who argues that Paul "uses sacrificial language and patterns to speak of the community itself as an offering on the 'day of Christ' (1:8, 2:15)."

⁵⁹ Although the wording of the two texts is almost verbatim, since Paul offers no introductory marker, it is an allusion (as throughout Philippians), rather than a citation. David Lincicum, *Paul and the Early Jewish Encounter with Deuteronomy* (Grand Rapids, MI: Baker, 2013), 119, argues for "the importance of not confining one's investigation of Paul's engagement with Deuteronomy to explicit quotations," but then surprisingly denies that this allusion in Phil 2:15 has sufficient "assertorial weight" to be treated with other, louder allusions to Deuteronomy in Paul.

⁶⁰ The MT of Deut 32:5 is notoriously difficult to analyze for comparison with the Greek. Still, it is evident that Paul's language draws on the LXX. Cf. Deut 32:5 LXX: "not to him [viz., God] children" (οὐκ αὐτῷ τέκνα).

⁶¹ Cf. Peter Wick, *Philipperbrief* (Stuttgart: Verlag W. Kohlhammer, 1994), 177, who argues forcefully: "eine Hauptfunktion des Briefes [ist] das Lob der Philipper," in line with the honorific emphasis of the Greco-Roman world. Such praise for the community, however, is of course subservient to the "oberste Ziel" of praising God himself. Similarly, Ralph Brucker, *"Christushymnen"*

In contrast to this encomiastic reading of Phil 2:15b that envisions praise on behalf of the Philippian believers for being honorably distinguished from their pagan environment, McAuley argues in light of the larger context from the Song of Moses that the phrase γενεᾶς σκολιᾶς καὶ διεστραμμένης, which appears in both Deut 32:5 and again in 32:20, "denotes God's judgment on Israel …; a 'crooked and perverse generation' is one that incurs God's displeasure."[62] Hence, McAuley posits that Paul's use of the phrase in Phil 2:15, now describing the unbelieving pagan world rather than Israel, "conveys a veiled threat or warning" against the Philippians themselves as God's people. This matches up with Rengstorf's view that Paul's use of the Pentateuchal γογγυσμός material highlights the notion of God's judgment. In the allusion to Israel's grumbling in 2:14, this implied judgment was thus raised as a prospect for the Philippian believers should they fall into Israel's sin of disbelief and rebellion.[63] Here in 2:15b, however, the judgment is directed against the Philippians' surrounding milieu (of whom they are "in the midst" [μέσον]), though the implication remains that, should the church cease to be "blameless" through ongoing obedience, they too would fade back into the twisted, disobedient masses who are under God's judgment. Paul has sharp words for such a faithless group: their end is ἀπώλεια (3:19; cf. 1:28); for the Philippians, however, Paul has confidence that their fate will be far different (1:28; 1:6).[64]

The Final Appeals of Paul and Moses

As a corollary to the "eschatological Israel" narrative running through Phil 2:12–18, some scholars have proposed a connection in this passage between Paul's ministry and that of Moses,[65] particularly in the congruence between their final appeals to God's people before their impending death.[66] On this reading, the link with Deuteronomy occurs even earlier, in Phil 2:12, where Paul speaks of his absence and calls for renewed

---

oder "epideiktische Passagen"?: *Studien zum Stilwechsel im Neuen Testament und seiner Umwelt*, FRLANT 176 (Göttingen: Vandenhoeck & Ruprecht, 1997), 320, describes the adjectives ἄμεμπτος and ἀκέραιος "als antizipierendes Lob."

[62] McAuley, *Scripture*, 207. McAuley, *Scripture*, 203–4, thus views Paul's allusion not as an anticipated affirmation for the Philippians but rather as a warning against the "dangers of disloyalty." I grant that one purpose for the use of the wilderness generation was as an *anti-model* to be avoided (in accord with how epideictic rhetoric regularly deploys negative models), but this does not exclude the corollary purpose, which is to praise the Philippians for succeeding where Israel failed.

[63] Cf. Paul's similar warning to the Corinthian community in 1 Cor 10:1–22.

[64] Cf. Paul's vision of eschatological realization for the Philippians' purity in 1:10–11.

[65] Describing Paul's ministry more generally, Jeffrey W. Aernie, *Is Paul Also among the Prophets?*, LNTS 467 (London: Bloomsbury, 2012), 157, argues that Paul uses the Mosaic tradition, in addition to other Jewish prophetic traditions, to show "that his ministry parallels the trajectory of the prophetic tradition." Similarly, Brian Rosner, "Deuteronomy in 1 and 2 Corinthians," in *Deuteronomy in the New Testament*, ed. Steve Moyise and Maarten J. J. Menken, LNTS 358 (London: A&C Black, 2007) 118–35, 135, adduces that "Paul found in Deuteronomy and Moses a typological model and a sympathetic ally." Cf. Jennings, *Partnership*, 111, who speaks of "Paul analogically pairing himself with Moses" in Phil 2:14.

[66] Beare, *Philippians*, 89: "Like Moses, Paul speaks to his people in the shadow of his impending departure from this life." Michael, *Philippians*, 99, argues that these verses "furnish clear evidence that Paul is here comparing and contrasting himself with Moses when he was giving to the children of Israel his parting injunctions as described in the closing chapters of Deuteronomy." Fred B. Craddock, *Philippians* (Louisville, KY: Westminster John Knox Press, 1985), 45, agrees: "It is quite

obedience on the part of the Philippians. For instance, Deut 31:29 LXX contains points of contact (of both similarity and dissonance) with Paul's appeal in Phil 2:12, declaring, "For I know that, after my demise, with lawlessness you will act lawlessly and turn aside from the way that I have commanded you. And the evils will come upon you at the end of days."[67] Both Moses and Paul show concern about how their respective communities will fare after their death; both are anxious about whether the group will maintain obedience. But Moses is almost resignedly pessimistic; he is confident (οἶδα) that Israel will apostatize, and that the ἔσχατον τῶν ἡμερῶν will find them suffering an evil fate.[68] Paul, on the other hand, is exuberantly optimistic.[69] He is confident (πεποιθώς) that the Philippians will succeed on the last day (Phil 1:6), that their past record of obedience (2:12) will be capped off with victory at the final assize (cf. 1:10–11; 2:16; 4:1).[70]

The reason such a vast gulf separates Paul's expectations from those of Moses is the position each minister occupies within the salvation-historical timetable. Moses had to deal with a hard-hearted Israel that lacked the indwelling power of the Spirit to enable obedience (cf. 2 Cor 3:6–18);[71] Paul writes to those among whom God is at work (Phil 2:13), whose identity "in Christ" implies that they will be able to remain faithful where Israel failed.[72] This is not to deny the possibility that the Philippians

---

obvious that Paul used for a model [in Phil 2:14–16] the farewell speech of Moses (Deut. 31:24–32:3)." Hans Dieter Betz, *Studies in Philippians*, WUNT 343 (Tübingen: Mohr Siebeck, 2015), 152, omits such a parallel, but argues nonetheless that this letter "is meant to be [Paul's] 'last word,'" classifying the letter within the genre of *praemeditatio mortis*.

[67] Beare and McAuley both point to Deut 31:27 LXX for a similar background, which states, "For I know your rebelliousness and your hard neck. For, while I am still alive among you today, you are being fractious concerning the things of God, how not also after my death?" This provides a contrast to Phil 2:12, since Moses insinuates that the Israelites have *disobeyed* in the past and will now *go on disobeying* in the future after he is gone. For Paul the matter is the reverse.

[68] Michael, *Philippians*, 101, notes how Moses "predicts with sorrow what will happen after his death," whereas Paul, "with a confidence springing from his experience of the unbroken obedience of the Philippians in the past, urges them all the more strenuously after his death to work out their own salvation."

[69] Craddock, *Philippians*, 45: "Paul has not adopted the negativity" of Moses's speech.

[70] See McAuley, *Scripture*, 210: "Unlike Moses, [Paul] is confident that their obedience is not dependent on his presence."

[71] On the dissimilarity between the ministries of Paul and Moses in 2 Corinthians see Scott J. Hafemann, *Paul, Moses, and the History of Israel*, WUNT 81 (Tübingen: Mohr Siebeck, 1995), 336–46.

[72] Compare as a parallel the promise of God's activity among the Philippians in 2:13 and the hope that Moses offers Israel in Deut 30 that after exile God himself will enable his people's obedience, with the result that he will "take delight over you" (εὐφρανθῆναι ἐπὶ σέ, Deut 30:9 LXX). Though the language is different than that describing God's "good pleasure" (ὑπὲρ τῆς εὐδοκίας) in Phil 2:13, conceptually the two ideas correlate in that God is pleased by the obedience that he himself has affected in his people. Stettler, *Heiligung*, 540, demonstrates how Paul presents the Philippians as taking up the task assigned to Israel: "Indem die Gemeinde im Gehorsam lebt, erfüllt sie den Auftrag Israels (vgl. Jes 42,6f; 49,6; 58,8-10), welchen dieses durch seine Untreue gegen Gott nicht erfüllt hatte (vgl. Phil 2,15b mit Dtn 32,5), und steht in der Erfüllung der eschatologischen Verheißung für das erneuerte Israel." Claude Tassin, "L'apostolat, un 'sacrifice'?" in *Le Sacrifice dans les Religions*, ed. Neusch (Paris: Beauchesne, 1994), 86–116, 113, refers to the daily sacrifice of the Philippians' obedience to the gospel (2:12) as ensuing from "la Nouvelle Alliance en laquelle Dieu donne à l'homme le *vouloir* et le *faire*," citing 2:13, which new covenant empowering "manqué par l'Israël du désert." Cf. John M. G. Barclay, "'By the Grace of God I Am What I Am': Grace and Agency in Philo and Paul," in *Divine and Human Agency in Paul and His Cultural Environment*, ed. Barclay and Gathercole (London: T&T Clark, 2007), 140–57, 152, for whom this passage reveals that "the believers' agency is entangled with divine agency from the roots up."

too could fall into the same trap of disloyalty and disbelief modeled by Israel (hence the imperatives of 2:12 and 2:14 and the implied warnings of 2:15-16). There is still considerable danger, which necessitates "fear and trembling." Yet, Paul is optimistic; he has seen the Philippians' obedience in action (1:6; 4:10) and he is certain that they will continue to display "the fruit of Christ" moving forward (1:10).

Paul's Deuteronomic Καύχημα in Philippians 2:16

The goal of the foregoing presentation of a predominantly Deuteronomic reading of Phil 2:12-18 has been to demonstrate the plausibility of reading Paul's καύχημα in Phil 2:16 within the framework of the ending of Deuteronomy (see Chapter 2).[73] That is to say, the generative source for the idea that obedience prompts divinely appropriated eschatological boasting on the day of judgment emerges from Paul's Scriptural tradition.[74] Thus, as the capstone to the Deuteronomic story of Israel's history of disobedience and eschatological restoration in Deut 26-32, now according to Paul being fulfilled in the lives of his Philippian converts, the apostle turns to the final outcome of their holy living, which is the establishing of *his boast* on the eschatological day of Christ's judgment (2:16b). That Paul's boasting in his work as an apostle is the climax of his argument in Phil 2:12-16 has long been recognized. Indeed, scholars often refer to the καύχημα in 2:16 as depicting Paul's *apostolic boast*.[75] For, this boasting by the apostle is "characteristically used by Paul in the context of the on-going work of the gospel itself."[76] And the legitimacy of such boasting is commonly supported by reference to Rom 15:17-18, where Paul explicitly grounds his apostolic boast (καύχησις) in Christ's working "through" (διά) him.[77]

But the Deuteronomic backdrop for this boasting in Phil 2:16 has not been sufficiently recognized. Although the grammar is compact, the phrase εἰς καύχημα

---

[73] Waters, *End of Deuteronomy*, argues for the undeniable influence of the latter chapters of Deuteronomy on Paul. While he points specifically to Deut 27-30 and 32 as providing the source material, I propose extending the influence to include the transitional material in Deut 26:16-19, which represents the bridge between the preceding law code and the ensuing appendices. Cf. Lincicum, *Deuteronomy*, 52-53, who argues that the "liturgical prominence of Deuteronomy in the Second Temple period" entails the likelihood "of Paul committing the book of Deuteronomy to memory," which could support our proposal that Paul's language of καύχημα in 2:16 is drawn from Deut 26:19 LXX.

[74] J. Sánchez Bosch, *"Gloriarse" segun san Pablo: Sentido y teología de καυχάομαι*, AnBib 40 (Rome: Biblical Institute Press, 1970), 120, similarly argues that the Greek Scriptures provide "the *concrete genesis*" of Paul's idea that either his churches constitute his boast or that he constitutes their boast. For a similar approach that views Paul's phrasing in Phil 2:16 as "Scriptural language," cf. Isaac D. Blois, "'What is my boast? Is it not you?': Εἰς καύχημα ἐμοί as Scriptural Language in Philippians 2,16," *EstBib* (forthcoming)."

[75] Bultmann, "καυχάομαι," *TDNT* 3.651. See already, Adolf von Harnack, "Das hohe Lied des Apostels Paulus von der Liebe," *SPAW* 1 (1911), 132-63, 144, noting how "sich Paulus (als Apostel) als zum Rühmen berechtigt ansieht."

[76] John Howard Schütz, *Paul and the Anatomy of Apostolic Authority*, SNTSMS 26 (Cambridge: Cambridge University Press, 1975), 233.

[77] C. K. Barrett, "Boasting (καυχᾶσθαι, κτλ.) in the Pauline Epistles," in *L'apôtre Paul: Personalité, style et conception du ministère*, ed. A. Vanhoye, BETL 73 (Leuven: University Press, 1986), 363-8, 367: "Because the grace and power of God are given to *him*, Paul, personally, his boasting in them must sometimes look like, and in a sense have to be, boasting in himself"; and further: "It is based not on Paul himself but on what God does through him (Rom 15:17f; 1 Cor 15:10, 31)." Cf. I. H. Marshall, "Should Christians Boast?" *BibSac* 159 (2002), 259-76, 266.

in 2:16b rightly denotes the culmination of Paul's argument in 2:12-16a.[78] That is, should the Philippians continue their obedience by doing all things *sans* grumbling and disputing, then they will become blameless, they will shine as lights, they will hold fast the gospel message, *so that* they will constitute a boast for their apostle. For, in the phrase εἰς καύχημα, the εἰς-preposition functions to introduce the predicate;[79] hence, the Philippians will serve "as a boast" for Paul on the final day.[80] The Philippians' becoming a boast (for Paul) is the ultimate end toward which their holy lifestyle tends, just as Israel's holiness was to result in their becoming a boast (for YHWH). As our study of the theme of mutual honor in Deuteronomy 26–32 revealed (see Chapter 2), the grammatical and conceptual structuring of Phil 2:14-16 reflects strong similarities with Deut 26:19, *activated by Paul's allusion in v. 15 to Deut 32:5*, in which Israel's obedience was to serve "as a boast" for YHWH:

καὶ εἶναί σε ὑπεράνω πάντων τῶν ἐθνῶν, ὡς ἐποίησέν σε ὀνομαστὸν καὶ **καύχημα** καὶ δόξαστόν, εἶναί σε λαὸν ἅγιον κυρίῳ τῷ θεῷ σου, καθὼς ἐλάλησεν. (Deut 26:19 LXX)

And for you to be high above all the nations, as he made you nameworthy and a boast and glorious, for you to be a holy people to the Lord your God, just as he has spoken.

Both Deut 26:19 and Phil 2:16b therefore display the "formula" observed by Sánchez Bosch in which "someone *is* a καύχημα for another person."[81] Whereas Sánchez Bosch points to the presence of this relational-boasting "formula" in 2 Cor 1:14 (καύχημα ὑμῶν ἐσμεν), I propose that the implied copula verb in the εἰς-clause of Phil 2:16b allows us to see the same formulaic understanding of one entity "serving as a καύχημα for another" here as well. Sánchez Bosch understands this type of a καύχημα as bearing an "objective" sense, by which he means that "there is a reference to the subject itself as the entity which *possesses* the object about which it boasts."[82] That is, in such uses of καύχημα, the focus is on the *relationship* between the subject and object of the boast.

---

[78] Marvin R. Vincent, *A Critical and Exegetical Commentary on the Epistles to the Philippians and to Philemon* (Edinburgh: T&T Clark, 1902), 70; Schapdick, *Heil*, 188 n. 302.

[79] BDAG, "εἰς," 290 (4d): εἰς can mark "vocation, use, or end indicated *for, as*"; and further in meaning 8, "The predicate nominative and the predicate accusative are sometimes replaced by εἰς with accusative under Semitic influence, which has strengthened Greek tendencies in the same direction." J. H. Moulton, *Grammar of New Testament Greek: Volume I Prolegomena*, 3rd ed. (Edinburgh: T&T Clark, 1967), 71–2, "common to nominative and accusative is the use of εἰς with accusative to replace a predicate, in such phrases as εἶναι εἰς and ἐγείρειν εἰς (Acts 8:23; 13:22)." Daniel B. Wallace, *Greek Grammar: Beyond the Basics* (Grand Rapids, MI: Zondervan, 1996), 47–8: "Εἰς + the accusative is occasionally found replacing the predicate nominative in the NT. Although this construction is found in the papyri, it is usually due to a Semitic influence (Hebrew לְ). This idiom is frequent in OT quotations." Wallace's observation pertains to our present case in light of our proposed background of Deut 26:19 for Phil 2:16, where the LXX's καύχημα likely renders the MT's לִתְהִלָּה. Moreover, in the many recurrences of the deuteronomic triad the *lamed* is usually rendered with εἰς: e.g., εἰς καύχημα (Jer 13:11), εἰς καύχημα (Zeph 3:19, 20).

[80] For this reading, see Max S. J. Zerwick, *A Grammatical Analysis of the Greek New Testament* (Rome: Biblical Institute Press, 2007), 597, who renders the εἰς: "to serve *as*."

[81] Sánchez Bosch, *Gloriarse*, 115: "alguien es καύχημα de otra persona."

[82] Sánchez Bosch, *Gloriarse*, 121.

Instead of a subjective boast that focuses on the *activity* of boasting, this is an objective boast, emphasizing that a second entity has been taken up into relationship with the primary subject. Hence, the fact that the blameless Philippians become a boast *for Paul* (ἐμοί) highlights the fact that they are in a relationship of shared honor, rather than solely focusing on Paul's activity of boasting.

The interconnection between Paul's efforts and those of the Philippians therefore becomes tantamount in this passage, since Paul's boast rests on both his converts' faithfulness (2:14-16a) and on his own faithfulness (2:16c). When the Philippians display faithfulness, Paul's ministry is vindicated; when Paul displays faithfulness, the Philippians are strengthened. Success by either party in this relationship results in success for the partner, thereby producing mutuality.[83] The fact that Paul directs his readers to Deut 32 in order to understand their identity and significance as the eschatologically restored "children of God" entails that they are obliged to fulfill the same expectation of covenant obedience that pertained to Israel. Moreover, just as God proffered to Israel the blessing of exaltation for obedience, so too the Philippians can expect that their obedience will bring about exaltation. And, in the same way that Israel's exaltation was described as their becoming a καύχημα for YHWH in Deut 26:19 LXX, so too the Philippians experience exaltation in the form of becoming a καύχημα in Phil 2:16. Their divinely enabled obedience earns the right to boast, but not for themselves; rather, just as in Deuteronomy, the earned boast is on behalf of another.[84]

The radical difference between Deuteronomy and Philippians, however, is that in Phil 2:15-16 the people's obedience brings about boasting, not *for God* (though this is not excluded, cf. Phil 3:3 in comparison to 1:11, 2:11, and 4:19-20)[85] but *for Paul*. Whereas in almost every instance of the Deuteronomic honorific triad (i.e., the existence of someone or something "for praise, for glory, for boasting"), this honor pertained *to YHWH* (cf. the use of the expressions ליהוה ǁ κυρίῳ in Deut 26:19; cf. too, e.g., Jer 13:11 and the survey in Chapter 2), Paul takes up the first-person dative pronoun ([ἐ]μοι) that normally marks God's share in the honor of Israel's obedience and *appropriates it to himself*.[86] One must wonder, with Silva, "how Paul can speak of

---

[83] This mirrors the mutuality reflected in the Greco-Roman discussion about friendship adduced above in Chapter 4. Cf. Seneca, *Ep.* 109.15, who speaks of a friend who "rejoice[s] in [the other's] advancement as if it were absolutely [his] own." On the value of comparing Paul and Seneca as letter writers, see E. Randolph Richards, "Some Observations on Paul and Seneca as Letter Writers," in *Paul and Seneca in Dialogue*, ed. Joseph R. Dodson and David E. Briones, APR 2 (Leiden: Brill, 2017), 49-72.

[84] Sánchez Bosch, *Gloriarse*, 120, observes that one never finds in profane Greek literature "the idea that one person might be the καύχημα of another," which idea he finds prominent in the LXX (e.g., Deut 26:19; Jer 13:11; Zeph 3:19, 20). While I agree that one is hard-pressed to find such an idea of mutual glory in Hellenistic texts via the term καύχημα, the idea that one individual might promote the glory of another is evident in the texts we have adduced in Part 2 of our study, though the idea is marked by other vocabulary.

[85] Alexander N. Kirk, *Departure of an Apostle: Paul's Death Anticipated and Remembered*, WUNT 2.406 (Tübingen: Mohr Siebeck, 2015), 171, shows how Paul's appropriation of boasting for himself does not conflict with his ability to boast in God, pointing to a "causative" relationship between them: "God alone is Paul's boast, but particularly in how his grace leads to Paul's integrity and sufficiency in ministry, and especially as that leads to the transformation of ... [Paul's] converts."

[86] Because of the linguistic similarities between Phil 2:16 (εἰς καύχημα ἐμοί) and Jer 13:11 LXX (μοι ... εἰς καύχημα), Sánchez Bosch, *Gloriarse*, 120-1, sees them as parallel, adding Zeph 3:19-20 LXX to this list as well (though noting the lack of μοι in those two verses). He cautions, however, that in

his eschatological boasting as apparently on the same level with God's glory?"[87] How is it that Paul can audaciously weave himself into this mutuality of the honor shared between God and his people?

Isaiah in Philippians 2:10-16

The answer to this question, and the key to understanding Paul's daring move of inserting *himself* within the matrix of honor enjoyed between God and the Philippians, lies in the apostle's understanding of his own mission in light of that of the Isaianic Servant. The apostle directs us to this Scriptural source by presenting two clear allusions to Isaiah in close succession in Phil 2:10-11 and 2:16.

Isaiah 45:24 in Philippians 2:10-11

The first allusion in Phil 2:10-11 is to Isa 45:23, where the worldwide submission that will be directed toward YHWH in the eschaton is now attributed to the exalted and vindicated Christ. This Isaianic text sets the stage for the eschatological perspective that runs throughout Phil 2, since Christ's eschatological exaltation demands that all creation, believers included, give to him the honor that is his prerogative.

Even this text, however, when viewed in its Isaianic context,[88] envisions the mutual glory that exists between God and his people. Directly following God's declaration that "*to me* (ἐμοί) every knee shall bow" (Isa 45:23 LXX) and "glory [will come] *to him*" (v. 24),[89] he promises that "in God (ἐν τῷ θεῷ) [Israel] shall be glorified" (v. 25).[90] Hence,

---

these three prophetic texts Israel's becoming a καύχημα is not the "ultimate end," but rather is only a *means* to promoting the knowledge of God among the nations. Therefore, Sánchez Bosch sees Sir 31:10 as a closer conceptual fit (despite being "more [linguistically] distant") with Paul's idea in Phil 2:16, since, in his view, both texts speak of a καύχημα in the context of ecclesial assessment ("before the church/congregation"). But *pace* Sánchez Bosch, the covenantal context of the Philippians passage leans toward a usage of καύχημα that sets the Philippians in comparison with a restored eschatological community of God's people, just like that offered (but then rejected) in Jer 13 and like that described in Zeph 3. Another fault in Sánchez Bosch's dismissal of these three prophetic texts as formative for Paul's presentation of his καύχημα in Phil 2:16 is his assertion that the interest of these texts in the Gentiles' "seeing" Israel's καύχημα and thereby being led into the praise of God separates them from the context of Philippians. This is simply false, not only because καύχημα necessarily involves a claim to honor *before others* but also because Paul is explicitly interested in the Philippians "shining amidst" (2:15) the surrounding pagan world.

[87] Silva, *Philippians*, 127.
[88] Peter Oakes, *Philippians: From People to Letter*, SNTSMS 110 (Cambridge: Cambridge University Press, 2001), 168-9, similarly draws on the wider Isaianic context to help understand Paul's message in Phil 2:10-11, though he actualizes the nations' submission to God (Isa 45:22), rather than Israel's exaltation by God (Isa 45:25).
[89] Nikolaus Walter, "Alttestamentliche Bezüge in christologischen Ausführungen des Paulus," in *Paulinische Christologie*, ed. Udo Schnelle, Thomas Söding, and Michael Labahn (Göttingen: Vandenhoeck & Ruprecht, 2000), 246-71, 267, notes how Isa 45:24 LXX supplies Paul with the *Stichwort* δόξα for the conclusion to the Christ hymn in 2:11. Pace Ralph P. Martin, *Hymn of Christ* (Downers Grove, IL: InterVarsity Press, 1997), 256, who states that "the influence of Isaiah ... is *unconscious*," arguing that the *auctor* of the hymn (not Paul) was a "pneumatic" who wrote "under the direct afflatus of the Spirit" and thus had no logical basis for using these allusive words.
[90] Oakes, *Philippians*, 168-70, cites the broader context of the allusion to Isa 45:24 LXX but does not elaborate on any implications flowing out of the ἐνδοξασθήσονται πᾶν ... Ισραηλ phrase in 45:25. J. Ross Wagner, *Heralds of the Good News: Isaiah and Paul in Concert in the Letter to the Romans,*

the very text to which Paul directs his readers in the conclusion of the Christ-hymn opens up the prospect of God's/Christ's glory as something in which his people can participate. Paul makes this apparent in 3:20–21, promising that God "will transform our humble bodies *to be like [Christ's] glorious body*."[91] In Philippians, glory flows from God to his eschatologically restored community of saints, which is precisely the move displayed in Isaiah's portrayal of the eschatological glory promised for God's people. And, far from standing at odds with God's own rightful possession of glory, this coheres seamlessly with the picture we have developed (see Chapter 3) of a mutuality of honor shared between God and his covenant people, both historically and eschatologically.

Paul and the Servant in Philippians 2:16

As we have seen in Chapter 3, this prospect of God's sure, eschatological glorification of his people appears regularly throughout the latter portion of Isaiah, and it is something that Paul draws on when he then describes his own ministry at verse 16 in terms of Isa 49:4: καὶ ἐγὼ εἶπα Κενῶς ἐκοπίασα καὶ εἰς μάταιον καὶ εἰς οὐδὲν ἔδωκα τὴν ἰσχύν μου, διὰ τοῦτο ἡ κρίσις μου παρὰ κυρίῳ, καὶ ὁ πόνος μου ἐναντίον τοῦ θεοῦ μου. For, as observed above, in 2:16bc Paul envisions the obedient and blameless Philippians as constituting his boast on the day of Christ:

εἰς καύχημα ἐμοὶ εἰς ἡμέραν Χριστοῦ, ὅτι οὐκ εἰς κενὸν ἔδραμον οὐδὲ εἰς κενὸν ἐκοπίασα.

(so that it/you may be) as a claim to honor for my benefit for the day of Christ, because I neither ran for nothing nor worked for nothing.

From a rhetorical and alliterative standpoint, the fourfold repetition of εἰς in 2:16bc, all here rendered woodenly with *for* to retain the rhetorical effect, is striking. While the second εἰς represents a telic marker (*for the day of Christ*), the first and the final two εἰς prepositions constitute the dual, interrelated outcomes of Paul's ministry efforts: he will have a boast and he will not have run in vain.

The reality of such a boast in Phil 2:16b is based on the fact, in v. 16c, that Paul has neither "run in vain, nor labored in vain" (cf. the causal ὅτι in v. 16c).[92] Harnack's

---

NovTSup 101 (Leiden: Brill, 2003), 339, similarly draws in the broader context from Isa 45:25 when discussing Paul's citation in Rom 14:11, where by "tapping into this larger Isaianic narrative" Paul portrays the "Romans' present life in Christ as the proleptic realization of the eschatological deliverance promised in Isaiah," and finds a comparison between Israel's "glorification" in Isa 45:25 and the Gentile believers' "glorification" in Rom 8:30 (both of which texts employ the δικ- and δοξ- verbs). As the argument here has made clear, this same "larger Isaianic narrative" and its significance for understanding the church as the realization of Isaiah's eschatological hope are at work in Phil 2:12–16.

[91] Cf. Peter Doble, "'Vile Bodies' or Transformed Persons?: Philippians 3.21 in Context," *JSNT* 86 (2002), 3–27, 27 n. 62, who argues against there being "a great gulf ... between their Lord's exaltation and the saints' transformation" into glory.

[92] Judith M. Gundry-Volf, *Paul and Perseverance: Staying In and Falling Away* (Louisville, KY: Westminster John Knox Press, 1990), 267, discusses the mutuality inherent within Paul's eschatological expectations vis-à-vis his ministry among his communities: "Paul's statements about laboring in vain express primarily ... self-concern. Yet the eschatological nature of the implications

seminal study of the term κοπιᾶν has demonstrated that for Paul this term indicates gospel ministry.[93] Often the apostle employs the κοπ- term in contexts where he entertains his own prospects for reward, frequently within eschatological settings (cf. 1 Cor 15:10; Gal 4:11; 1 Thess 3:5; 1 Cor 3:8 [alongside μισθός]; 2 Cor 10:15). The term κενός is a conspicuous member of Paul's idiolect (cf. Gal 2:2; 4:11; 1 Thess 3:5).[94] In Phil 2:16 the term appears twice in succession, within metaphors from the respective athletic and working-class word-fields. The second of these metaphors alludes to language from Isaiah's second Servant song (Isa 49:4).[95]

Paul's Isaianic Servant-Reward[96]

As we saw in our discussion of Isaiah in Chapter 3, the phrase that Paul takes up in Phil 2:16c from Isa 49:4 ("I have labored in vain") describes the Servant's lament over an unresponsive field of ministry. Moreover, this lament is the one negative statement surrounded by positive statements about the Servant's divine vocation and vindication. Most importantly, the second half of the Servant's declaration, which Paul does not incorporate within his allusion,[97] is that his "judgment is with the Lord"

---

of ineffective labor for Paul shows that the implications for his converts are also eschatological: they may be excluded from final salvation."

[93] Adolf von Harnack, "Κόπος (Κοπιᾶν, Οἱ Κοπιῶντες) im frühchristlichen Sprachgebrauch," *ZNW* 27 (1928), 1–10. Paul regularly employs the terms τρεχεῖν (1 Cor 9:26; Gal 2:2; 2 Thess 3:1) and κοπιᾶν (Rom 16:6, 12; 1 Cor 15:10; 16:16; Gal 4:11; Phil 2:16; 1 Thess 5:12) to describe his (or others') gospel efforts.

[94] Of the nineteen occurrences of κενός in the NT, eleven are in the undisputed Pauline epistles; the phrase εἰς κενόν appears only in Paul (2 Cor 6:1; Phil 2:16; Gal 2:2; 1 Thess 3:5). Gundry-Volf, *Perseverance*, 262, notes that Phil 2:16 is distinct from the other texts in which Paul brings up the possibility of having run "in vain," since here only is the phrase negated. She points out, in pp. 268–9, that "in Phil 2:16 the motif of futile service is not colored by fear but by confidence."

[95] Martin Brändl, *Der Agon bei Paulus*, WUNT 222 (Tübingen: Mohr Siebeck, 2006), 254, argues that Isa 49:4 provides "das spezifisch theologische Profil" from which one must necessarily interpret Paul's language of κοπιᾶν in Phil 2:16, since the Philippians' faithful behavior is specifically linked with "seine Jes 49,4 LXX aufgreifende Erwartung" (p. 256). Brändl, *Agon*, 260, notes a similar Isaianic connection in the running metaphor as well, pointing to Isa 40:31, where God's restoration of his people enables them to "run and not grow weary" (δραμοῦνται καὶ οὐ κοπιάσουσιν), and possibly even a reference to the "feet of those who bring good news" (πόδες εὐαγγελιζομένου) in Isa 52:7.

[96] For classic presentations of Paul's ministry being formed by the role of the Isaianic Servant, see Lucien Cerfaux, "Saint Paul et le 'Serviteur de Dieu' d'Isaïa," *RLC* 2, 439–54; and David M. Stanley, "The Theme of the Servant of Yahweh," *CBQ* 16 (1954), 415–18, 416: "Paul, whilst ever conscious that Christ Himself is the Servant *par excellence*, repeatedly reminds his listeners that in his own apostolic labours the work of the Servant is being carried forward." Mark Gignilliat, *Paul and Isaiah's Servants: Paul's Theological Reading of Isaiah 40–66 in 2 Corinthians 5.14–6.10*, LNTS 330 (London: T&T Clark, 2007), 52, treats "the issue of Paul's close identification with the Servant of Yahweh without collapsing the identity of the Servant of Isaiah 40–55 onto Paul." Gignilliat affirms the "definite overlap between Paul and the Servant of Isaiah 40–55" but argues that the category of "the servants of the Servant in Isaiah 53–66" provides for Paul an identity that is not collapsed with the Servant of Isa 40–55 (p. 53). Aernie, *Paul among the Prophets*, 139, views Paul's role as an amalgamation of multiple prophetic mantles, including but not exclusive to the Isaianic Servant, affirming that "Paul's ministry is in some way parallel to that of the servant, as well as to the rest of the prophetic tradition."

[97] Venantius de Leeuw, *De Ebed Jahweh-Profetieen: Historisch-Kritisch Onderzoek naar hun Ontstaan en hun Betekenis*, UCL 3.2 (Leuven: Van Gorcum, 1956), 30, speaks of Paul's "slightly out of tune" use of Isa 49:4 in Phil 2:16.

(49:4b).⁹⁸ Thus, by negating the Servant's lament via his positive statement in v. 16c,⁹⁹ Paul has essentially employed the Servant's lament from 49:4a in a way that lines up with the positive image from 49:4b.¹⁰⁰ Now, however, the Lord will not vindicate Paul's faithfulness *in spite* of the fact that he labored in vain, as with the Isaianic Servant, but precisely *because* Paul has *not* labored in vain.¹⁰¹

The apostle has Scriptural, Isaianic warrant to make such a change, however, since a later (eschatological) passage from Isaiah's prophecy makes just such a reversal of this image. In Isa 65:23, God promises to a renewed Israel that the covenant curses will be overturned and that they will experience anew the covenant blessings, one element of which is that they will "*not* labor in vain."¹⁰² Whereas the Servant lamented that he *has* labored in vain, both renewed Israel and now the apostle Paul exult that they have *not* labored in vain.¹⁰³ At the same time, while the Servant lamented over his lack of success, he remained confident that God would empower his labor; and, though Paul

---

⁹⁸ J. Ross Wagner, "Isaiah in Romans and Galatians," in *Isaiah in the New Testament*, ed. Steve Moyise and Maarten J. J. Menken (London: T&T Clark, 2005), 117–33, 132. Paul is not the only Jewish thinker to interpret Isa 49:4 eschatologically. See R. Abbihu (ca. 300 CE), who cites Isa 49:4 to describe the hope of divine reward awaiting him after death, and also GnR 62 (39ᵃ), both cited in Strack and Billerbeck, *Kommentar zum Neues Testament aus Talmud und Midrasch* (Munich: C. H. Beck, 1926), 3.220.

⁹⁹ Pace Terrance Callan, "Competition and Boasting: Toward a Psychological Portrait of Paul," *ST* 40.2 (1986), 137–56, 142, for whom Paul's numerous references to the possibility of having run in vain constitute a "fear of failure" that (negatively) reflects "Paul's unconsciously continuing to rely on himself." Rather, the phrase εἰς κενόν in Paul, reflecting as it does the parlance of the Isaianic Servant, conveys the apostle's understanding of his own ministry as continuing the *divinely empowered* ministry of the Servant (compare Isa 49:5, "my God shall be my *strength* [ἰσχύς]" with Phil 4:13, "*I have strength* [ἰσχύω] to do all things, through the one who empowers me"), a ministry that will undoubtedly succeed where the original Servant faced rejection because Christ has provided the Spirit who enables obedience among the people of the new covenant.

¹⁰⁰ Comfort, "Futility," *DPL* 321: "The second half of Isaiah 49:4 may stand behind Paul's expression of confidence [in Phil 2:16] that his ministry will be vindicated and he will 'boast' on the Day of Christ." For as McAuley, *Scripture*, 231, points out, "An initial intertextual pattern formed by Paul … could include God's approval of the servant despite his apparent failure." Markus Bockmuehl, *The Epistle to the Philippians*, BNTC 11 (Peabody, MA: Hendrickson, 1998), 159, also points to the Servant's assurance that his "toil" is before the Lord in Isa 49:4b as possibly formative for the apostle's understanding of his own apostolic labor. Detlef Häußer, *Der Brief des Paulus an die Philipper*, HTANT (Witten: SCM R.Brockhaus, 2016), 189, similarly argues that behind Paul's confidence in 2:16 stands Isa 49:4, in which the Servant's lament becomes absorbed "in dem Vertrauen auf Gott, dass er sein Recht und Lohn ist."

¹⁰¹ Brändl, *Agon*, 257, recognizes that the background of the Servant's reward (*Lohn*, משפטי פעלתי) in Isa 49:4 could lead to an understanding of καύχημα in Phil 2:16, though he understands the connection emerging from a common experience of success between Paul and the Servant, rather than taking into account the Servant's experience of failure.

¹⁰² Of the numerous uses of the *in vain* phrase in the LXX, Isa 65:23 is one of the rare occurrences in which the phrase is negated (i.e., *not* in vain). For use of the phrase εἰς κενός (alternately, διὰ κενῆς, κενῶς, εἰς κενά, εἰς τὸ κενόν) in its negative, vacuous capacity, see, e.g., Lev 26:16, 20; Isa 49:4; Job 2:9b LXX; 20:18; 39:16; T. Job 24:2; Wis 3:11. Antonio Pitta, *Lettera ai Filippesi: Nuova versione, introduzione e commento*, LBNT 11 (Milan: Paoline, 2010), 181–2, sees in Phil 2:16 an echo of Job 2:9LXX, where Job's wife laments having given birth "in vain."

¹⁰³ So too Silva, *Philippians*, 127: "Quite likely, Paul's language reflects the promise of Isa 65:17–25," and Todd Still, *Philippians & Philemon* (Macon, GA: Smyth & Helwys Bible Commentary, 2011), 79: "While Paul, like exiled Israel, sometimes thought his labor might be for naught (see Isa 49:4; cf. Hab 2:13), his eschatological and pastoral hope was that his apostolic ministry would not be in vain (cf. Isa 65:23)."

is experiencing the success of the gospel, he too reflects this same confidence. In Isa 49:5, the Servant exclaims: "I will be gathered and glorified (δοξασθήσομαι) before the Lord,[104] and my God shall become my strength (ἰσχύς)" (49:5 LXX, cf. Isa 41:10). Paul similarly affirms that he "has strength (ἰσχύω) through the one who enables (ἐνδυναμοῦντί)" him (Phil 4:13).

This assurance of support and reward for the Servant follows the trajectory of reward as developed throughout Isa 40–66. In the second Servant song, such an assured reward appears as the Servant's prerogative (κρίσις) in 49:4b. Paul taps into this tradition of the Servant's reward when speaking about his own ministry in Philippians (and elsewhere[105]). Just as the Servant was faithful to his task to call Israel to repentance and so could count on receiving divine exaltation when God brought about Israel's glory, so too the apostle expects that God will grant him glory once his ministry of fostering the exaltation of God's people in Philippi reaches its *telos*. The result of the Servant's faithfulness would eventually be a new covenant community that experiences the covenant blessing of labor that is fruit*ful*, not fruit*less* (Isa 65:23). Such fruitfulness is just what Paul expects both for his own continued ministry (cf. 1:22 with 2:16c) and for the Philippians' participation in that ministry (cf. 1:7, 11; 4:17).[106] Isaiah presents this nonfutility as a future, eschatological blessing, but Paul envisions himself already sharing in the eschatological reality of nonfutility because of his role as minister of the gospel of the risen and exalted Christ.

In Phil 2:16, Paul's inclusion of the καύχημα term as the positive counterpart to labor that is not εἰς κενόν allows him to conjoin the honorific language reserved for God's covenant people from Deut 26:19 LXX (cf. Jer 13:11; Zeph 3:19–20) with the exaltation promised for the ministry of the Isaianic Servant in Isa 49:4. This link between covenant honor and the honor facilitated by the Servant is not a Pauline *novum*; indeed, the Hebrew text of Isa 40–66 attests remarkable linguistic overlap with the honorific triad from Deut 26:19, with the terms "honor" (תהלה), "name" (שם), and "glory" (תפארת) recurring regularly (see Chapter 3). Moreover, while the Greek equivalents of two of these terms abound in LXX-Isaiah ([ἐν]δόξα and ὀνομαστός), the καυχ- word-group is conspicuously absent, which supports further the supposition

---

[104] Along with reiterating 49:3, this idea echoes various earlier divine declarations to his people: e.g., Isa 43:4; 45:24.

[105] For example, Gal 2:2; 1 Thess 2:1; 3:5; 2 Cor 6:1. Cf. Gal 4:11; 1 Cor 9:15; 15:10, 14, 58. Note the comment by Roy E. Ciampa, *The Presence and Function of Scripture in Galatians 1 and 2*, WUNT 102 (Tübingen: Mohr Siebeck, 1998), 131–2, that Isa 49:4 "is a favorite phrase of St. Paul's" (citing B. Lindars, *New Testament Apologetic: The Doctrinal Significance of the Old Testament Quotations* [London: SCM. Press, 1973], 223–4). Cf. Karl Olav Sandnes, *Paul—One of the Prophets?: A Contribution to the Apostle's Self-Understanding*, WUNT 2.43 (Tübingen: Mohr Siebeck, 1991), 218, who describes "not in vain" (1 Thess 2:1) as "a typical Pauline expression of biblical language … from Isa. 49:4."

[106] Paul, therefore, being on the other side of the eschatological divide, is expecting an outcome of his ministry that is *opposite* to that of the Servant. In contrast, Carl J. Bjerkelund, "'Vergeblich' als Missionsergebnis bei Paulus," in *God's Christ and His People*, ed. Jacob Jervell and Wayne A. Meeks (Oslo: Universitetsforlaget, 1977), 175–91, 181, finds in the Rabbinic literature confirmation that "'vergeblich' als charakterisierende Norm beibehalten wird, und dass es hier [viz., Isa 65:23] ausgesprochen die kommende Welt ist, die dem, was 'nicht vergeblich' ist."

that Paul derived the "boasting" motif in Phil 2:16 from Deut 26:19 LXX as read within its larger literary context.

Thus, by aligning himself with the role of the Isaianic Servant, Paul envisions himself sharing in the eschatological "reward" offered to the Servant. Isaiah's Servant figure, because of his divinely bestowed mission to Israel (and the nations) (cf. Isa 49:6), becomes a focal point for the exaltation previously offered to God's covenant people (cf. Deut 26:19; Isa 45:25). As the figurehead who represents Israel, the Servant is therefore often depicted in the same exalted, glorified terms applied to Israel (cf. the Servant "is glorified [δοξασθήσομαι]" [Isa 49:5], as Israel was to be made "glorious [δόξαστόν]" [Deut 26:19]). In his identity as Israel's representative and the embodiment of her glory, the Servant figure plays a significant role in bringing about Israel's eschatological glory through his ministry to restore her, and thereby gains for himself a distinctive reward (cf. Isa 49:4; 53:12).[107] This notion of the unique reward given by God to the Servant thus provides the framework within which Paul could envision *himself* as the beneficiary of the honorific καύχημα engendered by the Philippians' obedience.[108]

Against this backdrop of Deut 26:19 and Isa 49:4, the eschatological boast that Paul envisions as a reality on the day of Christ represents the culmination of the obedience displayed by the newly constituted children of God as they become blameless, pure, and faultless on the one hand, and by his own faithfulness on the other, both of which are represented in Phil 2:15-16. This "boast" is the same honorific reality that was offered to Israel when they entered into covenant with YHWH in Deut 26:16-19, but, as Phil 2:15 makes clear, is only now becoming attainable because of Christ's work in establishing a new community of faithful children in contrast with faithless Israel. It is a boast that is enjoyed mutually, as was true of the original promise in Deuteronomy. There, both God and his people participated in the exaltation that ensued from their (hoped for) obedience. Here in Philippians, as in Isaiah, three entities now participate in the exaltation arising from the believers' obedience: God/Christ, the Philippians, and Paul himself in his role as their apostolic "servant."

Conclusion

In this chapter, we have demonstrated that in Phil 2:16 Paul provides the corollary to Phil 1:26 in order to complete the picture of mutual honor that he shares with the Philippians. In so doing, the Scriptural framework of mutual honor between God and his people enumerated in the covenant relationship furnished the hope that obedience by God's people (now represented by the Philippians themselves) would engender a

---

[107] On the basis of these strong resonances with Isa 49 in Phil 2:16, A.-M. Denis, "La fonction apostolique et liturgie nouvelle en esprit," *RSPT* 42 (1958), 617–56, 622, argues that "Il est donc permis de voir dans le labeur de S. Paul le labeur des derniers temps, prélude de leur ultime accomplissement." Paul hopes to receive the honor accruing from his end-time labors when the day of Christ finally dawns.

[108] P. Genths, "Der Begriff des καύχημα bei Paulus," *NKZ* 38 (1928), 501–21, 511, calls attention to Paul's emphatic self-appropriation of the honor accruing from the Philippians' obedience: "ἐμοί hebt das Selbstgefühl des Apostels deutlich heraus."

mutual καύχημα between God, his people, and Paul (Deut 26:19 LXX; Isa 49:4). That this mutual honor could include Paul within its gamut is demonstrated by Paul's use of the Isaianic Servant material to describe his own role, placing him in the position of mediator between God and his people, with the prospect of participating in the glorious reward offered to the Servant (Isa 49:4). It remains to be seen in our final chapter how Paul makes use of this Scripturally warranted idea of a mutual boast, shared between himself, the Philippians, and God, in order to persuade them to stand firm, united for the gospel.

8

Mutual Honor as the Motivational Spur in Philippians

It has been shown that Paul has theological warrant from the Scriptures for presenting himself as sharing in the mutual honor between God and his people accruing from the Philippians' faithfulness. This comes from the Isaianic Servant's position as mediator of the bidirectional flow of honor between God and his covenant people, a role Paul sees himself sharing as an apostle of Christ. Another way of understanding this mutuality of honor shared between Paul and the Philippians, one that would have been evident to the Romanized audience in the letter, is through the cultural lens pertaining to the friendship and family relationships (see Part 2) established by Paul throughout the letter. In fact, the Scriptural and cultural frameworks are linked insofar as the covenant itself is based primarily on the familial tie between God as Father and Israel as his children.[1] Hence, as we saw in our discussion of Phil 1:26, Paul presents his relationship with the Philippians in terms that resonate strongly within the closely interrelated paradigms of friendship and family. This framework involved the expectation that friends and family pursued each other's honor.[2] Applied to Phil 2:12-16, this friendship and family expectation for mutual honor similarly explains how Paul's auditors would have found it natural that the honor ensuing from their own blameless behavior contributed toward the honor of Paul as their friend (1:5, 7; 2:1, etc.) and "brother" (cf. 1:12, 14; 2:25; 3:1, etc.). Indeed, they would have been delighted by this fact (cf. 4:10, 14-15), even as Paul experienced joy over the Philippians (cf. 1:3, 7-8; 4:1). And in Phil 2:17-18 Paul expresses that his faithfulness, even to the point of death, should lead to a mutual rejoicing among them.[3]

---

[1] Again, see F. M. Cross, "Kinship and Covenant in Ancient Israel," in *From Epic to Canon: History and Literature in Ancient Israel* (Baltimore, MD: Johns Hopkins Press, 1998), 3-21.

[2] Joseph H. Hellerman, "Brothers and Friends in Philippi: Family Honor in the Roman World and in Paul's Letter to the Philippians," *BTB* 39 (2009), 15-25, 20, points to inscriptions from ancient Philippi erected by one friend on behalf of another, arguing that friendship was thus a "social context in the colony of Philippi in which persons conferred, rather than vied for, honor." For an elaboration of this point, see Chapter 6.

[3] Recall Seneca's comment that friends "rejoice in [each other's] advancement as if it were absolutely [their] own" (*Ep.* 109.15); Cicero, *Amic.* 22, describes a friend as "someone whose joy in [your prosperity] would be equal to your own." Cf. Paul's admonition to the Roman Christ-followers to "rejoice with those who rejoice" (Rom 12:15).

Even more foundational than the friendship paradigm within Philippians is the family model, on which Paul again draws in Phil 2:12–18. In line with the first of his many references to the Philippians as "siblings" in 1:12, the apostle refers to them as "my beloved" in 2:12,[4] thereby reinforcing the familial bond as the basis for his exhortations in 2:12 and 14.[5] The result of this communally enjoyed familial honor in the mutual boast of 1:26 and 2:16 fits well the common Greco-Roman pattern of one family member's virtuous actions contributing toward the honor of the family as a whole.[6] That is, within the Philippians' cultural framework, it would have been no surprise that Paul's beloved brothers and sisters contribute toward his honor by means of their virtuous behavior and vice versa. This cultural framework and expectation are confirmed by the example of Epaphroditus in 2:25–30.[7] On the one hand, the Philippians are expected to receive great joy from his return to them, since Epaphroditus's faithfulness honors the Philippians as their emissary (cf. 2:29 with 4:17–18). On the other hand, the Philippians are expected to bestow honors on Epaphroditus for his faithfulness to God and his people in carrying out his role as Paul's brother and the Philippians' emissary, since doing so entailed great danger and almost caused his death (see Phil 2:29–30; the parallels to Christ and Paul are evident).[8]

Two things remain to be discussed in this final chapter. First, we will summarize how mutuality is achieved by the conjoining of Phil 1:26 and 2:16 and how this mutuality is in fact threefold in that God/Christ is brought into the bidirectional flow of honor between Paul and the Philippians. Second, we will then conclude by drawing out in more detail how Paul used this reality of mutual honor within the letter to motivate the Philippians. Specifically, we will observe how the apostle deployed the motif of mutual honor rhetorically to persuade his readers to respond favorably to his central command to pursue unity in the face of persecution and thereby prove themselves worthy citizens of Christ's kingdom (Phil 1:27–28; 2:2; cf. 4:2).[9] We begin, however,

---

[4] Reider Aasgaard, *"My Brothers and sisters!": Christian Siblingship in Paul*, JSNTSup 265 (London: T&T Clark, 2004), 282, speaks of the "close affinity" of the term ἀγαπητοί to the sibling address ἀδελφοί.

[5] Ralph Brucker, *"Christushymnen" oder "epideiktische Passagen"?: Studien zum Stilwechsel im Neuen Testament und seiner Umwelt*, FRLANT 176 (Göttingen: Vandenhoeck & Ruprecht, 1997), 320, notes how Paul's intensive praise for the addressees forms the basis for the following imperatives.

[6] Cf. Plutarch's assertion that a sibling serves as the perfect candidate to be "a sharer in all honourable enterprises" (*Mor.* 485C) so that together the siblings can attain honor for the family.

[7] Cf. Drake Williams III, "Honouring Epaphroditus: A Suffering and Faithful Servant Worthy of Admiration," in *Paul and His Social Relations*, ed. Stanley E. Porter and Christopher Land (Leiden: Brill, 2013), 333–55, 341, who argues: "Paul's writing about Epaphroditus indicates both a mutuality as well as distinction with regard to the Philippian congregation."

[8] See R. Alan Culpepper, "Co-Workers in Suffering: Philippians 2:19–30," *RevExp* 77 (1980), 349–58, 356: "Just as Christ had died as a servant and Paul faced death, Epaphroditus too had come near death as a result of his mission to serve."

[9] While the focus of the present study is on the motif of mutual honor as Paul's means to motivate his hearers to obedience, this is not the only tool Paul uses to bring about this goal. Additionally, one could point to the motivating power of deploying the narrative of Christ's humiliation and exaltation as a parallel to the kind of attitude to which Paul is calling the Philippians (cf. 2:5). That is, just as Christ's "obedience" (2:7) led to his exaltation by the Father (2:9–11), so too (cf. Paul's "therefore" in 2:12) the Philippians' "obedience" can also result in eschatological boasting/honor (2:16, on which see Morna Hooker, "Philippians," in *New Interpreter's Bible: Second Corinthians-Philemon*, vol. 11 [Nashville, TN: Abingdon Press, 2000], 469–549, 513). Similarly, Paul's gesture toward the Spirit's work already in the lives of these believers in 2:2 establishes the expectation that they will continue to walk in step with the new spiritual life into which they have been called.

with a presentation of the threefold nature of the mutuality of honor that Paul presents in the letter, which he then draws on when exhorting his readers.

Triple Mutuality of Honor in Philippians

The picture that emerges from our discussion of Phil 1:26 and Phil 2:16 is one of a balanced reciprocity of honor between Paul and the Philippian believers.[10] When held together, these passages demonstrate that Paul depicted himself in a relationship with this community, which anticipated that their actions would affect his honor and his actions theirs. We have also seen that this mutuality of honor has its theological basis in the reciprocal honor arising "vertically" from YHWH's covenant relationship with his people, a relationship within which Paul now situates his Gentile converts as "children of God" (2:15).[11] The mutuality of honor shared between God the Father and his children, however, allows room for Paul himself to participate in this honor by means of his identification with the Isaianic Servant. The mediation that the Servant undertakes to facilitate mutual honor for God and his people allows Paul to benefit from the honor accruing for God from the obedience of the Philippians (2:16) as well as allowing Paul to contribute toward God's honoring of the Philippians (1:26).

The same reality of mutual honor is evident in the Greco-Roman family model, by means of which the Philippian ἀδελφοί are expected to maintain the honor of their sibling Paul, and vice versa. Here too, however, the mutuality of honor reflected in the letter via the family model, in which Paul consistently refers to the Philippians as his "siblings," but never as his "children," presupposes the presence of God as the third party who establishes the relationship between the siblings (cf. God as "[our] Father" in 1:2; 2:11; 4:20). Just as the honor accruing from the Philippians' actions applies to their "brother," Paul, and as the honor accruing from Paul's actions applies to his Philippian "brothers and sisters," so too the mutual honor between siblings ultimately redounds to God their "Father" (1:11; 2:11; 4:20). Thus, the mutual honor reflected in the letter essentially entails a tridirectional flow of honor between Paul, the Philippians, and God/Christ.

Paul also portrays this three-way mutuality of honor in his third use of the καυχ- word group in the letter at Phil 3:3. In this passage, where the apostle sets the Christ community over against the evil workers in a series of contrasts, Paul describes believers (including himself in the first-person plural, "we") as those who "boast in Christ Jesus" (καυχώμενοι ἐν Χριστῷ Ἰησοῦ), as opposed to those who place their "confidence in the flesh" (ἐν σαρκὶ πεποιθότες). Here the activity of "boasting" is parallel to "finding confidence," both of which employ prepositional phrases using ἐν to designate the object or realm of such assurance. Here the boasting verb, in line with the overall emphasis of the passage on a self-presentation of honorific

---

[10] Frank W. Weidmann, *Philippians, 1 and 2 Thessalonians, and Philemon* (Louisville, KY: Westminster John Knox, 2013), 56, notes that in both 1:26 and 2:16, "the boasting is premised on the ongoing relationship of Paul to the community."

[11] Cf. I. H. Marshall, "Should Christians Boast?" *BibSac* 159 (2002), 259–76, 271, commenting on 2 Cor 1:14: "Evidently it is proper for believers to exult in one another as they see each other gain approval from God."

pedigree,[12] represents the activity of locating one's honor in someone or something. Whereas the two previous uses of the καυχ- lexeme depicted a flow of honor between Paul and the Philippians (though with Christ and God intimately involved),[13] here in 3:3 the flow of honor moves from both Paul and the Philippians explicitly to Christ.[14] That is, they locate their honor in Christ Jesus.

Even this experience of honor moving from Paul and the Philippians to God/Christ is mutual in the letter, however, in that the divine third party in the relationship reciprocates honor to both Paul and the Philippians. Paul is convinced that he will experience vindication from God through not being ashamed in his trial proceedings (1:20), as well as through his experience of the power of Christ's resurrection (3:10). Moreover, Paul looks forward to the prize that awaits him because of his divine calling in Christ (3:14). The Philippians as well can expect to receive honor from Christ when he returns. In a similar picture to that of the apostle's παρουσία in Phil 1:26, which also entailed honor for the Philippians, Christ's return from heaven will produce a glorious and powerful transformation for believers (3:20-21). Additionally, Paul promises a divine reciprocation of glory for the Philippians as a response to their generous financial participation in Paul's gospel ministry (4:19). This interconnected tripartite matrix of honor flowing between Paul, the Philippians, and God/Christ is depicted in the following diagram:

Trifold Mutuality of Honor in Philippians

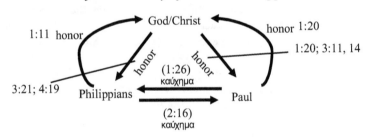

---

[12] On Paul's self-presentation in Phil 3, see Joseph H. Hellerman, *Reconstructing Honor in Roman Philippi: Carmen Christi as Cursus Pudorum*, SNTSMS 132 (Cambridge: Cambridge University Press, 2005), 121-7; Peter Pilhofer, *Philippi: Band I, Die erste christliche Gemeinde Europas*, WUNT 87 (Tübingen: Mohr Siebeck, 1995), 123-4. Francesco Bianchini, *L'elogio di sé in Cristo: L'utilizzo della περιαυτολογία nel contesto di Filippesi 3,1-4,1*, AnBib 164 (Rome: Biblical Institute Press, 2006), 5, speaks of the paradoxical use of the *periautologia* form by Paul, for whom "l'elogio di sé sino a trasformarlo in elogio di Cristo."

[13] In addition to Christ's central inclusion grammatically in 1:26, both 2:16 and 1:26 conceptually include Christ/God within the gamut of mutual honor between Paul and the Philippians. This is because God's activity enables the faithfulness that brings about the boasting in both cases. In 1:26 the Philippians' boast comes about through Paul's faithfulness, which is dependent on Christ who is his life (1:21) and who empowers him (4:13). In 2:16 Paul's boast comes about through the Philippians' faithfulness, which is dependent on God who works in them (2:13; cf. 1:6). Cf. G. Walter Hansen, *The Letter to the Philippians*, PNTC (Grand Rapids, MI: Eerdmans, 2009), 185-6.

[14] Bianchini, *L'elogio*, 248, argues that Paul's boast in 2:16 is closely recalled in 3:3, where the boast is experienced together by all believers.

All three entities are involved in the interchange of honor: God/Christ, the Philippians, and the apostle. Much as we saw in Isaiah, the three-way relational flow of honor between YHWH, Israel, and the Servant, so too here in Philippians the matrix of relations presents three parties in a threefold exchange of honor.

Paul's Radical Reversal of Honor

It is significant rhetorically, furthermore, that the honorific nature of this outcome for both the apostle and his community (and for God as the divine agent enabling the activity of each) is conveyed in 2:16 in language that has strong resonance within the Roman colony of Philippi. For instance, in addition to the motifs we have studied, Samuel Vollenweider sees in Paul's combination of the ideas of παρουσία and ἡμέρα Χριστοῦ in 2:12-16 a modeling after certain "politisch-festlicher Konventionen," which he too reconstructs in terms of honor: "Der wiederkehrende Christus verleiht dem Apostel im Blick auf dessen Wohltaten zugunsten der himmlischen Stadt einen Ehrenpreis."[15] This image of Paul as an honored benefactor in Phil 2:12-16 matches the picture we developed regarding Phil 1:26, where Paul's glorious arrival provided honor for the Philippians. In both cases, the picture of a glorious entrance into a colony by a dignitary, thereby acquiring honor for himself and for his retinue, would have been familiar to the Philippians.

The radical element in Paul's depiction, however, and this is where his thinking diverges drastically from the Roman culture in which he ministered and the Philippians dwelt, is that the benefactor for whom the beleaguered community is eagerly awaiting, in the case of both Paul (1:26; 2:12) and Christ (3:20), has assumed the form of a slave (cf. 1:1; 2:7). As Witherington describes it, "Paul has engineered a remapping of honor and shame," with the result that there are different criteria for "what one ought or ought not [to] boast about."[16] Paul maintains the importance of honor for both himself and for his communities in accordance with the surrounding culture,[17] but it is an honor that has been redefined by the humiliation and exaltation of Jesus Christ. Collange points to this same reversal of honor in 2:16:

> It is symptomatic how, in defining his ministry, the apostle does not have recourse to a vocabulary associated with honour, dignity, or glory, but on the contrary to words denoting effort and difficulties. Yet honour itself does come; not from the apostle himself or from his office but from others—from those who will be his pride in the "day of Christ."[18]

---

[15] Samuel Vollenweider, "Lob am Jüngsten Tag: zum Hintergrund der Gerichtserwartung im Philipperbrief," in *Beiträge zur urchristlichen Theologiegeschichte*, ed. Wolfgang Kraus, BZNW 163 (Berlin: de Gruyter, 2009), 307-17, 308.
[16] Ben Witherington III, *Paul's Letter to the Philippians: A Socio-Rhetorical Commentary* (Grand Rapids, MI: Eerdmans, 2011), 93.
[17] Cf. James R. Harrison, "Paul and the Roman Ideal of Glory," in *Letter to the Romans*, ed. U. Schnelle, BETL 226 (Leuven: Leuven University Press, 2009), 329-69, 363: "For Paul, the Romans are correct in highlighting ... the quest for glory ... But [for Paul] the allocation of δόξα for the believer is an eschatological gift."
[18] J.-F. Collange, *The Epistle of St. Paul to the Philippians*, trans. A. W. Heathcote (London: Epworth Press, 1979), 113.

Mutual Fame as the Motivational Spur in Philippians

We have established that Paul had good grounds, both theologically and culturally, for referring to the mutual honor that he shared with his Philippian converts. It now remains to look at the motivational power inherent in the reality of such a shared boast. We saw in Chapter 5 that ancient letter writers attempted to wield the power engendered by their relationship of mutual honor to sway friends and family to respond favorably to exhortation. Paul too wields the emotional pathos that such mutual honor possesses over his readers.[19]

By presenting the first half of their mutual honor in Phil 1:26, in which Paul shows that he is personally invested in furthering the honor of the Philippians, Paul establishes rapport with his readers. Rhetorically, Paul is establishing ethos, demonstrating his goodwill and thereby acquiring their trust, which is necessary for him to be able to issue commands.[20] As John Marshall defines it, ethos is "the relationship built up within the speech between the rhetor and the auditor which induces the auditor to believe the person speaking." Marshall argues that such ethos is established "by means of identification between" both parties.[21] Paul highlights this identification not only by asserting that he seeks the best interests of the Philippians[22] but also by displaying that he has actually forgone his own good in order to pursue theirs. As Watson observes, "Paul's show of concern which outweighs his own wishes provides an example of a life lived worthy of the gospel in spite of suffering (the central concern of Philippians)."[23]

Moreover, by pointing in Phil 1:26 to one half of the mutuality of honor, that is, *his* actions contributing toward *their* honor, Paul is also creating an expectation for the other corresponding half of the kinship ties he shares with the Philippians.[24] That

---

[19] On Philippians as containing the species of deliberative rhetoric, see Duane F. Watson, "A Rhetorical Analysis of Philippians and Its Implications for the Unity Question," *NovT* 30.1 (1988), 57–88, 59; cf. Demetrius K. Williams, *Enemies of the Cross of Christ: The Terminology of the Cross and Conflict in Philippians*, LNTS 223 (London: Sheffield Academic, 2002), 98–105. Peter-Ben Smit, *Paradigms of Being in Christ*, LNTS 476 (London: Bloomsbury T&T Clark, 2013), 34 n.181, notes that there are epideictic elements of Paul's rhetoric in Philippians (he points to "the implied praise of Christ in Phil. 2:5–11, Paul's praise of Timothy and Epaphroditus as well as of himself in … ch. 2 and in ch. 3"), though Smit argues that these elements "are all parts of overarching deliberative sections." See also George A. Kennedy, *New Testament Interpretation Through Rhetorical Criticism* (Chapel Hill: University of North Carolina Press, 1984), 77, who states that "Philippians is largely epideictic." Kennedy is followed by Claudio Basevi and Juan Chapa, "Philippians 2.6–11: The Rhetorical Function of a Pauline 'Hymn,'" in *Rhetoric and the New Testament*, ed. Stanley E. Porter and Thomas H. Olbricht, 338–56, LNTS 90 (London: Bloomsbury, 1993), 349: "[Philippians] belongs rather to the epideictic speech than to the deliberative one."

[20] John W. Marshall, "Paul's Ethical Appeal in Philippians," in Porter and Olbricht, *Rhetoric and the New Testament*, 357–74, 366, describes Paul's identification with the Philippians in, e.g., 1:26, as engendering the "trustworthiness he needs for a persuasive ethos."

[21] Marshall, "Ethical Appeal," 360.

[22] Marshall, "Ethical Appeal," 367: "Paul frequently uses affectionate language (ἀδελφός, ἀγαπητός, ἐπιπόθητος, etc.) to identify with and ingratiate himself to the audience."

[23] Duane F. Watson, "The Integration of Epistolary and Rhetorical Analysis of Philippians," in *Rhetorical Analysis of Scripture*, ed. Stanley E. Porter and Thomas H. Olbricht, LNTS 146 (Sheffield: Sheffield Academic Press, 1997) 398–426, 416.

[24] Cf. Craig S. Wansink, *Chained in Christ: The Experience and Rhetoric of Paul's Imprisonments*, LNTS 130 (Sheffield: Sheffield Academic Press, 1996), 125, who argues in reference to Phil 1:18b–26 that "Paul presents a pattern of behavior which he expects the Philippian community to follow."

is, after describing how *he* has furthered *their* honor, it would be natural for Paul to present how *they* can further *his* honor. As Jaquette notes, "Situated in the *exordium* to build his own *ethos* and elicit positive *pathos* from his readers, Paul's personal example [presented in 1:21-26] places the burden of the letter's paraenesis right up front."[25] This is precisely the element that emerges from Phil 2:12-16, where the Philippians are issued a command as Paul's "beloved," and are expected to respond in the way that siblings should, that is, to bolster Paul's honor.

Hence, whereas the reference to the Philippians' boast in 1:26 establishes ethos, the reference to Paul's boast in 2:16 garners pathos.[26] Much as Cicero[27] and Fronto[28] relied on their correspondents' concern for the writers' own glory as motivation for a positive response to their advice, so too Paul points to the honor that will accrue for himself as motivation for the Philippians to amend their behavior.[29] Paul has referred often in the letter to the "affections" that he feels toward the Philippians (1:8; 4:1) and his concern for their welfare (2:19). He presupposes that they feel the same goodwill toward himself (1:12; 2:25; 4:10), and so he capitalizes on their affection for him[30] by making his own joy and honor dependent upon their success (cf. 2:2, 16).[31] As Snyman notes, Paul's reference to the possibility of his own failure (εἰς κενόν) motivates the Philippians[32] because it represents "something that [they] would try to avoid at all cost, due to the close relationship between themselves and the apostle."[33] In the same way,

---

[25] J. L. Jaquette, "A Not-So-Noble Death: Figured Speech, Friendship and Suicide in Philippians 1:21-26," *NeoT* 28.1 (1994), 177-92, 186.

[26] Timothy C. Geoffrion, *The Rhetorical Purpose and the Political and Military Character of Philippians* (Lampeter: Mellen Biblical Press, 1993), 176, explains that Paul's "self-disclosure reinforces his sense of trustworthiness (*ethos*) and elicits an emotional response (*pathos*) of gratitude and admiration."

[27] For example, *Fam.* 9.14.4, where, if he follows Cicero's advice, Dolabella will "win such fame," while for Cicero himself it will be "something to boast about."

[28] For example, *Ad Verum Imp.* 2.4: "When I see you return with such great glory gained by your valour, I shall not have lived in vain."

[29] Richard M. Ryan and Edward L. Deci, "Intrinsic and Extrinsic Motivations: Classic Definitions and New Directions," *CEP* 25 (2000), 54-67, describe how providing intrinsic motivation, such as Paul does, through creating a sense of "relatedness" with the one issuing the commands, is more effective in garnering a favorable response. Carolyn Osiek, *Philippians, Philemon* (Nashville, TN: Abingdon, 2000), 72, finds in Paul's reference to his own honor the kind of rhetoric "expected ... to sway a crowd in oral or written communication."

[30] James W. Thompson, "Paul's Argument from Pathos in 2 Corinthians," in *Paul and Pathos*, ed. Thomas H. Olbricht and Jerry L. Sumney, SBLSymS 16 (Atlanta, GA: SBL, 2001), 131-45, 134, notes about Paul's similar statement in 2 Cor 1:14 that Paul uses pathos to "appeal to the emotions of his listeners, describing the bonds that unite them with him."

[31] A. H. Snyman, "Rhetorical Analysis of Phil 1:27-2:18," *VE* 26.3 (2005), 783-809, 801, makes a similar argument about Phil 2:12, where the presence/absence motif conveys "the close relationship between Paul and the Philippians" with the result that Paul "relies on the fact that the Philippians would act in a way consistent with this relationship ... Paul is convinced that they would try their best not to disappoint him."

[32] As stated above, although our study focuses on Paul's use of mutual honor, this is not say that such mutual honor is the *only* element motivating the Philippians to obedience. The example of Christ depicted in the hymn (Phil 2:5-11) immediately prior to the exhortations of 2:12 and 2:14 doubtlessly prompts Paul's ὥστε in 2:12, which introduces his command.

[33] Snyman, "Phil 1:27-2:18," 804. Cf. Geoffrion, *Military Character*, 177-8: "By articulating the nature and value of the network of relationships [viz., a common hope, joy, and future together] ... Paul implicitly offers the Philippians a great motivation to 'stand firm' in their allegiance to Christ, to him, and to one another." See also Stefan Schapdick, *Eschatisches Heil mit eschatischer*

Engberg-Pedersen describes how in 2:2 ("make *my joy* complete") "Paul is appealing to the already established partnership of love (2:1) between himself and the Philippians ... and using an affirmation of his own love for them ... as a basis for exhorting them to respond to him."[34] The same move happens in 2:16 as well, where now it is Paul's honor (καύχημα) that depends on the Philippians for its preservation.[35] This is not manipulative insofar as the flow of honor moves in the other direction as well, their honor is similarly dependent on his success (1:26). Paul has maintained his side of the mutual relationship; and now they must maintain theirs.

Such a deliberative purpose[36] in Paul's letter writing is, in fact, one of the key instances where our emphasis on mutuality within the letter plays a significant role. For whereas one can find numerous instances depicted in the letter where the Philippians' activities on behalf of Paul are mirrored by his on behalf of them, in the end, the Philippians are the ones who need to respond to the apostle's admonitions, not the other way around. Paul has already shown himself to be faithful and has displayed his commitment to continue to be so (cf. 1:12–26; 2:17–18; 3:8–16; 4:11–13). This corresponds with the rhetorical use of mutual honor we adduced from Roman letters between family and friends in Chapter 5. As such, it reflects the relational connectedness between Paul and the Philippians, which matches the friendship norms used by Cicero in his letters to friends like Cassius, Dolabella, and Plancus, or to his brother Quintus, with all of whom he stressed their mutuality in honor so as to influence their behavior.

In such friendly and family relationships, the one side of the relationship can deploy the theme of mutual honor rhetorically in order to influence the other side. Paul has already upheld his side of the relationship; he now seeks to persuade the Philippians to uphold theirs. So both the depiction of Paul's selflessness that leads to the Philippians' boasting (1:12–26)[37] and the depiction of the Philippians' selflessness that leads to

---

Anerkennung: Exegetische Untersuchungen zu Funktion und Sachgehalt der paulinischen Verkündigung vom eigenen Endgeschick im Rahmen seiner Korrespondenz an die Thessalonicher, Korinther und Philipper, BBB 164 (Göttingen: Vandenhoeck & Ruprecht, 2011), 190, who argues that, since the Philippians are emotionally bound to Paul, "sein eschatisches Wohl" can serve for the Philippians "als sinnvolle Handlungsmotivation."

[34] Troels Engberg-Pedersen, *Paul and the Stoics* (Edinburgh: T&T Clark, 2000), 112. Anke Inselmann, "Zum Affect der Freude im Philipperbrief," in *Der Philipperbrief in der hellenistisch-römischen Welt*, ed. Jörg Frey, Benjamin Schliesser and Veronika Niederhofer, WUNT 253 (Tübingen: Mohr Siebeck, 2015), 255–88, 271, compares Paul's command in 2:2 with the Aristotelian "ethische Ideal" of "Freundschaft unter Mitbürgern."

[35] Uta Poplutz, *Athlet des Evangeliums: Eine motivgeschichtliche Studie zur Wettkampfmetaphorik bei Paulus*, HBS 43 (Freiburg: Herder, 2004), 313, sees Paul's use of the "in vain" topos in Phil 2:16 functioning "als rhetorisches Mittel des Ansporns." Marshall, "Should Christians Boast?" 272, notes a similar strategy of encouragement in 2 Cor 7:4: "The fact that [Paul] ... exulted in their Christian growth should urge them on to greater things."

[36] See Ben Witherington III, *Friendship and Finances in Philippi: The Letter of Paul to the Philippians* (Valley Forge, PA: Trinity Press, 1994), 13; cf. Weidmann, *Philippians*, 15: "As letters intended to shape the future course of action, most of Paul's letters have points of similarity to the deliberative speech."

[37] Pace Stefano Bittasi, *Gli esempi necessari per discernere: Il significato argomentativo della struttura della lettera di Paolo ai Filippesi*, AnBib 153 (Rome: Biblical Institute Press, 2003), 47, who questions Paul's unselfish motives in Phil 1:12–26, calling attention to the fact that Paul's activity on behalf of the advance of the gospel and that of the Philippians is not a matter of self-renunciation but rather entails "the explicit affirmation that all of this results in the progress of Paul himself, in joy (1:18b),

Paul's boasting (2:12–18) ultimately come together in their purpose for motivating the Philippians to safeguard the honor of their "brother," Paul. While 1:26 refers to the selfless decisions that Paul has already made in favor of their honor, the outcome of 2:16 remains open: will the readers respond as the apostle hopes and expects they will? All of the rhetoric in the letter moves toward bringing this about.

One of the reasons Paul could rely on this tactic of referring to his own honor to motivate a favorable response from his auditors was because of his role as founder of the community.[38] As Holmberg has noted, "We can reasonably conclude that Paul thought of himself as the 'father' of all the churches he had founded," which entails numerous "obligations" from his communities, two of which are that they are to "be proud of their 'father'" and to "aim their actions at pleasing their 'father' (Phil 2:2, 16)."[39] We saw in our discussions of both Scriptural texts and the Greco-Roman cultural milieu that children contributed to the honor of their parents. In Phil 2:16, Paul draws on this familial sharing of honor since he begins his admonition by referring to the Philippians as "my beloved" (2:12) as a means to motivate the "children" to behave aright. Hence, just as "grandchildren are the στέφανος of the aged" (Prov 17:6a), so too the Philippians are Paul's στέφανος (Phil 4:1). Paul's indication that his fate rests on the obedience of the Philippians implicitly motivates them to obey (cf. 2:2, 16).[40] This mixing of imagery, in which Paul not only describes his relationship with the Philippians as that between siblings (ἀδελφοί) but also presents them as in a father–child relationship, is not in tension.[41] In either case, whether between siblings or between parent and child, there is a mutuality of honor in which both parties benefit.[42]

---

in his own salvation (1:19), and in the possibility of his being able to 'boast' about the Philippians (1:26)" (my translation). I agree that Paul benefits from the advance of the Philippians, but I do not see this as counteracting Paul's explicit declaration that he is choosing what the Philippians need rather than following his own preference (1:22–25).

[38] Cf. James Constantine Hanges, *Paul, Founder of Churches: A Study in Light of the Evidence for the Role of "Founder-Figures" in the Hellenistic-Roman Period*, WUNT 292 (Tübingen: Mohr Siebeck, 2012), 391, who speaks of "Paul's appropriation of the paradigm of the founder-figure," including "the persuasive model" (p. 393) that accompanies that paradigm.

[39] Bengt Holmberg, *Paul and Power: The Structure of Authority in the Primitive Church as Reflected in the Pauline Epistles* (Lund: Gleerup, 1978), 78. He notes that Paul's power is "not strictly formalized"; rather, by using the father–child metaphor for his relation vis-à-vis his churches, Paul's authority is both "milder and at the same time more demanding than a list of rights and obligations" (p. 79).

[40] As Ernest Best, *Paul and His Converts* (Edinburgh: T&T Clark, 1988), 44, remarks, "A parent may say to a child: 'Don't do that; if you do I'll look a fool in the eyes of people!' The child is expected to behave in a certain way not for its own good but for the parent's benefit." Jean-Noël Aletti, *Saint Paul Épître aux Philippiens: Introduction, traduction et commentaire*, EB 55 (Paris: J. Gabalda, 2005), 187, notes how Paul's interest in the Philippians' success is related to his fatherly role vis-à-vis them: "Bien des parents, dira-t-on, raisonnent ainsi, désirant que leurs enfants soient des modèles pour en tirer fierté devant leurs amis." Aletti goes on to argue that Paul's referring to his own boast is able "servir de motivation pour les inviter à la perfection."

[41] Andrew D. Clarke, "Equality or Mutuality? Paul's Use of 'Brother' Language," in *New Testament in its First Century Setting*, ed. P. J. Williams et al. (Grand Rapids, MI: Eerdmans, 2004), 151–64, 160, points to papyri in which one writes to a brother who is also "as a father."

[42] This is in line with David G. Horrell, "From ἀδελφοί to οἶκος θεοῦ: Social Transformation in Pauline Christianity," *JBL* 120 (2001), 293–311, 299, who argues that by using ἀδελφοί to refer to the Philippians "Paul both assumes and promotes the relationship between himself and his addressees ... as one between equal siblings, who share a sense of affection, mutual responsibility, and solidarity." Camille Focant, *Les letters aux Philippiens et à Philémon*, CBNT (Paris: Les Éditions du Cerf, 2015),

Paul's Dangerous Mutual Boast

Paul's opening himself up, however, to the possibility (and nonpossibility) of a mutual boast is not only useful rhetorically, it is also dangerous theologically.[43] It is dangerous because it means that for Paul his own eschatological fate is not in his hands alone.[44] Rather, he now depends upon the success of his converts for his ability to boast in his ministry's effectiveness.[45] His fate is bound together with their fate.[46] On the final day, they are essentially linked: if the Philippian believers fail, he has failed; if they shine, he will be victorious. Such vulnerability on the part of the apostle[47] is neither feigned nor merely rhetorical; it is not a tool for manipulation.[48] Rather, it represents the reality of existence in Christ as Paul has come to understand it,[49] since God has pledged to be at work in the gospel to redeem his people (1:6; 2:13; 3:12; 4:7, 13, 19). By partnering with the Philippians in a κοινωνία for the gospel (Phil 1:5), Paul has both expanded and constrained his own gospel ministry. He has expanded it because he experiences their help and support (1:7): in prayer (1:19), financial contributions (4:17), personnel (2:26), comfort (2:28), and perhaps even proclamation (2:16a).[50] It is constrained

---

129, concurs: "C'est de solidarité plus que d'ambition personnelle qu'il est ici question: leur réussite sera commune."

[43] Williams, *Enemies of the Cross*, 139, notes that here "Paul's appeal becomes quite personal."

[44] On the danger connected with the complex Roman notion of shame, see Robert A. Kaster, "The Shame of the Romans," TAPA 127 (1997), 1–19, 11: "The more exposed you were to *pudor*, the more embedded in the community you were, the more complete and multi-faceted was your social identity. The risk of *pudor* was in that respect desirable, even enviable. Yet at the same time the more exposed you were, the greater was the chance that you would falter."

[45] Reimund Bieringer, "Lasst euch mit Gott versöhnen: eine exegetische Untersuchung zu 2Kor 5,14-21 in seinem Kontext" (PhD diss., Leuven University, 1986), 2.276–277, summarizing Dowdy, explains that "[Paulus] rühmt sich seiner Gemeinden und will, daß sie sich seiner rühmen. Dies ist zum einen ein Ausdruck gegenseitigen Vertrauens und zum anderen ein Zeichen echter christlicher Freude."

[46] Ulrich B. Müller, *Philipper*, THKNT 11/1 (Leipzig: Evangelische Verlagsanstalt, 1993), 122: "Sein eschatologisches Geschick ist mit dem ihren verknüpft." Cf. John H. P. Reumann, *Philippians: A New Translation with Introduction and Commentary*, AB 33B (New Haven, CT: Yale University Press, 2008), 414, who argues that Paul and the Philippians "interrelate … in eschatological earnestness."

[47] See John M. G. Barclay, "Security and Self-Sufficiency," *Ex Auditu* 24 (2008), 60–72, 66, where while describing Paul's anxiety about the success of his churches, Barclay quips, "What surprises us is that this matters so much to him." M. Sydney Park, *Submission within the Godhead and the Church in the Epistle to the Philippians: An Exegetical and Theological Examination of the Concept of Submission in Philippians 2 and 3*, LNTS 361 (London: T&T Clark, 2007), 129, defines the submission displayed in Philippians by Christ, Paul, Timothy, and Epaphroditus as "a self-willed position of weakness and vulnerability." David E. Briones, *Paul's Financial Policy*, LNTS 494 (London: T&T Clark, 2013), 90, similarly notes how the mutual obligatory ties of Paul's κοινωνία with the Philippians entail that both parties are "vulnerably depending on one another to meet each other's needs."

[48] Osiek, *Philippians*, 72, notes that Paul "seems manipulative" at 2:16, since he implies that "it will be their fault" if his honor capsizes. Judith M. Gundry-Volf, *Paul and Perseverance: Staying In and Falling Away* (Louisville, KY: Westminster John Knox Press, 1990), 271, argues that references to the possibility of failure in Paul must be traced "to the apostle's failure to cooperate with the gospel as the power of salvation," rather than allowing for the possibility that "his converts might become apostates by cutting short the saving work of God begun in their lives." Against this interpretation, Barclay, "Security," 67, rightly asserts that "we cannot take [the apostle's] grief as merely an external show."

[49] Barclay, "Security," 70: "Mutual encouragement, mutual struggle, and mutual dependency are for Paul *core constituents* of life in Christ" (emphasis original).

[50] Barclay, "Security," 69, points to Phil 1:19 (among other texts) to demonstrate that "others appear to have an instrumental role in bringing about the 'safety' or 'rescue' for which Paul hopes: his 'security'

because any failure by them in the future would constitute the failure of Paul's own ministry labors (2:16c). Bieringer observes that, as a result, "Paul *has the courage* to present himself in a fairly weak and dependent position,"[51] since in relying on the Philippians he has opened himself up to the possibility of failure coming from outside his control. This is the unavoidable result from Paul's desire to establish a relationship of mutual dependence between himself and his churches.

But Paul's overall tone throughout the letter is not one of fear. Rather, it is one of confidence, fully convinced that the God who empowers his own ministry will empower the Philippians, thereby assuring their mutual boast on the day of Christ. Fee's description is apt:

> The final word, therefore, is not a word of doubt, but an affirmation: by their heeding these words he will have plenty of cause for "boasting" when they stand together before Christ at his Parousia.[52]

Conclusion

In this chapter, we have argued that the mutual boasting motif appearing in Philippians incorporates three parties within the matrix of honor established by the success of Paul and of the Philippians. In both cases, the honor of the one contributes to the honor of the other, while both parties are empowered by the very God who unites them in their partnership for the gospel, thereby allowing God/Christ to participate as the third recipient of honor emerging from the faithfulness of both Paul and the Philippians.

Additionally, we have argued that Paul lays the burden of maintaining this threefold mutual honor, shared by all three parties, on the Philippians in particular. After describing how *he* has upheld the honor of the group in Phil 1:25–26, the apostle calls for the Philippians, on *their* side, to uphold the honor of the group by demonstrating their faithfulness and obedience. Still, by appealing to the Philippians to guard his own honor, Paul displays a profound sense of vulnerability yet also trust that his "siblings" in Christ will prove victorious through the power of God working in them.

---

depends on God but *also* on the cooperation and support of fellow Christians to whom he appeals for help." Barclay goes on, in p. 70, in discussing Paul's κοινωνία with the Philippians, to describe how "the God on whose encouragement [Paul] relies supplies his needs *through others*, and he is desperately at a loss when they fail to play their part" (emphasis original).

[51] Reimund Bieringer, "Paul's Divine Jealousy: The Apostle and His Communities in Relationship," *LS* 17 (1992), 197–231, 216 (emphasis added).

[52] Fee, *Philippians*, 249.

9

Conclusion

This has been a study of the role of boasting (καύχημα) in Paul's letter to the Philippians. To that end, its focus has been on the pivotal passages of Phil 1:25-26 and 2:14-16, where Paul introduces this concept in the service of his central admonitions to the community. Led by these texts, the study has therefore focused on the theological source for boasting in the Scriptures and its rhetorical role in the letter as made clear in terms of the Philippians' cultural context. We have seen that in Philippians Paul's paraenesis is motivated by a mutuality of honor between God/Christ and the Philippians understood against the backdrop of Deut 26:19, but one that includes Paul within this relationship in light of his sharing the role of the Isaianic Servant in Isa 49:4, albeit now in the new eschatological reality brought about by the exaltation of Christ. God constitutes the foundational partner in their κοινωνία, enabling the faithfulness of each of the other parties and thereby assuring the καύχημα that each can then bestow upon the other, while Paul is the apostolic mediator of this boast.

In Part 1 of our study, we developed the Scriptural warrant for Paul's use of the mutual boasting motif by following two key allusions made by the apostle within the key hortatory section of Phil 2:12-16. The allusion in Phil 2:15 to Israel's unfaithfulness as reflected in the Song of Moses at Deut 32:5 ("blemished children, not his, have sinned, a generation, crooked and perverse") prompted a study into the wider context of the ending of Deuteronomy (Chapter 2). We argued, on the basis of the balanced presentation throughout Deut 26-32 of God's promise of blessing for Israel in response to covenant faithfulness and God's warning of cursing for Israel in response to covenant unfaithfulness, that a key component of Israel's covenant blessing was the emergence of a mutual honor (καύχημα, cf. Deut 26:19 and 10:21) shared between YHWH and Israel. We also showed how this theme of mutual honor enjoyed between God and people recurred as part of Israel's eschatological hope in the prophetic literature (e.g., Jer 13:11; 33:9; Zeph 3:19, 20). In Chapter 3, we followed Paul's allusion in Phil 2:16 to the Isaianic Servant's lament in Isa 49:4 that he had "labored in vain." We argued that this lament by the Servant taps into a larger theme running throughout Isa 40-66 reflecting Israel's hope of sharing in God's glory and of receiving a "reward" for faithfulness (Isa 49:5; 65:23).

In Part 2 of our study, we turned to developing the cultural context in which Paul's motif of mutual boasting would have been understood by the thoroughly Romanized Philippian believers. We argued in Chapter 4 that honor was both the most valued commodity in the Roman world at the time when Paul was writing and that it was an inherently sharable commodity when it was possessed in the context of friendship and family. Following from this aspect of honor as mutual, we argued in Chapter 5 that Roman letter writers made use of the rhetorical power of mutual honor as a way to motivate others to heed proffered advice. Hence, we discussed examples in which Cicero, in his letters to his brother and to other statesmen, referred to *his own honor* in order to spur them on to be guided by his direction in political matters. We additionally pointed to later writers, namely Seneca and Fronto, who mimicked Cicero in this tactic of appealing to their own honor in order to stimulate obedience.

Finally, in Part 3 we returned to Paul's own use of the mutual boasting motif in two key passages in Philippians to demonstrate how Paul establishes a mutuality of honor that both encompasses three parties (himself, the Philippians, and God/Christ) and that has its foundation in the Scriptural material we discussed in Part 1 and is culturally intelligible on the basis of the Greco-Roman material we discussed in Part 2. In Chapter 6, we began by providing a close reading of Phil 1:25–26, arguing that Paul here presents the first of a two-step presentation of the mutual honor emerging from his own and the Philippians' faithfulness, respectively. In Phil 1:26, it is the Philippians who are the primary beneficiaries of the καύχημα emerging from Paul's choice to remain alongside them in ministry (1:24), yet their boasting subsists "in [Paul] in Christ Jesus," thereby encompassing all three parties in the experience of honor. Then in Chapter 7 we focused on the denser passage of Phil 2:14–16, arguing that Paul provides here the complement to the prior passage in that it is his own καύχημα that emerges from the Philippians' obedience (2:12, 14). It is in this passage, moreover, that the Scriptural material from Part 1 becomes essential, since Paul's allusions both to Deuteronomy and Isaiah activate the mutual boast arising from covenant faithfulness (Deut 32:5; cf. Deut 26:19) along with the reward promised to the Servant (Isa 49:4), a role in which Paul himself now participates. The culmination of Part 3, indeed of the entire study, comes in Chapter 8 where we argued that Paul capitalizes on the mutuality inherent in the friendship and family paradigms in which he casts his relationship with the Philippians and with God himself in the letter. It is primarily on the basis of their familial relationship, since Paul and the Philippians are "siblings" (1:12, 14; 3:1, 13, 17; 4:1, 8) while God is their "Father" (1:2; 2:11; 4:20) and they his "children" (2:15), that they participate in a tripartite mutual honor.

Within this threefold mutuality, Paul declares in Phil 1:25–26 that he has already displayed his faithfulness within their friendship- and family-based relationship, thereby providing a boast for the Philippians. In Phil 2:14–16, Paul then moves to the rhetorical task of persuading the Philippians to fulfill their side of this relationship, prompting them to establish Paul's boast through their faithfulness. Throughout, Paul's theological argument from Scripture thus relies on pathos for its rhetorical force, since it is the emotional appeal of not wanting to fail their "brother" Paul that will spur the Philippians on to continue their life of faithful obedience. By continuing to cash in on their past record of obedience as Paul's friends and siblings, the apostle envisions an outcome of honor, enabled by God/Christ, that can be mutually shared between them. But it is an honor that stands radically opposed to the Roman ideal, since it waits for its recognition until the "day of Christ," the final, eschatological return of the once-slave now-vindicated Lord of the universe (cf. Phil 2:10–11 with 2:16 and 3:20–21).

Bibliography

Primary Literature

Aelius Aristides. 1981. *Aelius Aristides: Complete Works*. Translated by C. Behr. Leiden: E. J. Brill.
Aristotle. 1935. *Eudemian Ethics*. Translated by H. Rackham. LCL. Cambridge, MA: Harvard University Press.
Aristotle. 1926. *Nicomachean Ethics*. Translated by H. Rackham. LCL. Cambridge, MA: Harvard University Press.
Alt, A., O. Eißfeldt, P. Kahle, and R. Kittel, eds. 1997. *Biblia Hebraica Stuttgartensia*, 5th ed. Stuttgart: Deutsche Bibelgesellschaft.
Cicero. 1923. *On Friendship*. Translated by W. A. Falconer. LCL. Cambridge, MA: Harvard University Press.
Cicero. 1927. *Tusculan Disputations*. Translated by J. E. King. LCL. Cambridge, MA: Harvard University Press.
Cicero. 1956. *Epistulae ad Familiares*. Translated by D. R. Shackleton Bailey. LCL. Cambridge, MA: Harvard University Press.
Cicero. 1972. *Letters to Quintus and Brutus*. Translated by D. R. Shackleton Bailey. LCL. Cambridge, MA: Harvard University Press.
Cicero. 1999. *Letters to Atticus*. Translated by D. R. Shackleton Bailey. 4 vols. LCL. Cambridge, MA: Harvard University Press.
Epictetus. 1925, 1928. *Discourses, Fragments, The Enchiridion*. Translated by William A. Oldfather. 4 vols. LCL. New York: Putnam's Sons.
Field, Frederick. 1875. *Origenis Hexaplorum*. Oxford: Clarendon Press.
Fronto. 1919. *The Correspondence of Marcus Cornelius Fronto*. In Two Volumes. Translated by C. R. Haines. 3 vols. LCL. London: Heinemann.
Homer. 1924–5. *Iliad*. Translated by A. T. Murray. 2 vols. LCL. New York: Putnam's Sons.
Horace. 1926. *Satires*. Translated by H. Rushton Fairclough. LCL. Cambridge, MA: Harvard University Press.
Josephus. 1930. *Jewish Antiquities*. Translated by H. St. J. Thackeray. LCL. Cambridge, MA Harvard University Press.
Lucian. *Toxaris*. 1936. Translated by A. M. Harmon. LCL. Cambridge, MA: Harvard University Press.
Lucretius. 1924. *On the Nature of Things*. Translated by W. H. D. Rouse. LCL. Cambridge, MA: Harvard University Press.
Nestle-Aland. 2012. *Novum Testamentum Graece*. Edited by Barbara and Kurt Aland, Johannes Karavidopoulos, Carlo M. Martini, and Bruce M. Metzger, 28th ed. Stuttgart: Deutsche Bibelgesellschaft.
Philo of Alexandria. 1929–62. *On the Special Laws*. Translated by F. H. Colson et al. 10 vols. LCL. Cambridge, MA: Harvard University Press.
Pindar. 1969. *The Odes of Pindar*. Translated by C. M. Bowra. Suffolk: Penguin.

Pliny the Younger. 1969. *Letters*. Translated by B. Radice. 2 vols. LCL. Cambridge, MA: Harvard University Press.
Plutarch. 1914–26. *Comparatio Demosthenis et Ciceronis* (*Comp. Dem. Cic.*). In *Lives*. Volume 8. Translated by B. Perrin. 11 vols. LCL. Cambridge, MA: Harvard University Press.
Plutarch. 1927–69. *Moralia*. Translated by Frank Cole Babbitt et al. 15 vols. LCL. Cambridge, MA: Harvard University Press.
Ralphs, Alfred. 1996. *Septuaginta*. Stuttgart: Deutsche Bibelgesellschaft.
Sallust. 1921. *The War with Jugurtha*. Translated by J. C. Rolfe. LCL. Cambridge, MA: Harvard University Press.
Seneca. 1918–25. *Ad Lucilium Epistulae Morales*. Translated by R. M. Gummere. 3 vols. LCL. New York: Putnam's Sons. Revised edition 1943, 1953.
Seneca. 1928–35. *Moral Essays*. Translated by John W. Basore. 3 vols. LCL. New York: Putnam's Sons.
Valerius Maximus. 2000. Translated by D. R. Shackleton-Bailey. 5 vols. LCL. Cambridge, MA: Harvard University Press.
Vix, Jean-Luc. 2010. *Les Discours 30 à 34 d'Aelius Aristide*. Turnhout: Brepols.
Wevers, J. W. 1977. *Deuteronomium*. Göttingen: Vandenhoeck & Ruprecht.
Xenophon. 1918–25. *Memorabilia*. Translated by E. C. Marchant. 7 vols. LCL. Cambridge, MA: Harvard University Press.
Ziegler, Joseph. 1957. *Jeremias*. Septuaginta 15. Göttingen: Vandenhoeck & Ruprecht.
Ziegler, Joseph. 1983. *Isaias*. Septuaginta 14. Göttingen: Vandenhoeck & Ruprecht.

Secondary Literature

Aasgaard, Reider. 2002. "Role Ethics in Paul: The Significance of the Sibling Role for Paul's Ethical Thinking." *NTS* 48: 513–30.
Aasgaard, Reider. 2007. "Paul as Child: Children and Childhood in the Letters of the Apostle." *JBL* 126 129–59.
Aernie, Jeffrey W. 2012. *Is Paul Also Among the Prophets?: An Examination of the Relationship between Paul and the Old Testament Prophetic Tradition in 2 Corinthians*. LNTS 467. London: Bloomsbury.
Agosto, Efrain. 1996. "Paul's Use of Greco-Roman Conventions of Commendations." PhD diss., Boston University.
Aletti, Jean-Noël. 2005. *Saint Paul Épître aux Philippiens: Introduction, traduction et commentaire*. EB 55. Paris: J. Gabalda.
Alexander, Loveday. 1989. "Hellenistic Letter-Forms and the Structure of Philippians." *Journal for the Study of the New Testament* 37: 87–101.
Alkier, Stefan. 2015. "New Testament Studies on the Basis of Categorical Semiotics." In *Reading the Bible Intertextually*, edited by Richard B. Hays, Stefan Alkier, and Leroy A. Huizenga. Waco, TX: Baylor University Press, 223–48.
Anderson, Peter J. 2002. "'Fame Is the Spur': *Memoria, Gloria*, and Poetry among the Elite in Flavian Rome." PhD diss., University of Cincinnati.
Arnold, Bradley. 2014. *Christ as the* Telos *of Life*. WUNT 2.371. Tübingen: Mohr Siebeck.
Arzt-Grabner, Peter. 2002. "'Brothers' and 'Sisters' in Documentary Papyri and in Early Christianity." *RivBib* 50: 185–204.

Ascough, Richard S. 2003. *Paul's Macedonian Associations: The Social Context of Philippians and 1 Thessalonians*. WUNT 2.161. Tübingen: Mohr Siebeck.
Asting, Ragnar. 1925. "*Kauchesis*. Et bidrag til forståelsen av den religiøse selvfølelse hos Paulus." *NoTT* 26: 129–204.
Balsdon, J. P. V. D. 1960. "*Auctoritas, Dignitas, Otium*." *CQ* 10: 43–50.
Barclay, John M. G. 2007. "'By the Grace of God I Am What I Am': Grace and Agency in Philo and Paul." In *Divine and Human Agency in Paul and His Cultural Environment*, edited by John M. G. Barclay and Simon J. Gathercole. London: T&T Clark, 140–57.
Barclay, John M. G. 2008. "Security and Self-Sufficiency: A Comparison of Paul and Epictetus." *Ex Auditu* 24: 60–72.
Barclay, John M. G. 2015. *Paul and the Gift*. Grand Rapids, MI: Eerdmans.
Barrett, C. K. 1986. "Boasting (καυχᾶσθαι, κτλ.) in the Pauline Epistles." In *L'apôtre Paul: Personalité, style et conception du ministère*, edited by A. Vanhoye. BETL 73. Leuven: University Press, 363–8.
Barton, Carlin A. 2001. *Roman Honor: The Fire in Their Bones*. Berkeley: University of California Press.
Barton, John. 2013. "Déjà Lu: Intertextuality, Method or Theory?" In *Reading Job Intertextually*, edited by Katharine J. Dell and William L. Kynes, 1–16. London: T&T Clark, 2013.
Beale, G. K. 2012. *Handbook on the New Testament Use of the Old Testament*. Grand Rapids, MI: Baker.
Beare, F. W. 1969. *A Commentary on the Epistle to the Philippians*, 3rd ed. BNTC. London: Adam & Charles Black.
Becker, Eve-Marie. 2015. *Der Begriff der Demut bei Paulus*. Tübingen: Mohr Siebeck.
Beetham, Christopher A. 2008. *Echoes of Scripture in the Letter of Paul to the Colossians*. BIS 96. Leiden: Brill.
Begrich, Joachim. 1969. *Studien zu Deuterojesaja*. Edited by W. Zimmerli. TB 20. Munich: Chr. Kaiser Verlag.
Bell, Richard H. 1994. *Provoked to Jealousy: The Origin of the Jealousy Motif in Romans 9–11*. WUNT 2.63. Tübingen: Mohr Siebeck.
Bénétreau, Samuel. 2009. "Appellation et transcendance: Le nom mystérieux de *Philippiens* 2,9." *RHPhR* 89: 313–31.
Benner, Margareta. 1975. "The Emperor Says: Studies in the Rhetorical Style in Edicts of the Early Empire." PhD diss., Acta Universitas Gothoburgensis (Sweden).
Ben-Porat, Ziva. 1976. "The Poetics of Literary Allusion." *PTL* 1: 105–28.
Benjamin Fiore, S. J. 1985. "The Hortatory Function of Paul's Boasting." *EGLMBS* 5: 39–46.
Benjamin Fiore, S. J. 1990. "Invective in Romans and Philippians." *PEGLMBS* 10: 181–9.
Berger, Klaus. 1977. *Exegese des Neuen Testaments*. Heidelberg: Quelle & Meyer.
Bergey, Ronald. 2003. "Song of Moses (Deuteronomy 32:1–43) and Isaianic Prophecies: A Case of Early Intertextuality?" *JSOT* 28.1: 33–54.
Best, Ernest. 1988. *Paul and His Converts*. Edinburgh: T&T Clark.
Betz, H. D. 1978. "*De fraterno amore*." In *Plutarch's Ethical Writings and Early Christian Literature*, edited by H. D. Betz. SCHNT 4, 231–63. Leiden: Brill.
Betz, H. D. 2015. *Studies in Paul's Letter to the Philippians*. WUNT 343. Tübingen: Mohr Siebeck.
Beuken, W. A. M. 1974. "Confession of God's Exclusivity by All Mankind: A Reappraisal of Is. 45,18-25." *BijDragen* 35: 335–56.

Beuken, W. A. M. 1989. "Servant and Herald of Good Tidings: Isaiah 61 as an Interpretation of Isaiah 40–55." In *The Book of Isaiah, Le livre d'Isaïe*, edited by Jacques Vermeylen, 1989. BETL 81, 411–42. Leuven: University Press.

Bianchini, Francesco. 2006. *L'elogio di sé in Cristo: L'utilizzo della περιαυτολογία nel contesto di Filippesi 3,1-4,1*. AnBib 164. Rome: Biblical Institute Press.

Bieringer, Reimund. 1986. "'Lasst euch mit Gott versöhnen: eine exegetische Untersuchung zu 2Kor 5,14-21 in seinem Kontext." PhD diss., Catholic Leuven University, 4 vols.

Bieringer, Reimund. 1992. "Paul's Divine Jealousy: The Apostle and His Communities in Relationship." *LS* 17: 197–231.

Bittasi, Stefano. 2003. *Gli esempi necessari per discernere: Il significato argomentativo della struttura della lettera di Paolo al Filippesi*. AnBib 153. Rome: Biblical Institute Press.

Bittasi, Stefano. 2004. "La prigionia di Paolo nella lettera ai Filippesi e il problema di una sua morte possibile. 1." *RdT* 45: 19–34.

Bitzer, Lloyd F. 1968. "The Rhetorical Situation." *Philosophy & Rhetoric* 1.1: 1–14.

Bjerkelund, Carl J. 1977. "'Vergeblich' als Missionsergebnis bei Paulus." In *God's Christ and His People: Studies in Honour of Nils Alstrup Dahl*, edited by Jacob Jervell and Wayne A. Meeks, 175–91. Oslo: Universitetsforlaget.

Blois, Isaac D. 2020. "Formulas for (Dis)Honorable Installation in Deuteronomy 26:19 and 28:37: The Honorific Implications of Israel's Covenant (Un)Faithfulness." *CBQ* 82.3, 381–406.

Blois, Isaac D. 2020. "'What Is My Boast? Is It Not You?': Εἰς καύχημα ἐμοί as Scriptural Language in Philippians 2,16." *EstBib* (forthcoming).

Böckler, Annette. 2000. *Gott als Vater im Alten Testament: Traditionsgeschichtliche Untersuchungen zu Entstehung und Entwicklung eines Gottesbildes*. Kaiser: Gütersloher Verlagshaus.

Bockmuehl, Markus. 1998. *The Epistle to the Philippians*. BNTC 11. Peabody, MA: Hendrickson.

Bonnard, P.-E. 1950. *L'Épitre de saint Paul aux Philippiens*. CNT. Paris: Delachaux et Niestlé.

Bonnard, P.-E. 1972. *Le Second Isaïe: Son Disciple et Leurs Éditeurs, Isaïe 40–66*. EB. Paris: J. Gabalda.

Bordieu, Pierre. 1977. *Outline of a Theory of Practice*. Translated by R. Nice. Cambridge: Cambridge University Press.

Bormann, Lukas. 1995. *Philippi: Stadt und Christengemeinde zur Zeit des Paulus*. NovTSup 78. Leiden: Brill.

Bormann, Lukas. 2001. "Reflexionen über Sterben und Tod bei Paulus." In *Das Ende des Paulus: Historische, theologische und literaturgeschichtliche Aspekte*, edited by F. W. Horn, 307–30. BZNW 106. Berlin: de Gruyter.

Bormann, Lukas. 2002. "Das 'letzte Gericht'—ein abständiges Mythologumenon?" *ZNT* 9: 47–53.

Bormann, Lukas. 2006. "Triple Intertextuality in Philippians." In *The Intertextuality of the Epistles*, edited by Dennis MacDonald, Stanley E. Porter, and Thomas L. Brodie, 90–7. Sheffield: Sheffield Phoenix Press.

Bormann, Lukas. 2009. "Die Bedeutung des Philipperbriefs für die Paulustradition." In *Beiträge zur urchristlichen Theologiegeschichte*, edited by W. Kraus, 321–41. BZNW 163. Berlin: de Gruyter.

Bouttier, Michel. 1966. *Christianity According to Paul*. Translated by Frank Clarke. SBT 49. London: SCM Press.

Brändl, Martin. 2006. *Der Agon bei Paulus: Herkunft und Profil paulinischer Agonmetaphorik*. WUNT 222. Tübingen: Mohr Siebeck.
Braulik, Georg. 1992. *Deuteronomium II. (16,18-34,12)*. Würzburg: Echter Verlag.
Brélaz, Cédric. 2016. "Entre Philippe II, Auguste et Paul: la commémoration des origines dans la colonie romaine de Philippes." In *Une mémoire en acts: Espaces, figures et discours dans le monde romain*, edited by Stéphane Benoist, Anne Daguet-Gagey, and Christine Hoët-van Cauwenberghe, 119–38. Lille: Presses Universitaires du Septentrion.
Brélaz, Cédric. 2018. "First-Century Philippi: Contextualizing Paul's Visit." In *The First Urban Churches 4: Roman Philippi*, edited by James R. Harrison and L. L. Welborn, 153–88. WGRWSup 13. Atlanta: SBL Press.
Brélaz, Cédric. 2018. "Philippi: A Roman Colony within Its Regional Context." In *Les communautés du nord Égéen au temps de l'hégémonie romaine: Entre ruptures et continuités*, edited by Julien Fournier and Maria-Gabriella G. Parissaki, 163–82. Meletemata 77. Athens: National Hellenic Research Foundation.
Breytenbach, Cilliers, ed. 2015. *Paul's Graeco-Roman Context*. BETL 277. Leuven: Peeters.
Briones, David E. 2013. *Paul's Financial Policy: A Socio-Theological Approach*. LNTS 494. London: T&T Clark.
Brockington, L. H. 1951. "The Greek Translator of Isaiah and His Interest in ΔΟΞΑ." *VT* 1: 23–32.
Brown, Peter. 1978. *The Making of Late Antiquity*. Cambridge, MA: Harvard University Press.
Brucker, Ralph. 1997. *"Christushymnen" oder "epideiktische Passagen"?: Studien zum Stilwechsel im Neuen Testament und seiner Umwelt*. FRLANT 176. Göttingen: Vandenhoeck & Ruprecht.
Brueggemann, Walter. 1998. *Isaiah 40–66*. Louisville, KY: Westminster John Knox Press, 1998.
Brun, Lyder. 1922. "Zur Formel 'in Christus Jesus' im Brief des Paulus an die Philipper." *SO* 1: 19–37.
Brunt, P. A. 1988. *The Fall of the Roman Republic and Related Essays*. Oxford: Oxford University Press. Reprint 2004.
Bultmann, Rudolf. 1948. *Theologie des Neuen Testaments*. Tübingen: Mohr Siebeck.
Caird, G. B. 1987. *Paul's Letters from Prison in the Revised Standard Version*. NCB. Oxford: Oxford University Press.
Callan, Terrance. 1986. "Competition and Boasting: Toward a Psychological Portrait of Paul." *ST* 40.2: 137–56.
Carrez, Maurice. 1964. "La confiance en l'homme et la confiance en soi selon l'apôtre Paul." *RHPhR* 44: 191–9.
Ceccarelli, Paola. 2013. *Ancient Greek Letter Writing: A Cultural History (600 BC–150 BC)*. Oxford: Oxford University Press.
Cerfaux, Lucien. 1959. *Christ in the Theology of St. Paul*. Translated by Geoffrey Webb and Adrian Walker. New York: Herder and Herder.
Cerfaux, Lucien. 1951. "Saint Paul et le 'Serviteur de Dieu' d'Isaïa." *RLC* 2: 439–54.
Champlin, Edward. 1980. *Fronto and Antonine Rome*. London: Harvard University Press.
Charneux, Pierre. 1991. "En relisant les décrets argiens II." *BCH* 115: 297–323.
Chibici-Revneanu, Nicole. 2007. *Die Herrlichkeit des Verherrlichten: das Verständnis der δόξα im Johannesevangelium*. WUNT 2.231. Tübingen: Mohr Siebeck.
Ciampa, Roy E. 1998. *The Presence and Function of Scripture in Galatians 1 and 2*. WUNT 102. Tübingen: Mohr Siebeck.

Ciampa, Roy E. 2007. "Deuteronomy in Galatians and Romans." In *Deuteronomy in the New Testament*, edited by Steve Moyise and Maarten J. J. Menken, 99–117. LNTS 358. London: A&C Black.

Clarke, Andrew D. 2004. "Equality or Mutuality? Paul's Use of 'Brother' Language." In *The New Testament in its First Century Setting*, edited by P. J. Williams, Andrew D. Clarke, Peter M. Head, and David Instone-Brewer, 151–64. Grand Rapids, MI: Eerdmans.

Clarke, Andrew D. 2015. "The Source and Scope of Paul's Apostolic Authority." *CTR* 12.2: 3–22.

Collange, Jean-Francois. 1979. *The Epistle of St. Paul to the Philippians*. Translated by A. W. Heathcote. London: Epworth Press.

Connolly, A. L. 1979. "Minor Philological Notes." *New Documents*, 141–4.

Craddock, Fred B. 1985. *Philippians*. Louisville, KY: Westminster John Knox Press.

Craigie, Peter C. 1976. *The Book of Deuteronomy*. NICOT. Grand Rapids, MI: Eerdmans.

Cross, F. M. 1998. "Kinship and Covenant in Ancient Israel." In *From Epic to Canon: History and Literature in Ancient Israel*, 3–21. Baltimore, MD: Johns Hopkins University Press.

Culler, Jonathan. 1976. "Presupposition and Intertextuality." *MLN* 91.6: 1380–96.

Culpepper, R. Alan. Summer 1980. "Co-Workers in Suffering: Philippians 2:19–30." *RevExp* 77.3: 349–58.

Cuvillier, Élian. 1993. "L'homme entre mort et vie: L'existence humaine selon Philippiens 3." *Cat* 130: 43–55.

Dafni, Evangelia G. 2006. "Die sogenannten 'Ebed-Jahwe-Lieder in der Septuaginta." In *XII Congress of the International Organization for Septuagint and Cognate Studies: Leiden, 2004*, edited by Melvin K. H. Peters, 187–200. SCS 54. Leiden: Brill.

Danker, Frederick W. 1982. *Benefactor: Epigraphic Study of a Graeco-Roman and New Testament Semantic Field*. St. Louis, MO: Clayton.

Davis, Casey Wayne. 1999. *Oral Biblical Criticism: The Influence of the Principles of Orality on the Literary Structure of Philippians*. JSNTS 172. Sheffield: Sheffield Academic Press.

Davis, G. B. 1999. "True and False Boasting in 2 Cor 10–13." PhD diss., University of Cambridge.

Deissman, Adolf. 1892. *Die neutestamentliche Formel "in Christo Jesu."* Marburg: N. G. Elwert'sche Verlagsbuchhandlung.

Denis, A.-M. 1958. "La fonction apostolique et liturgie nouvelle en esprit: Étude thématique des métaphores pauliniennes du culte nouveau (suite)." *RSPT* 42: 617–56.

De Leeuw, Venantius. 1956. *De Ebed Jahweh-Profetieen: Historisch-Kritisch Onderzoek naar hun Ontstaan en hun Betekenis*. UCL 3.2. Leuven: Van Gorcum.

De Vaux, Roland. 1973. *Ancient Israel: Its Life and Institutions*. Translated by John McHugh. London: Darton, Longman & Todd.

De Vries, Simon J. 1968. "Origin of the Murmuring Tradition." *JBL* 87: 51–8.

Didier, Georges S. J. 1955. *Désintéressement du Chrétien: La rétribution dans la morale de saint Paul*. Théo 32. Paris: Aubier Éditions Montaigne.

Dietrich, Jan. 2009. "Über Ehre und Ehrgefühl im Alten Testament." In *Der Mensch im Alten Israel: Neue Forschungen zur altestamentlichen Anthropologie*, Edited by Bernd Janowski and Kathrin Liess with Niko Zaft, 419–52. HBS 59. Freiburg: Herder.

Dille, Sarah J. 2003. "Honor Restored: Honor, Shame and God as Redeeming Kinsman in Second Isaiah." In *Relating to the Text: Interdisciplinary and Form-Critical Insights on the Bible*, Edited by Timothy J. Sandoval and Carleen Mandolfo, 232–50. LOTS 384. London: T&T Clark International.

Dille, Sarah J. 2004. *Mixing Metaphors: God as Mother and Father in Deutero-Isaiah*. LOTS 398. London: T&T Clark International.

Doble, Peter. 2002. "'Vile Bodies' or Transformed Persons?: Philippians 3.21 in Context." *JSNT* 86: 3–27.

Dodd, Brian J. 1999. *Paul's Paradigmatic "I": Personal Example as Literary Strategy*. LNTS 177. Sheffield: Sheffield Academic Press.

Dodd, C. H. 1953. *According to the Scriptures: The Sub-Structure of New Testament Theology*. New York: Charles Scribner's.

Dogniez, Cécile, and Marguerite Harl. 1992. *Le deutéronome*. La Bible d'Alexandrie. Paris: Les Éditions du Cerf.

Dogniez, Cécile et al. 1999. *La bible d'alexandrie: Les douze prophètes 4–9*. Paris: Les Éditions du Cerf.

Donahoe, Kate C. 2008. "From Self-Praise to Self-Boasting: Paul's Unmasking of the Conflicting Rhetorico-Linguistic Phenomena in 1 Corinthians." PhD diss., University of St Andrews.

Dowdy, Barton Alexander. 1955. "The Meaning of Kauchasthai in the New Testament." PhD diss., Vanderbilt University.

Drexler, Hans. 1966. "*Dignitas*." In *Das Staatsdenken der Römer*, edited by Richard Klein, 231–54. WF 46. Darmstadt: Wissenschaftliche Buchgesellschaft.

Driver, S. R. 1902. *Deuteronomy*. ICC. Edinburgh: T&T Clark.

Droge, A. J. 1988. "*Mori Lucrum*: Paul and Ancient Theories of Suicide." *NovT* 30.3: 263–86.

Dupont, Jaques. 1952. ΣΥΝ ΧΡΙΣΤΩΙ: *L'union avec le Christ suivant Saint Paul*. Paris: Desclée.

Ebner, Martin. 1991. *Leidenslisten und Apostelbrief: Untersuchungen zu Form, Motivik und Funktion der Peristasenkataloge bei Paulus*. FB 66. Würzburg: Echter Verlag.

Edart, Jean-Baptiste. 2002. *L'épître aux Philippiens: Rhétorique et composition stylistique*. EB 45. Paris: J. Gabalda.

Edwards, Catharine. 2008. "Self-Scrutiny and Self-Transformation in Seneca's Letters." In *Oxford Readings in Seneca*, edited by John G. Fitch, 84–101. ORCS. Oxford: Oxford University Press.

Edwards, Catharine. 2015. "Absent Presence in Seneca's *Epistles*: Philosophy and Friendship." In *The Cambridge Companion to Seneca*, edited by Shadi Bartsch and Alessandro Schiesaro, 41–53. Cambridge: Cambridge University Press.

Edwards, Catharine. 2019. *Seneca: Selected Letters*. CGLC. Cambridge: Cambridge University Press.

Ehrensperger, Kathy. 2015. "Scriptural Reasoning: The Dynamic that Informed Paul's Theologizing." *JSR* 5.3: 1–16.

Ekblad Jr., Eugene Robert. 1999. *Isaiah's Servant Poems According to the Septuagint: An Exegetical and Theological Study*. BET 23. Leuven: Peeters.

Engberg-Pedersen, Troels. 2000. *Paul and the Stoics*. Edinburgh: T&T Clark.

Esler, Philip F. 1996. "Group Boundaries and Intergroup Conflict in Galatians: A New Reading of Galatians 5:13–6:10." In *Ethnicity and the Bible*, edited by Mark G. Brett, 215–40. BIS 19. Leiden: E. J. Brill.

Esler, Philip F. 2000. "'Keeping It in the Family': Culture, Kinship and Identity in 1 Thessalonians and Galatians." In *Families and Family Relations as Represented in Early Judaisms and Early Christianities: Texts and Fictions*, edited by Jan Willem van Henten and Athalya Brenner, 145–84. STAR 2. Leiden: Deo.

Esler, Philip F. 2002. "Family Imagery and Christian Identity in Gal 5:13 to 6:10." In *Constructing Early Christian Families: Family as Social Reality and Metaphor*, edited by H. Moxnes, 121–49. London: Routledge.

Esler, Philip F. 2005. "Paul and the *Agon*: Understanding a Pauline Motif in Its Cultural and Visual Context." In *Picturing the New Testament: Studies in Ancient Visual Images*, edited by Annette Weissenrieder, Friederike Wendt, and Petra von Gemünden, 356–85. WUNT 2.193. Tübingen: Mohr Siebeck.

Fatehi, Mehrdad. 2000. *The Spirit's Relation to the Risen Lord: An Examination of Its Christological Implications*. WUNT 2.128. Tübingen: Mohr Siebeck.

Fee, Gordon D. 1995. *Paul's Letter to the Philippians*. NICNT 46. Grand Rapids, MI: Eerdmans.

Fields, Dana. 2008. "Aristides and Plutarch on Self-Praise." In *Aelius Aristides between Greece, Rome, and the Gods*, edited by W. V. Harris and Brooke Holmes, 151–73. Leiden: Brill.

Finney, Mark T. 2011. *Honour and Conflict in the Ancient World: 1 Corinthians in Its Greco-Roman Social Setting*. LNTS 460. London: T&T Clark.

Fishbane, Michael. 1985. *Biblical Interpretation in Ancient Israel*. Oxford: Clarendon Press.

Fitzgerald, J. T., ed. 1996. *Friendship, Flattery, and Frankness of Speech*. NovTSup 82. Leiden: E. J. Brill.

Fitzgerald, J. T. 1996. "Philippians in the Light of Some Ancient Discussions of Friendship." In *Friendship, Flattery, and Frankness of Speech*, edited by J. T. Fitzgerald, 141–60. NovTSup 82. Leiden: E. J. Brill.

Fitzgerald, J. T. 2016. "Paul and Friendship." In *Paul in the Greco-Roman World*, 2nd ed., edited by J. Paul Sampley, 1.331–62. London: Bloomsbury.

Flexsenhar III, Michael, "The Provenance of Philippians and Why It Matters: Old Questions, New Approaches." *JSNT* 42.1 (2019): 18–45.

Focant, Camille. 2015. *Les letters aux Philippiens et à Philémon*. CBNT. Paris: Les Éditions du Cerf.

Forbes, Christopher. 1986. "Comparison, Self-Praise, and Irony: Paul's Boasting and the Conventions of Hellenistic Rhetoric." *NTS* 32: 1–30.

Forster, A. Haire. 1929. "Meaning of Δόξα in the Greek Bible." *ATR* 12: 311–16.

Foster, Paul. 2011. "Eschatology of the Thessalonian Correspondence." *JSPL* 1.1: 57–82.

Fortna, Robert T. 1990. "Philippians: Paul's Most Egocentric Letter." In *The Conversation Continues: Studies in Paul and John, in Honor of J. Loius Martyn*, edited by R. T. Fortna and B. R. Gaventa, 220–34. Nashville, TN: Abingdon.

Fowl, Stephen E. 2005. *Philippians*. THNTC. Grand Rapids, MI: Eerdmans.

Fowl, Stephen E. 2012. "The Use of Scripture in Philippians." In *Paul and Scripture: Extending the Argument*, edited by Christopher Stanley, 163–84. ECL 9. Atlanta, GA: Society of Biblical Literature.

Fredrickson, David E. 2013. *Eros and the Christ: Longing and Envy in Paul's Christology*. Minneapolis, MN: Fortress Press.

Freisenbruch, Annelise. 2007. "Back to Fronto: Doctor and Patient in His Correspondence with an Emperor." In *Ancient Letters: Classical and Late Antique Epistolography*, Edited by Ruth Morello and A. D. Morrison, 235–56. Oxford: Oxford University Press.

Frey, Jörg, and Benjamin Schliesser, with Veronika Niederhofer, eds. 2015. *Der Philipperbrief des Paulus in der hellenistisch-römischen Welt*. WUNT 1.253. Tübingen: Mohr Siebeck.

Fuchs, Eric. 1977. "Gloire de Dieu, Gloire de l'homme: essai sur les termes *kauchasthai, kauchēma, kauchēsis* dans la Septante." *RTP* 27: 321–32.

Fuchs, Eric. 1980. "La fablaisse, gloire de l'apostolat selon Paul: Étude sur 2 Corinthians 10–13." *ETR* 55: 231–53.
Funk, Robert W. 1966. *Language, Hermeneutic, and Word of God: The Problem of Language in the New Testament and Contemporary Theology*. New York: Harper & Row.
Funk, Robert W. 1967. "The Apostolic Parousia: Its Form and Significance." In *Christian History and Interpretation: Studies Presented to John Knox*, edited by William Reuben Farmer, 249–68. Cambridge: Cambridge University Press.
Garland, David E. 1985. "The Composition and Unity of Philippians: Some Neglected Literary Factors." *NovT* 27.2: 141–73.
Gathercole, Simon J. 2001. "After the New Perspective: Works, Justification and Boasting in Early Judaism and Romans 1–5." *TynBul* 52.2: 303–6.
Gathercole, Simon J. 2002. *Where Is Boasting?: Early Jewish Soteriology and Paul's Response in Romans 1–5*. Grand Rapids, MI: Eerdmans.
Gaventa, Beverly Roberts. 1985. "'Where Then Is Boasting?': Romans 3:27 and Its Contexts." *PEGLBS* 5: 57–66.
Genths, P. 1928. "Der Begriff des καύχημα bei Paulus." *NKZ* 38: 501–21.
Geoffrion, Timothy C. 1993. *The Rhetorical Purpose and the Political and Military Character of Philippians: A Call to Stand Firm*. Lampeter: Mellen Biblical Press.
Gerber, Christine. 2005. *Paulus und seine "Kinder": Studien zur Beziehungsmetaphorik der paulinischen Briefe*. BZNW 136. Berlin: de Gruyter.
Gerber, Christine. 2015."ΚΑΥΧΑΣΘΑΙ ΔΕΙ, ΟΥ ΣΥΜΦΕΡΟΝ ΜΕΝ... (2 Kor 12,1): Selbstlob bei Paulus vor dem Hintergrund der antiken Gepflogenheiten." In *Paul's Graeco-Roman Context*, edited by Cilliers Breytenbach, 213–51. BETL 277. Leuven: Peeters.
Gignilliat, Mark. 2007. *Paul and Isaiah's Servants: Paul's Theological Reading of Isaiah 40–66 in 2 Corinthians 5.14–6.10*. LNTS 330. London: T&T Clark.
Glancy, Jennifer A. 2004. "Boasting of Beatings (2 Corinthians 11:23–25)." *JBL* 123: 99–135.
Glatt-Gilad, David A. 2002. "Yahweh's Honor at Stake: A Divine Conundrum." *JSOT* 98: 63–74.
Goldingay, John, and David Payne. 2006. *Isaiah 40–55: Volume I*. ICC. London: T&T Clark International.
Grelot, Pierre. 1981. *Les poèmes du serviteur: De la lecture critique a l'herméneutique*. LD 103. Paris: Les Éditions du Cerf.
Griffin, Miriam T. 2013. *Seneca: A Philosopher in Politics*. Oxford: Clarendon Press.
Gulin, E. G. 1932. *Die Freude im Neuen Testament*. AASF B 26.2. Helsinki: Druckerei-A.G.
Gundry-Volf, Judith M. 1990. *Paul and Perseverance: Staying In and Falling Away*. Louisville, KY: Westminster John Knox Press.
Gupta Nijay K. 2008. "'I Will Not Be Put to Shame': Paul, the Philippians, and the Honourable Wish for Death." *Neot* 42.2: 253–67.
Hafemann, Scott J. 1995. *Paul, Moses, and the History of Israel: The Letter/Spirit Contrast and the Argument from Scripture in 2 Corinthians 3*. WUNT 81. Tübingen: Mohr Siebeck.
Hainz, Josef. 1982. *Koinonia: "Kirche" als Gemeinschaft bei Paulus*. Regensburg: Pustet.
Hall, Jon. 1998. "Cicero to Lucceius (*Fam.* 5.12) in Its Social Context: *Valde Bella*?" *CP* 93.4: 308–21.
Hall, Jon. 2009. *Politeness and Politics in Cicero's Letters*. Oxford: Oxford University Press.

Hanges, James Constantine. 2012. *Paul, Founder of Churches: A Study in Light of the Evidence for the Role of "Founder-Figures" in the Hellenistic-Roman Period*. WUNT 292. Tübingen: Mohr Siebeck.

Hansen, G. Walter. 2003. "Transformation of Relationships: Partnership, Citizenship, and Friendship in Philippi." In *New Testament Greek and Exegesis: Essays in Honor of Gerald F. Hawthorne*, edited by Amy M. Donaldson and Timothy B. Sailors, 181–204. Cambridge: Eerdmans.

Hansen, G. Walter. 2009. *The Letter to the Philippians*. PNTC. Grand Rapids, MI: Eerdmans.

Harrison, James R. 2009. "Paul and the Roman Ideal of Glory in the Epistle to the Romans." In *The Letter to the Romans*, edited by Udo Schnelle, 329–69. BETL 226. Leuven: Leuven University Press.

Harrison, James R. 2013. "Paul the 'Paradoxical' Parent: The Politics of Family Beneficence in First Century Context (2 Cor 12:14–16)." In *Theologizing in the Corinthian Conflict: Studies in the Exegesis and Theology of 2 Corinthians*, edited by R. Bieringer et al., 399–426. BTS 16. Leuven: Peeters.

Harrison, James R. 2015. "Paul and Ancient Civic Ethics: Redefining the Canon of Honour in the Graeco-Roman World." In *Paul's Graeco-Roman Context*, edited by Cilliers Breytenbach, 75–118. BETL 277. Leuven: Peeters.

Harrison, James R. 2018. "From Rome to the Colony of Philippi: Roman Boasting in Philippians 3:4–6 in Its Latin West and Philippian Epigraphic Context." In *The First Urban Churches 4: Roman Philippi*, 307–70, edited by James R. Harrison and L. L. Welborn. WGRWSup 13. Atlanta, GA: SBL Press.

Hatina, Thomas R. 1999. "Intertextuality and Historical Criticism in New Testament Studies." *BI* 7.1: 28–43.

Haury, Auguste. 1974. "Cicéron et la gloire: une pédagogie de la vertu." In *Mélanges de philosophie, de littérature et d'histoire ancienne offerts à Pierre Boyancé*, 401–17. Rome: École Française de Rome.

Häußer, Detlef. 2016. *Der Brief des Paulus an die Philipper*. HTANT. Witten: SCM R.Brockhaus.

Hawthorne, Gerald F., and Ralph P. Martin. 2004. *Philippians*. WBC 43. Revised Edition. Milton Keynes: Word Books.

Hays, Richard. 1989. *Echoes of Scripture in the Letters of Paul*. New Haven, CT: Yale University Press.

Hays, Richard. 2005. *Conversion of the Imagination: Paul as Interpreter of Israel's Scriptures*. Grand Rapids, MI: Eerdmans.

Heckel, Ulrich. 1993. *Kraft in Schwachheit: Untersuchungen zu 2. Kor 10–13*. WUNT 2.56. Tübingen: Mohr Siebeck.

Hellegouarc'h, Joseph. 1963. *Le Vocabulaire latin des relations et des partis politiques sous la République*. FLSHUL 11. Paris: Les Belles Lettres.

Hellerman, Joseph H. 2005. *Reconstructing Honor in Roman Philippi: Carmen Christi as Cursus Pudorum*. SNTSMS 132. Cambridge: Cambridge University Press.

Hellerman, Joseph H. 2009. "Brothers and Friends in Philippi: Family Honor in the Roman World and in Paul's Letter to the Philippians." *BTB* 39.1: 15–25.

Hermisson, H.-J. 1998. *Studien zu Prophetie und Weisheit: Gesammelte Aufsätze*. Edited by Jörg Barthel, Hannelore Jauss, and Klaus Koenen. FAT 23. Tübingen: Mohr Siebeck, 197–219.

Hermisson, H.-J. 2007. *Deuterojesaja*. BKAT XI.8. Neukirchen-Vluyn: Neukirchener Verlag.

Höffken, Peter. 2006. "Eine Bemerkung zu Jes 55,1-5: Zu buchinternen Bezügen des Abschnitts." *ZAW* 118.2: 239-49.
Holleaux, Maurice. 1933. "Une inscription de Séleucie-de-Piérie." *BCH* 57: 6-67.
Holmberg, Bengt. 1978. *Paul and Power: The Structure of Authority in the Primitive Church as Reflected in the Pauline Epistles*. Lund: Gleerup.
Hooker, Morna. 2000. "Philippians." In *New Interpreter's Bible: Second Corinthians-Philemon*, 469-549, Vol. 11. Nashville, TN: Abingdon Press.
Horrell, David G. 2001. "From ἀδελφοί to οἶκος θεοῦ: Social Transformation in Pauline Christianity." *JBL* 120: 293-311.
Huber (Bechtel), Lyn. 1983. "Biblical Experience of Shame/Shaming: The Social Experience of Shame/Shaming in Biblical Israel in Relation to its Use as Religious Metaphor." PhD diss., Drew University.
Hutchinson, G. O. 1998. *Cicero's Correspondence: A Literary Study*. Oxford: Clarendon Press.
Hutchinson, G. O. 2007. "Down to the Documents: Criticism and Papyrus Letters." In *Ancient Letters: Classical and Late Antique Epistolography*, edited by Ruth Morello and A. D. Morrison, 17-36. Oxford: Oxford University Press.
Hutter, Horst. 1978. *Politics as Friendship*. Waterloo: Wilfrid Laurier University Press.
Inselmann, Anke. 2015. "Zum Affect der Freude im Philipperbrief: Unter Berücksichtigung pragmatischer und psychologischer Zugänge." In *Der Philipperbrief des Paulus in der hellenistisch-römischen Welt*, edited by J. Frey, B. Schliesser, and Veronika Niederhofer, 255-88. WUNT 253. Tübingen: Mohr Siebeck.
Inwood, Brad. 2007. "Form in Seneca's Letters." In *Ancient Letters: Classical and Late Antique Epistolography*, edited by Ruth Morello and A. D. Morrison, 133-48. Oxford: Oxford University Press.
Jaquette, James L. 1994. "A Not-So-Noble Death,: Figured Speech, Friendship and Suicide in Philippians 1:21-26." *NeoT* 28.1: 177-92.
Jaquette, James L. 1996. "Life and Death, *Adiaphora*, and Paul's Rhetorical Strategies." *NovT* 38.1: 30-54.
Jennings, Mark A. 2018. *The Price of Partnership in the Letter of Paul to the Philippians: "Make My Joy Complete."* LNTS 578. London: Bloomsbury T&T Clark.
Jewett, Robert. 1970. "The Epistolary Thanksgiving and the Integrity of Philippians." *NovT* 12: 40-53.
Johnson, L. T. 2010. *The Writings of the New Testament*, 3rd ed. Minneapolis, MN: Fortress Press.
Johnson, Terry, and Christopher Dandeker. 1989. "Patronage: Relation and System." In *Patronage in Ancient Society*, edited by Andrew Wallace-Hadrill, 219-42. London: Routledge.
Jordan, Judith V., Alexandra G. Kaplan, Jean Baker Miller, Irene P. Stiver, and Janet L. Surrey, eds. 1991. *Women's Growth in Connection: Writings from the Stone Center*. New York: Guilford Press.
Judge, E. A. 1968. "Paul's Boasting in Relation to Contemporary Professional Practice." *ABR* 10: 37-50.
Judge, E. A. 2008. "Paul as a Radical Critic of Society." In *Social Distinctives of the Christians in the First Century*, edited by David M. Scholer, 99-115. Peabody, MA: Hendrickson.
Kaster, Robert A. 1997. "The Shame of the Romans." *TAPA* 127: 1-19.
Kennedy, George A. 1984. *New Testament Interpretation Through Rhetorical Criticism*. Chapel Hill: University of North Carolina Press.

Keown, Mark J. 2015. "The Use of the Old Testament in Philippians." In *All That the Prophets Have Declared: The Appropriation of Scripture in the Emergence of Christianity*, edited by Matthew R. Malcolm, 139–65. Milton Keynes: Paternoster.

Keown, Mark J. 2017. *Philippians 1:1–2:18*. EEC. Bellingham, WA: Lexham Press.

Kirk, Alexander N. 2015. *Departure of an Apostle: Paul's Death Anticipated and Remembered*. WUNT 2.406. Tübingen: Mohr Siebeck.

Klauck, Hans-Joseph. 1991. "Kirche als Freundesgemeinschaft: Auf Spurensuche im Neuen Testament." *MTZ* 42: 1–14.

Klauck, Hans-Joseph. 2003. "Letters in Cicero's Correspondence." In *Early Christianity and Classical Culture: Comparative Studies in Honor of Abraham J. Malherbe*, edited by J. T. Fitzgerald, T. H. Olbricht, and L. M. White, 131–55. NovTSup 110. Leiden: Brill, 2003.

Klauck, Hans-Joseph. 2006. *Ancient Letters and the New Testament*. Waco, TX: Baylor University Press.

Koskenniemi, Heikki. 1956. *Studien zur Idee und Phraseologie des griechischen Briefes bis 400 n. Chr.* Helsinki: Akateeminen Kirjakauppa.

Krentz, Edgar. 1993. "Military Language and Metaphors in Philippians." In *Origins and Method: Towards a New Understand of Judaism and Christianity*. FS John C. Hurd, edited by Bradley H. McLean, 105–27. LNTS 86. Sheffield: JSOT Press.

Krentz, Edgar. 2003. "Paul, Games, and the Military." In *Paul in the Greco-Roman World: A Handbook*, edited by J. Paul Sampley, 344–83. Harrisburg: Trinity Press International.

Kuhn, Annika B. 2015. "The Dynamics of Social Status and Prestige in Pliny, Juvevnal and Martial." In *Social Status and Prestige in the Graeco-Roman World*, edited by Annika B. Kuhn, 9–28. Stuttgart: Franz Steiner Verlag.

Labuschagne, Casper J. 1997. "The Setting of the Song of Moses in Deuteronomy." In *Deuteronomy and the Deuteronomic Literature*, edited by Marc Vervenne and Johan Lust, 111–29. BETL 133. Leuven: University Press.

Lambrecht, Jan. 1985. "Why Is Boasting Excluded? A Note on Rom 3:27 and 4:2." *ETL* 61: 365–9.

Lambrecht, Jan. 1998. "Paul's Boasting about the Corinthians: A Study of 2 Corinthians 8:24–9:5." *NovT* 40: 352–68.

Landy, Francis. 1993. "Construction of the Subject and the Symbolic Order: A Reading of the Last Three Suffering Servant Songs." In *Among the Prophets: Language, Image and Structure in the Prophetic Writing*, edited by P. R. Davies and D. J. A. Clines, 60–71. LOTS 144. Sheffield: JSOT Press.

Leach, Eleanor. 2006. "*An gravius aliquid scribam*: Roman *seniores* Write to *iuvenes*." *TAPA* 136: 247–67.

Leeman, A. D. 1949. *Gloria: Cicero's waardering van de roem en haar achtergrond in de Hellenistische Wijsbegeerte en de Romeinse samenleving*. Rotterdam: N. V. Drukkerij M. Wyt & Zonen.

Lendon, J. E. 1997. *Empire of Honour: The Art of Government in the Roman World*. Oxford: Clarendon Press.

Lightfoot, J. B. 1908. *Saint Paul's Epistle to the Philippians: A Revised Text with Introduction, Notes, and Dissertations*. London: MacMillan.

Lincicum, David. 2013. *Paul and the Early Jewish Encounter with Deuteronomy*. Grand Rapids, MI: Baker.

Lindars, Barnabas. 1973. *New Testament Apologetic: The Doctrinal Significance of the Old Testament Quotations*. London: SCM Press.

Lohfink, Norbert. 1969. "Dt. 26, 17–19 und die 'Bundesformel'." *ZkTh* 91: 517–53.

Lohfink, Norbert. 1982. *Great Themes from the Old Testament*. Translated by Robert Walls. Edinburgh: T&T Clark.

Lohmeyer, Ernst. 1954. *Die Briefe an die Philipper, Kolosser und an Philemon*. KEK. Göttingen: Vandenhoeck & Ruprecht.

Louw, I-Jin, and Eugene Nida. 1977. *A Translator's Handbook on Paul's Letter to the Philippians*. New York: United Bible Society.

Luyten, Jos. 1985. "Primeval and Eschatological Overtones in the Song of Moses (Dt 32,1-43)." In *Das Deuteronomium: Entstehung, Gestalt und Botschaft*, edited by N. Lohfink, 341-7. BETL 68. Leuven: Leuven University Press.

Lyons, George, and William H. Malas, Jr. 2007. "Paul and His Friends within the Greco-Roman Context." *WTJ* 42.1: 50-69.

MacMullen, Ramsay. 1986. "Personal Power in the Roman Empire." *AJP* 107: 512-24.

Maier, Michael P. 2015. *Völkerwallfahrt im Jesajabuch*. BZAW 474. Berlin: de Gruyter.

Malherbe, Abraham J. 2000. *The Letters to the Thessalonians*. AB 32b. Yale: Yale University Press.

Malina, Bruce J. 1983. *New Testament World: Insights from Cultural Anthropology*. London: SCM Press.

Marchal, Joseph A. 2005. "Mutuality Rhetorics and Feminist Interpretation: Examining Philippians and Arguing for our Lives." *BCT* 1.3: 1-16.

Marchal, Joseph A. 2006. "With Friends Like These …: A Feminist Rhetorical Reconsideration of Scholarship and the Letter to the Philippians." *JSNT* 29: 77-106.

Marchal, Joseph A. 2006. *Hierarchy, Unity, and Imitation: A Feminist Rhetorical Analysis of Power Dynamics in Paul's Letter to the Philippians*. SBLAB 24. Leiden: Brill.

Marchal, Joseph A. 2008. *The Politics of Heaven: Women, Gender and Empire in the Study of Paul*. Minneapolis, MN: Fortress Press.

Marshall, I. Howard. 2002. "Should Christians Boast?" *BibSac* 159: 259-76.

Marshall, John W. 1993. "Paul's Ethical Appeal in Philippians." In *Rhetoric and the New Testament: Essays from the 1992 Heidelberg Conference*, edited by Stanley E. Porter and Thomas H. Olbricht, 357-74. LNTS 90. Sheffield: Sheffield Academic Press

Martin, Ralph P. 1987. *The Epistle of Paul to the Philippians: An Introduction and Commentary*. Grand Rapids, MI: Eerdmans.

Martin, Ralph P. 1997. *A Hymn of Christ: Philippians 2:5-11 in Recent Interpretation & in the Setting of Early Christian Worship*. Downers Grove, IL: InterVarsity Press.

Mays, Andrew D. H. 1981. "Deuteronomy 4 and the Literary Criticism of Deuteronomy." *JBL* 100: 23-51.

McAuley, David. 2015. *Paul's Covert Use of Scripture: Intertextuality and Rhetorical Situation in Philippians 2:10-16*. Eugene, OR: Pickwick.

McConville, J. G. 2002. *Deuteronomy*. AOTCS 5. Downers Grove, IL: InterVarsity Press, 2002.

Mendecki, Norbert. 1991. "Deuteronomistische Redaktion von Zef 3,18-20?" *BN* 60: 27-32.

Mengestu, Abera M. 2013. *God as Father: Kinship Language and Identity Formation in Early Christianity*. Eugene, OR: Pickwick.

Merendino, Rosario Pius. 1980. "Jes 49,1-6: ein Gottesknechtslied?" *ZAW* 92: 236-48.

Metzner, Rainer. 2002. "In aller Freundschaft. Ein frühchristlicher Fall freundschaftlicher Gemeinschaft (Phil 2.25-30)." *NTS* 48: 111-31.

Michael, J. Hugh. 1939. *Philippians*. MNTC. London: Stodder and Houghton.

Michel, Andreas. 2007. "Deuteronomium 26,16-19 ein 'ewiger Bund." In *Für Immer Verbündet: Studien zur Bundestheologie der Bibel*, edited by Christoph Dohmen and Christian Frevel, 141–9. SB 211. Stuttgart: Katholisches Bibelwerk.

Michel, Otto. 1954. "Zur Exegese von Phil 2,5-11." In *Theologie als Glaubenswagnis*, edited by K. Elliger, A. Weiser, E. Würthwein, and O. Bauernfeind, 79–95. FS for Karl Heim. Hamburg: Furche-Verlag.

Mitchell, Alan C. 1997. "'Greet the Friends by Name': New Testament Evidence for the Greco-Roman Topos on Friendship." In *Greco-Roman Perspectives on Friendship*, edited by J. T. Fitzgerald, 225–62. RBS 34. Atlanta, GA: Scholars Press.

Montiglio, Silvia. 2010. *Silence in the Land of Logos*. Princeton, NJ: Princeton University Press.

Morello, Ruth, and A. D. Morrison, eds. 2007. *Ancient Letters: Classical and Late Antique Epistolography*. Oxford: Oxford University Press.

Morello, Ruth. 2013. "Writer and Addressee in Cicero's Letters." In *The Cambridge Companion to Cicero*, edited by Catherine E. W. Steel, 196–214. Cambridge: Cambridge University Press.

Motyer, James A. 1993. *The Prophecy of Isaiah*. Downers Grove, IL: InterVarsity Press.

Moulton, J. H., and G. Milligan. 1914–29. *The Vocabulary of the Greek New Testament: Illustrated from the Papyri and Other Non-Literary Sources*. London: Hodder and Stoughton.

Moulton, J. H. 1967. *Grammar of New Testament Greek: Volume I, Prolegomena*, 3rd ed. Edinburgh: T&T Clark.

Moxnes, Halvor. 1996. "Honor and Shame." In *The Social Sciences and New Testament Interpretation*, edited by Richard L. Rohrbaugh, 19–40. Peabody, MA: Hendrickson.

Müller, Ulrich B. 1993. *Der Brief des Paulus an die Philipper*. THKNT 11/1. Leipzig: Evangelische Verlagsanstalt.

Mullins, Terence. 1973. "Visit Talk in the New Testament Letters." *CBQ* 35: 350–8.

Nasrallah, Laura S. 2012. "Spatial Perspectives: Space and Archeology in Roman Philippi." In *Studying Paul's Letters: Contemporary Perspectives and Methods*, edited by Joseph A. Marchal, 53–74. Minneapolis, MN: Fortress Press.

Newton, Michael. 1985. *The Concept of Purity at Qumran and in the Letters of Paul*. SNTSMS 53. Cambridge: Cambridge University Press.

Neyrey, Jerome H. 2007. *Give God the Glory: Ancient Prayer and Worship in Cultural Perspective*. Grand Rapids, MI: Eerdmans.

Nikki, Nina. 2019. *Opponents and Identity in Philippians*. NovTSup 173. Leiden: Brill.

Nongbri, Brent. 2009. "Two Neglected Textual Variants in Philippians 1." *JBL* 128: 803–8.

North, C. R. 1964. *The Second Isaiah*. Oxford: Clarendon Press.

Oakes, Peter. 2000. "Quelle devrait être l'influence des échos intertextuels sur la traduction?" In *Intertextualités: La Bible en échos*, edited by Daniel Marguerat and Adrian Curtis, 251–87. Geneva: Labor et Fides.

Oakes, Peter. 2001. *Philippians: From People to Letter*. SNTSMS 110. Cambridge: Cambridge University Press.

Oakes, Peter. 2005. "Re-Mapping the Universe: Paul and the Emperor in 1 Thessalonians and Philippians." *JSNT* 27.3: 301–22.

Ogereau, Julian M. 2014. *Paul's Koinonia with the Philippians: A Socio-Historical Investigation of a Pauline Economic Partnership*. WUNT 2.377. Tübingen: Mohr Siebeck.

Öhler, Markus. 2017. "Rezeption des Alten Testaments im 1. Thessalonicherbrief und im Philipperbrief?" In *Paulinische*

Schriftrezeption: Grundlagen—Ausprägungen—Wirkungen—Wertungen, edited by Florian Wilk and Markus Öhler, 113–35. FRLANT 268. Göttingen: Vandenhoeck and Ruprecht.
Olley, John W. 1979. *"Righteousness" in the Septuagint of Isaiah*. SCS 8. Atlanta, GA: Scholars Press.
Olyan, Saul. 1996. "Honor, Shame and Covenant Relations: Honor Relations in Ancient Israel and Its Environment." *JBL* 115 (1996): 201–18.
Olyan, Saul. 2017. *Friendship in the Hebrew Bible*. New Haven, CT: Yale University Press.
Ortwein, Gudrun Guttenberger. 1999. *Status und Statusverzicht im Neuen Testament und seiner Umwelt*. NTOA 39. Göttingen: Vandenhoeck & Ruprecht.
Osiek, Carolyn. 2000. *Philippians, Philemon*. ANTC. Nashville, TN: Abingdon Press.
Oswalt, John. 1998. *Isaiah: Chapters 40–66*. NICOT. Grand Rapids, MI: Zondervan.
Pangle, Lorraine Smith. 2003. *Aristotle and the Philosophy of Friendship*. Cambridge: Cambridge University Press.
Pao, David W. 2002. *Thanksgiving: An Investigation of a Pauline Theme*. NSBT 13. Downers Grove, IL: InterVarsity Press.
Park, M. Sydney. 2007. *Submission within the Godhead and the Church in the Epistle to the Philippians: An Exegetical and Theological Examination of the Concept of Submission in Philippians 2 and 3*. LNTS 361. London: T&T Clark.
Patterson, Jane Lancaster. 2015. *Keeping the Feast: Metaphors of Sacrifice in 1 Corinthians and Philippians*. ECL 16. Atlanta, GA: SBL Press.
Pauritsch, Karl. 1971. *Die neue Gemeinde: Gott sammelt Ausgestossene und Arme (Jesaia 55–66)*. AnBib 47. Rome: Biblical Institute Press.
Pedersen, Johannes. 1991. *Israel: Its Life and Culture Volume I*. Atlanta, GA: Scholars Press.
Peristiany, John G., ed. 1966. *Honour and Shame: The Values of Mediterranean Society*. Chicago, IL: University of Chicago Press.
Perkins, Pheme. 1991. "Philippians: Theology for the Heavenly Politeuma." In *Pauline Theology Vol. I*, edited by J. Bassler, 89–104. Minneapolis, MN: Fortress Press.
Pernot, Laurent. Jan–June 1998. "Periautologia: Problèmes et méthodes de l'éloge de soi-même." *REG* 111: 101–24.
Perri, Carmela. 1978. "On Allusion." *Poetics* 7: 289–307.
Peterlin, Davorin. 1995. *Paul's Letter to the Philippians in the Light of Disunity in the Church*. NovTSup 79. Leiden: E. J. Brill.
Pialoux, Luc. 2017. *L'épître aux Philippiens: L'évangile du don et de l'amitié*. EB 75. Leuven: Peeters.
Pilhofer, Peter. 1995. *Philippi: Band I, Die erste christliche Gemeinde Europas*. WUNT 87. Tübingen: Mohr Siebeck.
Pilhofer, Peter. 2000. *Philippi. Band II: Katalog der Inschriften von Philippi*. WUNT 119. Tübingen: Mohr Siebeck.
Pitt-Rivers, Julian A. 1966. "Honour and Social Status." In *Honour and Shame: The Values of Mediterranean Society*, edited by John G. Peristiany, 19–77. Chicago, IL: University of Chicago Press.
Pitta, Antonio. 2010. *Lettera ai Filippesi: Nuova versione, introduzione e commento*. LBNT 11. Milan: Paoline.
Plevnik, Joseph. 1998. "Honor/Shame." In *Handbook of Biblical Social Values*, edited by John J. Pilch and Bruce J. Malina, 106–15. Peabody, MA: Hendrickson.
Poplutz, Uta. 2004. *Athlet des Evangeliums: Eine motivgeschichtliche Studie zur Wettkampfmetaphorik bei Paulus*. HBS 43. Freiburg: Herder.

Porter, Stanley E., and Christopher D. Stanley, eds. 2008. *As It Is Written: Studying Paul's Use of Scripture*. SBLSymS 50. Atlanta, GA: SBL Press.
Porter, Stanley E. 2008. "Allusions and Echoes." In *As It Is Written: Studying Paul's Use of Scripture*, edited by Stanley E. Porter and Christopher D. Stanley, 29–40. SBLSymS 50. Atlanta, GA: SBL Press.
Prümm, Karl S. J. 1962. *Diakonia Pneumatos, Band II: Theologie des zweiten Korintherbriefes*. Rome: Herder.
Raurell, Frederic. 1996. *"Doxa" en la teologia I: Antropologia dels LXX*. CSP 59. Barcelona: Herder.
Reed, Jeffrey T. 1997. *A Discourse Analysis of Philippians: Method and Rhetoric in the Debate over Literary Integrity*. LNTS 136. Sheffield: Sheffield Academic Press.
Rees, Roger. 2007. "Letters of Recommendation and the Rhetoric of Praise." In *Ancient Letters: Classical and Late Antique Epistolography*, edited by Ruth Morello and A. D. Morrison, 149–68. Oxford: Oxford University Press.
Reider, Joseph, and Nigel Turner. 1966. *An Index to Aquila*. VTSup 12. Leiden: Brill.
Reinl, Peter. 2003. "Plädoyer gegen die Schaffung neuer Ränder in der Gemeinde von Philippi: Phil 3,1b-11(21) und das kulturanthropologische Modell 'Ehre und Scham/Schande'." In *Randfiguren in der Mitte: Hermann-Josef Venetz zu Ehren*, edited by Max Küchler and Peter Reinl, 117–34. Luzern: Paulusverlag.
Rendtorff, Rolf. 1998. *The Covenant Formula: An Exegetical and Theological Investigation*. Translated by Margaret Kohl. Edinburgh: T&T Clark.
Reumann, John H. P. 1987. "The Theologies of 1 Thessalonians and Philippians: Contents, Comparison, and Composite." *SBLSP* 26: 521–36.
Reumann, John H. P. "Philippians, Especially Chapter 4, as a 'Letter of Friendship': Observations on a Checkered History of Scholarship." In *Friendship, Flattery, and Frankness of Speech*, edited by J. T. Fitzgerald, 83–106. NovTSup 82. Leiden: E. J. Brill.
Reumann, John H. P. 2006. "The (Greek) Old Testament in Philippians: 1:19 as Parade Example—Allusion, Echo, Proverb?" In *History and Exegesis*. FS Ellis, edited by Sang-Won Son, 189–200. London: T&T Clark.
Reumann, John H. P. 2008. *Philippians: A New Translation with Introduction and Commentary*. AB 33B. New Haven, CT: Yale University Press.
Richards, E. Randolph. 2017. "Some Observations on Paul and Seneca as Letter Writers." In *Paul and Seneca in Dialogue*, edited by Joseph R. Dodson and David E. Briones, 49–72. APR 2. Leiden: Brill.
Robert, Louis. 1971. *Les gladiateurs dans l'Orient grec*. Amsterdam: Adolf M. Hakkert. Reprint from *Biblitothèque de l'Ecole des Hautes Etudes 4th section, Sciences historiques et philologiques* 278. Limoges: A. Bontemps, 1940.
Rosell Nebreda, Sergio. 2011. *Christ Identity: A Social-Scientific Reading of Philippians 2.5–11*. FRLANT 242. Göttingen: Vandenhoeck & Ruprecht.
Rosner, Brian. 2007. "Deuteronomy in 1 and 2 Corinthians." In *Deuteronomy in the New Testament*, edited by Steve Moyise and Maarten J. J. Menken, 118–35. LNTS 358. London: A&C Black.
Rudd, Niall. 1992. "Stratagems of Vanity: Cicero, *Ad familiares* 5.12 and Pliny's Letters." In *Author and Audience in Latin Literature*, edited by Anthony John Woodman and Jonathan Powell, 18–32. Cambridge: Cambridge University Press.
Ryan, Richard M., and Edward L. Deci. 2000. "Intrinsic and Extrinsic Motivations: Classic Definitions and New Directions." *CEP* 25: 54–67.
Saller, Richard P. 1982. *Personal Patronage Under the Early Empire*. Cambridge: Cambridge University Press.

Saller, Richard P. 1989. "Patronage and Friendship in Early Imperial Rome: Drawing the Distinction." In *Patronage in Ancient Society*, edited by Andrew Wallace-Hadrill, 49–62. London: Routledge.
Salvesen, Alison. 1991. *Symmachus in the Pentateuch*. JSSM 15. Manchester: University of Manchester.
Sampley, J. Paul. 1980. *Pauline Partnership in Christ: Christian Community and Commitment in Light of Roman Law*. Philadelphia, PA: Fortress Press.
Sampley, J. Paul. 1988. "Paul, His Opponents in 2 Corinthians 10–13, and the Rhetorical Handbooks." In *The Social World of Formative Christianity and Judaism*. FS Howard Clark Kee, edited by Jacob Neusner, Peder Borgen, Ernest S. Frerichs, and Richard Horsley, 162–77. Philadelphia, PA: Fortress Press.
Sampley, J. Paul, ed. 2003. *Paul in the Greco-Roman World: A Handbook*. Harrisburg, PA: Trinity Press International.
Sampley, J. Paul, ed. 2016. *Paul in the Greco-Roman World: A Handbook*, 2nd ed., 2 vols. London: Bloomsbury..
Sánchez Bosch, Jorge. 1970. *"Gloriarse" segun San Pablo: Sentido y teología de καυχάομαι*. AnBib 40. Rome: Biblical Institute Press.
Sandnes, Karl Olav. 1991. *Paul, One of the Prophets?: A Contribution to the Apostle's Self-Understanding*. WUNT 2.43. Tübingen: Mohr Siebeck.
Schäfer, Klaus. 1989. *Gemeinde als "Bruderschaft": Ein Beitrag zum Kirchenverständnis des Paulus*. EH 333. Bern: Peter Lang.
Schapdick, Stefan. 2011. *Eschatisches Heil mit eschatischer Anerkennung: Exegetische Untersuchungen zu Funktion und Sachgehalt der paulinischen Verkündigung vom eigenen Endgeschick im Rahmen seiner Korrespondenz an die Thessalonicher, Korinther und Philipper*. BBB 164. Göttingen: Vandenhoeck & Ruprecht.
Schellenberg, Ryan S. 2013. *Rethinking Paul's Rhetorical Education: Comparative Rhetoric and 2 Corinthians 10–13*. ECL 10. Atlanta, GA: SBL Press.
Schenk, Wolfgang. 1984. *Die Philipperbriefe des Paulus: Kommentar*. Stuttgart: Kohlhammer.
Schmeller, Thomas. 1995. *Hierarchie und Egalität: Eine sozialgeschichtliche Untersuchung paulinischer Gemeinden und griechisch-römischer Vereine*. SB 162. Stuttgart: Verlag Katholisches Bibelwerk GmbH.
Schneider, Johannes. 1932. *Doxa: Eine bedeutungsgeschichtliche Studie*. BSGUF 3. Gütersloh: C. Bertelsmann.
Schliesser, Benjamin. "Paulus und 'seine' Philipper." 2014. In *Philipperbrief in der hellenistisch-römischen Welt*, edited by Jörg Frey, Benjamin Schliesser, and Veronika Niederhofer, 33–119. WUNT 253. Tübingen: Mohr Siebeck.
Schoon-Janssen, Johannes. 1991. *Umstrittene "Apologien" in den Paulusbriefen: Studien zur rhetorischen Situation des 1. Thessalonicherbriefes, des Galaterbriefes und des Philipperbriefes*. GTA 45. Göttingen: Vandenhoeck & Ruprecht.
Schreiner, Josef. 1974. "'Jer 9,22.23 als Hintergrund des paulinischen 'Sich-Rühmens.'" In *Biblische Randbemerkungen*. FS R. Schnackenburg, edited by H. Merklein and J. Lange, 530–42. Würzburg: Echter Verlag.
Schütz, John Howard. 1975. *Paul and the Anatomy of Apostolic Authority*. SNTSMS 26. Cambridge: Cambridge University Press.
Schwind, Rainer. 2007. *Gesichte der Herrlichkeit: Eine exegetisch-traditionsgeschichtliche Studie zur paulinischen und johanneischen Christologie*. HBS 50. Freiburg: Herder.
Seaford, Richard. 1994. *Reciprocity and Ritual: Homer and Tragedy in the Developing City-State*. Oxford: Clarendon Press.

Sevenster, J. N. 1961. *Paul and Seneca*. NovTSup 4. Leiden: E. J. Brill.
Silva, Moises. 2005. *Philippians*. BECNT 19. Grand Rapids, MI: Baker Academic.
Sisson, Russel B. 2003. "A Common Agōn: Ideology and Rhetorical Intertexture in Philippians." In *Fabrics of Discourse: FS V. K. Robbins*, edited by David B. Gowler, L. Gregory Bloomquist, and Duane F. Watson, 242–63. Harrisburg, PA: Trinity Press International.
Sherk, Robert K. 1984. *Rome and the Greek East to the Death of Augustus*. New York: Cambridge University Press.
Smend, Rudolf. 1963. *Die Bundesformel*. Zürich: EVZ-Verlag.
Smit, Peter-Ben. 2013. *Paradigms of Being in Christ: A Study of the Epistle to the Philippians*. LNTS 476. London: Bloomsbury T&T Clark.
Smit, Peter-Ben. 2014. "Paul, Plutarch and the Problematic Practice of Self-Praise (περιαυτολογία): The Case of Phil 3.2–21." *NTS* 60.3: 341–59.
Snyman, A. H. 2005. "Rhetorical Analysis of 1:12–26." *ATh* 25.1: 89–111.
Snyman, A. H. 2005. "Rhetorical Analysis of 1:27–2:18." *VE* 26.3: 783–809.
Spicq, Ceslas. 1994. *Theological Lexicon of the New Testament*. Translated and edited by James D. Ernest. 3 vols. Peabody, MA: Hendrickson.
Stanley, Christopher D. 1992. *Paul and the Language of Scripture: Citation Technique in the Pauline Epistles and Contemporary Literature*. SNTSMS 69. Cambridge: Cambridge University Press.
Stanley, Christopher D. *Arguing with Scripture: The Rhetoric of Quotations in the Letters of Paul*. London: T&T Clark, 2004.
Stanley, Christopher D, ed. 2012. *Paul and Scripture: Extending the Conversation*. ECL 9. Atlanta, GA: SBL Press.
Stanley, Christopher D. 2012. "What We Learned—and What We Didn't." In *Paul and Scripture: Extending the Conversation*, edited by Christopher D. Stanley, 321–30. ECL 9. Atlanta, GA: SBL Press.
Stanley, David M. 1954. "The Theme of the Servant of Yahweh." *CBQ* 16: 415–18.
Steel, Catherine E. W. 2004. *Reading Cicero*. London: Duckworth.
Steel, Catherine E. W, ed. 2013. *The Cambridge Companion to Cicero*. Cambridge: Cambridge University Press.
Stettler, Hanna. 2014. *Heiligung bei Paulus: Ein Beitrag aus biblisch-theologischer Sicht*. WUNT 2.368. Tübingen: Mohr Siebeck.
Stevenson, T. R. 1992. "Ideal Benefactor and the Father Analogy in Greek and Roman Thought." *CQ* 42 (1992): 421–36.
Still, Tod. 2011. *Philippians & Philemon*. Macon, GA: Smyth & Helwys Bible Commentary.
Stirewalt, M. Luther Jr. 2003. *Paul the Letter Writer*. Grand Rapids, MI: Eerdmans.
Stowers, Stanley K. 1986. *Letter Writing in Greco-Roman Antiquity*. LEC 5. Philadelphia, PA: Westminster John Knox Press.
Stowers, Stanley K. 1991."Friends and Enemies in the Politics of Heaven: Reading Theology in Philippians." In *Pauline Theology. Vol. 1: Thessalonians, Philippians, Galatians, Philemon*, edited by J. M. Bassler, 105–21. Minneapolis, MN: Fortress Press.
Strack, Hermann, and Paul Billerbeck. 1926. *Kommentar zum neuen Testament aus Talmud und Midrasch. Dritter Band: Die Briefe des Neuen Testaments und die Offenbarung Johannis*. Munich: C. H. Beck.
Stromberg, Jacob. 2009. "The Second Temple and the Isaianic Afterlife of the הסדי דוד (Isa 55:3–5)." *ZAW* 121: 242–55.
Sullivan, Francis A. 1941. "Cicero and Gloria." *TAPA* 72: 382–91.

Synofzik, Ernst. 1977. *Die Gericht- und Vergeltungsaussagen bei Paulus.* GTA 8. Göttingen: Vandenhoeck & Ruprecht.
Talstra, Eep. 1997. "Deuteronomy 31: Confusion or Conclusion? The Story of Moses' Threefold Succession." In *Deuteronomy and Deuteronomic Literature,* edited by Marc Vervenne and Johan Lust, 87–103. BETL 133. Leuven: University Press.
Tassin, Claude. 1994. "L'apostolat, un 'sacrifice'?" In *Le Sacrifice dans les Religions,* edited by Marcel Neusch, 86–116. Paris: Beauchesne.
Tellbe, Mikael. 2001. *Paul between Synagogue and State: Christians, Jews, and Civic Authorities in 1 Thessalonians, Romans, and Philippians.* CB 34. Stockholm: Almqvist & Wiksell.
Thielman, Frank S. 1994. *Paul and the Law: A Contextual Approach.* Downers Grove, IL: InterVarsity Press.
Thielman, Frank S. 2003. "Ephesus and the Literary Setting of Philippians." In *New Testament Greek and Exegesis: Essays in Honor of Gerald F. Hawthorne,* edited by Amy M. Donaldson and Timothy B. Sailors, 205–23. Grand Rapids, MI: Eerdmans.
Thompson, James W. 2001. "Paul's Argument from Pathos in 2 Corinthians." In *Paul and Pathos,* edited by Thomas H. Olbricht and Jerry L. Sumney, 131–45. SBLSymS 16. Atlanta, GA: SBL.
Thompson, James W. 2006. *Pastoral Ministry According to Paul: A Biblical Vision.* Grand Rapids, MI: Baker.
Thompson, James W. 2011. *Moral Formation According to Paul: The Context and Coherence of Pauline Ethics.* Grand Rapids, MI: Baker.
Thompson, Richard W. 1986. "Paul's Double Critique of Jewish Boasting: A Study of Rom 3:27 in Its Context." *Bib* 67: 520–31.
Tigay, Jeffrey H. 2003. *Deuteronomy.* JPS Torah Commentary. Philadelphia, PA: JPS.
Tooman, William A. 2011. *Gog of Magog: Reuse of Scripture and Compositional Technique in Ezekiel 38–39.* FAT 2.52. Tübingen: Mohr Siebeck.
Trapp, Michael. 2003. *Greek and Latin Letters: An Anthology with Translation.* Cambridge: Cambridge University Press.
Travis, S. H. 1973. "Paul's Boasting in 2 Corinthians 10–12." In *StuEv* 6, edited by Elizabeth A. Livingstone, 527–32. Berlin: Akademie Verlag.
Trebilco, Paul. 2011. *Self-Designations and Group Identity in the New Testament.* Cambridge: Cambridge University Press.
Troxel Ronald L. 2008. *LXX-Isaiah as Translation and Interpretation: Strategies of the Translator of the Septuagint of Isaiah.* JSJSup 124. Leiden: Brill.
Vahrenhorst, Martin. 2008. *Kultische Sprache in den Paulusbriefen.* WUNT 230. Tübingen: Mohr Siebeck.
Van der Kooij, Arie. 1997. "'The Servant of the Lord': A Particular Group of Jews in Egypt According to the Old Greek of Isaiah, Some Comments on LXX Isa 49:1-6 and Related Passages." In *Studies in the Book of Isaiah.* FS W. A. M. Beuken, edited by Jacques Van Ruiten and Marc Vervenne, 383–96. BETL 132. Leuven: Leuven University Press.
Van der Merwe C. H. J., J. A. Naudé, and J. H. Kroeze. 2000. *A Biblical Hebrew Reference Grammar.* Biblical Languages: Hebrew 3. Sheffield: Sheffield Academic Press.
Van Nijf, Onno. 2015. "Civic Mirrors: Honorific Inscriptions and the Politics of Prestige." In *Social Status and Prestige in the Graeco-Roman World,* edited by Annika B. Kuhn, 233–46. Stuttgart: Franz Steiner Verlag.
Veyne, Paul. 1990. *Bread and Circuses.* Translated by Brian Pearce. London: Penguin Press.
Vincent, Marvin R. 1902. *A Critical and Exegetical Commentary on the Epistles to the Philippians and to Philemon.* ICC. Edinburgh: T&T Clark.

Vollenweider, Samuel. 1994. "Die Waagschalen von Leben und Tod: Zum Antiken Hintergrund von Phil 1:21-26." *ZNW* 85.1-2: 93-115.

Vollenweider, Samuel. 2006. "Politische Theologie im Philipperbrief?" In *Paulus und Johannes: Exegetische Studien zur paulinischen und johanneischen Theologie und Literatur*, edited by Dieter Sänger and Ulrich Mell, 457-69. WUNT 198. Tübingen: Mohr Siebeck.

Vollenweider, Samuel. 2008. "'Der Name, der über jedem anderen Namen ist': Jesus als Träger des Gottesnamens im Neuen Testament." In *Gott nennen: Gottes Namen und Gott als Name*, edited by I. U. Dalferth and P. Stoellger, 173-86. RPT 35. Tübingen: Mohr Siebeck.

Vollenweider, Samuel. 2009. "Lob am Jüngsten Tag: zum Hintergrund der Gerichtserwartung im Philipperbrief." In *Beiträge zur urchristlichen Theologiegeschichte*, edited by Wolfgang Kraus, 307-17. BZNW 163. Berlin: de Gruyter.

Von Harnack, Adolf. 1911. "Das hohe Lied des Apostels Paulus von der Liebe (I. Kor. 13) und seine religionsgeschichtliche Bedeutung." *SPAW* 1: 132-63.

Von Harnack, Adolf. Jan 1928. "Κόπος (Κοπιαν, Οἱ Κοπιῶντες) im frühchristlichen Sprachgebrauch." *ZNW* 27: 1-10.

Von Rad, Gerhard. 1964. *Deuteronomium*. ATD 8. Göttingen: Vandenhoeck & Ruprecht.

Vos, Johan S. 2002. *Die Kunst der Argumentation bei Paulus: Studien zur antiken Rhetorik*. WUNT 149. Tübingen: Mohr Siebeck.

Vos, Johan S. 2005. "Philippians 1:12-26 and the Rhetoric of Success." In *Rhetoric, Ethic, and Moral Persuasion in Biblical Discourse: Essays from the 2002 Heidelberg Conference*, edited by Thomas Olbricht and Anders Eriksson, 274-83. ESEC 11. London: T&T Clark International.

Vouga, François. 2008. "L'épître aux Philippiens." In *Introduction au Nouveau Testament: Son histoire, son écriture, sa théologie*, edited by Daniel Marguerat, 251-64. Genève: Labor et Fides.

Wagner, J. Ross. 2003. *Heralds of the Good News: Isaiah and Paul in Concert in the Letter to the Romans*. NovTSup 101. Leiden: Brill.

Wagner, J. Ross. 2005. "Isaiah in Romans and Galatians." In *Isaiah in the New Testament*, edited by Steve Moyise and Maarten J. J. Menken, 117-33. London: T&T Clark.

Wagner, J. Ross. 2006. "Moses and Isaiah in Concert: Paul's Reading of Isaiah and Deuteronomy in the Letter to the Romans." In *"As Those Who Are Taught": The Interpretation of Isaiah from the LXX to the SBL*, edited by Claire Matthews McGinnis and Patricia K. Tull, 87-103. SBLSymS 27. Atlanta, GA: SBL Press.

Wagner, Thomas. 2012. *Gottes Herrlichkeit: Bedeutung und Verwendung des Begriffs kābôd im Alten Testament*. VTSup 151. Leiden: Brill.

Wallace, Daniel B. 1996. *Greek Grammar: Beyond the Basics*. Grand Rapids, MI: Zondervan.

Walter, Nikolaus. 1998. "Der Brief an die Philipper." In *Die Briefe an die Philipper, Thessalonicher und an Philemon*, edited by Nikolaus Walter, Eckart Reinmuth, and Peter Lampe, 11-101. NTD 8/2. Göttingen: Vandenhoeck & Ruprecht.

Walter, Nikolaus. 2000. "Alttestamentliche Bezüge in christologischen Ausführungen des Paulus." In *Paulinische Christologie: Exegetische Beiträge*. FS Hans Hübner, edited by Udo Schnelle, Thomas Söding, and Michael Labahn, 246-71. Göttingen: Vandenhoeck & Ruprecht.

Walton, Steve. 2013. "Paul, Patronage and Pay: What Do We Know about the Apostle's Financial Support?" In *Paul as Missionary: Identity, Activity, Theology and Practice*, edited by Trevor Burke and Brian Rosner, 220-33. LNTS 420. London: T&T Clark.

Wansink, Craig S. 1996. *Chained in Christ: The Experience and Rhetoric of Paul's Imprisonments*. LNTS 130. Sheffield: Sheffield Academic Press.
Ware, James P. 2011. *Paul and the Mission of the Church: Philippians in Ancient Jewish Context*. Grand Rapids, MI: Baker Academic.
Waters, Guy P. 2006. *The End of Deuteronomy in the Epistles of Paul*. WUNT 221. Tübingen: Mohr Siebeck.
Watkins, Thomas H. 1997. *L. Munatius Plancus: Serving and Surviving in the Roman Revolution*. ICSSup 7. Chicago, IL: Scholars Press.
Watson, Duane F. 1988. "A Rhetorical Analysis of Philippians and its Implications for the Unity Question." *NovT* 30.1: 57–88.
Watson, Duane F. 1997. "The Integration of Epistolary and Rhetorical Analysis of Philippians." In *The Rhetorical Analysis of Scripture: Essays from the 1995 London Conference*, edited by S. E. Porter and T. H. Olbricht, 398–426. LNTS 146. Sheffield: Sheffield Academic Press.
Watson, Duane F. 2005. "Paul's Boasting in 2 Corinthians 10–13." In *Rhetoric, Ethic, and Moral Persuasion in Biblical Discourse: Essays from the 2002 Heidelberg Conference*, edited by Thomas Olbricht and Anders Eriksson, 260–75. ESEC 11. London: T&T Clark International.
Watson, Duane F. 2003. "Paul and Boasting." In *Paul in the Greco-Roman World: A Handbook*, edited by J. Paul Sampley, 77–100. Harrisburg: Trinity Press International.
Watson, Duane F. 2016. "Paul and Boasting." In *Paul in the Greco-Roman World: A Handbook*, 2nd ed., edited by J. Paul Sampley, 90–112. London: Bloomsbury.
Watson, Francis B. 2009. "Mistranslation and the Death of Christ: Isaiah 53 LXX and its Pauline Reception." In *Translating the New Testament: Text, Translation, Theology*, edited by Stanley E. Porter and Mark J. Boda, 215–50. MNTS. Grand Rapids, MI: Eerdmans.
Wei, Ryan. 2013. "Fronto and the Rhetoric of Friendship." *CEA* 50: 67–93.
Weidmann, Frank W. 2013. *Philippians, 1 and 2 Thessalonians, and Philemon*. Louisville, KY: Westminster John Knox Press.
Weinfield, Moshe. 1972. *Deuteronomy and the Deuteronomic School*. Oxford: Clarendon Press.
Westermann, Claus. 1986. *Das Buch Jesaja 3*. ATD 19. Göttingen: Vandenhoeck & Ruprecht.
Westermann, Claus. 1969. *Isaiah 40–66: A Commentary*. OTL. Translated by David M. G. Stalker. Philadelphia, PA: Westminster Press.
Wevers, John William. 1995. *Notes on the Greek Text of Deuteronomy*. SCS 39. Atlanta, GA: Scholars Press.
White, John L. 1986. *Light from Ancient Letters*. Minneapolis, MN: Fortress Press.
White, L. Michael. 1990. "Morality between Two Worlds: A Paradigm of Friendship in Philippians." In *Greeks, Romans, and Christians*. FS Malherbe, edited by David L. Balch, Everett Ferguson, and Wayne A. Meeks, 201–15. Minneapolis, MN: Fortress Press.
White, Peter. 2010. *Cicero in Letters: Epistolary Relations of the Late Republic*. Oxford: Oxford University Press.
Whybray, R. Norman. 1975. *Isaiah 40–66*. NCBC. Edinburgh: Oliphants.
Wick, Peter. 1994. *Der Philipperbrief: Der formale Aufbau des Briefs als Schlüssel zum Verständnis seines Inhalts*. BWANT 135. Stuttgart: Verlag W. Kohlhammer.
Wilcox, Peter, and David Paton-Williams. 1988. "The Servant Songs in Deutero-Isaiah." *JSOT* 42: 79–102.

Wilcox, Amanda. 2012. *The Gift of Correspondence in Classical Rome*. Madison: University of Wisconsin Press.

Wilk, Florian. 1988. *Die Bedeutung des Jesajabuches für Paulus*. FRLANT 179. Göttingen: Vandenhoeck & Ruprecht.

Wilk, Florian. 2005. "Isaiah in 1 and 2 Corinthians." In *Isaiah in the New Testament*, edited by Steve Moyise and Maarten J. J. Menken, 133–58. London: T&T Clark.

Wilk, Florian. 2010. "Ruhm *coram Deo* bei Paulus?" *ZNW* 101: 55–77.

Williams, Craig A. 2012. *Reading Roman Friendship*. Cambridge: Cambridge University Press.

Williams, Demetrius K. 2002. *Enemies of the Cross of Christ: The Terminology of the Cross and Conflict in Philippians*. LNTS 223. London: Sheffield Academic.

Williams, H. H. Drake III. 2013. "Honouring Epaphroditus: A Suffering and Faithful Servant Worthy of Admiration." In *Paul and His Social Relations*, edited by Stanley E. Porter and Christopher Land, 333–55. Leiden: Brill.

Windsor, Lionel J. 2014. *Paul and the Vocation of Israel: How Paul's Jewish Identity Informs His Apostolic Ministry, with Special Reference to Romans*. BZNW 205. Berlin: de Gruyter.

Wischmeyer, Oda. 1986. "Das Adjektiv ΑΓΑΠΗΤΟΣ in den paulinischen Briefen, Eine Traditionsgeschichtliche Miszelle." *NTS* 32 (1986). 476–80.

Wiseman, Timothy Peter. 1962. "The Ambitions of Quintus Cicero." In *Studies on Cicero*, edited by John Ferguson, 34–41. Roma: Centro di studi Ciceroniani.

Witherington III, Ben. 1994. *Friendship and Finances in Philippi: The Letter of Paul to the Philippians*. Valley Forge, PA: Trinity Press International.

Witherington III, Ben. 2011. *Paul's Letter to the Philippians: A Socio-Rhetorical Commentary*. Grand Rapids, MI: Eerdmans.

Wojciechowski, Michael. 2006. "Paul and Plutarch on Boasting." *JGRChJ* 3: 99–109.

Wojtkowiak, Heiko. 2012. *Christologie und Ethik im Philipperbrief: Studien zur Handlungsorientierung einer frühchristlichen Gemeinde in paganer Umwelt*. FRLANT 243. Göttingen: Vandenhoeck & Ruprecht.

Wright, N. T. 2013. *Paul and the Faithfulness of God*. COQG 4. London: SPCK.

Wyss, Beatrice. 2014. "'Vater Gott und seine Kinder und Frauen.'" In *The Divine Father: Religious and Philosophical Concepts of Divine Parenthood in Antiquity*, edited by Felix Albrecht and Reinhard Feldmeier, 165–97. Leiden: Brill.

Young, E. J. 1965. *The Book of Isaiah*. NICOT, 3 vols. Grand Rapids, MI: Eerdmans, 1965.

Zeller, Dieter. 2006. "Selbstbezogenheit und Selbstdarstellung in den Paulusbriefen." In *Neues Testament und Hellenistische Umwelt*, 201–13. BBB 150. Göttingen: Philo.

Zerbe, Gordon Mark. 2016. *Philippians*. Believers Church Bible Commentary. Waterloo: Herald Press.

Zerbe, Gordon Mark. 2012. *Citizenship: Paul on Peace and Politics*. Winnipeg: CMU Press.

Zerwick, Max S. J. 2007. *A Grammatical Analysis of the Greek New Testament*, 5th ed. Rome: Biblical Institute Press.

Author Index

Aasgaard, Reider 31 n.172, 32, 85, 76, 152
Aernie, Jeffrey 65, 146 n.96
Agosto, Efrain 81 n.14
Aletti, Jean-Noel 159 n.4
Alexander, Loveday 31, 114 n.6
Alkier, Stefan 21 n.104
Anderson, Peter J. 79 n.2
Arnold, Bradley 1 n.4
Arzt-Grabner, Peter 31 n.173, 33 n.184
Ascough, Richard S. 27 n.138, 77 n.11
Asting, Ragnar 10, 11, 13, 118 n.23

Balsdon, J. P. V. D. 75 n.5
Barclay, John M. G. 14, 15, 140 n.72, 160 nn.47–9
Barrett, C. K. 141 n. 77
Barton, Carlin 82 n.17
Barton, John 20 n.101
Beale, G. K. 19, 26
Beare, F. W. 123, 133 n.26, 139 n.66, 140 n.67
Becker, Eve-Marie 8 n.24
Beetham, Christopher A. 19 n.94, 96, 26
Begrich, Joachim 69 n.66
Bell, Richard H. 41 n.2
Benetreau, Samuel 8 n.26
Benner, Margareta 80 nn.6–7, 95 n.11
Ben-Porat, Ziva 20, 21
Benjamin Fiore, S. J. 13 n.55, 18 n.89
Berger, Klaus 11 n.42, 13 n.57, 16 n.75
Bergey, Ronald 42 n.8
Best, Ernest 159 n.40
Betz, H. D. 2 n.5, 27 n.141, 83 n.27, 114 n.4, 118 n.22, 119 n.29, 122 nn.49–50, 140 n.66
Beuken, W. A. M. 60 n.15, 73 nn.90–1
Bianchini, Francesco 154 n.12, 154 n.14
Bieringer, Reimund 86 n.37, 160 n.45, 161
Bittasi, Stefano 117 n.21, 134 n.28, 158 n.37
Bitzer, Lloyd F. 22 n.112

Bjerkelund, Carl J. 148 n.106
Blois, Isaac D. 49 n.56, 54 n.77, 141 n.74
Böckler, Annette 43 n.9
Bockmuehl, Markus 25 n.131, 147 n.100
Bonnard, P.-E. 66 n.48, 133 n.23
Bordieu, Pierre 14 n.68
Bormann, Lukas 21, 29, 59 n.13, 115 n.9, 116 n.16, 123, 137 n.49
Bouttier, Michel 116
Brändl, Martin 73 n.88, 146 n.95
Braulik, Georg 47 n.36, 48 n.45
Brélaz, Cédric 3 n.6, 76 n.10
Breytenbach, Cilliers 13 n.55
Briones, David 30, 35, 122 n.49, 123 n.56, 160 n.47
Brockington, L. H. 5 n.14, 59 n.12
Brown, Peter 90 n.61
Brucker, Ralph 13 n.55, 138–9 n.61, 152 n.5
Brueggemann, Walter 58 n.5, 67 n.56
Brun, Lyder 118 n.24
Brunt, P. A. 75 n.5, 81 n. 12
Bultmann, Rudolf 11, 12, 13, 14, 48 n.48, 141 n.75

Caird, G. B. 132 n.16
Callan, Terrance 147 n.99
Carrez, Maurice 12 n.50
Cerfaux, Lucien 59 n.11, 110 n.1, 146 n.96
Champlin, Edward 105 n.52
Charneux, Pierre 80 n.6
Chibici-Revneanu, Nicole 38, 82 n.21
Ciampa, Roy E. 24, 148 n.105
Clarke, Andrew D. 30 n.165, 32 n.182, 159 n.41
Collange, Jean-Francois 155
Connolly, A. L. 132 n.18
Craddock, Fred B. 4 n.8, 33 n.185, 139 n.66, 140 n.69
Craigie, Peter C. 48 n.47

Cross, F. M. 6 n.17, 42 n.1, 43, 45 n.20, 126 n.74, 151 n.1
Culler, Jonathan 20, n.101
Culpepper, R. Alan 152 n.8
Cuvillier, Élian 12 n.50

Dafni, Evangelia G. 71 n.82
Danker, Frederick W. 8 n.27, 119, 120, 135
Davis, Casey Wayne 131 n.4
Davis, G. B. 10 n.32, 81 n.16
Deissman, Adolf 118 n.23
Denis, A.-M. 149 n.107
De Leeuw, Venantius 146 n.97
De Vaux, Roland 43
De Vries, Simon J. 133 n.22
Didier, Georges S. J. 117 n.20
Dietrich, Jan 38
Dille, Sarah J. 43, 67, 69 n.62
Doble, Peter 145 n.91
Dodd, Brian J. 118 n.28
Dodd, C. H. 19, 21
Dogniez, Cécile 47 n.29, 49, 52 n.69
Donahoe, Kate C. 10 n.32, 11 n.44, 18 n.88, 47
Dowdy, Barton Alexander 52 n.68, 52 n. 71, 53 n.73, 55 n.80, 58 n.8, 160 n.45
Drexler, Hans 76 n.8
Driver, S. R. 41 n.2
Droge, A. J. 119 n.32
Dupont, Jaques 119 n.31

Ebner, Martin 34, 35, 125 n.65
Edart, Jean-Baptiste 131
Edwards, Catharine 103 n.42, 104 n.44,
Ehrensperger, Kathy 23 n.122,
Ekblad Jr., Eugene Robert 71–2
Engberg-Pedersen, Troels 117 n.21, 121 n.42, 122 n.52, 158
Esler, Philip F 5 n.11, 8 n.30, 83 n.26, 127 nn.80–1

Fatehi, Mehrdad 22 n.113
Fee, Gordon D. 3, 4 n.8, 22, 23 n.118, 34, 114 n. 5, 116 n.15, 118 n.22, 131, 132 n.13, 134 n.29, 135, 161
Fields, Dana 90 n.61
Finney, Mark T. 8 .23, 11 n.42
Fishbane, Michael 20 n.99

Fitzgerald, J. T. 28, 103 n.39, 124 n.62, 126 n.72
Focant, Camille 3 n.7, 159 n.42
Forbes, Christopher 10n.34, 13 n.58
Forster, A. Haire 59 n.12
Fortna, Robert T. 113 n.3
Foster, Paul 1 n.1
Fowl, Stephen E. 4, 23, 24, 25, 26, 121 n.42, 127 n.82, 132 n.12, 134 n.30
Fredrickson, David E. 105 n.50, 124 n.64
Freisenbruch, Annelise 107
Frey, Jörg 158 n.34
Fuchs, Eric 10 n.32, 17, 53 n.72, 54, 58, 65 n.42, 66 n.53
Funk, Robert W. 116

Garland, David E. 7 n.18
Gathercole, Simon J. 10 n.33, 15, 16, 140 n.72
Gaventa, Beverly Roberts 10 n.35
Genths, P. 149 n.108
Geoffrion, Timothy C. 33 n.186, 121 n.43, 157 n.26
Gerber, Christine 13 n.55, 32, 33 n.185
Gignilliat, Mark 21, 71 n.77, 146 n.96
Glancy, Jennifer A. 10 n.32
Glatt-Gilad, David A. 38, 43 n.15
Goldingay, John 62
Grelot, Pierre 71
Griffin, Miriam T. 104 n.45
Gulin, E. G. 127 n.84
Gundry-Volf, Judith M. 145 n.92, 146 n.94, 160 n.48
Gupta Nijay K. 7 n.20, 8 n.23

Hafemann, Scott J. 140 n.71
Hainz, Josef 27
Hall, Jon 99 n.26, 100 n.29, 101 n.33, 102 n.36
Hanges, James Constantine 159 n.38
Hansen, G. Walter 34, 154 n.13
Harrison, James R. 1, 7 n.18, 8 n.29, 12 n.47, 86 n.37, 155 n.17
Hatina, Thomas R. 20 n.21
Haury, Auguste 83 n.23
Häußer, Detlef 4 n.7, 147 n.109
Hawthorne, Gerald F. 121 n.45
Hays, Richard 18, 19, 21, 22 n.113, 24 n.130, 26, 131 n.10

Heckel, Ulrich 10 n.32, 18 n.87, 47 n.30
Hellegouarc'h, Joseph 76 n.9, 114 n.8
Hellerman, Joseph H. 7 n.19, 76 n.7, 77 n.12, 83 n.26, 125, 126 n.71, 151 n.2, 154 n.12
Hermisson, H.-J. 66 n.50, 69 n.65, 69 n.66, 70, 71 n.80, 72 n.84, 73 n.89
Höffken, Peter 66 n52
Holleaux, Maurice 80 n.6
Holmberg, Bengt 32 n.183, 159
Hooker, Morna 152 n.9
Horrell, David G. 32 n.182, 159 n.42
Huber (Bechtel), Lyn 38 n.12, 42 n.7
Hutchinson, G. O. 94 n.7, 95 n.10, 96 n.13
Hutter, Horst 75 n.3, 81 n.15

Inselmann, Anke 158 n.34
Inwood, Brad 103 n.40

Jaquette, James L. 126 n.78, 157
Jennings, Mark A 7 n.18, 31 n.171, 115 n.12, 122 n.50, 129 n.1, 131 n.7, 132 n.15, 139 n.65
Jewett, Robert 7 n.18
Johnson, L. T. 26 n.136
Johnson, Terry 88 n.49
Jordan, Judith V. 4
Judge, E. A. 13, 14, 28, 60 n.16

Kaster, Robert A. 83 n.25, 160 n.44
Kennedy, George A. 156 n.19
Keown, Mark J. 22 n.113, 25 n.134, 120 n.37, 126 n.77, 130 n.2
Kirk, Alexander N. 118 n.27, 123 n.58, 143 n.85
Klauck, Hans-Joseph 31 n.172, 98 n.21, 103 n.39
Koskenniemi, Heikki 31 n.173
Krentz, Edgar 120
Kuhn, Annika B. 5 n.12, 76 n.6, 76 n.9

Labuschagne, Casper J. 2 n.2
Lambrecht, Jan 10 n.32, 10 n.35
Landy, Francis 68 n.61, 71 n.77
Leach, Eleanor 79 n.1, 98 n.22, 98 n.23, 101 n.32, 102 n.38
Leeman, A. D. 76 n.9, 96 n.12
Lendon, J. E. 75 n.3, 75 n.4, 76, 80 n.8, 82 n.17

Lightfoot, J. B. 118 n.25
Lincicum, David. 21, 138 n.59, 141 n.73
Lindars, Barnabas 148 n.105
Lohfink, Norbert 44 n.16, 45 n.23, 46
Lohmeyer, Ernst 22 n.110, 119, 120, 122 n.50, 133 n.23
Louw, I-Jin 117 n.22, 118 n.25
Luyten, Jos 44 n.16
Lyons, George 125 n.65

MacMullen, Ramsay 81 n.13
Maier, Michael P. 61 n.21
Malherbe, Abraham J. 103 n.41
Malina, Bruce J. 79 n.3, 83 n.23
Marchal, Joseph A. 26 n.135, 29, 30, 113 n.3, 117 n.20
Marshall, I. Howard. 141 n.77, 153 n.11
Marshall, John W. 33, 156, 158 n.35
Martin, Ralph P. 121 n.45, 144 n.89
Mays, Andrew D. H. 44 n.19
McAuley, David. 1 n.4, 22, 23, 24 n.129, 25, 132 n.12, 139, 140 n.67, 147 n.100
McConville, J. G. 46 n.26, 57
Mendecki, Norbert 54 n.76
Mengestu, Abera M. 137 n.51
Merendino, Rosario Pius 70 n.68, 70 n.74, 71 n.75
Metzner, Rainer 33 n.187, 124 n.62, 125 n.66
Michael, J. Hugh 132 n.15
Michel, Andreas 46 n.27, 49 n.55,
Michel, Otto 59 n.11, 110 n.1
Mitchell, Alan C. 28 n.152, 31 n.172
Montiglio, Silvia 121 n.44
Morello, Ruth 81 n.11, 94 n.7, 103 n.40, 107 n.66
Motyer, James A. 65 n.43, 73 n.88
Moulton, J. H. 115 n.10, 142 n.79
Moxnes, Halvor 5 n.11, 5 n.14
Müller, Ulrich B. 130 n.3, 160 n.46
Mullins, Terence 116 n.18

Nasrallah, Laura S. 26 n.135
Newton, Michael 134 n.32, 137 n.34
Neyrey, Jerome H. 8 n.25
Nikki, Nina 5 n.13
Nongbri, Brent 7 n.22
North, C. R. 63 n.31

Oakes, Peter 1 n.2, 22, 23, 36, 135 n.42, 144 n.88
Ogereau, Julian M. 26 n.136
Öhler, Markus 22 n.113
Olley, John W. 63, 66 n.49
Olyan, Saul 38, 39 n.14, 45 n.22, 54 n.78, 67
Ortwein, Gudrun Guttenberger 37 n.1
Osiek, Carolyn 117 n.22, 157 n.29, 160 n.48
Oswalt, John 61, 65 n.46

Pangle, Lorraine Smith 86 n.36, 87 n.41, 88 n.51
Paton-Williams, David 72 n.85
Pao, David W. 133
Park, M. Sydney 30, 160 n.47
Patterson, Jane Lancaster 1 n.4, 138 n.58
Pauritsch, Karl 67
Pedersen, Johannes 51 n.60
Peristiany, John G. 5 n.12
Perkins, Pheme 123 n.57
Pernot, Laurent 90 n.61
Perri, Carmela 20 n.102
Peterlin, Davorin 118 n.27
Pialoux, Luc 4 n.8, 31 n.171, 34 n.189, 114 n.7, 119 n.33
Pilhofer, Peter 125 n.70, 154 n.12
Pitt-Rivers, Julian A. 5, 11, 79 n.4, 81 n.16
Pitta, Antonio 3 n.7, 146 n.102
Plevnik, Joseph 5 n.11
Poplutz, Uta 158 n.35
Porter, Stanley E. 21 n.103, 25 n.133
Prümm, Karl S. 8 n.28

Raurell, Frederic 47, 48, 49 n.50, 72
Reed, Jeffrey T. 3 n.5, 18 n.89
Rees, Roger 81 n.11
Reider, Joseph 65 n.42, 65 n.47
Reinl, Peter 5 n.13
Rendtorff, Rolf 45, 46
Reumann, John H. P. 3 n.7, 28, 30 n.168, 118 n.26, 122 n.51, 131 n.9, 132 n.12, 160 n.46
Richards, E. Randolph 143 n.83
Robert, Louis 121 n.44
Rosell Nebreda, Sergio 1 n.4, 7 n.19, 28, 29, 137 n.50
Rosner, Brian 139 n.65
Rudd, Niall 82 n.19
Ryan, Richard M 157 n.29

Saller, Richard P. 87 n.44, 88 n.49
Salvesen, Alison 42 n.6
Sampley, J. Paul 10 n.34, 13 n.58, 27, 28 n.149, 34
Sánchez Bosch, Jorge 10 n.39, 48 n.38, 62 n.27, 141 n.74
Sandnes, Karl Olav 148 n.105
Schäfer, Klaus 32 n.179
Schapdick, Stefan 9 n.31, 115 n.11, 121 n.46, 122 n.49, 136 n.47, 137 n.54, 142 n.78, 157 n.33
Schellenberg, Ryan S. 10 n.34
Schenk, Wolfgang 7 n.22, 122 n.49, 133
Schmeller, Thomas 123
Schneider, Johannes 52 n.71
Schliesser, Benjamin 1 n.4, 26, 27
Schoon-Janssen, Johannes 21, 22 n.108, 133 n.26
Schreiner, Josef 16, 47 n.29, 48 n.48, 53 n.72, 56, 57 n.4, 58 n.9, 63 n.34
Schütz, John Howard 127 n.83, 141 n.76
Schwind, Rainer 72 n.86
Seaford, Richard 88 n.48
Sevenster, J. N. 28
Sherk, Robert K. 80 n.5
Silva, Moises 115 n.10, 131 n.5, 133 n.23, 143, 144 n.87, 147 n.103
Sisson, Russel B. 103 n.41, 113 n.2, 122 n.52
Smend, Rudolf 45 n.21
Smit, Peter-Ben 13, 14, 117 n.20, 133 n.21, 156 n.19
Snyman, A. H. 157
Spicq, Ceslas 5–6 n.15, 12 n.52, 56 n.90
Stanley, Christopher D. 18, 21 n.103, 23 n.120, 25
Stanley, David M. 146 n.96
Steel, Catherine E. W. 96 n.14
Stettler, Hanna 132 n.17, 136 n.44, 140 n.72
Stevenson, T. R. 86 n.37
Still, Tod 147 n.103
Stirewalt, M. Luther Jr.
Stowers, Stanley K. 28, 93 n.3, 94 n.6, 124 n.63
Strack, Hermann 147 n.98
Stromberg, Jacob 64
Sullivan, Francis A. 96 n.17, 114 n.8
Synofzik, Ernst 116 n.14, 136 n.46

Author Index

Talstra, Eep 41 n.2
Tassin, Claude 140 n.72
Tellbe, Mikael 7 n.21, 120 n.39, 121 nn.47–8
Thielman, Frank S. 7 n.18, 136
Thompson, James W. 134 n.31, 136 n.45, 157 n.30
Thompson, Richard W. 10 n.35
Tigay, Jeffrey H. 55 n.84
Tooman, William A. 19–20
Trapp, Michael 93 nn.1–2, 95 n.9
Travis, S. H. 10 n.32
Trebilco, Paul 33
Troxel Ronald L. 53 n.74, 59 n.10

Vahrenhorst, Martin 134 n.32, 135 n.39
Van der Kooij, Arie 71 n.83
Van Nijf, Onno. 75 n.6, 80 n.6
Veyne, Paul 75 n.4
Vincent, Marvin R. 142 n.78
Vollenweider, Samuel 8 n.26, 26 n.135, 119 n.30, 155
Von Harnack, Adolf 69 n.67, 141 n.75, 145–6
Von Rad, Gerhard 37, 48 n.39, 61
Vos, Johan S. 120 n.38, 121 n.45
Vouga, François 34 n.194

Wagner, J. Ross 20, 25 n.130, 131 n.11, 144 n.90, 147 n.98
Wagner, Thomas 38 n.6, 64 n.39
Wallace, Daniel B. 51 n.57, 52 n.70, 142 n.79
Walter, Nikolaus. 133 n.20, 144 n.89
Walton, Steve 29
Wansink, Craig S. 156 n.24
Ware, James P. 24, 64 n.40, 132 n.14, 137
Waters, Guy P. 22 n.110, 137 n.51, 141 n.73
Watkins, Thomas H. 100 n.30

Watson, Duane F. 13–15, 103 n.41, 113 n.2, 156
Watson, Francis B. 58 n.10
Wei, Ryan 106 n.58
Weidmann, Frank W. 3 n.7, 153 n.10, 158 n.36
Weinfield, Moshe 49 n.53
Westermann, Claus 64, 66–7, 70 n.71
Wevers, John William 42 nn.3–6, 47 nn.33–4
White, John L. 31 n.173, 94, 95 n.9, 114 n.6, 123 n.57
White, L. Michael 18 n.90, 27–8, 103 n.39, 124 n.62
White, Peter 96 n.16, 99 n.24, 101 n.32, 102 n.36
Whybray, R. Norman 57 n.1, 65 n.45
Wick, Peter 3 n.5, 22 n.110, 31 n.174, 138 n.61
Wilcox, Peter 72 n.85
Wilcox, Amanda 81 n.9, 96 n.15, 104–5
Wilk, Florian 20 n.98, 22 n.113, 118 n.24
Williams, Craig A. 99 n.25, 105 n.50
Williams, Demetrius K. 156 n.19
Williams, H. H. Drake III 152 n.7
Windsor, Lionel J. 70 n.70
Wischmeyer, Oda 126 n.77
Wiseman, Timothy Peter 97 n.18
Witherington III, Ben 32, 155, 158 n.36
Wojtkowiak, Heiko 1 n.4, 7 n.19, 134 n.27
Wright, N. T. ix, 19 n.98, 39 n.15
Wyss, Beatrice 137 n.49

Young, E. J. 65 n.44

Zeller, Dieter 17
Zerbe, Gordon Mark 120 n.39
Zerwick, Max S. J. 142 n.80

Ancient Sources Index

Aristides

Concerning a Remark in Passing
20   90 n.61

Funeral Address in Honor of Alexander
32.5   90
32.12   90
32.20   90

Aristotle

Nicomachean Ethics
1155a   6 n.16
1155b   87 n.45
1158a   87 n.39
1159b   87 n.39
1161b   86 n.36, 124 n.65
1166a   87 n.43
1167a   87 n.38
1168a   88 n.47, 125 n.69
1168b   124 n.65

Eudemian Ethics
7.6.9   87 n.41, 89 n.53
7.12.15   88 n.52
7.12.19   87 n.41

Cicero

Ad Atticum
1.15.1   97 n.19
1.15.2   75

Ad Familiares
5.12.8   82 n.19
7.31   89 n.56
9.14.1   99
9.14.2   99
9.14.3   99, 100
9.14.4   100, 157 n.27
9.14.8   100
10.1.3   102
10.3.2   101
10.3.3   101
10.3.4   102
10.4.2-3   102
10.5.2-3   102
10.7.2   102
10.12.1   102
10.19.2   102
10.23.7   102
12.7.1   98
12.12.2   98
12.13.1   98
12.23.2   75 n.5
15.14.6   98

Ad Quintum Fratrem
1.1.4-44   97
1.1   101 n.34

Amicitia
11-12   137 n.49
20   87 n.40
22   87 n.44, 89 n.55, 151 n.3
31   88 n.50
57   87 n.45
69-70   125 n.69

De Officiis
1.56   88 n.48, 89
1.58   87 n.39
1.85   88 n.46
3.24   87 n.46
3.52   87 n.46

Dream of Scipio
13   137 n.49

Pro Sestio
38   114 n.8

Republic
6.13   137 n.49

Tusculanae Disputationes
2.24.58   75 n. 2

Dio Chrysostom

Orations
31.159   107 n.70

Diogenes Laertius

Philosophoi Bioi
8.10   124 n.65
10.11   124 n.65

Epictetus

Diatribai
2.22   84 n.28

Fronto

Ad Amicos
81 n.10

Ad Antoninum Imperium
1.2.1-2   106

Epistulae Graecae
5.4   84 n.29
5.8   84 n.29
7.2   105
7.2-4   106

Ad Marcus Caesarem
1.5.4   105
1.8.7   75, 105
3.3   106
5.59   105-6

Ad Verum Imp.
2.1   106
2.1.13   105 n.51
2.2   106

2.4   107, 157 n.28

Herodotus

History
2.177   138 n.56

Homer

Iliad
6.476-79   85

Horace

Satires
1.6.23-24   76 n.7

Josephus

Antiquities of the Jews
4.303   39 n.15

Lucian

Toxaris
53   87 n.42, 89 n.57

Lucretius

De Rerum Natura
5.1120-1130   82 n.20

Philo

Confusion of Tongues
145   137 n.49

Special Laws
1.311   12
1.318   137 n.49
2.236   37
4.164   12 n.47

De Vita Mosis
2.288   39 n.15

Pindar

Isthmian Odes
5.51   121 n.44

Olympian Odes
9.38   121 n.44

Nemean Odes
9.7   121 n.44

Plato

Lysis
207c   124 n.65

Meno
97e   119 n.35

Pliny

Epistulae
2.9.1   81 n.13

Plutarch

Comparison of Demosthenes and Cicero
2.2   82 n. 18

Moralia
95A   87 n.38
96F   87 n.42
484D   84, 126 n.79
484E   84
485C   84, 152 n.6
486E   83
487D   83-4, 126 n. 79
478B-492D   83 n.27
539E-F   14
540A   82 n.19

Sallust

Bellum Jugurthinum
85.40   75 n.6

Seneca

De Clementia
1.14.2   85 n.32

De Beneficiis
2.15.1   86 n.34
2.22.1   87 n.44
2.32.2   87 n.38
3.17.3   88 n.50
3.29.3   86
3.36.2   86
3.38.2   86

Epistulae ad Morales
20.1   103 n.41
34   103-4
35   104
109.1, 4-6   104 n.47
109.15   89, 143 n. 83, 151 n.3

Suetonius

Julius Caesar
88   137 n.49

Valerius Maximus

De Factis
5.5.1   85
5.5.2   85
5.7   85
8.14.5   76 n.7

Xenophon

Mem.
2.6.26   87 n.40
2.6.35   89 n.56, 125 n.67

Scripture Index

Jewish Scriptures

Genesis
6:4	51 n.60
8:21	18 n. 89
11:4	51 n.60
12:2	51 n.60
17:1	23, 135

Exodus
4:22	137
15:24	132, 133 n.19
16:2	132, 133 n.19
16:7	132, 133 n.19
16:8	133 n.19
17:3	133 n.19
19:5	47 n.35, 49 n.57
19:5-6	49, 51 n.57
19:6	136
24:16	38
28:2	50, 51, 53
28:40	50, 51, 53
29:1	138 n.55
32:9	55 n.85
33:3	55 n.65
33:5	55 n.65
33:12	37
34:9	55 n.65

Leviticus
1:3, 10	138 n.55
23:12	137 n.54
26:16	72, 147 n.102
26:31-33	54 n.77

Numbers
6:14	137 n.54
11: 1	132, 133 n.19
14:2	23 n.115, 133 n.19
14:27, 29, 36	132
15: 5	23 n.115
16:11	132, 133 n.19
17:20, 25	133 n.19
19:2	137 n.54
28:3	138 n.55

Deuteronomy
1:27	32, 133 n.19
4:1	44 n.18
4:20	44, 55 n.83
4:45	44 n.18
5:1	44 n.18
7:6	136, 44, 49 n.57, 136 n.45
7:13	46 n.28
7:20	46 n.28
9:13	55 n.85
9:26	55 n.83
9:27	55 n.85
9:29	44, 55 n.83
10:12-22	55
10:21	12, 13, 16, 17, 51, 53, 55, 56, 58 n.6, 65, 109,
11:13	46 n.28
11:26	46 n.28
11:32	44 n.18
12:1	44 n.18
14:1	137
14:2	44, 49 n.57, 136 n.45
14:21	44
15:6	46 n.28
15:21	137 n.53
18:2	55 n.83
26:16	44
26:16-19	6, 39, 41, 42, 44, 47, 55, 141 n.73

26:18-19	6, 20, 46, 54,	18:28	23 n.115
26:19	2, 6, 13. 16, 17, 19,	20:11	63 n.34
	26, 46 n.23, 48,	21:11	58 n.6
	49, 49, 50, 51, 52,		
	53, 54, 55 n.80, 56,	*2 Kings*	
	57, 58, 59, 65,	22:19	54 n.77
	67, 73, 74, 109, 110,		
	136, 142, 143, 148,	*1 Chronicles*	
	149, 150, 163, 168	14:27	51 n.60
27:9	44	16:27	17, 52 n.71
28:1	46 n.21	16:33	11
28:1-14	46	16:35	52 n.71, 63 n.34
28:9	49 n.57	17:21	51 n.60
28:13	47 n.34	22:5	48, 50, 53,
28:37	49, 54	29:11	17, 56, 58 n.7
29:12	44		
29:13	44	*Esther*	
30:9	46 n.28, 140 n.72	8:12 n LXX	134 n.32
30:16	46 n.28		
31:6	132 n.15	*Job*	
31: 8	132 n.15	1:1	134 n.32, 135 n.33
31:24	140	1:8	134 n.32
31:27	132 n.15, 134 n.26,	2:3	134 n.32, 135 n.35
	140 n.67	2:9	70 n.67, 147
31:29	132 n.15, 140	4:17	134 n.32, 135 n.34
32:1-43	44, 167	9:20	134 n.32, 135 n.33
32:1	176	11:4	134 n.32, 135 n.34
31:24-32:3	140 n.66	12:4	135 n.33
32:4-5	42	13:16	18 n.89, 22 n.107,
32:5	2, 18, 19, 20,		23
	22 n.107, 23, 25, 26,	15:14	134 n.32, 135 n.33
	42 n.6, 60, 109, 132,	20:18	70
	133 n.23, 137, 138,	22:3	134 n.32
	139, 142, 163, 164	22:19	135 n.33
32:8-9	44	24:2	147
32:28-29	132 n.15	33:9	134 n.32, 135 n.34
32:30	43 n.13, 60	39:16	70
32:43	43, 132 n.15		
		Psalms	
Joshua		5:11	11 n.46, 63
9:18	133 n.19	8:7 LXX	18 n.89
		9:25	132 n.17
1 Samuel		15:2	137-8
2:30	38	18:23	137
		18:26	136 n.44
1 Kings		18:31	138 n.55
8:51	55 n.83	19:8	138 n.55
8:53	55 n.83	20:11	132 n.17
9:7	54 n.77	21:26 LXX	51 n.58

Scripture Index

29:1	37	11:30	18 n.89
31:23	69	16:30	132 n.17
32:11	63 n.34	16:31	58 n.7, 66 n.48
33	22 n.113	17:6	58 n.7, 159
33:12	55 n.83	17:12	132 n.17
34:2	63 n.33	19:11	58 n.7
34:20	132 n.17	20:7	138
35	22	22:11	138
35:4	132 n.17	25:14	58 n.6, 63 n.34
36:18	138 n.55	27:1	58 n.6, 63 n.34
37:18	137		
49:7	58 n.6, 63	*Isaiah*	
51:3 LXX	11 n.46	1:2	57 n.1
52:3	58 n.6, 63	3:18	59 n.11
56:5	63 n.34	4:2	50, 52 n.63, 65
58:13	70	6:9-10	70
58:16	133	10:12	59 n.11
63:12	63 n.34	10:15	65 n.43
64:5	138 n.55	13:19	59 n.11
66:2	37	20:5	59 n.11
66:18	69	28:5	50, 52 n.64, 65
69:28	18 n.89	29:10	70 n.70
89:18	52 n.67, 56 n.90	29:24	133
93:11	132 n.17	30:5	70
97:7	58 n.6, 63	30:9-11	70 n.70
101:2	138 n.55	30:12	133
105:3	63 n.34	40:5	37, 61
105:25	133	40:10	70, 71 n.81, 73
109:20	70	40:18	60 n.16
118:59	132 n.17	40:26	70
119:1, 80	138 n.55	40:27	70 n.68, 72
127:1	70	40:28	60 n.16
127:3	37	40:29	70
127:5	37	40:31	70, 146
135:4	47 n.35	41:1	60, 70
138:5	37	41:4	60 n.16
139:3	132 n.17	41:8-9	68 n.59
144	22 n.113	41:10	69 n.64, 148
145:18	18 n.89	41:11–16	63
148:14	51 n.58	41:16	6, 58 n.9, 61, 62
149:5	11, 63 n.34	41:17	59-60, 62
		41:21–24	60
Proverbs		42:1	68 n.59
3:9	18 n.89	42:3-4	70 n.70
4:9	66 n.48	42:5	60 n.16
10:16	70 n.69	42:6	24, 69 n.64, 70, 140 n.72
11:5	138 n.55		
11:18	70 n.69	42:7	2
11:20	138	42:8	60-1

42:12	61, 68	49:1–6	68–9, 71, 183
42:16	60 n.16	49:3	61, 65, 66 n.52, 68,
42:17	60		72, 74, 148
42:21	61, 74	49:4	6, 18, 19, 22, 24, 25,
42:24	47		26, 39, 68, 69, 70–4,
43:4	74, 148		109, 110, 145, 146,
43:7	61, 74		147, 148, 149,
43:9	60 n.16		150, 163, 164
43:10	60, 68	49:5	61, 68-9, 74,
43:11	60		147-9, 163
43:13	60	49:5–6	2
43:21	61, 74	49:6-12	70 n.70
43:22-24	70 n.70	49:6	68, 140, 149
43:25	74	49:7	70
43:28	54 n.77	49:8	71, 74
44:1-2	68 n.60	49:14	72
44:6, 8	60	50:6	70 n.70
44:9–20	60	50:7	70 n.70, 146 n.95
44:21	68 n.60	50:10	68 n.60
44:23	61, 65, 66 n.52, 74	51:3	60 n.16
44:26	68 n.60	52:1	59 n.11
45:4	62, 68	52:7	146
45:5-22	60	52:13	24, 68, 70, 74
45:7-18	60 n.16	52:13-53:12	24
45:12	60 n.16	52:14	59, 70
45:16	60	53:1–4	70
45:20	60	53:3	18
45:21	60 n.16	53:4	72 n.83
45:22	144	53:8	73
45:22–23	24	53:7–9	70
45:23	18, 22, 23, 25, 144	53:10–12	70 n.70
45:23–24	55 n.87	53:11	18, 68, 72–3
45:24	7, 22, 23, 63,	53:12	24, 73-4, 149
	144, 148	54:13	74
45:25	61, 62, 63, 74 144,	54:17	68 n.60
	145, 149	55:3–5	64, 182
46:6–7	60	55:5	58 n.9, 61, 65-6, 74
46:9	60	55:13	61
46:12	70 n.70	56:5	61 n.24
46:13	52, 61, 66, 74	56:6	68 n.59
48:1	70 n.70	56:7	18
48:4	70	56:10-12	70 n.70
48:8	70 n.70	57:4	70 n.70
48:9	60, 61, 74	57:17	70 n.70
48:11	37, 61, 74	58:2	70 n.70
48:12	60 n.16	58:8-10	140 n.72
48:18	70 n.70	59:3-8	70 n.70
48:20	68 n.60	59:19	68 n.59
49:1–5	68	60:1	74

60:1-3	64 n.39	*Jeremiah*	
60:2	61	3:19	137
60:3	65 n.44	4:2	63
60:6	61	9:22	58 n.6, 47, 57,
60:7	58-60, 64-7		63, 181
60:9	51 n.60, 61, 64-8	9:22–23	16
60:13	64-5, 67	9:22–24	18
60:15	67 n.56, 74	9:23	63
60:18	58 n.9, 59 n.11, 60, 74	10:16	55
		13:11	17, 48, 49, 50, 51, 52, 54, 56 n.90,
60:19	6, 50, 52 n.65, 58 n.9, 60, 63-5, 109		58 n.6, 110, 142, 143, 148, 163
60:21	61, 64-5, 66 n.52, 74	13:16	37
61:3	59 n.11, 61, 64-6, 74	13:18	66
		13:40	48
61:8	70 n.69, 71-3	17:14	51, 56 n.90, 58 n.6
61:9	74	18:16	54 n.77
61:10	64 n.38	24:9	54
61:11	74	25:9	54 n.77
62:1-3	64 n.39	27:38 LXX	58 n.6
62:2	61 n.24, 63, 74	28:58	70
62:3	52 n.66, 59, 62, 64-6, 109	31:16	70
		32:18 LXX	54 n.77
62:7	51, 58-60, 67, 73	32:20	51 n.60
62:11	70 n.69, 71, 73	33:9	48, 54, 163
62:44	65	49:18 LXX	54 n.77
63:7	61, 74	51:19	55
63:8	57 n.1		
63:10	70 n.70	*Lamentations*	
63:12	51 n.60, 61, 64	3:39	133
63:14	51 n.60, 52, 53, 58 n.9, 59, 61, 64	*Ezekiel*	
63:15	64 n.38	5:14-5	54 n.77
63:17	55 n.83, 68, 70	16:12	58 n.7, 66 n.48
64:5-7	70 n.70	16:14	51 n.60
64:10	64 n.38	16:17	58 n.7
65:2, 3, 11	70 n.70	16:39	58 n.7
65:7	70-1	23:26	58 n.7
65:8-15	68 n.60	23:42	58 n.7, 66 n.48
65:15	74	24:25	58 n.7
65:17–25	147	28:15	138 n.55
65:21	73	34:29	51 n.60
65:22	72-3	38–39	20, 183
65:23	6, 70-3, 147, 148, 163	39:13	51 n.61
		43:23	138 n.55
66:5	61 n.23		
66:14	68 n.60	*Daniel*	
		1:4	138 n.55

12:3	18 n.89, 22 n.107	50:11	58 n.7
		50:20	58 n.7
Hosea			
2:1	137	*Judith*	
4:7	18, 23	5:22	133 n.19
		15:9	121 n.44
Joel			
2:17	54 n.77, 55 n.83	*Wisdom of Solomon*	
		2:22	137-8
Micah		3:11	147 n.102
6:16	54 n.77	10:5	136
		10:15	134 n.32
Habakkuk		18:21	134 n.32
2:13	147 n.103		
		Jubilees	
Zephaniah		1:24-25	41 n.1
2:15	54 n.77		
3:19-20	13, 48, 50, 51, 53,	*Testament of Job*	
	56 n.90, 58 n.6,	24:2	147 n.102
	142 n.79, 143 n.84		
	148, 163	**New Testament**	
Zechariah		*Luke*	
2:9	61	13:17	64
10:12	11		
12:7	56 n.90, 58 n.7	*Acts*	
		8:23	142
Malachi		13:22	142
3:17	47 n.35		
		Romans	
1 Maccabees		1:1	68
4:42	138 n.55	1–5	15, 173
		2:17	11
Sirach		2:23	11
1:11	11, 56 n.90	3:27	10, 16, 173,
7:28	86 n.35		176, 183
9:16	11, 58 n.7, 122	8:30	145
10:22	11, 58 n.7	10	25 n.130
10:25	133 n.19	12:15	151
11:4	58 n.6	14:11	145
31:8	138 n.55	15:17	16, 122, 141
31:10	58 n.7	15:17–18	12, 141
31:24	133 n.19	16:6	146
38:25	58 n.6	16:12	146
39:8	12		
40:19	138 n.55	*1 Corinthians*	
44:7	58 n.7	1:8	136
45:7-8, 12	53 n.73	1:19	11
48:4	58 n.7	1:31	16

Scripture Index

3:8	146	1:2	126, 134
4:7	11	1:3	33 n.188, 151
5:8	136	1:3-11	113
9:15	148	1:5.	26–8, 114–5, 151, 160
9:26	146		119
10:1–22	139	1:5-7	
15:10	141, 146, 148	1:6	138, 140–1, 154, 160
15:14	148		
15:31	16, 141	1:7	26–8, 115, 124, 148, 151, 160
15:58	148		151
16:16	146	1:7-8	
		1:8	33 n.188, 124, 138, 157
2 Corinthians			119
1:14	12, 116, 127, 142, 153, 157	1:9	122, 132 n.15
		1:9-10	130 n.5, 134, 139 n.64, 140
3:6–18	140	1:9-11	
4:5	68		134-6, 141
5:12	12	1:10	7, 18, 54, 110, 119, 135, 143, 148, 153-4
6:1	16, 148	1:11	
7:4	158		
7:14	12		27, 114, 126, 151-2, 157
8:24	10, 176	1:12	
9:2	12		96 n.17, 113-4, 121, 184
9:5	10, 176	1:12–26	
10-13	14		151
10:15	146	1:14	119
10:17	16	1:16	158
11:2	136	1:18	119 n.33, 123, 156
11:23–25	10, 173	1:18-26	22, 33 n.188, 115, 134, 160
12:14–16	174	1:19	
		1:20	8, 22, 154
Galatians		1:21	118, 123, 154, 157
1:10	68	1:21-24	117 n.20
2:2	146, 148	1:21–26	7, 118, 157, 175
4:11	146, 148	1:22	119 n.32, 148
5:13	83, 171	1:22–26	119, 159
6	14	1:23	33 n.188, 119
6:4	11	1:24	119, 164
6:10	171	1:25	116 n.17
6:13	12	1:25–26	7, 18, 113, 115, 117, 119, 121, 123, 125, 127, 161
Ephesians			
1:4	136	1:26	7, 9, 12–3, 16–8, 62 n.29, 124, 125, 127
4:13	136		
5:27	136	1:27	7-8, 28, 96 n.17, 114–5, 120, 123–5, 129
Philippians			
1:1	68 n.60, 120–1, 126, 130, 136, 154, 175	1:27-28	152

1:27-2:18	114, 129	2:17	117 n.20, 124, 132 n.15
1:28	64 n.37, 132 n.15, 138	2:17-18	33 n.188, 124, 151, 158
1:30	115, 119, 125	2:18	120, 126, 130, 134, 175
2	42 n.8		
2:1	26, 151, 158	2:19	157
2:1-4	32	2:19-30	152, 170
2:2	28, 34, 115, 124, 129, 152, 157-8	2:19-20	115
2:3	8, 134 n.28	2:20	28, 117
2:4	117	2:22	7-8, 68 n.60, 120
2:5	129-30, 152	2:23	115
2:5-11	130, 156, 177	2:24	123
2:6-9	24	2:25	27, 117, 120, 151, 157
2:7	59 n.11, 120-1, 152, 154	2:26	160
2:8	8	2:25-30	152
2:9	8	2:28	124, 160
2:9-11	121, 134	2:29	7-8, 123 n.58
2:10	22, 24, 55 n.87, 130 n.4	2:29-30	152
		3	14
2:10-11	7, 131, 144, 164	3:1	5, 27, 117 n.20, 126, 134, 151
2:10-16	7, 1, 22, 144, 177		
2:11	8, 143-4, 153	3:3	17, 18, 109, 143, 153-4
2:12	28, 111, 114-5, 23-5, 129 n.2, 152, 154	3:4-6	7, 12, 18, 174
		3:8-12	130 n.4, 158
2:12-13	119	3:10	26, 28, 34, 154
2:12-16	18, 36, 155	3:11	154
2:12-18	5, 7, 25, 131, 132, 152	3:12	130 n.4, 160
		3:12-16	9
2:13	110, 119, 132 n.15, 140, 154, 160	3:13	26
		3:14	8, 154
2:14	44, 132, 152	3:17	8, 26, 117, 125-6
2:14-15	132	3:19	7 n.20, 9, 18 n.89, 64 n.37, 139
2:14-16	7, 18, 19, 22, 58, 129, 130, 131, 133, 135, 137, 139, 141, 143, 145, 147, 149, 164		
		3:20	155
		3:20-21	9, 119, 145, 154
		3:21	18 n.89, 54, 164
		4:1	8, 27, 66 n.48, 105 n.52, 120, 124, 126, 140, 151, 157, 159
2:15	7, 19, 20, 22, 126, 134, 138		
2:15-16	9	4:2	28, 115, 152
2:16	3, 7, 8, 12, 16-7, 19, 20, 22, 24, 63 n.34, 96 n.17, 103 n.41, 107 n.69, 115, 141, 145, 160	4:3	9, 18 n.89, 119-20
		4:4	134
		4:5	22 n.113
		4:5-6	18 n.89
		4:6	134
2:16-18	114 n.5	4:7	160

4:8	7 n.20, 9, 27, 126	4:20	9, 34 n.189, 110, 153
4:8-9	28		
4:9	115	4:21	136
4:10	115, 124, 141, 151, 157	*Colossians*	
4:10-23	34 n.194	1:22	136 n.46
4:11-13	158		
4:13	35, 69 n.64, 119, 123, 147–8, 154, 160	*1 Thessalonians*	
		2:1	148 n.105
		2:19	66 n.48
4:14	124-5	2:19-20	12, 116 n.14
4:14-15	26, 28, 125 n.65, 151	2:20	103 n.41
		3:1	146 n.93
4:14-18	115, 117	3:5	146, 148 n.105
4:17	73 n.92, 117 n.20, 119, 148, 160	3:13	136 n.46
		5:12	146 n.93
4:17-18	152		
4:18	18 n.89, 34 n.189, 136, 138	*2 Peter*	
		3:14	136 n.46
4:19	22 n.113, 34 n.189, 154, 160	*Jude*	
4:19-20	143	24	136

Subject Index

Abraham 23, 135-6
advantages/interests 37, 85-8, 96, 114, 117 n.20, 156
allusion 18-26, 63 n.34, 72, 109-10, 131-46, 163-4
Aquila 53 n.72, 58 n.9, 59, 65, 110 n.1
associations 37 n.138
athletics 9 n.30, 121 n.44, 123 n.57, 146
authority 29-32, 70 n.70, 101 n.33, 107 n.66, 159 n.39

beloved 42, 126, 152, 156 n.22, 157, 159
benefaction 8 n.27, 9, 79-80, 86, 88, 90 n.61, 102, 110, 135, 155
  endangered benefactor 119-20
blameless 130-1, 134-6, 139, 142-3, 145, 149, 151
blessing(s) 39, 46, 51-2, 54-6, 72 n.87, 73, 84, 115, 143, 148, 163
boasting 1-6, 9-18, 52 n.71, 55 n.80, 62, 63 n.34, 90, 113, 115-16, 118, 121-7, 143, 149, 153-4, 163-4
  apostolic boasting 131, 141
  arrogant boasting 7 n.19, 10, 12, 30, 63 n.33, 65, 82, 113
  eschatological boasting 11-12, 16, 17, 35, 116, 141, 144, 149, 152 n.9
  mutual (reciprocal) 1, 4, 12, 19
    boasting 26, 33 n.185, 39, 56, 85, 109-15, 142, 158-61

children of god 42-3, 126, 130-1, 137-9, 143, 149, 151, 153, 163-4
Christ Hymn 8, 23, 29, 55 n.87, 59 n.11, 120, 130, 144 n.89, 145, 157 n.32
citizen(ship) 3 n.6, 8, 79-80, 82 n.21, 90, 99, 114 n.8, 129, 135, 152
civic oration 76, 79, 107
competition 14, 75 n.3, 81 n.16, 82, 89, 127 n.80, 147 n.99

covenant 2, 6, 24, 38-56, 109-10, 126 n.74, 135-64
  covenant blessings 72, 110, 147-8, 163
  covenant curses 72
  covenant honor 38, 67-8
  new covenant 24, 54, 140 n.72, 147 n.99, 148
crown (στέφανος) 8, 52 n.64, 53 n.73, 65, 66 n.48, 80, 99, 103, 123
cultic purity 134 n.32, 136 n.54, 138

dependence 35, 107 n.68, 154 n.13, 157-61
disobedience 54-5, 72, 133 n.23, 134 n.26, 139, 141

election 15, 17, 49 n.53, 62, 126, 136 n.45
emotions 76, 94-5, 101, 107, 124, 156-8, 164
emperor 75, 95 n.11, 105-6, 137 n.49
Epaphroditus 7 n.20, 8, 33, 119 n.34, 120 n.39, 152, 156 n.19, 160 n.47
equality 27, 30, 32, 86
eschatology 1-2, 8, 11, 15 n.72, 37, 39, 44 n.16, 61, 115 n.10, 122, 134, 148, 160, 163-4
  day of Christ 1, 16, 24, 122, 130-1, 134, 136, 138, 141, 145, 147 n.100, 149, 155, 161, 164
  eschatological 131, 139, 141
  judgment
    eschatological 54, 60, 64-7, 72-3,
  restoration 110, 137, 140 n.72, 143, 145
ethos 7 n.19, 126 n.78, 156-7
exaltation
  of Believers 143, 148
  of Christ 23, 25, 144, 145 n.91, 152 n.9, 155, 163
  of Isaiah's Servant 23, 148-9
  of Israel 46-8, 51, 54, 62-9, 73-4, 143, 149
exile 44, 57, 97, 140 n.72, 147 n.103

Subject Index

faith 12, 70, 114, 117, 120-7,
faithfulness 3, 8, 17, 24, 41-3, 52, 56, 71-4, 110, 131, 135, 137 n.51, 140, 143, 146 n.95, 147-54, 161, 163-4
family 5-6, 36, 43, 57, 79 n.2, 82-5, 123-7, 151-3
    father-child 31 n.172, 32, 37, 39, 43, 84 n.28, 101-2, 106, 153, 159
    fictive kinship 31-2, 120
    kinship 6, 15, 27, 41 n.1, 43, 45 n.20, 88 n.48, 120, 125-6, 137 n.50, 156
    siblings 6, 27, 31-3, 36, 38, 85-6, 110, 125-6, 152-3, 157, 159, 161, 164
financial support 9, 114-15, 123 n.57, 154, 160
fear 55, 62, 68 n.60, 111, 122, 126, 141, 146 n.94, 147 n.99, 161
friendship/*philia* 4 n.9, 6, 22 n.109, 26-39, 81-98, 101-6, 110-11, 114, 120, 124-6, 135 n.40, 143 n.83, 151-2, 158
fruit 52 n.63, 65 n.44, 73, 90, 119, 131, 141, 148
futility/in vain 39, 68-70, 72-3, 107, 130-1, 145-8, 147 n.100, 148, 157 n.28, 158 n.35, 163

glory 1, 5-13, 38, 47-56, 57-8, 60-74, 75, 83-5, 96 n.12
    כבוד 37-8, 49 n.54, 50-1, 59, 61, 64 n.39
    δόξα 52, 64 n.38, 82 n.21, 84 n.28, 89-90
    eschatological glory 1, 44, 57, 64
    mutual glory 39, 57-8, 61, 63, 67-8, 72, 74, 91
    תפארת 46, 49-54, 57-9, 64 n.38, 65-6, 148
gospel 4 n.9, 7 n.18, 22 n.109, 27 n.141, 33 n.185, 34, 56, 76, 96 n.17, 114, 119, 123, 133 n.21, 141, 146, 154, 158 n.37, 160
grace 7 n.19, 12-15, 55, 136 n.46
group identity 7 n.21, 29, 33 n.184, 43, 82-3, 88 n.48
grumbling 44, 130-9, 142

Hexapla 59, 65 n.42, 66-7, 109 n.1
hierarchy 29-33, 39, 95, 113, 122-3

holiness 6, 25, 42, 45, 46 n.23, 48 n.46, 51 n.62, 55, 62, 136, 142
honor 1, 7, 11, 37-8, 75, 135
    acquired honor 38, 79
    family honor 36, 43, 57, 82-5, 123, 151
    inherited honor 79, 83, 97
    mutual honor 1-2, 5, 10, 41, 68, 93, 113, 129
honorific triad 46-54, 57-60, 65-6, 142-3, 148
hope 1, 54, 61, 64 n.40, 74, 113, 140 n.72, 145 n.90, 163

intertextual 19-23, 147 n.100
Isaianic Servant 2, 23-6, 39, 58, 65 n.43, 68-74, 110, 144-55, 163-4

joy 12, 14 n.65, 33, 52 n.71, 73, 75, 86-9, 99, 103 n.41, 104-6, 113, 120-1, 123, 133 n.21, 151-2, 157-8
    divine judgment 15, 17, 45, 60, 70, 131, 133, 139, 141, 146

labor 14, 16, 68-73, 115 n.12, 119, 131, 145-9, 161, 163
letter 7, 24, 28, 31-3, 93, 95, 114, 126, 129, 140 n.66, 143 n.83
    epistolary conventions 105 n.50, 116, 125, 158, 81 n.15, 93 n.3, 103
    epistolary persona 98, 102, 107 n.68, 119 n.32
    recommendation letter 80-1, 98 n.21
light 24, 65, 71, 83 n.24, 130, 137 n.49, 142

manipulation 29-30, 102 n.37, 113, 158, 160
mediator 2, 39, 58, 68, 70 n.71, 74, 122, 150, 151, 153, 163
military 7 n.19, 63, 77 n.10, 98, 120-1, 124
mindset 129, 156 n.24
model/example 6, 8, 27-9, 54 80 n.6, 105 n.51, 110, 115, 117, 119, 121, 122 n.52, 132-41, 152, 156-7
moral discernment 104 n.44, 119
Moses 55, 86 n.71, 133 n.26, 140
motivation 7, 15, 46, 75 n.4, 79, 88, 94-111, 156-8
murmuring 132 n.18, 133

name 8 n.25, 9, 37-8, 47-9, 51, 57, 59-60, 67 n.59, 69, 82 n.19, 142, 148

obedience 4, 19-20, 26, 39, 45-6, 48-9, 54-5, 58, 74, 95 n.11, 110, 115 n.11, 131, 133-4, 139-43, 147 n.99, 149, 152-3, 159
opponents/enemies 5 n.13, 7 n.20, 8, 37, 43, 62-4, 70 n.72

pain/toil 71, 87, 107, 147 n.100
partnership/κοινωνία 2, 4, 7 n.18, 26-35, 84, 87, 88 n.48, 90, 99, 124-5, 158, 160-3
pathos 111, 126 n.78, 105 n.52, 129, 156-7, 164
patronage (patron/client) 6, 29-30, 81, 87-8, 100, 115 n.9, 123
persecution 4, 152
persuasion 2, 7 n.18, 29, 76, 80 n.7, 81, 93-8, 110-11, 101, 105, 107, 108 n.70, 111, 150, 152, 158, 164
pilgrimage of Nations 60, 62, 64, 66
praise 5, 7, 9, 11, 16, 47, 49, 51-2, 54-63, 67, 73, 80, 84 n.29, 97, 99, 103, 109, 135, 138 n.61, 139, 143-4, 152 n.5, 156 n.19
prayer 7-8, 113, 115, 134, 160
presence/absence 28, 30, 49, 114-9, 122-3, 125, 140 n.70, 153, 157
pride 10-2, 38, 52, 56, 65, 86, 88-90, 106, 108, 118 n.25, 125 n.67, 127 n.83, 155
priestly garments 51-3
prison 113-4, 121
progress/advance 14 n.65, 81 n. 13, 84, 88-9, 96, 102-5, 113-5, 120-1, 143 n.83, 151 n.3, 158-9 n.37
Prophet(s) 37, 54, 61, 64 n.40, 71 n.77, 131, 139 n.65, 144 n.86, 146 n.96, 163
purity 7, 61, 122, 130-1, 134-5, 137-9, 149

rebellion 43, 57 n.1, 133 n.22, 136, 139
reciprocity 6, 35, 38 n.9, 67, 87-8, 113, 153
renunciation 7 n.19, 30 n.163, 158 n.37
reputation 5, 7-8, 37-8, 41, 51, 79 n.4, 81, 84, 90, 96 n.14, 121, 135
resurrection 9, 154

rhetoric 3-4, 7, 9, 22, 26 n.135, 28, 38, 152, 156
   deliberative 156 n.19, 158
   epideictic 139 n.62, 156 n.19
   rhetorical theory 10, 13, 15, 17, 94
   rhetorical 2, 24, 29, 77, 93,
   strategy 96-100, 103-7, 129
righteousness 11, 42, 60, 70 n.69, 119, 135, 136 n.44, 138
reward/recompense 2, 15, 17, 26, 37, 48, 54, 68-73, 79, 86, 102, 106, 110, 129, 138, 146-50, 163-4
Roman Colony 3 n.6, 7 n.19,
   of Philippi 29 n.159, 76-7, 126, 151 n.2, 155
Roman Republic 82 n.22, 96-7, 99, 101
Roman trial 7, 115 n.9, 119, 124 n.60, 154

sacrifice 8 n.29, 30, 88, 110, 117-20, 127, 129, 137-8, 140 n.72
salvation/σωτηρία 11, 14, 35, 44 n.16, 63 n.32, 64, 66, 71, 98, 111, 114 n.6, 115, 122 n.52, 126, 129, 146 n.92, 159 n.37, 160 n.48
Second Temple 1, 11, 15, 18, 19 n.98, Judaism 21 n.105, 39, 137, 141 n.73
self-presentation 13 n.48, 14-15, 82, (*periautologia*) 90 n.61, 117, 120 n.36, 153-4, 157 n.26
servanthood/service 15, 33, 55, 60, 71, 80 n.5, 85, 87 n.46, 102, 114 n.8, 117, 119-20, 130, 135, 146 n.94, 152 n.8
servant song(s) 24, 68-73, 146, 148
shame 7, 9, 18 n.88, 37, 38, 41, 42 n.7, 44, 54, 62-4, 69, 74, 83 n.25, 97, 121 n.42, 138, 154-5, 160 n.44
slave(s)/slavery 76, 119-21, 155, 164
soul 73, 87, 137 n.49
spirit 15, 34, 74, 87 n.46, 104 n.44, 137, 140, 144 n.89, 147 n.99, 152 n.9
societas 26-7, 34
solidarity 29, 33-4, 82, 84, 159 n.42
Song of Moses 26, 38 n.10, 39, 41-4, 57, 132, 138-9, 163
status 5, 7 n.19, 17, 27 n.141, 28-30, 33 n.184, 38, 43, 46, 49 n.54, 51, 54-5,

Subject Index

62, 69, 76 n.9, 77 n.11, 95, 97, 99,
116, 120, 130, 135-7
strength 15, 52 n.67, 62, 68-9, 71, 73, 104,
143, 147 n.99, 148
suffering 23, 34, 117 n.20, 133 n.21, 140
suicide 119 n.32, 157 n.25
swear allegiance 55
Symmachus 58, 65-7
Syncrisis 116, 119 n.30

teacher-student 89-91, 100, 104, 107, 115
thanksgiving 12-3, 69 n.66, 113

Theodotion 58 n.9, 67, 73
torah/law 12 n.47, 16-7, 43-5, 138 n.55,
141 n.73

vindication 9, 16, 23, 44 n.16, 63-5, 120,
124 n.60, 143-4, 146-7, 154, 164
virtue 6, 8-9, 28, 86, 88, 90, 105, 121
n.41, 135
vulnerability 160-1

wilderness 55, 132-4, 136-7, 139 n.62

CPSIA information can be obtained
at www.ICGtesting.com
Printed in the USA
LVHW012003130522
718732LV00022B/1740